MW01010614

Events Industry Council

MANUAL

9TH EDITION

Executive Editor
Mariela McIlwraith, CMP, CMM, MBA

Published by the Events Industry Council
Washington, DC, USA
January 2014

Events Industry Council
1120 20th Street NW
Suite 750
Washington, DC 20036
USA
+1 202 712 9059
info@eventscouncil.org
eventscouncil.org

Library of Congress Catalog Card Numbers: 2014901332

Printed in the United States of America

ISBN: 9780970692306

Contents

Contents

From the CEO

On behalf of the Events Industry Council's Board of Directors and the CMP Governance Commission, I am proud to offer this edition of the Events Industry Council Manual. Since 1961, we have published this Manual to provide guidance to industry professionals and to assist candidates preparing for the Certified Meeting Professional (CMP) exam.

Totaling $621 billion (USD), the events industry has a significant global economic impact, contributes more than 10 million direct jobs and draws 1.5 billion participants globally to its meetings.* With this magnitude, professionalism is fundamental not only for our own organisations, but also for all industries that rely on the power of face-to-face events. It is more important now than ever before to speak about the lasting legacy impact of events.

This Manual provides guidance that ranges from high-level strategy to successful logistics execution. Today's event professionals are expected to understand how meetings and events support an organisation's strategic mission and deliver business results. In addition, they are called upon to manage increasingly complex financial, sourcing and contracting operations. They must know how to manage risk, how to engage stakeholders around the world, how to leverage new technology and how to embrace a commitment to sustainability as a reflection of organisational values.

This Manual helps professionals develop such knowledge. The CMP International Standards provide the foundation upon which the CMP exam and this Manual are based. Periodically, the International Standards are updated to reflect changes in the industry, thus also requiring an updated Manual to reflect those developments.

Updating the Manual was a team effort. We recruited more than 50 volunteer authors and reviewers to lend their expertise in each of the knowledge areas. To that end, they have worked diligently to ensure that this Manual would continue to be the recognised authority in the meetings industry, and we are grateful to each of them.

The Events Industry Council also administers the well-respected and sought after CMP designation with the help and support of dedicated volunteers. Event professionals from all aspects of the industry give their time and expertise to ensure that the CMP programme reflects current and emerging practices. On behalf of the Events Industry Council, we thank them for their contribution to our industry's professional growth.

Sincerely,

Amy Calvert

Amy Calvert
Chief Executive Officer
Events Industry Council

*According to the Events Industry Council's 2018 Global Economic Significance of Business Events study.

From the Executive Editor

It has been just over 50 years since the first edition of this Manual was published. During this time, our industry has evolved considerably. While many of the topics covered in the Manual are timeless, the ways in which these topics are approached have changed to reflect our progress. Greater emphasis is now placed on the delivery of strategic value to the organisations hosting meetings and events, as a reflection of the importance of the work that we do to enhance organisational success.

This Manual is a snapshot of today's best practices—the skills, knowledge and techniques currently applied by industry professionals to deliver successful meetings and events. We recognise as well that there is continuous innovation occurring in our industry and have incorporated this through sections on decision-making processes in rapidly developing areas such as technology and social media.

This edition also reflects the revised Certified Meeting Professional International Standards (CMP-IS). New sections have been added to align with the CMP-IS, and are indicative of the expanded role of our industry. We have drawn from expertise in other fields, including sustainability management, human resources and project management to inform our body of knowledge.

I am grateful for the support of the many volunteers and member organisations from around the world that have contributed to this Manual.

Sincerely,

Mariela McIlwraith, CMP, CMM, MBA
Executive Editor
Events Industry Council Manual, 9th Edition

About the Events Industry Council Manual, 9ᵗʰ Edition

Like any professional publication, the Events Industry Council Manual is periodically updated to keep it current. The Events Industry Council Manual uses the CMP International Standards (CMP-IS) as the benchmark for currency in professional practice in the meetings industry. The CMP-IS is the body of knowledge on which the CMP exam is based. In 2012, the CMP International Standards were updated. The Manual has been updated to reflect the changes to the CMP-IS.

What was updated in the 9ᵗʰ Edition?

The Events Industry Council has updated both the CMP exam as well as the Manual to ensure that it is more internationally focused. In addition, the Events Industry Council Manual and the Events Industry Council International Manual were combined in the 9ᵗʰ Edition. The 9ᵗʰ Edition is also now organised to follow the 10 domains in the CMP-IS. So now, for instance, the first chapter is about "Strategic Planning," which is the first of the 10 domains. Finally, the Events Industry Council will be offering both a print and eBook version of the Manual. This will be the first time the Manual will be available in eBook format. These changes all reflect recommendations from diverse sets of focus groups including CMPs, recent candidates, international CMPs and those involved in facilitating structured exam preparation groups.

Who contributed to the 9ᵗʰ Edition of the Manual?

The Events Industry Council asked an international group of subject matter experts from each of the 10 domains and 30 sub-domains to lend their knowledge. A total of 51 content experts lent their time and expertise to ensuring that the text reflected current and best practices for each domain area. A second group of content experts reviewed the text to ensure that all areas of a certain subject were covered.

How will the Manual help me prepare for the CMP exam?

The CMP exam is an experience-based exam designed to test applied knowledge, not a candidate's ability to memorise. This means you need practical experience in the meeting management field to be successful on the CMP exam. The Manual will help you understand the body of knowledge and current and effective practices, particularly any domains where you don't have direct experience. The Events Industry Council highly recommends you start your study regime by reviewing the CMP-IS and making an assessment of your experience in each of the 10 domains.

Conventions Used in the Manual

One of the greatest challenges in writing for an international audience is determining the terminology and conventions that are most globally relevant. For this Manual, conventions have been selected for greatest global relevance including decisions related to terminology, measurements and currencies.

Terminology:

- **Event:** This will be the primary term used in the Manual as it encompasses meetings as well as the many other types of events that comprise our industry.
- **Planner:** This will be the primary term (not meeting planner or meeting professional) to describe the event organiser.
- **Meeting Professional and Event Professional:** These will be used as the generic terms to refer to the variety of different roles that exist in our industry. For example, in a situation when we could be referring to either or both planners and suppliers, meeting professional will be used. In some cases, the term event professional may also be used if describing a broader range of professionals.
- **Event Owner:** This will be used to refer to the person(s) or organisation that is the host of the event. For example, the Events Industry Council is the event owner of the CMP Conclave. (When referring specifically to a meeting, meeting owner is also acceptable.)
- **Supplier:** This term will be used to refer to the many event professionals that provide services or goods for the event industry, including hotels, venues and event technology providers. In North America, the term "vendor" is often used to refer to a supplier.
- **Venue:** This will be used to refer to the specific location where a meeting or event is held, such as in a hotel, convention centre or conference centre. In North America, the term "facility" is often used to refer to a venue.
- **Attendee:** This will be used as the generic term for those attending or participating in events. There may be cases when the specific use of participant, delegate, guest or passenger may be more specific and may be used. As an example, when referring to someone with voting privileges, delegate will be used.

Formatting Guidelines

In order to support the global nature of our industry, formatting guidelines were selected to be as broadly applicable as possible. To this end, the following guidelines have been followed:

- Global English spelling has been used.
- A dual format of measurement is presented.
- Time will be indicated using the 24-hour format (e.g., 13:00)
- In most cases, currency symbols are not used, unless they are incorporated in examples referring to exchange rates between currencies.

About the Contributors

More than 50 industry professionals contributed to the creation of this Manual. This included representatives from Events Industry Council member organisations, authors, reviewers and focus group participants.

We also recognise that we stand on the shoulders of giants: the authors and reviewers of past editions. Although this Manual is predominantly new material, it builds on the work in the 8th Edition and in the International Manual.

The authors and reviewers of specific skills are acknowledged in their respective chapters. In addition, the Executive Editor, four principal reviewers and an Events Industry Council liaison were responsible for reviewing all of the materials.

Executive Editor

Mariela McIlwraith, CMP, CMM, MBA
President, Meeting Change (Canada)

Principal Reviewers

M. Theresa (Terri) Breining, CMP, CMM
Principal, The Breining Group LLC (USA)

Eric Rozenberg, CMM, CMP, HOEM, FONSAT
President, Swantegy; Executive Director, BOB.tv; Managing Director, Culture22 (Belgium/USA)

Tyra W. Hilliard, PhD, JD, CMP
Speaker, Educator and Multipreneur (USA)

Roger Simons, CMP
Group Sustainability Manager, MCI Group (Singapore)

Authors and Reviewers

- Richard Aaron, MFA, CMP, CSEP, BizBash Media (USA)
- MaryAnne P. Bobrow, CAE, CMP, CMM, CHE, Bobrow Associates, Inc. (USA)
- M. Theresa Breining, CMP, CMM, Breining Group LLC (USA)
- Lakisha Campbell, CAE, National Association of Home Builders (USA)
- Paul Cook, CMP, Planet Planit Ltd. (UK)
- Linda Dhawan, CMP, Experient, a Maritz Travel Company (USA)
- Matt DiSalvo, CMP, SER Exposition Services (USA)
- Joan L. Eisenstodt, Eisenstodt Associates, LLC (USA)

- Tahira Endean, CMP, Cantrav Services Inc. (Canada)
- Jennifer George Lion, CMP, PMP, Experient, a Maritz Travel Company (USA)
- Elizabeth Glau, CMP, Building Blocks Social Media (USA)
- Karen Gonzales, CMP, Destination Marketing Association International (USA)
- Ann Gravette, CMP, CSSBB, Maritz Travel Company (USA)
- Tyra W. Hilliard, PhD, JD, CMP, University of Alabama (USA)
- Dale Hudson, IMEX Group (UK)
- Jeff Hurt , Velvet Chainsaw (USA)
- Joanne H. Joham, CMP, CMM, International Congress and Convention Association (USA)
- Tamara Kennedy-Hill, CMP, Travel Portland (USA)
- Michael Lynn, CEM, CME, CMM, CMP, CPC, CPECP, L-3 Communications, Integrated Systems Group (USA)
- Carole McKellar, MA, CMM, FCIPD, HelmsBriscoe (UK)
- Shawna McKinley, MAEEC, MeetGreen (Canada)
- Walter Méndez Rojas, MBA, MPM (Costa Rica)
- Dr. Rodolfo Musco, CMM, CMP, Motivation & Events S.a.s. (Italy)
- Ksenija Polla, CMP, International Congress and Convention Association (Netherlands)
- Chris Prieto, CMP, International Congress and Convention Association (South Africa)
- Colleen A. Rickenbacher, CMP, CSEP, CPC, CTA, CPECP, Colleen Rickenbacher, Inc. (USA)
- Eric Rozenberg, CMP, CMM, Swantegy, Culture22 Communications Group, BOB.tv, (Belgium/USA)
- Dr. Jorge Sancho Zeledón, MBA (Costa Rica)
- Pat Schaumann, CMP, CSEP, DMCP, Meeting IQ, Present China (USA)
- Nicole Schray, Experient, a Maritz Travel Company (USA)
- Arlene Sheff, CMP, Strategic Meeting Consulting (USA)
- Marilee Sonneman, CMP, DMCP, Spotlight Events Consulting (USA)
- Amy Spatrisano, CMP, MeetGreen (USA)
- Tracy Stuckrath, CSEP, CMM, CHC, Thrive! Meetings and Events (USA)
- Andrea Sullivan, MA, BrainStrength Systems (USA)
- Erin Tench, CMM, CMP, The Pennsylvania State University (USA)
- Glenn Thayer, The Voice of Meetings and Events (USA)
- Cara Tracy, CMP, CMM (USA)
- Jon Trask, CMP, CMM, AVforPlanners (USA)
- Maarten Vanneste, CMM, Meeting Support Institute (Belgium)
- Bonnie Wallsh, MA, CMP, CMM, Bonnie Wallsh Associates, LLC (USA)
- Nancy Zavada, CMP, MeetGreen (USA)
- Karen Zimmerman, CMP, Maritz Travel (USA)

Other Contributors

Dr. B. J. Reed, Professor, Dept. of Media Studies and Director, Teaching & Learning Center from the University of Wisconsin – Platteville, Judy Cleary and Gayle Dahlman provided substantive and copy editing services for this Manual. Erika Abrams provided graphic design services. Bernice Eisen provided indexing services.

Focus Group Participants

We are grateful to the support of the focus group participants at IMEX Frankfurt 2013, who reviewed draft chapters and provided important guidance on the Manual.

- Karen Gonzales, CMP (US)
- Dale Hudson (UK)
- Joanne Joham, CMP (US)
- Tamara Kennedy-Hill, CMP (US)
- Walter Mendez (Costa Rica)
- Kristin Mirabal, CMP (US)
- Dr. Rodolfo Musco, CMM, CMP (Italy)
- Ksenija Polla, CMP (Netherlands)
- Chris Prieto, CMP (South Africa)
- Luis Sanchez (Colombia)
- Jorge Sancho (Costa Rica)
- Amy Spatrisano, CMP (US)
- Sherilou Tokvam, CMP (Germany)

We also thank the participants of the July 2012 focus group in St. Louis, Missouri who provided formative input for the Manual. The participants included:

- Patty Barnett, CMP (USA)
- Jason Doerge, CMP (USA)
- Julie Holtgrave, CMP (USA)
- Joanne Joham, CMP (USA)
- Ching Ching Lin, CMP (Taiwan)
- Bonnie Lipinski, CMP (USA)
- Aaron Missner, CMP (USA)
- Gary Murakami, CMP (USA)
- Carol Norfleet, CMP (USA)
- Faye Pastor, CMP (USA)
- Adrienne Six, CMP (USA)
- Jon Trask, CMP (USA)
- Denise Tedrow, CMP (USA)
- Tara Thebeau, CMP (USA)
- Dee Walsh, CMP (USA)

Other Acknowledgments

In addition to those mentioned above and in the chapters, there are a few people who provided extra support in the creation of this Manual. Joan Eisenstodt answered numerous questions and provided invaluable guidance on several topics in this book. Cathy Breden (IAEE), Ron Gulaskey (CLIA), Diana Hakenholz (ACCED-I), Phil Gin (ACCED-I), Suzanne Rose Bennett (ACCED-I), Brigid Neff (ACCED-I), Suzette Escobar (ACCED-I), Adrian Segar and Jeff Hurt also either proofread materials or answered questions related to their areas of expertise. Elizabeth Henderson provided project management support and guidance for the Manual. We are grateful for their support and contributions.

About the Events Industry Council

Advancing the Events Industry   www.eventscouncil.org

Mission and Overview

The events industry makes a substantial contribution to the global economy, stimulating job growth and providing jobs for millions of people. Face-to-face meetings reinforce the "solid human connections" critical to driving business growth. The Events Industry Council champions the economic and social value of the industry and provides a vibrant, collaborative platform to address critical issues to ensure a thriving events industry. Representing more than 30 member organisations with over 103,500 individuals and 19,500 organizations, the Events Industry Council promotes high standards and professionalism in the events industry. The Certified Meeting Professional (CMP) programme awards the CMP credential which is recognised globally as the badge of excellence in the events industry. The four other signature programmes of the Events Industry Council focus on Sustainability, Industry Insights, Knowledge, and Leadership and represent the key initiatives, assets, services and products for the Council.

Value

As a federation representing diverse voices in the events industry, the Events Industry Council serves as a nucleus and a trusted authority with a global reach, advocating the importance of the industry through a united voice, making the profession stronger and reinforcing its importance and relevance.

Programmes and Services

Certified Meeting Professional (CMP) Programme

Promoting professionalism is at the core of the Events Industry Council's mission. We encourage investing in professional development and set the benchmark for excellence through the administration of the CMP programme. The foremost certification available for meeting and event professionals, the CMP designation recognises individuals who have demonstrated their proficiency through a combination of education, experience and passing a rigorous exam. Established in 1985, the Events Industry Council has certified more than 21,000 professionals in 51 countries and territories since inception. These leaders have earned the CMP designation and are considered the leading experts in the global events industry.

CMP Healthcare Subspecialty (CMP-HC)

The Events Industry Council is committed to growth and anticipating the needs of the industry and the professionals working in it. The healthcare and life sciences sector continues to grow and, with it, the demand for specialised meeting professionals increases. The Events Industry Council developed the CMP-HC certification programme for CMPs working in the healthcare meetings industry. A subspecialty of the CMP Programme, it is designed to identify those who have mastered the knowledge needed to be a successful healthcare/life sciences meeting professional and is available only to those who hold a current CMP certification.

Signature Programmes

Sustainability

The Events Industry Council's Sustainability Initiative seeks to inspire, educate and support event professionals of all levels and disciplines in transforming the global meetings industry towards sustainability. We champion the implementation of sustainability practices that support the triple bottom line of people, planet and profit. The Sustainability Initiative champions the development and adoption of industry standards, and provides education, resources, industry research and recognition of industry leadership.

Industry Insights

The Events Industry Council is committed to advancing the industry through the development of voluntary standards, best practices and research. The Event Industry Council's Standards Committee is focused on developing best practices for professional meeting management. This initiative creates and promotes development and implementation of industry-wide accepted practices, the benefits of which include time and cost savings, ease of communication, streamlined systems and processes, enhanced professionalism and superior results.

The Events Industry Council's Research Committee oversees the council's signature research study on the Economic Significance of Meetings to the U.S. Economy, whose model has been replicated in more than 10 countries. Future studies will seek to measure the global events industry impact.

Knowledge

The Events Industry Council's focus on knowledge includes creation and repository of education, learning, accreditation, certification and career development resources to advance, elevate, and educate industry professionals. The Events Industry Council hosts regular webinars focused on various industry topics and hosts the annual CMP Conclave conference held specifically for Certified Meeting Professionals (CMPs).

Leadership

The Events Industry Council is comprised of more than 30 member organisations representing over 103,500 individuals and 19,500 firms and is governed by a board of directors with representatives from the member organisations. The Council is a collaborative platform for industry thought leaders to bring forth issues and trends for discussion and action as an industry body.

The Hall of Leaders recognition programme draws attention to the contributions that the meetings industry has made to the larger society as a whole by highlighting the specific achievements of industry pioneers and emerging leaders who not only changed the landscape of the profession, but changed the culture of business as well.

Since 1985, the Events Industry Council has promoted industry excellence and innovation by inducting industry pioneers with a lifetime of achievement into the Hall of Leaders and, more recently, recognising the real-time accomplishments of emerging leaders and industry supporters with the Pacesetter Award. Nominations are submitted either by Events Industry Council member organisations or the general industry community and honorees are recognised during a culminating awards ceremony and their stories housed virtually at www.eventscouncil.org.

Serving as a bridge connecting the industry's rich history to its exciting future, the Hall of Leaders helps encourage meetings professionals to connect with the stories of pioneers and inspires them to take innovative approaches to tackle current issues.

Strategic Planning

Events have the potential to be of great strategic value to organisations when they are designed and implemented with a strong focus on the objectives of the organisation. In fact, most event professionals have a much greater strategic influence than they might believe. By asking good questions, they can help shape the specific objectives of an event, which then directs all other decisions and activities. An event professional must understand the organisation's strategy and support it through the event. By making all of the logistical decisions within the context of the organisation and the business environment in which it operates, event professionals will host more effective events.

This chapter will focus on the role of the event professional in delivering on an organisation's strategic objectives in a way that drives the **business value** of the event. Business value is not measured only by the financial bottom line, but on what outcomes are expected by the business. For some, this will mean exceptional education or brand positioning while, for others, the value will be the quality of the contacts made through networking or sales generated by the event. These are only a few examples of what can be defined as the business value of the event.

Strategy involves the "what" and "why" of a meeting, which drives the "how" or the planning of the meeting.

SKILL 1: MANAGE STRATEGIC PLAN FOR MEETING OR EVENT

Learning Outcomes

- Determine the feasibility of an event.
- Develop a mission statement, goals, and objectives for an event.
- Identify the requirements to carry out an event successfully.

1

- Monitor a strategic plan for an event.
- Create a financial summary for an event.

Strategic planning is the process by which an organisation develops its long range plan of action. The role of the event professional with respect to strategic planning will vary depending on the organisation. This role can be viewed as a continuum from a development role to an implementation role. At the development end of the continuum, the event professional will be involved in actively setting strategic goals, as well as designing the event to meet stated objectives. At the implementation end of the continuum, the event professional responds to the strategic direction set by the organisation. In these cases, the event professional will be involved in designing the event to deliver on the organisation's goals, but will not be involved in setting those goals.

Example: Development Role in Strategic Planning

In some cases, the event professional will be a part of an organisation's senior leadership and will be actively involved in that organisation's strategic planning process and the development of the goals for the organisation. The development role answers the question: How will we achieve our organisation's mission through our meetings?

Example: Implementation Role in Strategic Planning

Event professionals are typically involved in implementing all or part of the strategic plan. In these cases, their role is to fully understand the strategic goals for the organisation and the event, and then to develop objectives to achieve those goals. Although not involved in setting the strategy for the organisation or event, this role is nevertheless highly strategic in nature. The implementation role answers the questions: How will this event achieve organisational goals? How do we best achieve the defined event goals to meet organisational performance expectations?

Strategic Planning

A strategic plan is a long range call to action for a company or organisation. Strategic planning for events includes three distinct elements: discovery, analysis, and planning.

Discovery: Know the Organisation

The focus of an event professional should be on supporting the organisation's core strategic purpose. That means acquiring a deep understanding of the organisation—the trends that are affecting it, its business objectives and strategies, historical and cultural issues, and the current formal and informal processes that exist.

The answers to the following questions will provide you with a profile of the total environment—a necessity for creating a sound strategic plan.

- Purpose of the event
  - Why is the event being held? What is the purpose?
  - What needs are being met though this event?
- Internal assessment
  - What are the organisational goals?
  - How are decisions made in the organisation?
  - What approvals and processes are needed in relation to meetings?
  - What types of events have been held, and how effective have they been?
  - What is the business cycle, and how will this affect the ability to deliver the event?
  - What are the core culture and brand values? Are issues such as quality or sustainability important?

- Business environment
  - What are the best practices employed by similar organisations (not necessarily competitive ones)?
  - What is the current economic, political, and regulatory climate, and how are events perceived and operated in this context?
  - What partnerships or collaborations are in place that might support the event?
  - What area of the country or globe is a key focus for my organisation?

Analysis

Disciplined management requires a sound foundation of data. Depending on the size, type and culture of the organisation, a variety of information on past events should be collected, such as:

- The types of events and the specific events that have been held historically
- The results of previous events—whether goals and targets (including financial and non-financial) were met
- The various ways decisions were made—by whom, and how total spending, purpose, and outcomes were treated
- Total direct and indirect costs for events
- Amount of internal resources involved with cost allocations
- Number, quality, and suitability of suppliers, partners, and alliances in the supply chain
- The financial, human, and technological resources available for delivering the event
- The current policies, processes, practices, templates, and tools for the selection, planning, financial tracking, risk management, and execution aspects of the event

Planning

Once the discovery and analysis phases are completed, development of the event's strategic plan begins. Elements of the strategic plan that will be detailed in the following sections include:

- Mission statement, goals, and objectives for the event
- Business environment analysis
- Implementation plan
- Sales, marketing, and communication plan
- Financial plan
- Success measures or key performance indicators (KPIs)

Sub Skill 1.01 – Develop Mission Statement, Goals, and Objectives of Meeting or Event

In order to develop your strategic plan, you will need to have a clear understanding of your mission statement, goals, and objectives. These elements are compared in Figure 1.

Creating SMART Objectives

A common methodology for developing objectives is called SMART, focused on five criteria for effective objective setting:

- Specific—should call out actions, results, behaviours that are to be achieved
- Measurable—what element of the objective is to be measured, and how
- Attainable—challenging goals, yet realistic and within reach
- Relevant—focused on what matters to the organisation and participants
- Time-based—achievable by a certain time

Focus on Strategic Meetings Management

The following section is adapted with permission from *Events Industry Council Manual, 8th edition.* Many organisations have focused on the development of a structure that facilitates greater efficiencies in the planning process. This structure, often referred to as strategic meetings management, involves developing and applying an organised system of policies, procedures, and tools that enable an organisation to reduce costs, leverage overall spending, and provide optimum service levels related to meetings. Strategic meetings management is not about the end product—events—but rather about engaging in a disciplined practice to ensure that the end product maximizes resources and supports organisational strategies.

A thorough strategic meetings management plan (SMMP) is an ongoing activity, developed as resources allow, over time. It is not necessary—or even possible—to implement all of its components at once.

Strategic meetings management incorporates fundamental concepts accepted as good practice in any business unit:

- Business planning and strategy
    - How do you maximize the organisation's resources to achieve the objectives?
    - What events should the organisation hold? Of those, which should be managed by the internal events department, which can be delegated to staff outside the event planning function such as administrative assistants, and which should be outsourced?
    - What is the level of willingness among senior management to invest in a programme that cedes control from individual departments and/or individuals?
- Organisation and execution
    - What competencies should you keep within your department? What ones should you handle by partnering with other internal groups? What ones should you outsource?
    - What process changes are required to establish or improve strategic meetings management?
    - How can technology be used to achieve lower costs and add greater value?
- Trust and transparency
    - What metrics should you employ to demonstrate value provided to the organisation?
    - How do you best communicate that value?
    - How do you build trust with all event stakeholders inside and outside of the organisation?

On a day-to-day level, the events department engages in these activities:

- Ensuring a solid business proposition for each individual event, which typically includes strategic messaging, branding, and establishing content objectives.
- Designing and organizing, which typically includes creative design and theme development; coordinating and communicating with stakeholders; managing, facilitating, and monitoring staff; and measuring and reporting results.
- Operating on a logistical and tactical level, which typically includes site selection, food and beverage, ground transportation, etc.

Examples of SMART objectives include the following:

- *Sales focused:* Sales staff shall increase year-end sales by 10 percent over the previous year following the sales training event.
- *Education focused:* Training course participants will raise their average test scores by 15 percent over pre-course assessments.
- *Exhibit focused:* Sales staff will generate a 10 percent increase in leads from the exhibit by the end of the tradeshow.

Figure 1. Comparison of Mission Statement, Goals, and Objectives.

Mission Statement	The mission statement defines the purpose of the organisation. It generally remains unchanged over time.
Goals	Goals are broad and general; they are expected to be achieved over a long-term horizon. Goals are used to achieve the mission.
Objectives	Objectives are specific and narrow and used to achieve a goal. Objectives tie directly to evaluation measures.

- *Sustainability focused:* Travel-related carbon emissions will be reduced by 10 percent over previous year.

In some organisations, the SMARTER methodology is utilised, which adds two additional elements:

- Ethical
- Recorded

Sub Skill 1.02 – Determine Feasibility of Meeting or Event

Before embarking on plans for a new event, or deciding whether or not to continue with one that is offered on a regular or cyclical basis (monthly, quarterly, annually, bi-annually, etc.), determine the feasibility of the event. In order to determine this feasibility, a number of factors need to be considered.

Internal Factors

- **History.** The first place to look is the organisation's history. This will include assessing what meetings have been successful, and for which segments of the intended audience. Also assess how attendance figures fluctuated over the years. If the event has shown regular growth and positive business results, you may want to continue in a similar format. If however, the meeting or result is showing declining financial, attendance, or satisfaction results, the feasibility should be examined more carefully to determine if the event should continue or if it should be changed to meet market needs.

- **Financial feasibility.** You will need to conduct a cost and revenue analysis, using best and worst case scenarios. It is recommended that you work with a financial expert to make sure your assumptions are reasonable. Costs should be estimated based on the destination where your event will be held, as this will have a significant impact. In addition to understanding event costs, you will also need to identify potential revenue sources. Examples include ticket or registration sales, sponsorships, internal resources, or grants.

- **Role of the event in the organisation's finances and overall strategy.** For some organisations, particularly in the association and exhibition sectors, events can form a primary profit centre. If this is the case, much greater care needs to be taken when determining the feasibility of the event, as it will have broad implications for the organisation's overall financial health. For an effective decision, strategic meeting management requires a clear understanding of what the organisation expects from the event.

- **Availability of human resources.** Does your organisation have the internal skills and available time to implement the event? Alternatively, is hiring an external organisation (outsourcing) an option? A strategic plan may appear very promising on paper, but if there is insufficient time or expertise to implement the plan, it is unlikely to succeed.

- **Commitment.** In order to be successful, a meeting generally needs support of senior leadership as well as those tasked with planning and executing the event.
- **Marketing and brand considerations.** An event should enhance and support the brand positioning of the host organisation (partners and sponsors).

External Factors

- **Audience.** A profile of prospective participants is also needed. This will answer who they are, what their needs are, where else they are getting the information, as well as the training and networking opportunities that your meeting might provide. You will also want to determine your possible competition, as well as partners and sponsors, by determining who provides products and services to this audience.
- **Industry.** Researching what similar organisations are doing successfully, what needs aren't being met with other meetings, and what trends are appearing in the industry you work in and in business generally can be very valuable in assessing the feasibility of a meeting.
- **Economic context.** An analysis of the economic climate is critical. It will answer key questions such as whether or not budget cuts may affect internal or external revenue sources (including sponsorship and registration or ticket sales), as well as the types of programmes that will be most attractive and how events will be perceived.
- **Applicable legislation or regulatory requirements.** In some cases, notably with government or healthcare-related meetings, there may be legislation or regulations that will have an impact on attendance, spending, or acceptable activities and practices.
- **Economic and social impacts on hosting communities.** What will be the short-term, medium-term, and long-term economic and social impact of the event on the hosting community or communities? How does this affect the feasibility of the event?
- **Risks (internal or external).** Finally, you should also identify potential risks and develop contingency plans for them, should they occur.

Sub Skill 1.03 – Determine Requirements to Carry Out Meeting or Event

Producing an event requires several resources. An important step in strategic planning is to determine these requirements and their availability for your event. The types of requirements that you will need to assess are covered in Figure 2.

Sub Skill 1.04 – Develop Financial Summary

A financial summary is a fundamental part of your strategic plan. It answers:

- How will the event be funded (internal resources, ticket or registration sales, sponsorship, other)?
- What is the financial goal of the event (to make a profit, to be revenue neutral, or is there an acceptable investment level on behalf of the host organisation)?
- What is the event budget, including all costs and revenues as well as internal overhead costs for the people/material involved?
- How will the event respond to budget shortfalls?
- How will the event address cash flow concerns related to paying deposits and expenses?
- Which currency will be used, and how will you cover the exchange rate risk (if applicable)?

Figure 2. Requirements for the Event.

Requirement	Considerations
Financial resources	▪ What are the financial requirements for producing your event? ▪ Will your event be funded through registration fees, sponsorship, internal sources, or other sources? ▪ When will you be required to make payments, and how will you ensure that the cash is available at that time?
Human resources	▪ Who will be responsible for producing the event or portions of it, and do they have the appropriate skills and time to do so effectively? ▪ What departments will need to be consulted or involved in the planning of the event, and are they available to do so? For example, will you need support from your procurement or marketing departments? ▪ For international events, does your team have an appropriate understanding of the destination, culture, taxes, strength of currency and cross-cultural communication?
Marketing and public relations resources	▪ How does this event reflect and enhance stakeholder relations with your organisation? ▪ To whom will your event be promoted? ▪ How will your event be promoted? ▪ What resources do you have to promote your event? ▪ Are there any restrictions or guidelines that you will need to follow in promoting your event? ▪ How will event promotion efforts be evaluated?
Technology requirements	▪ What are the pre-event technology requirements for your event? Examples include a Web site, registration tools, and programme management tools. ▪ What are the on-site technology requirements for your event? Examples include audiovisual technology, mobile applications, virtual meeting support, and Internet access. ▪ What are the post-event technology requirements for your event? Examples include post-event survey tools. ▪ What technical expertise and staffing will be required to produce your event?
Logistical requirements	▪ What are your destination and venue requirements? ▪ What resources will your participants require, such as accommodation, food and beverage, interpretation services, and accessibility requirements, as well as resources for health, wellness, and spiritual needs?
Event-specific resources	▪ Depending on the nature of your event, you may require specific resources such as educational content or entertainment. ▪ Depending on stakeholder relations, what resources might your event need to use (e.g., an organisational mascot)?
Legal or regulatory requirements	▪ What are the legal or regulatory considerations for your event? ▪ With whom do contracts need to be negotiated and executed? ▪ What state/province/country's laws are applicable? ▪ What permits or other regulatory requirements need to be procured?
Evaluation resources	▪ How will you evaluate the success of your event? ▪ Which stakeholders are tied to the achievement of the meeting objectives? ▪ What are the measurements that must be captured?
Sustainability resources	▪ What are the key sustainability challenges in your destination and for your event, such as water scarcity, lack of recycling facilities or indigenous rights? ▪ What resources are required in order to implement your sustainability plan?
Safety and security resources	▪ Have venue and destination risks been assessed and analysed? ▪ Is outside security needed? ▪ What are the insurance requirements?

To develop your financial summary, you'll need to analyse:

- Historical income and expense statements, as well as cash flow statements from previous events (if applicable).
- Budget for best and worst case scenarios for revenues and expenses.
- Do any of the financial decisions relating to a meeting or series of meetings impact policies at an organisation? For example, including a fee for family members is an implicit invitation to family members to participate and should be considered.

Obtaining advice from someone with financial expertise is advised.

For managing events with foreign currency, you should have a basic knowledge of the currency you'll be dealing with and some history of its stability. More information on this topic can be found in Domain D: Financial Management.

Sub Skill 1.05 – Monitor Strategic Plan

An important step in ensuring the success of a strategic plan is to monitor it carefully. The ability to monitor the plan requires:

- **Measurable objectives.** Look at each objective and key performance indicator (KPI) for your event and answer: How will we know if we've accomplished that objective or KPI?
- **Monitoring tools and processes.** Determine in advance how you will monitor the strategic plan. For example, you may need specific financial reports at pre-determined times to ascertain if the event is on track to reach the objectives. The frequency of monitoring may increase as the event dates get closer.

Figure 3. Key Performance Indicators for an Event.

Objective Area	Examples of Applicable Key Performance Indicators
Financial	▪ Budget versus actual revenues and expenses ▪ Value of sponsorship revenues – both cash and in-kind
Registration	▪ Registration numbers at pre-determined milestone dates ▪ Final registration numbers
Education	▪ Post-event survey results about speakers and content ▪ Test scores of participants
Exhibitors	▪ Number and quality of leads generated (if "quality" is clearly defined)
Motivation	▪ Staff satisfaction survey scores
Sustainability	▪ Waste diversion rate ▪ Percentage of local/organic food served ▪ Participation rates in a community service project
Planning	▪ Meeting milestone dates in the critical path
Marketing	▪ Social media statistics (for example, number of tweets, use of the event hashtag) ▪ Web site visits ▪ Response to e-mail and mailing campaigns
Evaluation	▪ Response rates to surveys?

- **Feedback and modification processes.** As part of your monitoring process, you might determine that your plan needs to be revised in order to achieve your goals and objectives. If this is the case, you need a process in place to communicate to the relevant parties any needed changes. Any changes should be recorded and include details such as the date, rationale, and implementation plan.

Key performance indicators

Key performance indicators (KPIs) are quantifiable measurements of critical success factors for an organisation. KPIs can be applied to events in order to measure how effectively goals and objectives are being met. Examples of KPIs that apply to events are shown in Figure 3. These will need to be tailored based on the event type and organisational objectives.

Contributing Authors

M. Theresa Breining. CMP, CMM
Principal, Breining Group, LLC
Greater San Diego Area, CA, USA
Member of Meeting Professionals International (MPI)

Eric Rozenberg, CMP, CMM
President, Swantegy
Managing Director Event Strategy Practice, Culture22 Communications Group
Executive Director BtoB Events Network, BOB.tv
Brussels, Belgium and Miami/Fort Lauderdale, FL, USA
Member of Meeting Professionals International (MPI)

Reviewer

Tamara Kennedy-Hill, CMP
Director of Community Relations, Travel Portland
Portland, OR, USA
Member of Green Meeting Industry Council (GMIC)

Skill 1:
Endpoints

Terminology

Business value
Key performance indicators (KPIs)
SMART and SMARTER objectives
Strategic meeting management plan (SMMP)
Strategic planning

Additional Resources

1. Kim, W.C., & Mauborgne, R. (2005). *Blue ocean strategy: How to create uncontested market space and make the competition irrelevant.* Boston: Harvard Business School.

Skill 1: Review Questions

1. Describe the differences between a mission statement, goals, and objectives for an event.
2. What are the internal and external factors that need to be considered when determining the feasibility of an event?
3. What types of requirements are needed to carry out an event?
4. What information is included in a financial summary for an event?
5. What are key performance indicators (KPIs)? How are they used to measure how well the goals and objectives for an event are being met?

SKILL 2: DEVELOP SUSTAINABILITY PLAN FOR EVENT

Learning Outcomes

- Identify how to implement a sustainability management plan.
- Provide examples of how to demonstrate environmental sustainability.
- Provide examples of social responsibility.

Sustainable or "green" events help to reduce the impact of events on the environment and can improve the financial outcomes for organisations. By implementing a **sustainability management plan** and demonstrating **environmental responsibility**, event professionals can produce meetings that are more sensitive to the environment and make positive contributions in the communities in which events are held. Using environmentally responsible practices reduces the consumption of resources and can position the event host organisation as a responsible business. The benefits can include:

- Economic savings through the efficient use of resources and the reduction of waste
- Reducing corporate risks by protecting reputations and being in compliance with standards and laws
- Contributing to favourable community legacies, which can support brand trust and loyalty
- Positioning the brand as a thought leader or innovator in its industry and a responsible business that considers its impact on the environment and society
- Positive public relations opportunities from meaningful community service projects
- Participant and worker health from the improvement of air quality and the elimination of chemicals

What Are Sustainable Events?

When most people think of being sustainable, green or environmentally sensitive, specific actions like recycling, serving local/organic food, or reducing printing are usually the first things that come to mind. However, a sustainable event or event goes beyond the individual practices that are implemented. The International Organisation for Standardization's *20121 Event Sustainability Management Systems* (ISO 20121) defines a sustainable event as "An event with a balanced approach to economic activity, environmental responsibility and social progress."

Sustainable events also incorporate social aspects, including fair labour practices, socially responsible procurement practices, charitable contributions, and humanitarian efforts. There are many ways that a meeting can have a positive impact in the community where it is held. Well-planned volunteer activities can be effective team-building activities that are positive for the community and offer public relations benefits to the host.

For the purposes of this section, green and environmentally and socially responsible meetings are included in the term "sustainable events."

Sub Skill 2.01 – Implement Sustainability Management Plan

A sustainability management plan should be integrated into the strategic planning for events as early in the process as possible to improve the outcomes.

A sustainability management plan for an event considers environmental, social and economic factors related to the production of the event and integrates these factors into the planning process.

Implementing sustainable practices can begin with the 4 Rs: Rethink, Reduce, Re-use, Recycle. These four principles can be applied to most resource consumption at events. For example, considering paper use results in the following:

- Rethink: Replacing on-site printed materials with a mobile application
- Reduce: Printing materials using both sides of the paper
- Re-use: Printing signs without dates to allow for re-use at multiple events
- Recycle: Recycling printed materials after the event

Sustainability and Cost Savings

For an event professional, sustainable event practices offer a variety of cost-saving opportunities without compromising quality. For example, selecting sleeping accommodations within walking distance of event venues can reduce transportation. Replacing printed materials with on-line versions or mobile applications is often more economical. Venues and hotels often have significant savings by implementing energy efficiency, water conversation and waste management practices. Caterers, food service providers, and general service contractors have ample opportunities as well. For example, condiments served in bulk containers instead of individual containers can offer substantial savings. By providing on-line exhibitor kits, general services contractors save money in production time, mailing, and staff time by not having to produce printed versions.

These are a few of the economic savings realized from implementing sustainable event practices. Suppliers should examine how and what they provide to their clients and customers and look for ways to implement more sustainable practices. Consider alternatives that provide the same or greater level of service while minimizing the negative effects on the environment.

Sustainable choices do not necessarily cost more than non-green selections. Event professionals should track the cost savings and then evaluate what "saved" funds can be reallocated to other goods that might cost marginally more but support the brand positioning of the event.

Sustainable Event Standards

In 2012, three separate but related bodies of work were launched in the events industry:

- *Accepted Practices EXchange/ASTM Environmentally Sustainable Meeting Standards*

Community Service Projects

Including a social legacy project or contributing positively to the community where the event is held is an important aspect of a sustainable event. A social legacy project can involve contributions such as donating food or leftover supplies to community organisations; arranging to clean up a park, river or beach; or painting a school building. The legacy can also consist of a financial contribution to a local charity.

In developing the community service projects, five criteria to consider from the "MAUDE Framework for Community Service Projects" (adapted from Henderson & McIlwraith, 2013) are:

- Is the project *meaningful* in the longterm?
- Is the project *aligned* with the organisation's vision, mission and values?
- Does the project leverage the organisation's unique *skills* or resources?
- Does the project address a *destination-specific* need?
- Is the project *engaging* for stakeholders?

When developing a community service project, event professionals should consult with their insurance provider and risk management team to verify whether projects are covered by existing insurance or if additional insurance will be required.

- International Organisation for Standardization's *20121 Event Sustainability Management Systems* (ISO 20121);
- *Global Reporting Initiative Event Organisers Sector Supplement* (GRI EOSS).

Each of these works addresses related approaches to sustainable event and meeting practices. They share a common purpose to create an accepted, customary approach to integrating sustainability into the meetings industry. The goal is that by adopting those processes, producing sustainable events will become the expected norm.

The APEX/ASTM Environmentally Sustainable Meeting Standards were developed by industry professionals, both planners and suppliers, from North America and Europe. The standards are a series of specific performance requirements, often with metrics for both the planner and supplier to satisfy in nine areas of event management: accommodations, audiovisual, communications, destination selection, exhibits, food and beverage, meeting venue, on-site office and transportation (see Figure 1).

Figure 1. APEX/ASTM Standards (APEX/ASTM, 2012, p. 1).

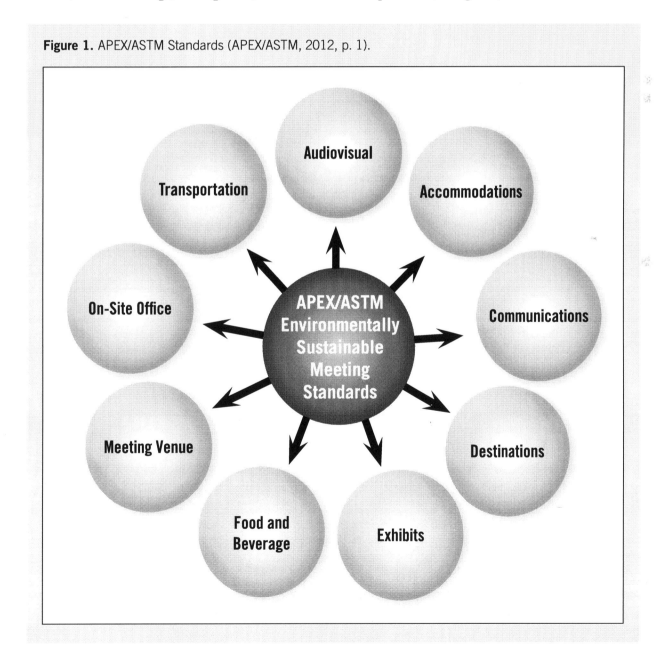

Figure 2. Comparison of Major Sustainable Event Standards and Protocols.

APEX/ASTM	ISO 20121	GRI EOSS
■ Prescriptive checklist approach with nine standards containng metrics for event professionals and suppliers	■ Process-oriented management programme for event organisers	■ Reporting protocol for sustainability measures

The ISO 20121 is a process-oriented management programme developed by the International Organisation for Standardization (ISO). This international standard programme requires organisations to have defined systems in place to implement sustainable practices. Unlike the APEX/ASTM standards, ISO 20121 does not require a specific, predetermined set of performance requirements. Instead, ISO 20121 requires processes to track and record performance.

The GRI EOSS is an international protocol for reporting on sustainable events. It is not a standard like APEX/ASTM or ISO 20121. The GRI EOSS guides event organisers on what and how to report on economic, environmental, and social outcomes. The intent is for events to have a systematic way of reporting elements such as advocacy, resource allocation, ethical fundraising, diversity, feedback mechanisms for complaints, and evaluation.

Simply stated, APEX/ASTM is a prescriptive checklist that mandates certain activities and metrics; ISO 20121 is oriented toward overall management processes; and GRI EOSS is a reporting protocol. They can be implemented separately or in conjunction with each other. Planning a sustainable event does not require any of these programmes; they are voluntary. Increasingly, however, government or grant-funded events are accompanied by mandates to have a robust and verifiable focus on sustainability.

Getting Started with a Sustainability Plan for an Event

Event professionals should understand how introducing a sustainability plan to their meeting will fit into their company or client's mission and values. Chances are some environmental commitment or corporate social responsibility statement may already exist. For example, the 3M Web site under "Sustainability" states "3M actively contributes to sustainable development through environmental protection, social responsibility, and economic progress" (3M Sustainability, 2013).

As with any other strategy or planning activity, the sustainability plan should consider and be grounded in the goals and objectives of the meeting. Be sure to include conversations about the environmental and social impacts of the event and sustainability issues in the destination (i.e., homelessness, water scarcity or lack of recycling infrastructure). Once the concepts around an event are established, creating a sustainability policy to frame your approach is an essential next step. During this process, make sure sustainable event practices are incorporated.

If this is the first time an organisation is developing a sustainability plan, its level of commitment will need to be established. Once the organisation's level of support is known, event professionals can determine what sustainable strategies or practices to put into place.

Here are some fundamental questions to consider before crafting a sustainability policy.

- **Why does the organisation want to incorporate sustainability?** The answers received may be different than expected and will shape the approach taken.
- **What are the areas of greatest impact for this particular event?** This helps to prioritize issues, such as food waste, paper consumption or travel-related carbon emissions.
- **How much is the organisation willing to contribute financially?** In addition to the cost savings inherent in many sustainable event practices, event professionals must know if their organisation is willing to spend more resources on recommended sustainable practices.
- **Is this a one-time effort or part of the organisation's core brand values?** This question clarifies the company's long-term commitment and purpose for adopting sustainability. The event professional can build on any level of commitment.
- **Is the organisation open to changing standard practices in established events or new events to explore new approaches and ideas?** This will provide critical direction and focus on where to spend time and resources. For example, if the attendees are used to having multipage documents available at the event, eliminating the documents or even reducing the size of them will require alternatives to satisfy the needs and expectations of attendees. An organisation might make a limited number of the large programme document available only upon request, while the downloadable alternative is automatically sent via e-mail to all registered attendees.

Elements of a Sustainability Plan for an Event

A sustainability plan for an event should have the following sections (this will satisfy both the ISO 20121 and APEX/ASTM standards):

- **Vision:** A concise statement that describes the ideal outcome, product or service.
- **Principles**: A list of principles that are most relevant to you will help you know how to best respond to an opportunity or challenge in a way that aligns with your sustainability vision. In this section you may also want to reference important protocols or commitments your company may already have.
- **Important Issues:** There are many important and differing issues in the world. Which ones are most important to your organisation, your stakeholders and your event destination? Here is one way to understand how issues and principles are different: *Issues* are the things you think are important to address; *principles* guide how you approach and respond to issues.
- **Objectives:** Your sustainability plan should include specific SMART objectives (see Sub Skill 1.01 – Develop Mission Statement, Goals and Objectives of Meeting or Event).
- **Actions and Initiatives:** The sustainability plan should include specific actions related to the issues and objectives identified in the previous section.
- **Measurement and Reporting:** The plan should also include specific actions regarding measuring the results and communicating these results to your stakeholders.

Effectively implementing a sustainability plan requires the following steps:

- **Developing guidelines:** Specific guidelines for all of the suppliers used for an event should be created. The APEX/ASTM standards can be used as a basis for the guidelines. It is important that clear guidelines are included in the RFP (Request for Proposal) stage of planning. This will make negotiating, contracting and implementing the practices much easier.
- **Communicating objectives internally:** Event professionals will need to communicate expectations for the event very clearly, especially if sustainable practices are new. It is essential to

inform stakeholders of the sustainable event practices. Start with your own organisation and ensure that everyone involved in the implementation of the event is aware of the policies and practices that are being put into place to produce a more sustainable event.

- **Negotiating sustainable practices:** Expected sustainability-related practices by suppliers should be negotiated in advance of the event and included in the contracts. The contract should also include expected repercussions if the obligations are not met.

- **Informing attendees:** Attendees will get engaged in what is being done if the what, why, and how are communicated to them. Let them know why the organisation is doing things differently, and why it is important to make a change on the event Web site, in e-blasts and on-site.

- **On-site verification:** Negotiated sustainable practices should be verified on-site to ensure that they are implemented. The effectiveness of sustainable event practices integrated into the concept and design of the event should be assessed (e.g., was recycling contaminated?) as part of the verification process, and discrepancies should be remedied, if possible.

- **Promoting the sustainable event practices**: Informing the media about sustainability efforts could offer a press-worthy angle to the meeting. Caution: Be sure you are transparent and genuine, and do not overstate what you're actually committed to and expecting to have happen.

Sub Skill 2.02 – Demonstrate Environmental Responsibility

From carbon emissions to waste management, events have many impacts that can be significant for the environment. These impacts vary in incidence and severity from event to event, and it is important for event professionals to be able recognise the impacts and apply techniques for reducing them. The remainder of this section provides sustainable event practice examples that are compliant with the APEX/ASTM Environmentally Sustainable Meeting Standards Level 1. They do not reflect the full list of APEX/ASTM standards.

Destination
The choice of destination for an event will significantly influence the environmental impact of the event. Following are some sustainable event practices for destination selection:

Understand the event's purpose and the attendees' geographic locations. Location can have a substantial impact on the environmental footprint of an event. Evaluate the amount of air travel required by calculating how close the destination is to the anticipated attendance base, with a goal of minimizing travel. Use this information as one of the factors, along with the most appropriate destination for the type of event and suitability for meeting the event goals, when choosing a destination.

Include environmental criteria in the RFP and contracts. When sending out the RFP for an event, event professionals should include environmental criteria and specify the importance of the criteria in the site-selection process. Determine if waste diversion programmes, such as recycling or composting, are available and request a programme with a large number of waste streams implemented in the venues being considered.

Obtain a list of environmentally responsible organisations. Ask the destination marketing organisation (DMO) for a list of venues, properties, and suppliers that have environmental practices in place. Many DMOs will have this readily available.

Evaluate all aspects of the city and venue. Weigh all the factors related to the city. Is the city's mass transit system adequate and is it linked to the airport? Does the city have hotels, restaurants and other services within walking distance of the convention centre or venue, or easily accessible by public transportation?

Venue

Event venues with active sustainability initiatives offer significant opportunities to reduce the event's negative environmental impact. As with other sourcing processes, evaluating sustainable venues early in the event planning process will improve results of the sustainable initiatives.

Send an RFP with the minimum guidelines.   Consider asking the venues if they have the following:

- **Environmental management programme or certification.** Has the property been certified by a third-party organisation or have they established an environmental management programme and training for all staff?
- **Recycling and waste diversion.** Does the venue have a recycling programme for cardboard, paper, metal, glass, and plastics? Does the venue have a composter or food digester? If not, is one available to them and will they ensure that it is implemented for the event?
- **Cleaning supplies and protocols.** Ask what percentage of the cleaning supplies and paper products are certified sustainable or eco-friendly.
- **Building equipment and systems.** Are the heating, ventilation and air conditioning (HVAC), lighting and water systems efficient?
- **Local community partnership and support.** Does the venue regularly support local charities or provide the opportunity to donate leftover food or materials to groups in need?

Include environmental commitment as a factor in rating properties.   Weigh each hotel or venue's environmental policies and procedures along with other determining factors. Ask venues that do not already have policies in place if it is possible to establish them for the meeting and if they will continue them after the requesting group checks out.

Include environmental practices and policies in site inspections.   Request a back-of-the-house tour as part of the site inspection. Tour areas where waste is sorted and where it is stored before it is collected. Take a look at the kitchen to see the amount of individual packaging used, as well as the venue's recycling or composting efforts and where they store food for donation to local food banks. Determine whether local facilities process the compost or recycling materials to ensure that your sorting efforts do not end up in a landfill.

Specify environmental and social programmes in the contract.   Include a clause in the contract outlining the environmental and social programmes to be in place during the event; be clear about the impact of non-compliance. These initiatives should be reviewed in the pre-event meetings and verified on-site.

Ensure that practices are occurring and the measurable data is being tracked.   Once on-site for the event, tour the back-of-the-house again to see how sustainable practices are being implemented. Ask for measured data, such as the waste diversion rate or energy and water use. If multiple groups are in-house, actual numbers may be difficult to obtain; in that case, ask for estimates based on the percentage or size of the meeting in comparison to others using the facility.

Accommodation

In many instances the event venue will contain both the event space and the guest accommodations, making the initial steps less time-consuming for the event planner. Many times, however,

---

the accommodations are separate from the event venue. When this is the case, the event professional should consider social and environmental criteria when selecting accommodations. Considerations include:

- Environmental certifications.
- Efficient energy and water use.
- Availability of a linen and towel re-use programme.
- Programmes to donate unused amenities or dispensers for soap and shampoo (eliminating single-use bottles).
- In-room and property recycling programmes.
- Environmentally friendly cleaning products and supplies.
- Non-smoking areas.
- Paperless registration and communication.

Transportation

Even when the event destination is sustainable, participants, meeting supplies, food, exhibit booths, and audiovisual equipment still must travel to an event location. Minimizing transportation and working with companies to provide the most environmentally responsible transportation options will never completely eliminate emissions or waste. However, measures can be taken to minimize the negative impact of transportation in the following areas:

Participants.   People make many of their own transportation decisions when coming to the event. Educate participants in the promotional materials and registration information, providing resources so their decisions can be as environmentally responsible as possible. The following suggestions reflect some sustainable event practices:

- Alert attendees to environmentally preferable transportation, such as mass transit, ridesharing and alternatives to air travel such as rail. Provide information about local public transit or arrange for transfers to transport attendees to and from the airport and the hotel or meeting venue.
- Provide public transit passes and maps in attendees' welcome packets.
- Encourage attendees to walk or cycle to events and allow sufficient time for them to do so.
- Provide carbon-offset opportunities for attendees during the registration process and on-site.
- Provide a schedule of transfers between venues to increase passenger loads and minimize the frequency of trips.

Transportation suppliers.   Inform potential transportation companies of the sponsoring organisation's sustainability commitment and initiatives. Ask about their sustainable practices. Include a clause in the contract with the transportation provider that confirms its commitment to comply with the requests (e.g., operating a no-idling policy in which vehicles are turned off when not in use). Compliance with this policy should be enforced through contractual clauses and on-site verification.

Ground transportation.   The following are questions to ask potential ground transportation companies:

- Do they perform environmentally responsible maintenance and recycle used oil, batteries, antifreeze, and tires?
- Do they have a no-idling policy (if weather permits) and routinely train drivers?
- Do they offer fuel-efficient or alternative-fuel vehicles? Or, are they willing to use bio-diesel fuel in their existing vehicles?

Shipping freight.   When choosing a freight forwarder, consider options to reduce transportation-related carbon emissions. In the United States, look for carriers that are EPA Smartway Certified. Also ask about consolidating deliveries, reducing waste, and recycling packaging. Use the questions in the air or ground transportation sections to choose a forwarder.

Carbon Offsets.   Carbon offsets are part of a holistic carbon management system and can be used to create carbon-neutral events, Although it is likely impossible to eliminate all carbon emissions related to an event, even with comprehensive environmental initiatives, carbon offsets can be purchased to mitigate the effects of the carbon emissions. A carbon offset is a way of counteracting the carbon emitted when the use of fossil fuel causes greenhouse gas emissions. Offsets commonly involve investing in projects such as renewable energy, tree planting, and energy-efficient projects. Before using carbon offsets, you will need to determine what your impact is and how it will be measured. Calculate the average attendee transport distance to the event and the estimated event-related carbon emissions. There are various programmes available to calculate the emissions caused by the energy use associated with events. Carbon offsets can be funded through voluntary participant contributions, as a sponsorship opportunity, or as part of the event budget.

Food and Beverage

The choices meeting managers make about food and beverage are critical to the well-being of their guests, the budget, and the planet. Event professionals have the responsibility for making these food choices for the large number of people attending their events. These choices have become increasingly complicated as guests have come to expect food that fits their daily way of life, whether that is vegetarian, organic, or one of the many other options. There is a growing trend in the food industry to celebrate local food businesses and know where our food comes from.

Here are a few suggestions to make those decisions easier:

- **Choose food in season**. Choosing food in season in the local area has great benefits. Buying locally grown products helps support the local communities and offers fresher, seasonal, and regional choices with less transportation-related emissions. It is also a great way to celebrate the local flavours of the region.
- **Choose seafood from sustainable fisheries**. Increased consumer demand for seafood is depleting fish stocks around the world and harming the health of the oceans. Ask your caterer to ensure that all seafood meets sustainable criteria. Resources for assessing sustainable seafood include Australian Marine Stewardship Council (Australia), Marine Stewardship Council (UK), OceanWise (Canada), Seafood Watch (USA) and the World Wildlife Federation Sustainable Seafood Consumer Guides (global).
- **Choose certified fair trade, organic products.** Sustainable coffee and cocoa bean harvesting should be taken into account when ordering coffee. Farmers should be paid a fair wage and both commodities should be certified. Other products that can be sourced as fair trade certified include sugar, bananas, chocolate, tea, and olive oil to name only a few.
- **Bulk food and beverage.** Look for opportunities to save both money and packaging by choosing food that doesn't require individual packaging.
- **Offer vegetarian and vegan options.** Each meal should have both of these options available to participants. Alternatively, make the whole meal a hearty vegetarian entrée by working with the chef. Costs for vegetarian meals are quite often lower than those for meals with meat.
- **Order food based on the history of the attendees' preferences and behaviours.** Guaranteed numbers for food and beverage functions should be based on historical trends for the group. For example, do attendees typically arrive after breakfast has been served? For recurring

events, attendance history for each food function should be available in post-event reports from prior instances of the event. If there is no history for the group, ask attendees to sign up for meals in advance. This will save both money and food.

- **Require that unused food be donated.** Donating leftover food from events is an important component of social responsibility. There are some misconceptions surrounding food donation and legal liability. Many countries have legislation that protects food donors that act in good faith. Regulations related to food donations should be researched in the location where your event is being held and proper food handling practices, as determined by the applicable health department, should be in place.

- **Ganging menus.** This practice involves two or more groups in the same venue using the same menus. This can significantly reduce waste and cost.

- **Purchasing, packaging, and serving.** A good deal of the food and beverage waste is in the packaging and the serving. The waste can be reduced by requesting minimal packaging on food products, avoiding the use of polystyrene (Styrofoam), and reducing the amount of disposable service ware. If disposables are required, offer recyclable, compostable or biodegradable options. Other recommendations include replacing individual water bottles with large pitchers, containers or water stations, and requesting cloth or compostable napkins with a high post-consumer recycled content.

- **Reduce, re-use, and recycle.** The venue or caterer should recycle paper, glass, plastics, cans, aluminum, corrugated boxes, and kitchen oil. Food and food-contaminated paper waste should be composted.

Exhibit Production

Exhibitions offer a tremendous opportunity to minimize their negative environmental impact and support communities by the choices made by the organisers, venue, general services contractor, and exhibitors. Collaboration among those suppliers is crucial to creating an environmentally and socially responsible exhibition. With respect to exhibitions, environmental factors to consider are energy and water usage, transportation-related carbon emissions, waste generated, and the products and services purchased to produce the show. Examples of practices that can improve an exhibition's environmental impact include:

- Communicating and monitoring expectations of environmental practices by exhibitors, including minimizing packaging, selecting environmentally preferred promotional products, and using reusable booth materials.

- Selecting venues with existing energy and water conservation infrastructure and waste diversion practices (such as recycling and composting).

- Printing on recycled paper with vegetable or soy-based inks, or replacing printed materials with on-line materials.

- Recycling, composting or donating leftover materials.

- Using recycled, recyclable or reusable, and/or sustainably cleaned exhibition materials, such as drapes and carpets.

- Minimizing packing materials and shipping, and choosing environmentally preferable options for both.

- Measuring and reporting environmental impact, and using this information to set goals for future exhibitions.

- Offering electronic lead capture for exhibitors.

Communication and Marketing

Environmental practices related to communication and marketing can be broadly categorized into three areas: marketing materials, communicating environmental practices, and attendee engagement. Examples of each are provided below:

Marketing and Communication Materials:

- Use electronic versions of materials such as registration forms, media and sponsorship packages, and surveys whenever practical.
- Make sure that e-mail and mailing lists are kept up to date to avoid sending printed materials to out-of-date contacts.
- When printing, double-side materials and use recycled products.
- Purchase marketing materials from a sustainable source.
- Utilise durable, reusable signage systems made from recycled/recyclable materials.
- After the event, repurpose used signs into other products.

Communicating Environmental Practices:

- Include information on environmental impact in the post event report (PER).
- Produce a case study with quantifiable results of environmental practices.
- Issue a press release that highlights environmental achievements.
- Consider applying for sustainable event awards or other media opportunities to communicate your environmental practices.

Engaging Attendees in Environmental Practices:

- Appoint waste management advisors to assist attendees in placing discarded items into the correct recycling and composting stations.
- Provide walking and public transportation maps so attendees can visit the city without renting a car.
- Inform attendees of the hotel's linen re-use programmes, daily housekeeping options, in-room recycling containers, and energy conservation efforts. Also suggest they decline a daily paper unless they intend to read and recycle it.
- Ask attendees to bring their favourite water bottle or coffee cup from home.
- Include questions in the formal evaluation about the event's environmental stewardship, attendees' participation, and their suggestions on how to build on your success.

On-site Procedures

The following practices apply to an on-site office and any other areas under the responsibility of the organiser, including registration or Internet cafes at a conference or event. While these recommendations are not comprehensive and do not consider all aspects of a workspace, they can be applied directly to any work environment. Many of the practices previously discussed in this chapter related to waste management, energy and water conservation, and using environmentally preferable products apply to this area as well. Examples of on-site practices to improve the impact on the environment include:

- **Office Equipment:** Select energy efficient equipment that is Energy Star™ certified and acquired locally to minimize transportation requirements. Select equipment that will reduce your paper consumption, such as copiers that print double-sided and a tablet for event team members, which can replace a printed event specifications guide (this has the added benefit of making real-time updates possible).

- **Communications:** Use recycled paper on flipcharts and substitute printed handouts with electronic versions unless necessary for educational purposes. Use reusable or electronic signage, including using the hotel's in-room television station to publish information.
- **Recycling and Repurposing:** Make sure to use the venue's recycling systems to recover cardboard, paper, glass, cans, glass, batteries, and toner cartridges. Donate all leftover supplies (including conference bags) to a school or charitable organisation. Save pre-event shipping containers for use after the event.
- **Staff Travel:** Create a travel plan for staff that maximizes the use of public transportation to attend the event. When lodging is required, make sure it is within a mile of the meeting venue. Hire local staff where possible to minimize travel.

Audiovisual

Audiovisual (AV) and event technology can be energy intensive. A number of practices can be implemented to reduce energy consumption and improve overall sustainability of the event. In consultation with the event technology supplier, practices include:

- Use energy-saving equipment and make sure these features are enabled.
- Turn off unnecessary equipment.
- Make floor plans and event diagrams available electronically.
- Ship only what is needed by ground not air or procure equipment locally.
- Use local labour for set-up and removal.
- Recycle batteries from equipment.
- Donate surplus equipment that cannot be re-used.
- Select lighting with reduced energy requirements.
- Enable virtual participation in the event through hybrid meeting technology.

References

3M, Inc. (2013). Retrieved from http://solutions.3m.com/wps/portal/3M/en_U.S./3M-Company/Information/

APEX/ASTM Environmentally Sustainable Meeting Standards. (2012). Events Industry Council. Retrieved from http://www.eventscouncil.org/APEX.aspx

Henderson, E., and McIlwraith, M. (2013). *Ethics and Corporate Social Responsibility in the Events Industry.* Hoboken: John Wiley & Sons.

ISO 20121 Event Sustainability Management System. (2012). International Organisation for Standardization. Retrieved from: http://www.iso.org/iso/catalogue_detail?csnumber=54552

Contributing Authors

Amy Spatrisano, CMP
Principal, MeetGreen®
Portland, OR, USA
Founder and Member of Green Meeting Industry Council (GMIC)

Nancy Zavada, CMP
Principal, MeetGreen®
Portland, OR, USA
Founder and Member of Green Meeting Industry Council (GMIC)

Reviewer

Tamara Kennedy-Hill, CMP
Director of Community Relations, Travel Portland
Portland, OR, USA
Member of Green Meeting Industry Council (GMIC)

Skill 2:
Endpoints

Terminology

Environmental responsibility

Environmentally preferable product

Fair Trade

Ganging menus

No-idling policy

Sustainability management plan

Sustainable or green events

Waste diversion

Additional Resources

1. ASAE and the Centre for Association Leadership Convene Green Alliance at http://www.convenegreen.com

2. APEX/ASTM Environmentally Sustainable Meeting Standards at http://www.eventscouncil.org/APEX/APEXASTM.aspx

3. Events Industry Council Sustainability Resources (www.eicsustainability.org)

4. Global Reporting Initiative Event Organisers Sector Supplement (GRI EOSS) at https://www.globalreporting.org/reporting/sector-guidance/event-organisers/Pages/default.aspx

5. International Standard Organisation 20121 Event Sustainability Systems Standard (ISO 20121) at http://www.iso.org/iso/catalogue_detail?csnumber=54552

6. Saving Green by Going Green, Nancy Zavada, Amy Spatrisano and Shawna McKinley (www.meetgreen.com)

7. Simple Steps to Green Meetings and Events, Amy Spatrisano and Nancy Zavada (www.meetgreen.com)

Skill 2: Review Questions

1. What is a sustainable event?

2. What are the benefits of a sustainable event?

3. What are three major sustainable event standards and protocols, and how do they compare to each other?

4. What are ten ways to improve the environmental and social responsibility of an event?

SKILL 3: DEVELOP BUSINESS CONTINUITY OR LONG-TERM VIABILITY PLAN OF MEETING OR EVENT

Learning Outcomes

- Explain how to develop an evaluation plan for an event.
- Describe how to measure an event's return on investment.
- Identify the steps necessary to evaluate/audit an event.

Business continuity refers to the ability of an organisation to continue to operate during and after an emergency, crisis, or disaster occurs. Simply put, can your business stay afloat if the worst happens? Business continuity planning is complementary to, but not the same as, **contingency planning**. While contingency planning addresses the ability of the event professional to carry off the event as planned, business continuity planning addresses the business as a whole.

To begin business continuity planning, a business must first determine its critical business functions. That is, what are those operational aspects without which the business cannot operate and without which the business will have no customers, clients, or members? Critical business functions will vary from one organisation to another and may even vary among businesses of the same type. For example, if a hotel faces a crisis, some of the first things that must be operational are data systems (to keep information secure), communication systems, and basic utilities. After that, perhaps the hotel will focus on food and beverage operations, housekeeping, and security for guests who are (and may be stuck) in-house. Clearly, things like banquet operations, the swimming pool, and sales are farther down the list because they are not critical to the health and safety of staff or guests, nor are they operations without which the hotel cannot operate, at least until the crisis is over.

Business continuity plans will vary greatly between, for example, a corporation and an independent event planner. Some of the most common elements are a place to work (physical plant—power, water, roof over your head, a desk to work at) and communications (phones, computers). These elements are common to almost all kinds of businesses. From there, plans vary.

To begin business continuity planning, the key question is to ask is "If the worst happened, what would we need to continue providing (product or services) to our customers, clients, or members?" Most businesses will need experts to help them determine their business continuity needs. Arrangements need to be made in advance to ensure minimal disruption to business operations. For example, data backup systems, a plan for employees to work from home or an alternative location, communication systems and protocols require advance arrangements. After a crisis occurs is the worst time to start piecing things together.

Determining the long-term viability of an event is related to the concept of business continuity. It answers, "Can the event continue under the currently forecasted conditions?"

To begin assessing the long-term viability of an event, you will need to consider financial aspects such as forecasted revenues and expenses, the economic context and how it may affect the event, and changes to the business environment (such as new technology) and whether they will positively or negatively affect the event. Most fundamentally, the viability of the event will be determined by whether or not it meets the goals and objectives set out for it. Viability is not only measured by the business factors listed above, it also considers the long-term impact on the natural environment and society.

Sub Skill 3.01 – Develop Evaluation Plan

Events should have a plan for evaluating effectiveness for the stakeholders. The evaluation should encompass both successes and challenges and is an ongoing process that serves as a planning tool for innovation and improvement. Evaluations can be costly and time-consuming for event organisers and participants, so should be undertaken only if there is a plan to learn or benefit from the evaluation. Evaluation instruments and reports should be created with the end user's needs in mind.

The first step in developing an **evaluation plan** is to establish how success is defined. For any given event, success is likely to be interpreted differently based on the stakeholder. The meeting owner may be interested in financial performance, while the participants may measure success based on the value of the education or the networking. The destination may measure success based on the economic impact to the local businesses.

Once you understand what success looks like for each of the stakeholders, you can proceed to determine the measurable objectives for the various event stakeholders. Ideally, these will follow SMART criteria (see Sub Skill 1.01 – Develop Mission Statement, Goals and Objectives of Meeting or Event). Examples of measurements based on objectives for different stakeholders are shown in Figure 1.

Figure 1. Measurements Based on Stakeholders and Their Objectives.

Stakeholder	Measurement
Meeting owner	Achievement of the purpose of the event
Participants	Satisfaction scores on evaluations
Exhibitors	Quality and quantity of leads

Sub Skill 3.02 – Measure Return on Investment

If we don't know how we've done, then the strategic planning exercise is just an exercise. Measurement is an essential part of strategic planning. It answers the critical question "Did we accomplish what we set out to accomplish?"

Measuring return on investment informs stakeholders in a commonly understood business format of the financial success of the event.

Return on investment is calculated as:

ROI (%) = Net Monetary Benefits/Meeting Costs x 100

Beyond the information that is typically measured for most meetings—such as achieving financial goals or attendance projections—there are six data types that can be measured in the meetings and events field as part of the Phillips ROI Methodology (Phillips, Breining and Phillips, 2008) (see Figure 2).

The most important element of any meaningful measurement is the development of clear and measurable objectives, and the development of those objectives is the determination of the level to which each will be measured (see Figure 3).

Additional information on measuring return on investment can be found in Sub Skill 14.04—Measure Event Success.

Figure 2.   Data Types in Meetings and Events from the Phillips ROI Methodology.

0	Inputs/Indicators: measures event basics, such as the number of attendees, costs and efficiencies.
1	Reaction and Perceived Value: tracks attendee reaction to the event and intention for follow-up action.
2	Learning: measures what participants learned during the programme.
3	Application and Implementation: measures how attendees apply what they learned during the programme.
4	Impact and Consequences: considers the changes to the business, such as productivity, revenue or employee engagement.
5	Return on Investment: measures the ratio of business impacts to meeting costs.
6	Intangibles: measures the benefits from an event that cannot or should not be converted into monetary values, such as leadership skills or customer satisfaction. *(Phillips, Breining and Phillips, 2008)*

Figure 3.   Examples of Measurements Across Meeting Types.

Event Type	Objective	Measurement
Corporate Sales Meeting	Increase of sales for meeting participants	Sales figures for participants compared to sales figures for those that didn't participate in the meeting
Association Annual Meeting	Increase in member retention	Membership figures for those that attended the meeting against those that did not
Exhibition	Shorter lead time to secure business for exhibitors	Comparing closing times with customers attending the exhibit against customers not attending
Internal Staff Training	Higher levels of customer satisfaction	Feedback scores from customers working with employees attending training vs. those that did not participate

Sub Skill 3.03 – Evaluate/Audit Meeting or Event

The following section is adapted with permission from the *Events Industry Council Manual, 8th Edition.*

What should you evaluate?

What you should evaluate will depend on the nature of the event, the needs of the stakeholders, and how the data will be used. For recurring events, consistent evaluation formats will allow you to compare results over time. Some typically measured elements include those shown in Figure 4.

Timing and sequencing of data collection

Evaluations often take place after the event. While this may be necessary to measure some impacts of the event, waiting until the conclusion of the programme to collect data means you will not be able to make any needed adjustments during the event to improve results. Data collection can be undertaken during three distinct phases: pre-event, on-site, and post-event.

Pre-event data. Surveying your participants prior to your event allows you to shape the programme to their needs. Examples of pre-event data that can be collected ahead of time to enhance your programme include:

Figure 4.   Measured Elements of Events.

Financial results	• Profit or loss • Attendance • Hotel room pick-up
Programme elements	• Speakers • Satisfaction with content, formats and length • Achievement of learning objectives • Scheduling • Recommendations for future events
Exhibits	• Quality and quantity of the exhibitors • Quality and quantity of the visitors • Exhibit services • Hours of operation • Facilities
Site and logistics	• Destination and venue • Technology infrastructure • Quality of the food and beverage • Ability to meet dietary requirements • Meeting facilities • Environmental attributes • Accessibility
Services	• Availability and quality of venue, technical and audiovisual staff • Transportation and tour operators
Other elements	• Entertainment and recreational activities • Sustainability—conformity to standards such as ISO 20121 and APEX/ASTM

- For educational events: topics or speakers that participants would like included
- For exhibits: exhibitors or product areas the visitors would like to see
- For training programmes: pre-training assessments that can be used to gauge learning

On-site data. Evaluations conducted on-site typically result in rich data as the concepts and ideas are fresh in people's minds. Many event mobile applications will include evaluation tools, allowing you to receive real-time evaluation data. Paper evaluations may also be collected following each session. Evaluations, if reviewed during the programme, can also allow you to make adjustments to improve participant satisfaction and comfort. Examples of on-site data that can be collected include:

- Site and venue aspects such as heat, lighting, and sound
- Programme content
- Understanding of content delivered (in training sessions)
- Satisfaction levels

Post-event data. Most evaluations are conducted after the event itself, primarily through electronic means, though this should be tailored to the audience. Aspects such as programme content can be reevaluated post event to measure longer-term impact.

Examples of post-event data that can be used to shape future events include:

- Achievement of stakeholder objectives
- Impact of event (see **return on investment** section above)
- Programme content
- Satisfaction with the venue and destination
- Recommendations for future events

Resource Requirements and Evaluation Formats

Required resources will depend on the types of evaluations that are conducted. Pre-event evaluations are often done electronically, and they can be integrated with registration or ticket sales to improve the number of responses. On-site evaluations may require staffing to distribute and collect evaluation forms, or may form part of a mobile application. Alternatively, electronic evaluations can be distributed at the end of each day and would require access to a distribution mechanism. Post-event evaluation requirements for data collection may involve electronic distribution, or mail-in surveys, phone surveys, and focus groups.

Data is only valuable if it is interpreted and converted into knowledge. Therefore, resources should be allocated not only to collect data but also to review and share the results and to develop recommendations from them.

Conducting surveys

The following section is adapted with permission from the *Events Industry Council Manual, 8th edition*.

Surveys and **questionnaires** are the most popular type of evaluation tools for events. They can be conducted on-site, through the mail, by phone, fax, or on-line. They are typically easy to prepare and distribute through inexpensive on-line tools. Surveys are given to the respondent and the respondent answers directly on the survey. Questionnaires are typically administered in person or by phone, but a person reads the questions to the respondent and marks the respondents answers. The respondent does not write on the questionnaire itself.

Advantages of surveys include their ease of use, creation, and distribution. However, they may have low response rates if conducted after the event and may result in biased responses if questions are worded in a way that suggests how they should be answered (e.g., "Was the food plentiful?" or "Was the room environment large enough for the number of participants?").

Questionnaires offer the advantage of allowing the respondent to hear the questions completely (instead of being able to skim and perhaps misunderstand questions), but the person reading the questions must take care to avoid adding words or changing the nature of the questions, which might skew the results (e.g., putting emphasis on a word or phrase inadvertently, which might indicate how the respondent should answer the question). Additionally, questionnaires can encourage inaccurate responses when the respondent is either favourably or unfavourably influenced by interaction with the person asking the questions. Surveys are often less expensive to administer, but questionnaires provide a more personal touch.

An event evaluation is only as good as the questions and how they are asked. Be familiar with how to write an objective question, how to accurately tabulate responses, and how to interpret the results. If you are using on-line survey tools, data security should also be considered, particularly if personal information is being collected. When questionnaires are used, having privacy for responses may be a concern.

Types of data. Two types of data are typically collected through surveys: **quantitative data**, sometimes referred to as "hard data," and **qualitative data**, also called "soft data."

Quantitative data is represented numerically, allowing comparison of data by assigning ranks or scores or by determining averages and frequencies of responses. Respondents are given a selection of responses to a question and must choose the response that most closely represents their opinion. These responses can be analysed to provide numerical data. For example, you might ask, "Did you receive value for the cost of this event registration?" with response options of "Yes" or "No." This allows you to count the number of affirmative and negative responses and arrive at the percentage of people who answered "Yes," and those who answered "No." Quantitative data is often used in executive summaries, promotions, and membership materials.

Qualitative data is a descriptive record of participants' observations or behaviour. It allows participants to answer in their own words. For example, you might ask, "What did you enjoy most about the event?" and provide several blank lines to allow for a response. Qualitative responses to open-ended questions are often viewed as anecdotal and not as valuable as quantitative data. That is incorrect. Qualitative data adds the *why* to the *what*. If 95 percent of attendees said the event provided value (quantitative data), compiling a list of what they enjoyed most tells what provided that value (qualitative data). Researchers advise collecting both quantitative and qualitative data, referred to as "mixed methods research." For most purposes, though, limit the number of qualitative questions, because they are time-consuming for the respondent to complete and for the evaluators to review.

Types of questions.   There are four basic formats for survey questions:

1. *Open-ended question*—offers unlimited response options. For example, "What is your opinion of the accommodations provided at this event?"

2. *Checklist*—a list of items for participants to check off responses. For example, "Which of the following activities did you attend? (check all that apply)" Also known as a multi-select question.
   - ❏ Opening reception
   - ❏ Networking lunch
   - ❏ Closing reception

3. *Two-way question*—offers alternative response options such as "Yes" or "No." For example, "Did you attend the awards banquet?" Typically known as a closed-end question.

4. *Multiple choice question*—respondent selects one from a variety of options. For example, "What is your preferred location for next year's event?" This is another type of closed-end question. It becomes slightly more open if you allow "Other" and a blank line for input.
   - ❏ Buenos Aires
   - ❏ London
   - ❏ New York
   - ❏ Shanghai
   - ❏ Other: _____

Respondents will be able to answer more quickly and with less confusion if the question format remains consistent. However, this can also lead to less reliable responses (e.g., selecting all of the first items in the various questions). Be sure response options allow respondents to give adequate and correct answers to the specific questions asked.

Survey design.   Some general guidelines for designing surveys include:

- Only ask for information (including personal information such as age or income) that is relevant and will have a useful purpose.

- Keep it short and easy to complete, especially for evaluations that must be completed quickly. Limit this to the most important information for assessing the goals and objectives of the event.
- Ask specific questions, each addressing a single topic. Do not ask, "How do you rate the meals and accommodation?" What if the accommodation was excellent but the meals were poor?
- Avoid professional jargon, abbreviations, and acronyms.
- Put difficult or time-consuming questions at the end of the survey. Attendees who have invested several minutes in filling out an evaluation are more likely to complete it. Even if they skip a difficult question, they are more likely to return the survey.
- Avoid asking for the respondent's name. Make it optional. Many people are reluctant to be completely honest if their responses can be traced.
- Include a contact name and your organisation's address and fax number on the evaluation form so it can be returned if not collected on-site.
- Number all questions; this will speed up coding of the data.
- Make the survey readable and visually simple.
- If the surveys are being conducted electronically, use a tool that allows you to filter the questions based on earlier responses. For example, if the respondent indicates that he or she is an exhibitor, a different question would appear depending on whether the person selected "yes" or "no."
- If possible, offer to make the evaluation results available to respondents.

Sub Skill 3.04 – Evaluate Effectiveness of Risk Management Plan

If we don't take the time to outline a risk management plan, we not only are completely unprepared in the event of unexpected challenges, but we also lose our credibility with our business partners, who routinely develop risk management plans for other business ventures. Risk management is outlined in detail in Domain C: Risk Management.

The risk management plan should be evaluated to verify that it includes the possibilities for the following potential risks:

- Accident or illness of attendees, speakers, or entertainers
- Natural disasters
- Civil unrest
- Inability for attendees, speakers, or entertainers to travel to meeting
- Other risks specific to the organisation

The likelihood of each risk should be assessed and then a contingency should be outlined for each. Those with a higher likelihood of occurring should have more elaborate plans with a variety of possible actions should they occur.

Evaluating a risk management plan is often difficult until a crisis, emergency, or disaster has occurred and the plan has been put into action. Only then can the event professional truly see what worked and what did not. However, the plan can be critiqued on the basis of thoroughness, clarity, organisation, and relevance.

Absent an actual crisis, disaster, or emergency, one evaluation method is to learn from the mistakes of others. The reactions, responses, and results of other organisations, meetings, and events that have been involved in a crisis, emergency, or disaster can often provide illustrations of errors or omissions to a risk management plan. Likewise, staying current on best practices in risk management is useful and reviewing the risk management plan at least once a year to update it as necessary is prudent.

Practicing elements of the risk management plan through drills or tabletop exercises can be a useful way to evaluate the risk management plan, but it is not without flaws. For example, one event professional's company regularly practiced a building evacuation plan. They modified the plan as issues arose during the drills (e.g., evacuating persons with disabilities, identifying a gathering point after evacuation, who would carry the contact list). When there was an actual emergency that required evacuation, however, the staff discovered that the lights in the stairwells did not come on when the power went out! They never would have known about this flaw in the plan had it not been put to use. To correct it, they arranged for the stairwell lights to be put on the backup generator and for employees to have emergency flashlights at their desks.

Reference

Phillips, J. J., Breining, M. T., & Phillips, P. P. (2008). *Return on investment in meetings and events: Tools and techniques to measure the success of all types of meetings and events.* Amsterdam: Elsevier/Butterworth-Heinemann.

Contributing Authors

M. Theresa Breining. CMP, CMM
Principal, Breining Group, LLC
Greater San Diego Area, CA, USA
Member of Meeting Professionals International (MPI)

Tyra W. Hilliard, PhD, JD, CMP
Associate Professor, Restaurant, Hotel, and Meeting Management
The University of Alabama
Tuscaloosa, AL USA
Member of Meeting Professionals International (MPI), Professional Convention Management Association (PCMA)

Eric Rozenberg, CMP, CMM
President, Swantegy
Managing Director Event Strategy Practice, Culture22 Communications Group
Executive Director BtoB Events Network, BOB.tv
Brussels, Belgium and Miami/Fort Lauderdale, USA
Member of Meeting Professionals International (MPI)

Reviewer

Tamara Kennedy-Hill, CMP
Director of Community Relations, Travel Portland
Portland, OR, USA
Member of Green Meeting Industry Council (GMIC)

Skill 3:
Endpoints

Terminology

Business continuity
Contingency planning
Qualitative data
Quantitative data
Questionnaires
Return on investment
Surveys

Skill 3: Review Questions

1. Compare business continuity planning and contingency planning.
2. How is return on investment calculated, and what are the five levels of measurement for events?
3. What are the three phases of data collection, and what is measured during each phase?
4. What should be included in a risk management plan?

DOMAIN

B

Project Management

When planning an event, the event professional is undertaking the management of a project from beginning to end. In addition to managing all logistical aspects of the event, the event professional is also responsible for budgetary control, resource deployment, and schedule management. **Project management** is broadly defined as "the application of knowledge, skills, tools and techniques to project activities to meet the project requirements" (*PMBOK Guide*, 2008, p.6). This chapter provides a framework for fundamental project management principles and how they may be applied to the event management realm.

SKILL 4: PLAN MEETING OR EVENT PROJECT

Learning Outcomes

- Use project management methods to develop an event plan.
- Develop quality standards, policies, and procedures.
- Identify a suitable theme for an event.
- Develop a procurement plan for the acquisition of goods and services.
- Establish a critical path for an event.
- Identify the elements of an integrated communication plan.
- Develop evaluation procedures for an event.

Early in the event planning process, the organisation will decide whether to hold the event and authorize a team to proceed with planning. The decision may be made based on financial criteria such as costs, break-even potential, or expected profitability. It may also be based on non-financial criteria such as the need to disseminate information, to meet with stakeholders, or to train a team. When authorization to hold the event is granted, the next step is developing a clear understanding of the reasons for holding the meeting, as well as the objectives, **key performance indicators** (KPIs), and how KPIs will be measured. This may require meeting with event stakeholders. Key stakeholders in the planning of an event could include the event professional, the planning team, executive leaders, members and/or employees, key volunteers, supplier partners, exhibitors, sponsors, attendees, and the local community. The organisation must understand the requirements of event stakeholders and balance their competing demands throughout the planning process. Please see Domain F. Stakeholder Management for more information on this topic.

In managing the event, an event professional will inevitably encounter challenges, restrictions, or shortages. In the project management discipline, these demands are referred to as **"constraints,"** as shown in Figure 1. Generally, constraints fall into one of three categories: time, cost, or performance.

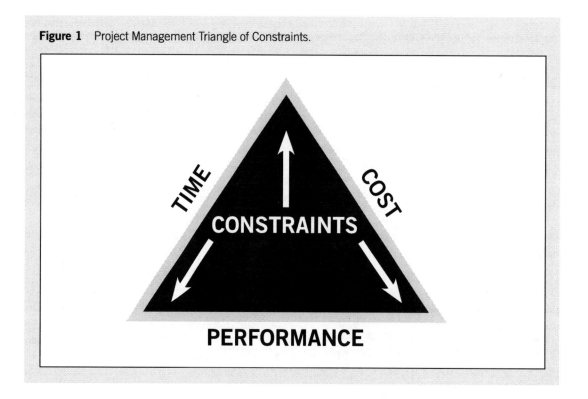

Figure 1   Project Management Triangle of Constraints.

Understanding an event's goals and objectives, requirements, stakeholders, and constraints will allow the event professional to clarify the scope of the event. **Project scope** is defined as "the work that must be performed to deliver a product, service or result with the specified features and functions" (*PMBOK Guide*, 2008, p. 103). The event professional must fully understand the project scope and communicate that with pertinent stakeholders. This will ensure that the event stays on course throughout the planning process.

Once a clear project scope has been established, an event professional can undertake detailed programme planning, which commences another stage in the event's lifecycle. According to the *Event Management Body of Knowledge* and shown in Figure 2, event management consists of five phases (CTHRC, p. 5):

Figure 2 Event Management Phases.

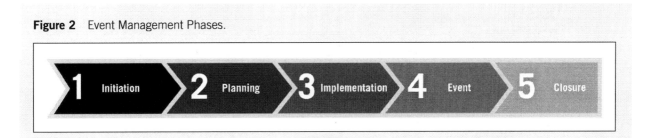

During the initiation phase, research is conducted and the basic event purpose is established; then the scope is outlined, and goals and objectives are defined. During this phase, the commitment of resources is established and risk management strategies are instituted. From there, the planning phase begins and the requirements and specifications for the event are determined, using risk planning as the structure for making decisions. The implementation phase occurs when all the goods and services are contracted and coordinated, synchronizing all the operational and logistical requirements of an event. Next, the event itself is held and risk monitoring and controls are prioritized. Finally, during the closure phase, event production is shut down, contractual obligations are completed, feedback is collected, and the event is evaluated. An important aspect is recording and sharing across key stakeholders the lessons learned during the project to improve future events.

Sub Skill 4.01 – Develop Project Plan

One of the first steps an event professional should take after a decision has been made to go forward with an event is to create a **project plan**. A project plan documents how a project will be completed within a certain timeframe. The project plan, in the simplest terms, serves as the roadmap for planning a project. Project plans come in various forms, and the event professional normally customises his/her versions to his/her preference, organisational needs, and the type of event.

- **Small event**. A project plan for a small event may be a simple document. It will include tasks that need to be completed in order to meet the objectives of the event (i.e., space usage, speakers, event technology needs, and more). It will likely have one person coordinating all tasks, as opposed to larger events, which typically involve a team of people coordinating various aspects of the project.

- **Large event**. Large events may include more tasks around speaker management, "in conjunction with" or unanticipated ("pop up") events, and working with numerous suppliers. Multiple team members may work on the same plan to ensure uniformity and completion of tasks by set deadlines. If the event is sufficiently complex, the event professional may coordinate the efforts of multiple teams.

- **Incentive programme**. A project plan for an incentive trip is likely to include hotels and suppliers, as well as many tasks relevant to leisure activities, spas, golf, and other activities or elements.

- **Exhibitions**. Exhibitions bring the need for tasks associated with sponsors, general service contractor, exhibitors, and more.

- **Product launch**. A product launch event will have tasks related to the marketing of a product, the public relations behind the event, customer relations, and more.

- **Training/educational events**. The content of a project plan for training and education events may get into details of content management, skill practice, and training materials.

Event Management Systems and the Project Plan

Many event professionals use spreadsheets or databases to manage their projects. In addition, many event management systems, available on-line or as downloadable software, can facilitate the creation of a project plan. A typical plan can be created and customised by event type and then automatically generated for each event. These plans will produce reminders of important tasks for the event professional, allowing him or her to manage multiple event timelines through one system. An event management company can call upon its information systems department to learn about products on the market that provide such functionality. Automation of task management is a best practice and provides an event professional with an efficient tool to manage numerous milestones and deadlines associated with a project.

Frequently used in project management, a **Gantt chart** provides a graphical illustration of a schedule that helps to plan, coordinate, and track specific tasks in a project. Gantt charts can be created using spreadsheet software.

Regardless of the format and/or technology selected, an event professional should refer to his/her project plan on a regular basis. Throughout the event lifecycle, progress should be monitored and adjustments made while effectively managing time, costs, and performance. If the plan needs to be adapted, those changes should be communicated to affected stakeholders. An event professional should assess carefully the measure by which he/she knows a specific task/deliverable is complete. Measurements should be concrete and ideally will fit the SMART criteria. For more information on SMART criteria, see Domain A. Strategic Planning.

Sub Skill 4.02 – Develop Quality Standards, Policies, and Procedures

To ensure the quality of an event, the event professional should establish documented standards, policies, and procedures. Creating **standard operating procedures** (SOPs) and checklists ensures that team members perform tasks with consistency and meet anticipated outcomes. Policies and procedures that are documented and housed in a central location accessible to all team members leads to higher quality deliverables.

Quality management includes managing overall project quality; it can also measure the quality of each project deliverable. The *PMBOK Guide* provides a general overview based on the following three processes:

- **Quality planning.** In simple terms, quality planning is a proactive and documented approach to ensure that tasks are done right the first time. Event professionals can use a simple spreadsheet or document to record how they plan to avoid error, waste, and/or service failure. This documentation is referred to as a quality management plan. An example would be listing the materials that should be compiled for attendees and distributed when they arrive at the event.

- **Quality assurance.** Quality assurance, or auditing the quality requirements, provides confidence that the project quality was planned, that results are reliable, and that the quality level established will be achieved. Quality audits or assessments are used to determine whether quality controls are being defined and applied properly. The focus during this stage is on preventing problems from occurring, such as monitoring that all materials for the registration packages are delivered, organised, and ready to be assembled.

- **Quality control.** This is an iterative process that should be performed throughout the project life to track and monitor the results of the project. Following this process will determine whether the results are complying with the standards previously defined in the quality management plan. Quality control is focused on detecting flaws; for example, inspecting assembled registration materials to identify incomplete packages before they are delivered to the attendee.

Figure 3. Simple Gantt Chart for an Event.

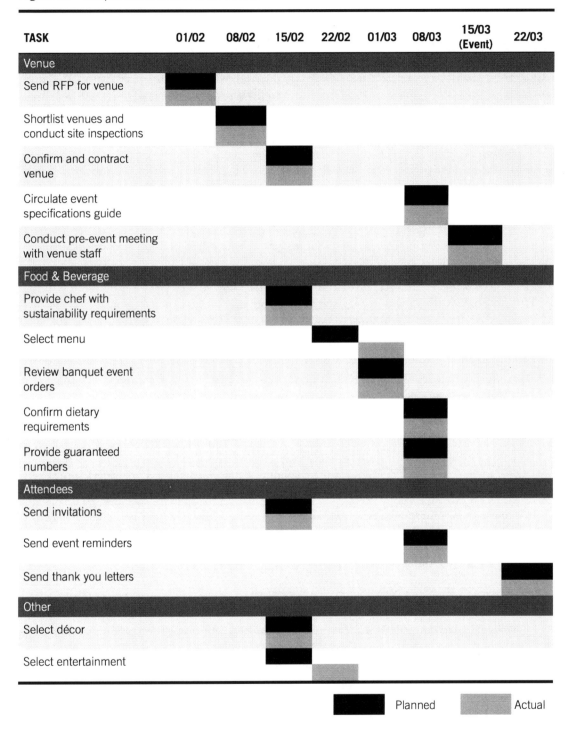

TASK	01/02	08/02	15/02	22/02	01/03	08/03	15/03 (Event)	22/03
Venue								
Send RFP for venue	■							
Shortlist venues and conduct site inspections		■						
Confirm and contract venue			■					
Circulate event specifications guide						■		
Conduct pre-event meeting with venue staff							■	
Food & Beverage								
Provide chef with sustainability requirements			■					
Select menu				■				
Review banquet event orders					■			
Confirm dietary requirements						■		
Provide guaranteed numbers						■		
Attendees								
Send invitations			■					
Send event reminders						■		
Send thank you letters								■
Other								
Select décor			■					
Select entertainment			■					

■ Planned   ▨ Actual

Sub Skill 4.03 – Develop Theme for Meeting or Event

Developing the theme for an event should be done early in the planning process, as it will influence many of the planning decisions that will need to be made. The theme can serve as a foundation around which the event professional selects event components, including, but not limited to, marketing pieces, décor, food, speakers, and activities.

More information on the development of an event theme can be found in Domain G. Meeting or Event Design.

Sub Skill 4.04 – Develop Procurement Plan (Acquisition of Goods and Services)

Most projects need to procure goods and services, regardless of project size or degree of complexity. Project procurement management includes planning, executing, and closing each purchase required for an event, and the event professional must manage each detail of these purchases or have a system that enables oversight for purchases carried out by another person or department. Many organisations have a procurement process in place. In these cases, the event professional will confer with the procurement department to follow established policies and procedures, will include a procurement specialist on the project team, or will put someone in charge of these tasks.

Organizing an event typically requires an extensive amount of acquisitions, including materials or services from external suppliers – such as renting venues, arranging catering, confirming event technology equipment, blocking hotel rooms, arranging transportation (air/land), printing materials, and securing personnel to execute the project. These may involve multiple contracts or subcontracts. See Sub Skill 5.02 for more information on contracts.

As defined by the *PMBOK Guide* (2008), in order to create the project procurement plan, four processes must be followed: planning, conducting, administering, and closing procurements.

- **Plan procurements.** In this process, the event professional and/or project team identifies the required goods and services needed to reach project objectives and determines if these are available in-house or through an external supplier. In planning procurements, the project manager should define "what, how much, and when" to procure. Suppliers also need to be identified and their potential impact on the project needs to be estimated. Various supplier networks and destination management organisations (DMOs) allow a buyer to research reputable suppliers and submit electronic requests for proposals (e-RFPs)

- **Conduct procurements.** After an event professional has sent RFPs to potential suppliers, he or she moves to the step of securing the goods and services. This phase focuses on obtaining responses along with selecting and assigning a contract to a selected supplier. If, during this phase, the bids received do not meet the minimum requirements, a secondary RFP process may be required.

- **Administer procurements.** Administering the procurements is the process of managing the relationship between one's organisation and all engaged and contracted suppliers. This phase includes evaluating the performance of the contract and verifying changes and adjustments as needed during the relationship, such as incorporating milestone dates into the project plan to ensure timely delivery of goods, services, and payments.

- **Close procurements.** Closing procurements is the formal conclusion of the acquisitions process. At this point, all work is verified to confirm accomplishment according to requirements and quality previously established. Upon verification, deliverables are accepted and the acquisition process can then be closed. On-site staff should closely compare the contracts with what is actually received on-site.

Selecting suppliers

Complying with the organisation's procurement process and building a solid framework by which suppliers are selected are important tasks for event professionals. Many organisations classify suppliers in some manner, such as "approved," "preferred," or "exclusive." Suppliers are usually given a status by the procurement department (if applicable). The event professional should work collaboratively with procurement specialists to influence this list.

Prior to engaging a supplier, the event professional should have thorough knowledge of the suppliers':

- History/longevity
- Mission, vision, values/alignment with that of the hosting organisation
- Financial stability
- Insurance, licenses, and bonding
- Staff expertise, credentials, and training received
- Reliability/age of equipment
- Overall professionalism of staff
- Security and reliability of technologies utilised
- References and testimonials
- Policies and processes
- Commitment to sustainability and ethical business

In some cases, this information may be provided when the supplier applies for specific status with the organisation, such as being designated an "approved supplier." If the information isn't secured then, or if it needs to be updated, the event professional should collect this information, which is usually done through the RFP process.

Request for Proposals (RFP)

The Events Industry Council's APEX Web site features an RFP Workbook that, provides the necessary information for single property and citywide events, event technology, DMC and transportation services, and official service contractors. The workbook is downloadable from the APEX Web site on a complimentary basis. By its very structure, the cover page of the workbook, once complete, auto-populates repetitive information to the other worksheets within the workbook. The workbook covers all of the major points that should be included in a quality RFP and allows the planner to identify specific needs and concessions, such as venues, hotel brands, price points, and other information. The APEX RFP Workbook provides potential responders with timelines, criteria for selection, and other information important for the responder in order to prepare an adequate proposal response. As with any RFP, if a prospective responder has questions on specific issues, they are provided with appropriate contact information. While criteria are typically quantifiable, using mathematical formulas and grids to make the process objective, the responder is seldom given detailed insight into the grading system for review of RFPs.

When the RFP is intended for international suppliers, it must contain terminology easy to interpret and translate into other languages. Also, all requests must be framed within the limits of local laws where the service will be contracted and carried out. For example, if the RFP is requesting the services of a professional translator, the procurement requirements must show a balanced description between the organisation's requirements (organisation origin) and the laws of the country where the service will be required. To further illustrate this point, consider the following example: ABC Company needs to contract the services of a bilingual English-Spanish translator. One major requirement for the organisation is a government-granted accreditation for the professional. However, this accreditation is not recognised in the country where the service will be hired and delivered. In this case, the RFP should not consider this requirement for recruitment. If the planner is unfamiliar with the laws in other countries, it is important to seek advice from individuals or companies, such as professional congress organizers (PCOs) familiar with laws and regulations of the country under consideration.

Sub Skill 4.05 – Establish Milestones and Critical Path

Mapping out the tasks from start to finish helps the event professional to visualize the scope of the project. In the project management discipline, a **work breakdown structure (WBS)** is initially drafted. The work breakdown structure organises and describes in detail the total scope of the project.

While not all-encompassing, Figure 4 is an example of a work breakdown structure for a number of areas that the event professional could oversee in the planning and execution of an event.

By subdividing the project into bite-sized pieces, the process of defining activities within each of these subsets becomes more manageable. The WBS is essentially a snapshot of the project scope and scale, and it forms the basis for estimating, scheduling, executing, monitoring, and controlling project work.

Steps in developing the WBS include the following:

1. *Determine tasks and milestones.* The WBS can illustrate the interdependence of tasks and facilitate identification of milestones that directly impact the planning of an event. For example, the registration department will work closely with the information technology department to decide when the on-line registration site will go live, as well as the expiration dates for early registration discounts. Identified in the planning process, **milestones** are key events that occur during the project and ultimately drive the project schedule. Examples of milestones in the meeting planning discipline include the date when registration is launched for an event project, the date when the final event specifications guide is shared with suppliers and facility partners, and the date when a room list is due to the hotel for processing.

2. *Estimate resources.* Resources include any materials, people, equipment, or supplies required for the event. One of the event professional's most important jobs is acquiring the best and most appropriate resources to support successful delivery of the event. While project management software can assist with facets of resource estimation, including scheduling, the event professional must select the best available or most suitable resources to support successful project execution. In a project schedule or timeline, each activity or task should be assigned to specific resources or stakeholders. It is the project manager's responsibility to ensure that all team members clearly understand the scope of the tasks they have been assigned before project execution begins.

Finally, an event professional must anticipate the amount of time needed to complete each of the tasks and assign a unit of time to each activity in the project schedule. The process, known as **forecasting**, will ultimately produce a project schedule or timeline that determines how long the project will take to complete from beginning to end.

The **critical path** represents the chain of activities that must begin on time and stay on track in order to achieve project milestones and ultimately execute the project on time. Tasks that are not part of the critical path may have some flexibility in terms of start or completion times; all critical path tasks must begin and end on time to ensure that the project ends on time. Any delays in achieving critical path tasks could negatively impact the overall project and result in added costs. Once the critical path is established, the event professional should schedule regular reviews of the critical path tasks with project team members, as well as any stakeholder groups that may influence the project schedule.

Sub Skill 4.06 – Develop Integrated Communication Plan

A communication plan should be created in the planning phase of the event. From that point, it becomes a living, breathing document, that guides the project manager and stakeholders throughout the life of the project. The thorough communication plan will contain goals and objectives, tools and tactics, and evaluation techniques. A simple approach to communication starts with a **communication matrix**, which requires answers to the following questions:

- *What* needs to be communicated?
- To *whom* does the content need to be communicated?
- *Who* is responsible for delivering the content?
- *When and how often* will the content be communicated?
- *How* will the content be communicated?
- *Why* does this information need to be communicated?

The event professional should ask the people receiving communications about their expectations regarding content and timing. This information can be used to develop the communication matrix. See Figure 5 for a sample of a simple communication matrix.

After a communication plan has been created, it should be reviewed and approved by key stakeholders, then made available in an easily accessible location, so team members can reference it often. It should be kept current and reposted or circulateed as needed. To start the communication plan, the event professional should determine whether a communication plan was utilised on a past project or whether any peers have templates they prefer to use.

The phrase "integrated communication" has a specific meaning for marketing, public relations, and communication professionals. To professionals in those disciplines, "integrated" refers to a seamless blend of messages so the organisation develops a positive and similar image across stakeholder groups. Therefore, the event professional must collaborate with marketing, public relations, and communication colleagues within the organisation throughout the event's lifecycle. For more information on integrated communication, see Skill 24: Manage Marketing Plan.

Sub Skill 4.07 – Develop Evaluation/Audit Procedures

Evaluation is a process of determining current values and setting changes by comparing the current project status with the plan. The processes for event evaluation are set during the planning stage; however, they can be adjusted or modified while the project is running, as long as those adjustments are based on improving the collection of data, not on influencing the results.

The project monitoring phase generates data relatively early in the project's lifecycle. Events may be evaluated based on a number of criteria, including whether or not the event was successful in:

- Meeting the event goals and objectives
- Meeting financial goals (if applicable)
- Meeting attendance goals and attendee satisfaction
- Meeting sponsorship goals and sponsor satisfaction

Prior to the event, the event professional should determine how the event will be evaluated based on selected criteria. Information on event evaluation procedures can be found in Sub Skill 3.01 – Develop Evaluation Plan and Sub Skill 14.04 – Measure Event Success.

In addition to evaluations, many event professionals will arrange for their events to be audited.

The goal of an evaluation process is to offer maximum transparency, while the goal of an audit is to offer maximum accountability. Both help establish an event's sustainability and establish the organisation's sense of social responsibility.

Although commonly thought of from a financial perspective, audits can be used to assess various aspects of an event, including sustainability, legal compliance, and ethical standards compliance.

Figure 4.   Work Breakdown Structure Example. (Courtesy of Experient, a Maritz Travel Company; used with permission.)

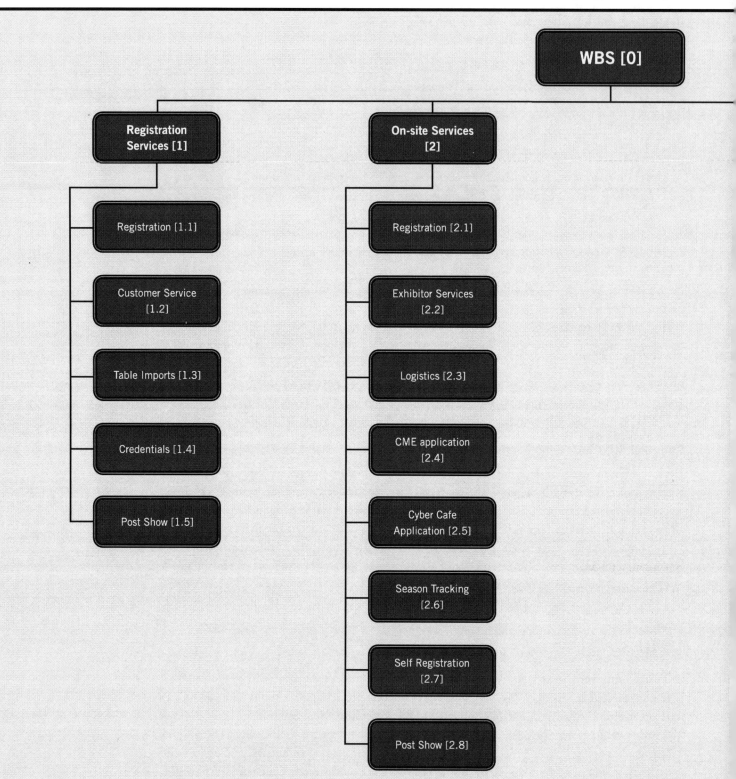

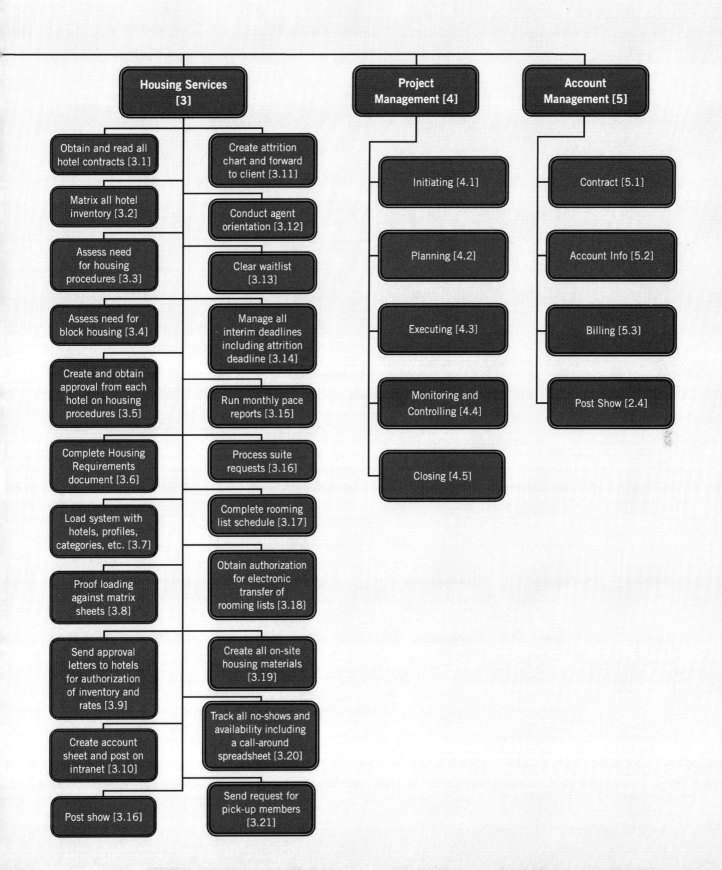

Housing Services [3]

- Obtain and read all hotel contracts [3.1]
- Matrix all hotel inventory [3.2]
- Assess need for housing procedures [3.3]
- Assess need for block housing [3.4]
- Create and obtain approval from each hotel on housing procedures [3.5]
- Complete Housing Requirements document [3.6]
- Load system with hotels, profiles, categories, etc. [3.7]
- Proof loading against matrix sheets [3.8]
- Send approval letters to hotels for authorization of inventory and rates [3.9]
- Create account sheet and post on intranet [3.10]
- Post show [3.16]

- Create attrition chart and forward to client [3.11]
- Conduct agent orientation [3.12]
- Clear waitlist [3.13]
- Manage all interim deadlines including attrition deadline [3.14]
- Run monthly pace reports [3.15]
- Process suite requests [3.16]
- Complete rooming list schedule [3.17]
- Obtain authorization for electronic transfer of rooming lists [3.18]
- Create all on-site housing materials [3.19]
- Track all no-shows and availability including a call-around spreadsheet [3.20]
- Send request for pick-up members [3.21]

Project Management [4]

- Initiating [4.1]
- Planning [4.2]
- Executing [4.3]
- Monitoring and Controlling [4.4]
- Closing [4.5]

Account Management [5]

- Contract [5.1]
- Account Info [5.2]
- Billing [5.3]
- Post Show [2.4]

Figure 5.   Sample Communication Matrix.

What	By Whom	To Whom	When/How Often	How	Why
Sponsor updates	Bob Johnson	Sponsors	Twice monthly	Meeting *Dashboard Report*	Advise sponsors of event status
Stakeholder meetings	Priti Khan	Stakeholders (see charter)	Monthly	Meetings	Ensure stakeholder engagement and approval
Budget review	Bob Johnson	CEO and CFO	First and third Tuesday of each month at 13:00 p.m. EST	Conference call with screen sharing	Budget approval
Attendee invitations	Bob Johnson	Invited guests	Launching on May 1	Registration site	Increase attendance
Attendee communication	Penny Sitz	Registered guests	Ongoing	Established phone line and e-mail box	Advise attendees of on-site information
Supplier relations	Bob Johnson	All employees	As needed, daily	E-mail/phone	Advise suppliers of any changes
Event owner updates	Rosa Day	All employees	Weekly, 09:00 on Tuesdays	Phone	Event owner approval of plans and budget
Full team updates	Priti Kahn	Marketing, production, operations	Weekly, 10:00 on Tuesdays	Conference call line	Review event plan
On-site staff communications	Bob Johnson	Staff	Briefing on July 1, 13:00 p.m. EST	Classroom sessions on-site	Ensure event is properly executed

The goal for a financial audit is to determine whether resources were appropriately requested, assigned, and utilised during the project. Whether the event was produced at cost (no profit), broke even, or was a profit-generating venture, an audit is a necessary and useful procedure. It helps stakeholders determine whether this project was managed appropriately to meet the stated objectives.

Audits can be internal, external, or combined. Usually event audits are internal and are performed by project team members. However, when a project is large or complex, involves funds from an external source (such as a government-sponsored grant), or has numerous sponsors, an external audit may be required by the stakeholders.

Any evaluation or audit process requires the designation of personnel who will carry out the assigned tasks, usually members of the project team, other personnel from within the organisation, or an outside and interested party. Some organisations, for instance, rely on volunteer evaluators who are knowledgeable in the industry but who have no vested interest in the event. The primary characteristics of an evaluator are objectivity and neutrality. This requires careful selection of evaluators or auditors, and they should not be selected based upon a biased interest of any stakeholder.

Audits should be scheduled as part of the planning process. While scheduling audits to occur after the event may seem logical, earlier data collection can be important to project success. Data collection and analysis may help early identification of problems and might allow corrective actions before the event concludes. For example, scheduling inspections while the event is ongoing allows the auditor to observe behaviour that could be changed. To expand this example, consider an on-site sustainability audit. With early warning through the audit process, the event professional can determine whether energy conservation and waste management processes are being followed, and corrective action can be taken as needed.

If an event team wants the most objective audits possible, it is wise to contract with a third-party auditing firm. Auditors who are external to the organisation help facilitate a more reliable process. The biggest disadvantage, however, to engaging an external auditor is the cost and area of specialization. However, when transparency and project performance are critical for image management, auditing costs can be built into the event budget during planning and a sound case can be made to justify this expenditure. Reliability and credibility of the findings are important, so the external auditor should be above reproach, with a sterling reputation as an auditing consultant.

During the planning phase, the event professionals should identify critical success factors that guide the evaluation and audit processes. Below is a series of factors that could be essential for your event to reach a positive outcome:

- Project statement for objectives, goals, and mission
- Scope statement (clearly defines the work breakdown structure (WBS) in parts or work packages)
- Effective planning from the project start
- Project support from project promoters/owners
- Financial support
- Competent manager and event team
- Stakeholder identification and management
- Use of appropriate technology
- Agenda and/or programme development
- Sponsorship programmes
- Cost management
- Quality management
- Risk management

In summary, developing project evaluation and audit procedures is a mandatory task for event professionals, as these tools support monitoring and controlling the event throughout its lifecycle; taking corrective actions when necessary; and anticipating potential issues in the rest of the lifecycle. Audits must be conducted throughout the lifecycle of the event (i.e., before, during and after the event). Evaluation and audit processes should not be construed as tools for punishment; the aim is to improve the outcome and address deficiencies in processes and procedures in a timely manner. Every proficient event professional should strive to practice sound auditing and evaluation principles and methodology, as they support effective decision making, ensure continuous improvement, and facilitate application of lessons learned.

Once the event evaluation and audit are concluded, it may be beneficial to report the results to the event's stakeholders. The Events Industry Council provides on-line resources for **post-event reporting (PER)**. These include recommendations for summarizing information related to the event's logistics, budget, contact information, hotel and room-block details, food and beverage orders, function and exhibit space details, and future event dates, as well as reporting protocols.

References

Events Industry Council. (2006). *APEX Contracts Accepted Practices*. Retrieved from http://www.eventscouncil.org/APEX/RequestsforProposals.aspx

Event Management Body of Knowledge (EMBOK): An Introduction. (2013). Retrieved from http://www.embok.org/

Project Management Institute. (2008). *A Guide to the Project Management Body of Knowledge (PMBOK Guide)*, 4th ed. Newtown Square, PA: Project Management Institute.

Contributing Authors

Jennifer George Lion, CMP, PMP
Director, Project Management, Experient, a Maritz Travel Company
St. Louis, MO, USA
Member of Professional Convention Management Association (PCMA)

Ann Gravette, CMP, CSSBB
Director, Process Improvement and Training, Maritz Travel Company
St. Louis, MO, USA
Member of International Special Events Society (ISES), Meeting Professionals International (MPI)

Walter Méndez Rojas, MBA, MPM
General Director, ATP® Internacional
San Jose, Costa Rica

Dr. Jorge Sancho Zeledón, MBA
New Business Development Director, ATP® Internacional
San Jose, Costa Rica

Reviewers

MaryAnne P. Bobrow, CAE, CMP, CMM, CHE
President, Bobrow Associates, Inc.
Citrus Heights, CA, USA
Member of American Society of Association Executives (ASAE), International Association of Exhibitions and Events (IAEE), Meeting Professionals International (MPI), Professional Convention Management Association (PCMA)

Ksenija Polla, CMP
Director of Association Relations, International Congress and Convention Association (ICCA)
Amsterdam, Netherlands
Member of American Society of Association Executives (ASAE)

Skill 4:
Endpoints

Terminology

Communication matrix

Constraints

Contract

Critical path

Gantt chart

Integrated communication

Key performance indicator (KPI)

Post-event report (PER)

Stakeholder

Standard operating procedure (SOP)

Work breakdown structure (WBS)

Additional Resources

1. RFP Workbook from APEX at http://www.eventscouncil.org/APEX/RequestsforProposals.aspx

2. Contracts information from APEX at http://www.eventscouncil.org/APEX/RequestsforProposals.aspx

3. Post-event reporting document from APEX at http://www.eventscouncil.org/APEX/AdditionalResources.aspx

Skill 4: Review Questions

1. According to the *Event Management Body of Knowledge*, what are the five phases of the event management process?

2. What are the four processes of the project procurement plan?

3. What is a critical path?

4. When creating a communication plan, what should an event professional ask and answer?

SKILL 5: MANAGE MEETING OR EVENT PROJECT

Learning Outcomes

- Know how to manage a critical path.
- Explore contract management.
- Describe implementation of an event.

Sub Skill 5.01 – Manage Critical Path

Once the event professional calculates the critical path for the event during the planning process, priority is given to identified tasks to ensure their timely completion. The event professional can ensure this is the case by creating a framework for regular review of project deadlines and deliverables with appropriate stakeholders, whether they are staff, contractors, or volunteers.

Since multiple stakeholders carry out event-related tasks along the critical path, a team organisation chart elaborating roles and responsibilities should be created. This will ensure that these stakeholders understand their individual roles, as well as the roles of others.

Additionally, the event professional is encouraged to create a **project status report** to capture regular updates concerning event progress, including such items as registration numbers, confirmed exhibitors and sponsors, and financials. Traditionally, updates are collected on a weekly basis from the project team and a brief summary is included in the project status report so event planning is captured for historical purposes. The project status report is a vehicle for the event professional to manage execution of the critical path. Any potential risks can be called out in this document as well. As an example, a weekly project status report on registrations for an annual conference can determine whether the number of registered attendees is on track to reach registration goals, or if adjustments should be made to the marketing campaign or event budget to reflect updated projections.

The event professional can monitor and control progress by setting up a regular meeting or conversation with project team members on a weekly or biweekly basis; this contact could take the form of a face-to-face meeting, a conference call, or videoconference. During these conversations, the event professional should receive progress updates on assigned tasks, paying particular attention to critical path activities and milestones. If potential delays with critical path tasks are noted, the event professional can make adjustments to correct the possible delay, avoid it, or mitigate the impact of that delay on other elements of the critical path. By conducting a regular review of deadlines and deliverables with team members, the event professional can effectively manage the critical path.

Despite a project team's best efforts, unforeseen changes or issues can occur in the project plan. Changes that alter the critical path and expand the project's scope are called "scope creep." When an event professional encounters scope creep, the potential impacts to the event budget, schedule, or resources must be determined. Then corrective action can be taken to limit or avoid negative effects or provide more resources to cover the altered scope. An example of scope creep would be the addition of a daylong sales team training meeting to a product launch. The additional expense and planning required to add the training session could jeopardize the product launch event, and decisions will need to be made to address this.

Taking a practical example, imagine a scenario in which an event professional is required to submit the final **event specifications guide** (ESG) to a venue by a specific date. One day prior to the submission deadline, the event professional has not received the electrical and telecommunications requirements from the individual overseeing the on-site registration area. The submission of the ESG represents a task along the project critical path. The event professional knows that failure to receive this important component will potentially delay submission of the ESG to the venue and may result in additional fees. In this instance, the event professional should reach out to the individual to explain the importance of receiving this information in a timely manner and, if necessary, offer assistance in compiling this information so that this critical path task is completed on track. With clear communication, the event professional can often mitigate project risks.

Ultimately, the best way to minimize potential delays and risks as they relate to the project schedule and critical path is by keeping all key stakeholders informed about event progress. One of the most important roles of the event professional is to facilitate communication among key stakeholders. In the end, an event professional who regularly monitors the project schedule and keeps pertinent stakeholders informed stands a much better chance of keeping on track with project deadlines and deliverables.

Sub Skill 5.02 – Manage Contracts

Managing contracts is a large part of event management, given the scope of detail and suppliers involved. Establishing contractual relations with suppliers involves a good amount of a project team's time. Some countries allow oral agreements as binding contracts when closed by a handshake in the presence of witnesses. A written contract may be required, however, in some situations and countries. The information provided in this section pertains to written contracts, which are recommended in event management between the parties involved.

The Contract

The Events Industry Council's APEX *Contract Accepted Practices* defines a contract as "an agreement between two or more parties that creates in each party a duty to do or not do something and a right to performance of the other's duty or a remedy for the breach of the other's duty" (Events Industry Council, 2006). A contract defines the rights and duties of the contracting parties. A well-written contract should be a clear roadmap of the parties' expectations and responsibilities.

Resources for drafting contracts and conducting negotiations can be found on the Events Industry Council's APEX Web site. Some of these pertinent best practices include:

- The initial contract should be carefully reviewed and clauses that need modification should be identified.
- The signing parties should be identified if they have authority to legally bind their organisation.
- Event professionals are encouraged to have legal counsel review the contract terms.
- All contracts should be in writing. While some oral contracts may be binding, they are not recommended.
- Contract language should be straightforward and understandable. Although there are some legal "terms of art" in which precise language is important, using plain language that is understandable by both parties is generally preferable and limits ambiguities and misunderstandings.
- Negotiations should always be done in good faith and in accordance with ethical business practices.
- Contracts should clearly identify how the risks are allocated between the parties. (Events Industry Council, 2006)

Contracts should be obtained from every supplier engaged, including—but not limited to—venue, hotels, restaurants, destination management companies, audiovisual companies, transportation companies, entertainers, technology suppliers, and others engaged in the project. Hotels generally offer a contract at point of commitment to cover their sleeping rooms and function space. Details of initial contracts received from suppliers can and should be negotiated; they are not rigid as presented, and the event professional should tailor the contract to his or her needs and critical timeline.

The event professional should consult his/her event contracts often and comply with their outlined responsibilities. As modifications are made to original contracts, the event professional must communicate additions, cancellations, or modifications to a contract and request that the supplier send a **contract amendment** or a **contract addendum**. An amendment is a change to an existing contract document, while an addendum adds a document to the original contract. Upon receiving amendments or addendums, the event professional must carefully review and countersign them. Important dates from contracts should be incorporated into the critical path.

Negotiating Contracts

Because contracts are a necessary and consistent part of the events industry, every event professional should develop his/her negotiation skills. Negotiation, oral and written, will be conducted throughout the lifecycle of the event. The event professional who lacks the ability to negotiate or the time and skill to review contracts (and/or have an attorney review them) may sign contracts that are less favourable to his or her company. Generally, neither of the negotiating parties gets everything they are seeking, but the process of negotiation ensures that each party has the opportunity to specify what their most important issues are. Each party should be prepared to give something up, as long as something useful is captured in return.

An event professional can prepare for negotiation by knowing:

- With whom he/she will negotiate and what their level of authority is
- What he/she hopes and needs to obtain from the negotiation
- What the other party hopes and needs to obtain from the negotiation
- What both parties are willing to concede
- What the value of the business is
- What the history of the business is
- How much time one has (more time generally equals more power/options)
- What other options exist, as this may provide negotiation leverage

Begin negotiation with a clear idea of what you must have, what you would like to have, and what you can give. Being able to give something helps show the other party that you are flexible and willing to cooperate. This can create a much better negotiating atmosphere than one party refusing to change anything in the contract or contract proposal.

Contract Elements

Some specific items should be included in event contracts. They are organised below in the areas of general contract information, event space, sleeping rooms, food and beverage functions, event technology, and other legal and miscellaneous clauses. (The following section is adapted, with permission, from the *Events Industry Council Manual, 8th edition*).

General Contract Information and Clauses

- Names of parties in agreement
- Status of the signatory party – in many cases, this will be reflected as an "agent of record for [client name]"
- Date contract issued

- Date by which contract must be signed and returned
- Detailed list of items and services being rendered (i.e., hotel room block, function space, food and beverage, ground services, equipment, staff, etc.), including concessions
- Details of all fees and charges (including taxes, service fees, rental fees, item costs, commissions/rebates offered, etc.)
- Payment schedule (amounts and due dates)
- Cancellation schedule and potential for penalties or attrition fees, in addition to rebooking or resold clauses
- All legal clauses (including *force majeure*, damages, indemnification, liabilities, insurance requirements, dispute resolution, etc.)

Contract Information for Event Spaces

- Function space requirements, room rental and set-up charges, including specific rooms to be utilised for the event (if possible) and set-up and tear-down times
- Convention services and equipment provided by the facility, including bandwidth specifics (if applicable)
- Jurisdiction and responsibilities of any unions under contract with the facility
- Requirements for booth storage, set-up, and dismantling (if applicable)
- Security, hours of operation, services, and key rules and regulations
- Requirements for disclosure regarding competitive or multiple events that could have a negative impact on the event. (Note: If exclusive access is required to the facility, it should be specified in the agreement.)
- Protection from material deterioration of the facility's condition. (Note: Often contracts give the group the right to cancel the event without paying damages in the event of material deterioration. The clause should also address the venue's obligations if it is undergoing renovations or construction during the event.)
- Information about exclusive services policies and requirements that the venue provide reasonable notice of any new exclusive service and an opportunity to accept or reject it. (Note: The contract should specify whether outside suppliers—such as event technology suppliers—are allowed and the conditions under which they may work at the facility.)
- Information on the right to sell merchandise or refreshments (may be referred to as concessions) on-site to individuals in conjunction with the event and any applicable income-sharing requirements

Contract Information for Sleeping Rooms

- Numbers and types of guest rooms being reserved
- Details on room reservation and confirmation procedures, including whether reservations will be made by rooming list, housing bureau, or individually by attendees
- Guarantee and deposit requirements
- Specific room rates (or formula by which rates will be computed) for the group, including room taxes, early departure fees, and other charges, such as resort fees and in-room Internet usage
- Commissions or rebates that are included in the room rate
- Any complimentary room policy and special room requirements and rates for very important persons (VIPs), staff and suppliers

- Cut-off dates when any rooms not reserved in the room block will be released, and whether the group room rate will be available after this cut-off date. (Note: This section of the contract should also address what happens to rooms not reserved within a block after the reservation cut-off date—released back to the hotel for sale to other guests, continue to be made available to the group at the agreed-upon rate, or charged to the group's account.)
- Policy for determining whether a block was filled, including reservations made outside of the normal reservation procedures established under the contract, and whether reservations for rooms used before or after the event will be counted in the total cumulative room block
- Policy regarding lower room rates potentially being available on-line
- Attrition penalties if the room block is not filled
- Room block review provisions through which the room block may be adjusted without penalty
- Provisions for what takes place if a guest is relocated, often referred to as "walking the guest" as a result of overbooking or other causes such as emergency maintenance. (Note: In the event the hotel cannot accommodate an attendee with a confirmed reservation, the contract should provide information on what alternative accommodations will be provided, the provision for ground transportation, relocation back to the hotel as soon as a room is available, attribution of the room night to the room block, and other possible concessions.)

Contract Information for Food and Beverage Functions

- The projected number and type of food and beverage functions
- Dates by which the group must confirm function space to be used, approximate attendance, menus and beverage service, and guaranteed attendance
- The date on which food and beverage costs will be confirmed
- Details on gratuities, service charges, and taxes
- Minimum attendance or monetary value requirements, if applicable, and how these are calculated; for example, are taxes and gratuities or service charges included in the minimum?
- Method of calculating the damages that will be paid if the expected minimums are not met. (Note: This might be a sliding scale for meeting room fees or an attrition calculation.)

Contract Information for Event Technology Providers

- Scope of work outline, along with provisions and staffing levels for set-up and dismantling
- Costs for Internet access, power and rigging. (Note: This may need to be included in the venue contract and not the event technology provider's contract.)
- Availability to provide on-site support and to fulfill technology requests made on-site
- Fees for equipment and staffing, including overtime or holiday staffing
- Provisions for meeting local certification requirements
- Licensing information, including specifications on software installed on any computers and music licensing
- Specifications about bandwidth requirements, if applicable

Other Legal and Miscellaneous Clauses

- Billing: Billing arrangements include method of payment, time of payment, any deposit requirements, names of authorized signatories to the master account, and any discounts for early payment of the master account.

- Termination: The contract should specify who can terminate it, under what circumstances the contract can be terminated without liability, the requirements for notice of termination, and any costs involved in termination. Termination clauses are provisions that excuse non-performance of the contract without liability. For example, *force majeure* (see below) or Act of God clauses protect the parties in the event that a contract cannot be performed because of causes that are outside the control of the parties and cannot be avoided.
- Cancellation: Cancellation policies should be included in all contracts. Generally, a cancellation clause outlines the damages to be paid to the non-cancelling party if a cancellation occurs. This can include a liquidated damage clause that stipulates the amount of damages in the event of cancellation. However, the absence of a liquidated damage provision does not mean that either party can cancel without liability. Cancellation by the event sponsor often is covered in contracts. Many contracts, however, fail to address what happens if the event venue cancels or otherwise breaches its obligations. The event sponsor can negotiate to include a liquidated damage clause for such cancellation. In calculating the amount of liquidated damages, the cost of relocating the event and any impact on attendance should be taken into consideration.
- *Force majeure*: Circumstance in which a contractual obligation is excused due to a factor not within the control of either party that makes performance impossible or commercially impracticable and the risk of which has not otherwise been allocated.
- Attrition: Many contracts have attrition clauses to address when a contract is fulfilled but one party does not fulfill all its obligations, such as failure to fill a room block or food and beverage volume as specified in the contract. An attrition clause is not required in order to have a binding contract. If there is no attrition clause, it does not mean that in the event of attrition there will be no damages, but rather that damages will be determined by a court. Event professionals should be aware that in such cases, the group may become obligated to pay for the entire unused portion of its room block. That is why it is important for the group to make sure all hotel contracts have attrition clauses, which typically allow some percentage of slippage (often 10 percent or 20 percent) from the contracted guest room or food and beverage commitment.
- Indemnification: Many contracts specify who is liable for any injuries that may occur under the contract and set a limit on the amount of liability. Under an indemnification clause, one party agrees to protect another party from liability as a result of a lawsuit by a third party. The clause usually is written so that a party whose negligence causes a liability provides such protection to the other party. It is essential that if the event sponsor is indemnifying the venue, the venue also indemnifies the sponsor. The two indemnification clauses should be essentially identical to ensure that each is getting the same protection. Because some jurisdictions provide for indemnification as a matter of law, some contracts do not contain indemnification clauses. Moreover, some government-related entities, such as convention centres, are unable to agree to indemnify because of local laws.
- Insurance: The contract should address whether both parties have appropriate insurance policies. Additional information on insurance can be found in Domain C: Risk Management.
- Dispute resolution and governing law: The contract may specify where and how any dispute is to be resolved. Generally, if parties cannot resolve a dispute, a party must file a claim in court to enforce its rights. A contract can also specify that the parties will use an alternative dispute resolution (ADR) procedure instead of going through the process of filing a complaint and pursuing the claim in court. It is essential that the contract state clearly how

and where disputes are to be resolved. There are several types of ADR procedures available, including arbitration, mediation and private use of retired judges. Also consider where a dispute will be resolved and specify which jurisdiction's laws will apply in interpreting the contract.

Banquet Event Orders (BEOs)

Later in the planning process, as details are being solidified, the venue's convention services department generally issues **banquet event orders** (BEOs), which thoroughly outline event details (food and beverage, room set-up, basic AV, décor, etc.), with all costs quoted. The BEOs become the final authority on-site for every item and service rendered. Hotel staff members refer to the documents on a daily basis and deliver services based upon the captured details. BEOs are generally produced by the convention services team from the ESG and are sent to the event professional approximately 14-30 days before the event start date, depending on the venue and event complexity. These BEOs must be carefully proofread and cross-checked, to ensure that all items match the ESG, event budget, and other project documents. Enlisting another "set of eyes" to doublecheck them can be helpful. The event professional should also compare the details to any published content to ensure that what the event stakeholders expect is indeed what the supplier plans to deliver. The event professional generally signs the BEOs to indicate agreement.

Sub Skill 5.03 – Manage Implementation of Meeting or Event

Moving from the planning process, the event professional will continue to manage the project into its operational phase. The implementation of the meeting or event generally begins when the staff arrives on location. At this time, the event professional should hold a team-training meeting or advance briefing. This meeting normally takes place three to five days in advance of the official event start date. A detailed agenda should be created and should include a thorough presentation of the event's logistics:

- goals and objectives
- stakeholder profiles and needs
- day-to-day itinerary
- recent changes to the documented ESG or BEOs
- assigned staff responsibilities
- documentation (contracts, budget, floor plans, menus, etc.)

Once the event staff and key stakeholders are informed, an event **pre-conference meeting** (pre-con) should happen. This meeting is standard within the industry and widely practiced at major hotels and event venues. The pre-con reviews responsibility of the overall event to the extended team and generally includes major suppliers. The pre-con is ideally scheduled 48-72 hours before the attendees' arrival. During the pre-con, team members gather to ensure that everyone involved is on the same page and know all the details of the event operations. The following people should attend a pre-con meeting:

- event owner/event professional
- travel staff (area leads for billing, housing, food and beverage, etc.)
- hotel/venue management team (sales, catering, convention services manager)
- hotel/venue departmental leads (front desk, housekeeping, set-up, audiovisual, accounting)
- suppliers as deemed necessary (event technology, destination management company, entertainment representatives, general services contractor)

A pre-con is typically led by the event professional, who begins by providing an overview of the group and the event. He or she generally provides details on the event goals and objectives, event inclusions, stakeholder involvement, expectations, and event details. After an overview of the overall event, he/she leads a detailed walk-through of the event's daily itinerary, and all team members gain consensus on their understanding and commitment to perform their duties as required to make the event a success. Identified team members should actively participate in the meeting and ask clarifying questions to ensure agreement and understanding.

Managing costs is a top priority within the implementation of events. The event budget must clearly match all contracts and BEOs. On-site staff must be aware of budget requirements and manage against them. The event professional often has the ultimate responsibility over the budget; however, other stakeholders may also need to have an understanding of event financials. Solid procurement practices generally require staff to record actual items and services received compared to what was planned and budgeted. For instance, if a planner budgeted for buffet tables and the attendee count decreased, meriting the need for only two tables, records should be kept to indicate such changes. In some cases, variances need to be recorded for regulatory disclosures and transparency reporting. Event professionals should document in advance how on-site additions or changes will be handled and who is authorized to make changes, and should advise staff accordingly. To protect the budget, the meeting organiser should require that all additional goods and services requested be approved in writing by one or two designated persons. This requirement can also be included in contracts with facilities and suppliers. See the Financial Management domain for more information about budget management.

Change management is typically required as an event is implemented. While the event professional strives to comply with the highest quality standards, plans often need to be altered on-site. An evening function may be extended. An event may have to be moved indoors due to inclement weather. An exhibitor may require a different booth location. The change possibilities are endless. The event professional needs to establish a formal process through which changes are handled. He or she should approve and record such changes.

Communication during an event operation is, of course, key to the event's success. The event professional should schedule daily meetings with those he/she deems necessary on-site. Staff members who oversee areas (housing, meetings, food and beverage, exhibitions, etc.) normally are invited to attend the daily meetings. Schedule a stand-up meeting early in the morning to discuss the day's events and needs. Conduct a more in-depth meeting in the evening hours, while the meeting attendees are occupied and a large number of staff members are available. This longer meeting provides an opportunity to discuss what is going well, what needs improvement, changes, action items, and overall expectations/needs, and to look at the coming day's details and flow.

Onboarding staff, managing change, and communicating clearly and often during an event operation leads to successful event outcomes.

References

Blum, B.A. (2007). *Contracts: Examples & Explanations.* New York, NY: Aspen Publishers.

Events Industry Council. (2006). *APEX Contracts Accepted Practices.* Retrieved from http://www.eventscouncil.org/APEX/RequestsforProposals.aspx

Events Industry Council Manual, 8th ed. (2008). Alexandria, VA: Events Industry Council.

Kerzner, Harold, Ph.D. (2006). *Project Management, A Systems Approach to Planning, Scheduling and Controlling,* 9th edition. Hoboken, NJ: John Wiley & Sons, Inc.

Project Management Institute, (2008). *A Guide to the Project Management Body of Knowledge (PMBOK Guide),* 4th edition. Newtown Square, PA: Project Management Institute, Inc.

Contributing Authors

Jennifer George Lion, CMP, PMP
Director, Project Management, Experient, a Maritz Travel Company
St. Louis, MO, USA
Member of Professional Convention Management Association (PCMA)

Ann Gravette, CMP, CSSBB
Director, Process Improvement and Training, Maritz Travel Company
St. Louis, MO, USA
Member of International Special Events Society (ISES), Meeting Professionals International (MPI)

Walter Méndez Rojas, MBA, MPM
General Director, ATP® Internacional
San Jose, Costa Rica

Dr. Jorge Sancho Zeledón, MBA
New Business Development Director, ATP® Internacional
San Jose, Costa Rica

Reviewers

MaryAnne P. Bobrow, CAE, CMP, CMM, CHE
President, Bobrow Associates, Inc.
Citrus Heights, CA, USA
Member of American Society of Association Executives (ASAE), International Association of Exhibitions and Events (IAEE), Meeting Professionals International (MPI), Professional Convention Management Association (PCMA)

Ksenija Polla, CMP
Director of Association Relations, International Congress and Convention Association (ICCA)
Amsterdam, Netherlands
Member of American Society of Association Executives (ASAE)

Skill 5:
Endpoints

Terminology

Banquet event order (BEO)

Contract addendum

Contract amendment

Event specifications guide (ESG)

Pre-conference meeting

Project status report (PSR)

Scope creep

Additional Resources

1. Project Management Institute Web site at http://www.pmi.org/
2. Event specifications guide from APEX at http://www.eventscouncil.org/APEX/
   AcceptedPractices.aspx
3. Contracts information from APEX at http://www.eventscouncil.org/APEX/AdditionalResources.aspx

Skill 5: Review Questions

1. What is the best way to minimize potential delays and risks as they relate to the project schedule and critical path?
2. What is a contract and what should it include?
3. What is an event specifications guide (ESG) and what should it include?
4. How is the banquet event order different from the ESG?

Risk Management

Risk management, as applied to the events industry, is the ongoing process of assessing the risks that may threaten attendees, the meeting or event itself, the organiser, or partner-suppliers, and applying the appropriate measures to manage the probability and consequences of such risks. The term "risk" refers only to the possibility that something may occur and not to the occurrence itself. So for example, there is a *risk* that an *emergency, crisis,* or *disaster* may occur.

This chapter is devoted to serious risks that may threaten life, health, property, or the financial viability of a meeting, business, or organisation. It does not address minor inconveniences such as running out of asparagus on the buffet or having the bulb on the projector go out in the middle of a session. It does apply to things like natural disasters, political unrest, assault on persons, building collapses, power outages, and similar major occurrences.

As applied to risks, crises, and disasters, risk management is not just a plan, but a programme and process that is integrated into the way meetings and events are planned and organised. There are four basic stages of risk management: (1) preparedness, (2) response, (3) recovery, and (4) mitigation (Mileti, 1999).

Each stage flows into the next to keep risk management an ongoing process and not a one-time activity of writing a risk management plan, buying insurance, or hiring security. Instead, it is all these activities and more, regularly reviewed and updated based on changes in the environment, politics, the meeting, the organisations involved, and many other factors.

Figure 1   Four Stages of Risk Management.

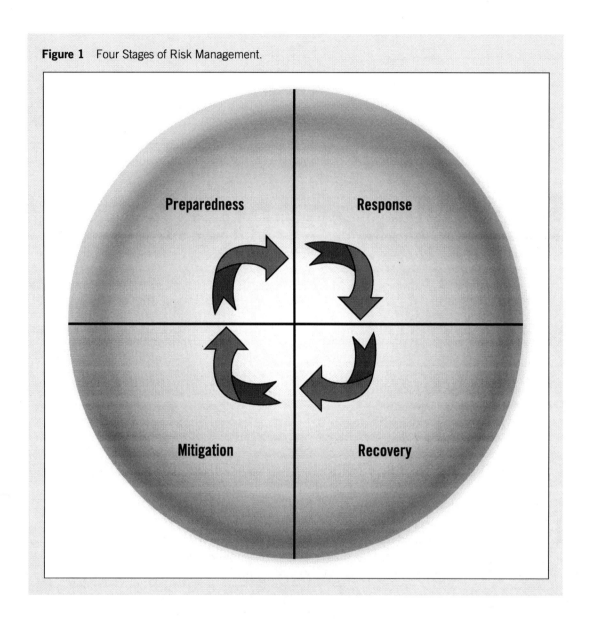

SKILL 6: MANAGE RISK MANAGEMENT PLAN

Learning Outcomes

- Learn how to identify risks related to meetings and events
- Learn how to analyse risks related to meetings and events
- Determine how to develop a risk management and implementation plan
- Learn how to develop and implement an emergency response plan
- Understand how to arrange security for meetings and events

Sub Skill 6.01 – Identify Risks

Risk assessment (or **risk identification**) is the process of identifying the risks specific to the destination, meeting or business event being planned. This is the point at which the event professional creates a list of all of the risks associated with his or her meeting, facility, or business. This is the first step in a four-step risk management process:

1. Risk assessment (identify risk)
2. Risk analysis (analyse risks)
3. Crisis planning (developing the risk management plan)
4. Crisis response (implementing, when needed, the planned responses to the specific crisis that occurs)

The first step in risk assessment is to consider how various aspects of a meeting or event may invite risk. That is, what vulnerabilities are inherent in the meeting or event based on factors such as destination, venue, programme, participants, and so on? Table 1 gives some examples. For any particular meeting or event, there may be more meeting aspects to consider and each may have different risks, so this process must be undertaken for each meeting and for each instance of a recurring meeting.

The risk assessment process must consider both internal vulnerabilities and external threats. Table 1 illustrates some of each.

SWOT Analysis

Another way to undertake this process might be to use a SWOT (strengths, weaknesses, opportunities, threats) analysis. In a SWOT analysis, strengths and weaknesses are internal to the meeting or event itself, including factors pertaining to the host organisation, the programme, the participants, and other stakeholders. Opportunities and threats are external to the meeting or event, including elements related to the destination, venue, or other groups.

The risk assessment and the SWOT analysis will yield similar results regarding the risks. The advantage of the SWOT analysis is that it also provides an opportunity for meeting and event professionals to consider what *mitigation* measures they have in place. What are their internal capabilities, and which ones will help reduce the likelihood of a crisis occurring or reduce the severity of the consequences if it does occur? Table 2 provides an example of a SWOT analysis.

In some sense, this combines risk assessment with the beginning of the *risk analysis* phase of the process (see next section). Event professionals should use whichever method makes the most sense to them.

Table 1 Risk Assessment Example.

Meeting Aspect	Risk (or vulnerability)
Destination	▪ Choosing a destination known for political instability ▪ Visas required for most attendees to travel to the destination
Venue	▪ City centre location has history of crime against tourists ▪ Resort remotely located and minimum two hours from nearest hospital ▪ Several other groups will be using the convention centre, including one that may be a protest target
Attendees	▪ Heavy drinkers ▪ Elderly group ▪ Youth programme
Programme	▪ Political speaker may draw negative press, picketers ▪ Fun run or other physical programme may create health and safety risk
Other	▪ Human rights record of destination conflicts with organisers' commitment to social responsibility

Table 2 SWOT Analysis Example.

Strengths (internal)	Weaknesses (internal)
■ Ample planning time to inform attendees about the need for a visa for travel ■ International attendees who are savvy about travel	■ Heavy drinkers ■ Elderly group ■ Youth programme ■ Political speaker may draw negative press, picketers ■ Fun run or other physical programme may create injury risk
Opportunities (external)	**Threats (external)**
■ Venue staff is trained in appropriate alcoholic beverage service protocols ■ Destination management company communicates which other groups may be meeting in the city or venue at the same time ■ Venue has on-site medical doctor/nurse and clinic ■ City centre location so off-site events can be held nearby; attendees won't walk long distances at night	■ Choosing destination known for political instability ■ Visas required for most attendees to travel to the destination ■ City centre location has history of crime against tourists ■ Several other groups will be using the convention centre, including one that may be a protest target

The international standards for managing risk have been set by the International Organisation for Standardization (ISO) via the 31000: 2009 report. Kevin Knight (2012), an expert in the field of risk management from Australia, wrote, "In many jurisdictions, emergency preparedness planning focuses on the sudden onset of natural hazards.... Of course, not all emergency events are caused by nature. However, consequences from emergency events may be similar, regardless of the trigger involved. It is therefore imperative that the final document adopts an all-hazards approach and provides a method that is suitable for considering other sources of risk. These include disease (human, animal and plant), insect/vermin plague, and those risks arising from technological and other human sources...." (para. 19).

To illustrate best practices, organisations in several countries have developed emergency management manuals for large events (although they do not always apply to meetings and conferences). Emergency Management Australia (1999) has published a manual for emergency management practices specifically geared toward large events. Similar to this manual is the Canadian Office of Critical Infrastructure Protection and Emergency Preparedness (1994) Emergency Perparedness Guidelines for Mass, Crowd-Intensive Events. In the United States, the National Fire Protection Association (NFPA) Standard on Disaster/Emergency Management and Business Continuity (2007) suggests combining threats into three categories: (1) natural disasters, (2) human-caused, and (3) technological. This step is useful because threats in each of these categories are likely to have similar responses, so they can be grouped together in the risk management plan. This is also a good way to doublecheck that you have identified everything you need in your risk assessment.

The risk assessment process is important because if something were to happen and someone or something was injured, damaged or lost, one of the first legal inquiries would be whether the event professional did his or her best in planning the meeting. That is, did he or she use **due diligence** in choosing the destination or venue? Did he or she choose reputable vendors to provide catering, motor coach transportation, or other services? In the United States, this standard is related to the **reasonable prudent person** standard, which basically asks, "Did this event professional do what a reasonably prudent event professional with similar experience and training would do under the same circumstances?" Other countries may have different specific legal standards, but the idea of **negligence** (even if called something else) or failure to use due care is nearly universal.

Part of determining risk for a particular meeting or event requires knowing the laws, contract requirements, ordinances, permits, and licenses specific to the country, destination, venue, activities, and services of the meeting or event. For example, a meeting planner needs to know the disability laws (or lack thereof) of the country in which the meeting or event is held. The UN Convention on the Rights of Persons with Disabilities and its Optional Protocol went into effect in 2008. There are currently 91 signatories to the Convention, which affirms the rights of equal enjoyment of persons with disabilities but only 76 signatories to the Optional Protocol, which provides a complaint mechanism for violations of the Convention (United Nations Treaty Collection, 2013). Thus, not all countries abide by the convention and some countries have their own laws addressing disability rights. The United States, for example, has the Americans with Disabilities Act (ADA) law and copious guidance from the government on following it (U.S. Department of Justice, 2013). Similarly, most of the United Kingdom is covered by the Equality Act of 2010, which also comes with guidance (Gov.UK, 2013).

When determining risks for a meeting, consult with others. Talk to colleagues who have held similar meetings or met in the destination or venue previously. Conversations between the planner and the venues or supplier-partners are also helpful at this stage.

In certain situations, it may be particularly important to get legal advice as well as advice from insurance or accounting representatives. In the case of international meetings, talking to someone more familiar with the destination, culture, and current state of affairs in the destination—such as a regulatory body, destination management company, or tourism bureau—could be critical to the success of the meeting in an emergency situation.

Sub Skill 6.02 – Analyse Risks

You cannot plan for every single risk that might occur. Even the most experienced planners with the most sophisticated risk management plans may not have considered possibilities such as the Eyjafjallajökull volcano in Iceland, which erupted in April 2010, resulting in the cancellation of thousands of flights and stranding tens of thousands of meeting and event attendees and travelers in and out of Europe for several days (Hatch & Kovaleski, 2010). Thus, in the risk analysis phase, consider all the risks identified in the risk assessment phase and then narrow them down.

To begin this process, the meeting or event professional examines damage, loss, or liability exposure, potential, and timing. Table 3 gives an example of this process.

The content in each of these categories may vary depending on whether a meeting or event is hosted by a corporation, an association or non-profit organisation, or another type of organisation, such as a government agency.

Accepting, Managing, and Avoiding Risk

The event professional has three choices when facing risk:

1. Accept/ignore the risk
2. Manage/mitigate the risk (which includes transferring the risk to someone else, such as through insurance or contracts)
3. Avoid the risk

Table 3   Risk Analysis of Damage, Loss, or Liability Exposure.

What is exposed to damage, loss, or liability?	▪ Property ▪ Persons ▪ Cash ▪ Reputation ▪ Environment
What could cause damage, loss, or liability?	▪ Natural disaster ▪ Human-caused event ▪ Technological event
Who could suffer damage, loss, or liability?	▪ Meeting organiser ▪ Venue ▪ Destination ▪ Attendees ▪ Exhibitors ▪ Sponsors ▪ Members ▪ Shareholders ▪ Other meeting stakeholders
When might damage, loss, or liability occur?	▪ Before the meeting ▪ During the meeting ▪ After the meeting

Which category a particular crisis, disaster, or emergency falls into depends in large part on the probability or likelihood that the risk will occur and the potential consequences if the risk actually does occur.

Accepting or ignoring the risk is a choice that is likely made if the probability of the risk occurring is very small or, if it does occur, the consequences would be minimal. Managing or mitigating the risk is what is done with crises, disasters, or emergencies that have either a high probability of occurring or significant potential consequences. The risks that are to be avoided, if possible, are those that have both a high probability of occurring and high consequences if they do occur. This is graphically depicted in Figure 2.

Most crises, disasters, and emergencies cannot be avoided. For example, a event professional certainly wants to avoid a hotel fire. However, it is beyond the control of the parties if the fire is started by an arsonist (human cause), an electrical fire (technological cause), or a lightning strike (natural disaster). Although the event professional would like to avoid that risk, the reality is that the best that can be done is to manage/mitigate the risk by making sure the hotel has been properly inspected; identifying where fire extinguishers or sprinkler systems are; being aware of the number of emergency exits and their width, that emergency lighting is correctly working, and procedures in case the fire alarm goes off; and having insurance to cover any damage resulting from fire.

The event professional may be able to avoid a risk such as a hurricane or typhoon, however, by not choosing a coastal destination during hurricane season for the meeting or event. The risk of travel disruption due to snow can be avoided by changing meeting dates to spring or summer. Even in these examples, however, risk still exists that the hurricane or snow will disrupt travel to or from the meeting destination.

Although it sounds as though the meeting or event professional is shirking responsibilities, certainly some risks are either so unlikely to occur or would have such minimal repercussions if they

Figure 2 Probability-Consequences Grid.

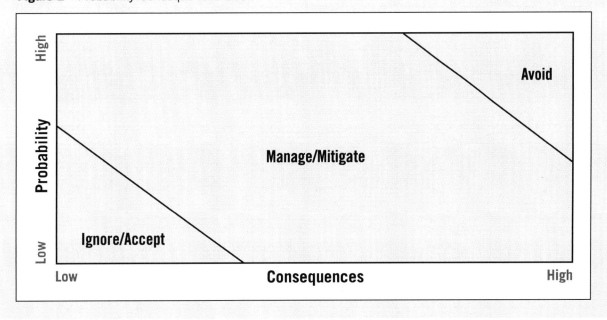

did occur that the organisation simply acknowledges the risk and moves on. Doing business of any kind is a risk. Getting out of bed in the morning is a risk. For example, perhaps there is a risk that someone will get a minor laceration or bruise during the team-building exercise. It frequently happens, but other than perhaps applying a bandage, this may be a risk the meeting or event professional chooses to ignore. This is a low consequences risk.

Likewise, the planner might say the risk of a meeting being affected by a meteor shower is so unlikely (low probability) that she or he is going to ignore that risk. Of course, in February 2013, a meteor shower did physical damage in Russia and injured over 1,000 people (Black, Milanova, & Smith-Spark, 2013). So risks that are ignored or accepted can happen. It is up to the meeting or event professional to decide whether the risk is worth spending limited time or resources on to manage/mitigate or avoid.

Most of the meeting or event professional's time is spent on managing or mitigating risks. This means putting into place measures that will:

1. Reduce the probability that the crisis, disaster, or emergency will occur.

2. Reduce the consequences if the crisis, disaster, or emergency does occur.

3. Transfer all or some of the risk to another party.

This is done through a variety of means, including developing and implementing a risk management plan, hiring security, using the services of experts to help manage specific risks, negotiating strong contracts, purchasing insurance policies, and simply thorough professional planning. Some of these techniques may fall into multiple categories. Table 4 provides some examples but is by no means exhaustive.

Planning and servicing meetings or events are risky activities. So most of the meeting or event professional's risk management efforts are spent reducing the probability of crises, disasters, and emergencies occurring or reducing the consequences of those that do occur. However, there are a few ways to transfer all or part of the risk to someone else. This is desirable, of course, because it reduces the drain on resources or cash for the meeting or event host (the organisation).

Table 4   Risk Management or Mitigation Techniques.

Reduce probability of the risk occurring	Reduce consequences if the risk occurs	Transfer risk to another party
▪ Incorporating risk management into each phase of planning ▪ Choosing a safe destination and venue ▪ Ensuring that the venue provides adequate security and staff or hiring externally	▪ Contracts (e.g., attrition, cancellation, *force majeure*) ▪ Provide security ▪ Waivers of liability ▪ Having medical or safety personnel and equipment on-site ▪ Using third-party suppliers for risky activities	▪ Insurance ▪ Contracts (e.g., indemnification clause) ▪ Using third-party suppliers with specialised training, insurance and equipment for risky activities

Insurance is one way to transfer at least some of the (mostly financial) risk to the insurance company. By paying an insurance premium, the event professional can take out a policy that requires the insurance company to pay out in the event of certain circumstances. There are many different types of insurance policies and they vary not only from country to country but from insurance company to insurance company. More details about some of the common types of insurance policies are in the next section.

Likewise, contract clauses such as **indemnification, attrition, cancellation,** and ***force majeure*** transfer or apportion risk between the policies. Indemnification clauses, in particular, are closely tied to insurance coverage amounts, as the parties will sometimes agree to indemnify one another up to the amount of insurance they carry.

Risk management should never be thought of as "another" thing for the busy meeting or event professional to do. Instead it should be integrated into every stage of the planning and execution of the meeting or event. Some of the tools available to help mitigate and manage risk are described in the next section.

Before embarking on risk management for meetings or events, however, the meeting or event professional must understand their organisation's *risk profile*. That is, how willing is the organisation to take risks? Some organisations are very risk averse, while others are willing to take more risks under the philosophy of "no risk, no reward." While hopefully no organisation is willing to take great risks with people's lives and health, a risk-averse organisation might avoid including activities such as ziplining, white water rafting, or hot air balloon rides out of fear of liability, financial repercussions, and damage to reputation if someone got injured. An organisation willing to take more risk might want to have these types of activities because they know they will have a positive impact on attendees' perception of the meeting or event. Even the latter group, however, is likely to want appropriate insurance and waivers of liability to manage the risk. A waiver of liability is a legal document signed by a person participating in an event or activity that verifies that the participant acknowledges and assumes the risks involved in participating. To be enforceable, a waiver of liability must be very carefully written. In a dispute, if it is found that a participant was not fully informed of or could not have understood the risks they were assuming, the waiver may not be enforceable.

Another issue to consider is what risk management measures are required by the city, state, province, or country in which the meeting or event is being held. The organiser must comply with the laws and regulations of the jurisdiction in which the meeting or event is being held. It is well established in most countries that ignorance of the law is no defense. If you are doing business in that country, you are deemed to be familiar with the law of doing business there. Each jurisdiction may have its own requirements regarding things like:

- Permits
- Licenses
- Insurance
- Accommodation for persons with disabilities
- Waivers of liability
- Health and safety of employees
- Food safety
- Unions
- Approval of exhibition floor plans
- Capacity limits

Before selecting risk management techniques, evaluate all available options to manage the best possible outcome—whether "best" in this case means it will reduce the risk most significantly, is the most cost-effective option, addresses the highest number of risks, or is the one approved by the organisation's decision-makers. Likewise, risk management techniques must be regularly evaluated following a meeting or event. For some risks, several different techniques must be tried before choosing the one that is most effective and cost-effective and least disruptive to the meeting, event, or organisation.

Sub Skill 6.03 – Develop Management and Implementation Plan

A meeting or event professional has no greater responsibility than ensuring the health and safety of attendees by developing and implementing a risk management plan. Just creating a plan is not sufficient—risk management needs to be infused into all aspects of meeting and event management, and the plan should be a living document that is regularly reviewed, tested where appropriate, and updated.

The event planner is not alone in the risk management process. Other stakeholders, both internal and external, who may have direct responsibilities or expertise in crisis planning should be consulted in the development and coordination of the risk management plan. They include:

- Internal risk management department
- Public relations team or firm
- Suppliers, including the event venue and transportation companies
- Local authorities, including emergency response services such as the fire department, police, and ambulance services
- Insurance providers, who may conduct site inspections and provide valuable resources to the meeting or event planner

Consultation and communication with local authorities and experts is vital in developing the risk management plan.

Elements of a Risk Management Plan

A risk management plan should include the following elements:

- Chain of command. It should be clear who is in charge of making decisions and under which circumstances. It should also be clear whom to contact if the primary decision maker is not available.
- Emergency and control procedures. (See Sub Skill 6.04 – Develop and Implement Emergency Response Plan for more information.)
- Spokesperson. The meeting or event planner should know who will be the spokesperson in the event of an emergency. This person should receive media and crisis communication training.

- Implementation strategies. This section will outline the activities that need to occur, such as safety inspections and incident reports, any resources that are required, and contingency measures.

Assessing and Communicating the Risk Management Plan

It's not enough to just create a plan; the plan also needs to be monitored and tested. This could include drills and reviewing incident reports. Very often, those who are tasked with implementing the risk management plan have important insights about the effectiveness of the plan. Thus, frontline staff and all those who are tasked with implementing the risk management plan should be consulted and involved in the assessment of the plan.

The plan also needs to be communicated to key stakeholders to ensure that everyone knows how to respond in the event that the plan needs to be put into action.

Event Insurance

As mentioned in the previous section, meeting and event professionals can transfer risk through the purchase of insurance. From an ethical perspective, meeting and event professionals should be actively involved in risk management, regardless of whether they have purchased insurance.

There are many types of insurance available for events, and it is important to research the types that apply in the jurisdiction where your event is being held. (Note: The term in Europe is "insurance cover;" the term in the United States is "insurance coverage.") Event planners should discuss their specific needs with an experienced industry insurance agent. In some jurisdictions it may also be advisable to consult an attorney or lawyer. As insurance requirements will vary significantly, it is helpful to review the following criteria to determine your specific needs:

Examples of insurance types that apply to meetings and events, to limit liability and protect against losses, are listed below. Applicability and terminology may vary by jurisdiction.

Table 5   Determining Insurance Needs.

Who	<ul><li>Who should be insured? This may include the meeting or event organiser, suppliers, vendors, and exhibitors.</li><li>Who is responsible? Depending on the jurisdiction, negligence may or may not be a requirement in order to be found liable.</li><li>Who should be consulted? Working with an insurance professional with event industry expertise is highly recommended.</li><li>Who is covered under the policy? Be clear about who is covered, including participants and staff, as well as sponsors, exhibitors, temporary staff, and volunteers.</li></ul>
What	<ul><li>What types of insurance are required for your event?</li><li>What restrictions (if any) apply to the cover?</li></ul>
Where	<ul><li>Where is your event being held, and what are the legal requirements in that particular jurisdiction?</li></ul>
When	<ul><li>When is the insurance in effect? Be sure to include pre- and post-meeting or event dates, including move-in and move-out dates.</li><li>When should insurance be acquired? Acquiring insurance early in the process is necessary to provide protection in cases of risks such as natural disasters that may have an impact on your event even if they occur several months before the meeting or event opens.</li></ul>
Why	<ul><li>Why is insurance needed? To determine this, analyse your specific risk factors.</li></ul>
How	<ul><li>How will the insurance be acquired and managed?</li></ul>

Table 6 Types of Insurance.

Commercial general liability/public liability	Provides protection against claims involving bodily injury and property damage. Consider a high limit. It protects the business from damage or loss that occurs on business premises or sometimes "temporarily off business premises." Some venues may have a minimum insurance requirement.
Umbrella policies	An umbrella policy is essentially insurance to cover gaps in coverage under the primary insurance policies. Since most claims will be covered by the primary insurance policies, umbrella coverage is relatively inexpensive, but can provide much-needed extra protection. This type of insurance is more common in the United States.
Fire liability	Under the terms of a facility contract, the event sponsor may be held responsible for fire damage to the building caused by negligence. Fire legal liability insurance provides protection. Be certain the contract releases the event sponsor from other damage to the building, including damage caused by an exhibitor. Ask the facility to add your organisation's name to the building's fire insurance or its all-risk policy.
Medical liability	Medical payment insurance provides reimbursement of medical expenses for injuries that occur at the site (excluding those suffered by employees and sometimes volunteers), regardless of your legal liability. If you maintain a first-aid station, know whether medical malpractice insurance will protect you and the nurses, doctors or paramedics staffing the station against claims for failure to render proper or adequate medical assistance. Primarily applies in the United States.
Independent contractor liability	Require all contractors to provide a certificate of insurance showing that they carry worker's compensation (or employer's liability) and general liability insurance (with a liability limit of at least $1 million or your local currency equivalent). Add independent contractors liability insurance to protect you against any suit brought against you or the event sponsor as a result of negligence on the part of an independent contractor. Primarily applies in the United States.
Products liability/ host and alcohol liability	If you operate a food concession or serve food and drink at a reception or dinner, products liability insurance can protect your group against claims such as food poisoning. Host liability or alcohol liability (depending on local laws) insurance protects the event sponsor against claims resulting from serving alcoholic beverages and may be required in certain jurisdictions.
Additional insured	If a group rents or charters buses, automobiles, boats or aircraft, there is a substantial liability exposure for injury to persons and damage to property. During contract negotiations for such vehicles, ask to have your organisation named as an additional insured on the lessor's insurance policy for liability, property damage and medical payments, and have the contract stipulate that the organisation shall not be held liable for damage to the vehicle itself. If the lessor's insurance company will not include your organisation as an additional insured, obtain that insurance yourself. Make sure your organisation is named as co-insured on any vendor's policy, above and beyond any coverage it may have. Also, require the insurance company to give notice of any non-renewal or cancellation of the policy or rider.
Valuable papers and records	Before mailing, event materials may be stored at a printer's place of business or warehouse, which may be insured in case of damage. However, valuable papers and records insurance is available to pay for the cost of reproducing any papers, pamphlets or records (or any part thereof) as a result of damage by fire, water, vandalism, etc.
On-site office	The computers, laptops, mobile devices , walkie-talkies and other equipment a group owns or rents for use at the event facility can be insured against loss or damage by fire, theft, explosion, water damage, vandalism and malicious mischief. Ask for office contents coverage. During the course of an event, a group may collect cheques. Daily deposits are recommended, but burglary and robbery insurance is available to cover cash and cheques as an additional precaution.
Exhibits	Exhibitors can insure their exhibit property through a special programme that may be offered on a voluntary basis for coverage at the exhibition site as well as in transit to and from. If the exhibitor's own general liability insurance does not extend to the exhibition site, liability insurance can be purchased, as well as insurance to cover a potential loss in the event that booth property does not arrive.

continued

Table 6   Types of Insurance.

Employers' liability/ worker's compensation	The event sponsor's worker's compensation (or employer's liability) policy probably covers employees who work at the event. If temporary on-site staff is put on the payroll, keep a record of salaries and the jobs performed. The insurance company will ask for this information during the audit at the end of the policy term. Also available is accidental death and dismemberment insurance, as well as accidental medical payment insurance for volunteers.
Travel	Delegates and guests should be made aware that the organisation sponsoring the event is not responsible for their personal property. You can, however, offer for purchase travel insurance for the term of the meeting or event, including travel to and from it.
Non-appearance	Events can be insured against non-appearance by speakers or entertainers. A contract with a celebrity may contain a clause that indicates that he or she does not have to appear in the case of sickness or travel-related delays. Insurance may cover any losses incurred as a result. The circumstances when the insurance applies must be clearly stated in the policy and understood by both parties.
Event cancellation	Cancellation insurance protects a group against loss of revenue if the event is interrupted or cannot be held because of fire, weather, a strike, or other insured hazard. The insurance also can pay for reasonable extra expenses incurred because of adverse circumstances, as long as the extra expenses are approved by the insurer in advance. For example, a taxi strike may require a group to hire buses to pick people up at airports. Insurance is available that would reimburse for this added expense.
Enforced reduced attendance	This is an extension that protects you from lower than expected attendance due to certain circumstances beyond your control (but not low attendance due to insufficient marketing, for example). Events vulnerable to the disruption of travel, particularly those involving flying overseas, need this coverage. Caution: This should not be construed as insurance against attrition. It effectively pays on a *force majeure* incident. Problems like prospective participants' fear of travel, higher airfare, or similar issues, although beyond your control, are typically not included in this coverage.
Property damage	You need to insure your own property that you take on-site to an event. You are responsible for any property for which you hold direct responsibility as well, such as rented audiovisual equipment, marquees or plants. In addition to the above, there may be a need for further property damage cover when the venue makes you responsible for damage to the venue.
Money insurance	If your event has a paying public, attendance or delegate fees are paid by cheque or cash, and those monies may be vulnerable to theft on-site or during transit to or from a bank. Your risk terminates, incidentally, from the moment the money is handed to an approved security organisation. Money insurance indemnifies you against the loss of the cash or cheques while at the venue or in direct transit to or from the bank.
Third-party losses	Research will usually be necessary into the liability of the event organiser for any losses incurred by subcontractors when an event is cancelled through natural causes (e.g., hurricanes, earthquakes). These can be covered by insurance if they are specified in advance.

Sub Skill 6.04 – Develop and Implement Emergency Response Plan

In the event of an emergency on-site at a meeting or business event, the meeting or event planner should have an easily accessible and readable written plan for emergency response. The worst time to make decisions about how to respond to an emergency is after the emergency has occurred. It is much better to think about what could happen, plan for it, and practice those plans before even going on-site. Remember that a meeting facility and destination may have its own plan, so the planner should consult and coordinate with representatives from the venue and destination to decrease the risk of creating greater chaos if an emergency occurs.

Threat Assessment

The risk assessment process is part of threat assessment, but threat assessment is more specific and must be customised for each meeting, venue, destination, and programme. Threat assessment is just what it sounds like—the process of assessing the threats to people, property, the organisation, the meeting, or any of the other at-risk elements identified during the risk assessment.

As mentioned previously and illustrated in Table 2, threat assessment varies by organisation, programme, destination, time and many other factors. This is why it is so important to conduct the SWOT analysis for each meeting or event. There may be no perceived risk in holding a meeting in a certain destination, but if a bombing of a downtown hotel occurs later today, a threat is created or escalated that may not have been there before. Threats can change in a moment's time and so must be monitored on an ongoing basis.

Capability Assessment

Capability assessment is likewise part of risk assessment and risk analysis. Capabilities and threats can be viewed as two sides of a coin. Just as threats are the negative risk-creating aspects of the meeting components, capabilities are the positive risk-reducing aspects of the meeting components.

Some of the elements illustrated in the strengths and opportunities section of Table 2 are capabilities. Capabilities are elements already in place that may assist in emergency response should it be necessary. Things like fire extinguishers in a meeting facility, a hardwired sprinkler system, automated external defibrillators (AEDs), security personnel, and staff trained in emergency response are examples of capabilities.

Confer with Authorities

To create an emergency response plan that will actually work in the event of an emergency, a event professional must confer with the proper facility and destination authorities. Some of the elements that need to be discussed are:

- Venue access
  - What are the entrances from which the venue can be accessed?
  - How are these entrances managed/controlled/monitored?
  - What are the accessibility points to the meeting space?
  - Who has access to the meeting space?
  - What is the most direct access for emergency responders?
- Venue information
  - What alarm(s) will be sounded (e.g., one type of alarm, or one for evacuation and one for sheltering in place?). Are there visual alarms for hearing-impaired guests?
  - Is there a public address system that will explain the appropriate response to guests and participants?
  - Does the public address system reach hotel or meeting rooms or just hallways and public areas?
  - What are the evacuation routes? How will guests and attendees be directed to the proper evacuation exit?
  - Where will evacuated guests and attendees gather? What process does the venue have, if any, to determine whether everyone has evacuated?
  - How does the venue handle the evacuation of persons with disabilities?

- On-site medical personnel and equipment
  - Is there an on-site physician, nurse, or emergency medical technician? If so, where are they located and during what hours?
  - Where are first-aid stations located? How are they equipped?
  - Are there automated external defibrillators (AEDs) on-site? If so, where? Who is authorized to use them?
- Off-site medical care
  - Where is the nearest hospital or other medical facility? Where is the nearest 24-hour dental clinic?
  - What is the telephone number to reach destination emergency services?
- Communication
  - What is the preferred mode of communication to reach security in the event of an emergency? Police? Fire? Emergency medical technicians?
  - Are there "house" phones in the meeting space? If so, where? Is there a "dial-out" number, or are they strictly for internal communications?
  - How can key facility and destination staff be reached after traditional business hours?
  - Verify the policy that the meeting planner is to be contacted as soon as any attendee emergency arises.
  - Who is designated to speak to the media?
  - How will you verify the status of all attendees (including your staff) and reach or help them reach their loved ones?

There may be other questions that a event professional wants to ask and have clarified, but at least the above should be asked verbally or in a questionnaire or checklist. For any meeting or business event, there may be other important questions. For example, for a meeting that includes guests from different countries, questions about the locations of the embassies may need to be asked.

Emergency Response Plans

Emergency response plans should be created for potential emergencies, crises, and disasters. Rather than trying to create a separate plan for every type of emergency, crisis, or disaster imaginable, group your response plans by the type of response. For example, fire, carbon monoxide, or gas leak will all require a similar response, culminating in evacuation. Consider whether these can be grouped into one emergency response that can include all of the steps, from hearing the alarm to taking precautions regarding breathing in dangerous elements to evacuating and gathering in one spot.

Make emergency response plans easy to follow. Although there are many things that need to be done in an emergency, the emergency response plan should focus on two main things: (1) getting people out of harm's way and (2) contacting the proper emergency responder (e.g., fire, police, ambulance). In general, emergency response plans should be no more than 10 steps. Too many steps or detailed instructions can slow down peoples' responses or confuse them and may actually make the emergency worse. The threat assessment should give the meeting or event professional an idea of what kinds of emergencies should be in the emergency response plan. Fire, political protest or bomb threat, medical emergency, assault, and other threats deemed to be most likely in the risk analysis are the ones to address first. Others may be included based on the specific meeting or event, venue, or destination.

Communication

In the event of emergency, crisis, or disaster, effective and concise communication are critical. In this very connected society, there are many means of communication, including telephone, e-mail, social media, television, radio, and Internet. In a disaster or catastrophe (such as the September 11, 2001 attack on New York City and Washington, DC, or the 2004 Asian tsunami), one or more of these communication channels may be completely unavailable. For example, mobile telephone towers may be down or a power outage may render television unusable. Even if the mechanical aspects work, sometimes traffic overloads from the sheer volume of calls, e-mail, or social media may render the system unavailable for a time.

Even in an emergency that doesn't rise to the level of a disaster or catastrophe, efficient and effective communication is critical. Internal communication between the meeting or event planner and staff, and external communication between the meeting or event planner and the facility, must be immediate and available. In an emergency, have several levels and types of communication systems available. For example, ideally, a landline (e.g., a house phone) could be used to contact the hotel personnel, mobile phone numbers could have been exchanged, and perhaps hand-held radios could be utilised to facilitate communication.

Some strategies and tools that should be in place before a meeting or event begins include:

- meeting or event planner has direct telephone extensions for key venue staff;
- mobile phone numbers, e-mails, and social media sites have been exchanged between meeting organiser staff and key facility staff;
- meeting or event planner has numbers for summoning destination emergency response providers;
- meeting or event planners have a system for contacting everyone within their organisation;
- hand-held radio channels—one for regular communication and a different one for emergency communication—have been established; and
- emergency outgoing voice-mail messages and Web site are created and in place to inform people outside the organisation of the emergency response status.

Contingency Plans

Contingency plans should be created in the event that a meeting or event has to be postponed, cancelled, relocated, or significantly modified due to an emergency, crisis, or disaster. Create these contingency plans in advance rather than puzzling through what should be done once the emergency occurs. For example, having a plan for delay, cancellation, or relocation of an event due to inclement weather should be done well before the start date of the event.

To be most effective, contingency plans should have a clear activation indicator. This means answering the question "At what point do we implement Plan B?" before the meeting even starts. Tie these activation indicators to a specific defined measure. For example, the contingency plan for weather may have an activation indicator that the event will be canceled if, 24 hours prior to the event, the weather forecast calls for 2 inches (5 cm) of snow. It should also have a specific activation indicator communication channel. Continuing the example of snow, whose weather forecast are we going to follow? Will we tune in to a specific radio station? Will we watch a specific television station? Will we seek information from the U.S. National Oceanic and Atmospheric Administration (NOAA) or an international equivalent?

Only after these things have been established can we determine what the contingency plan contains. While some determinations can only be made at the time of the occurrence, many decisions can be made in advance. For example, a secondary location for the event, confirmed as available on that date and time, must be identified in advance. The decision to relocate the event will be made at a time closer to the event, but the research on the alternative location should be done in advance.

Business Continuity Plans

Business continuity plans are a key consideration for risk management. See Skill 3: Develop Business Continuity or Long-Term Viability Plan of Meeting or Event.

Sub Skill 6.05 – Arrange Security

Every meeting or event has unique security needs. In the risk assessment and analysis phases, the meeting planner should be able to determine specific security needs by evaluating numerous aspects of the meeting or event (see Table 7 Determining Security Needs).

Types of Security

The type of security needed for a meeting or event will vary by the elements in Table 7. A meeting or event professional should not assume that security provided by the venue is necessarily adequate, though the country, type of venue, and rating of a hotel (whether the U.S.-based AAA

Table 7 Determining Security Needs.

Meeting or event characteristic	Specific examples
Type of meeting or event	<ul><li>Conference</li><li>Corporate product launch</li><li>Exhibition</li><li>Incentive programme</li></ul>
Hours of operation	<ul><li>Set-up and/or load-in</li><li>Hours of meeting or event</li><li>Down times between days</li><li>Breakdown and/or load-out</li></ul>
Destination	<ul><li>Destination in which another language or languages are prominently spoken</li><li>Political and civil unrest</li><li>Terrorism risk</li><li>Destination in which theft or loss will not be covered by standard insurance</li></ul>
Venue	<ul><li>Number and nature of entrances and exits</li><li>Public building that non-attendees may legally enter</li></ul>
Activities	<ul><li>Physically strenuous activities (e.g., ropes course, team-building activities)</li><li>Unfamiliar or potentially dangerous activities (e.g., hot air ballooning, ziplining, sky diving)</li><li>Risk of theft</li></ul>
Participants	<ul><li>VIPs</li><li>Famous participants (e.g., celebrities, political figures)</li><li>Youth</li></ul>
Insurance requirements	<ul><li>Certain security requirements may have to be met to maintain validity of insurance policies.</li></ul>

rating, Europe's HotelStars, or another rating type) will provide differing levels of security. Many meetings or events require one or more types of supplemental security. There are six types of security:

1. **Contracted.** When an outside company is hired to provide uniformed or non-uniformed security personnel for a meeting or event, the service is contracted. Security personnel may or may not carry weapons, depending on the applicable laws in the country or state of the event.
2. **Law enforcement.** On- or off-duty law enforcement officers may be used and may be uniformed or in plain clothes (under cover).
3. **Peer.** Trained security personnel that may be of a similar age and appearance as the meeting or event participants are "peers." Peer security personnel are generally dressed as the meeting or event attendees are, although they are clearly designated as security.
4. **Personal.** Also known as "bodyguards," personal security may be assigned to one person or to a small group of people.
5. **Proprietary.** Security personnel employed by (or hired by) a venue, company, or organisation with a defined scope of responsibility.
6. **Volunteer.** Unpaid volunteers with a variety of responsibilities. Volunteer security often provide information, direct traffic, and check credentials at entrances but rarely handle situations that rise to the level of danger, including theft or physical risk. (Silvers, 2008)

Whatever type of security is used, meeting and event professionals must be sure that they are well informed and well trained regarding expected services. Meeting and event professionals should use only licensed, bonded, and insured services when hiring professional security, and should check for pertinent accreditation or other credentials as required by insurance carriers or to ensure legitimacy in the jurisdiction. Security companies should be willing to provide references prior to hire, as well as a copy of their certificate of insurance.

If professional security services are used, allow the security company to help develop (or at least review) emergency response procedures for the high probability and high consequence risks identified in the risk analysis. If local, the security service may have its own emergency response procedures. The meeting or event professional should be willing to adapt his or her own procedures to those the security company has already developed, especially if those procedures have been tested and proven effective, or at least to discuss emergency response procedures (and include the venue and/or destination in the discussion) so that everyone agrees on the appropriate response in a security situation.

Channels of communication—both internal (between security and the meeting or event organiser and facility) and external (between security and the meeting or event organiser and local authorities)—should be established well in advance of the meeting or event. The purchase or rental of certain communication equipment may be needed. Include these needs in the request for proposals for security services, as the bidding security companies may have different recommendations and may or may not include communication equipment in their quoted cost and scope of services.

Local Authorities
Local authorities should be informed about some meetings or events, especially if the meeting or event has a significant risk factor (e.g., is very large or will be attended by one or more persons likely to draw attention from media or picketers, including a parade or protest). Discuss risks with fire and police authorities prior to the meeting or event. It not only alerts them so they can staff properly and be prepared to respond, it may also alert the planner to permits,

licenses, or registrations that have to be submitted in order to lawfully hold certain activities on public property.

Many international meeting and event planners routinely inform the embassy or consulate in the country in which they will be gathering so that if there is a security or consular issue, the embassy is forewarned and can be prepared to render aid or assistance. It is recommended that individual travelers do the same. For example, the U.S. Department of State maintains the Smart Traveler Enrollment Program (travel.state.gov) for U.S. travelers to register their international travels. Upon registering, the traveler receives any travel alerts or warnings about their destination country.

Incident Reporting

If an incident occurs at a meeting or event, it is crucial to have an incident report form completed—even if the danger is averted or someone says they would prefer not to. An incident report form completed at the time of an incident is the best record of what occurred and can be used later against a charge of negligence. In many instances, the venue and the meeting or event organiser (or designated security personnel) may complete separate incident report forms. Because either or both may be accused of negligence, the separate incident report forms protect them individually. A process for completing, reporting, and managing incident reports and follow-up should be determined prior to any incident, ideally when the risk management plan is developed.

References

Black, P., Milanova, B., & Smith-Spark, L. (2013, February 15). Russian meteor blast injures at least 1,000, authorities say. *CNN*. Retrieved from http://www.cnn.com/2013/02/15/world/europe/russia-meteor-shower

Canada Office of Critical Infrastructure Protection and Emergency Preparedness. (1994). Emergency preparedness guidelines for mass, crowd-intensive events.

Emergency Management Australia. (1999). Safe and healthy mass gatherings—A health, medical and safety planning manual for public events. *Australian Emergency Manuals Series*.

Gov.UK. (2013). Guide: Disability rights. Retrieved from https://www.gov.uk/rights-disabled-person

Hatch, S., & Kovaleski, D. (2010, April 20). Eruption disruption: Meetings scramble after flight cancellations. *MeetingsNet*. Retrieved from http://meetingsnet.com/corporate-meetings/eruption-disruption-meetings-scramble-after-flight-cancellations

HotelStars.EU. (2013). HotelStars Union. Retrieved from http://www.hotelstars.eu/en/

Knight, K. W. (2012). Get ready, set, go! - Managing disruptions in emergency situations. Retrieved from http://www.iso.org/iso/home/news_index/news_archive/news.htm?Refid=Ref1576

Mileti, D. S. (1999). *Disasters by design: A reassessment of natural hazards in the United States*. Washington, DC: Joseph Henry Press.

National Fire Protection Association (NFPA). (2007). Standard on disaster/emergency management and business continuity. Quincy, MA: NFPA.

Silvers, J. R. (2008). *Risk management for meetings and events*. Burlington, MA: Butterworth-Heinemann.

United Nations. (n.d.). *Treaty collection*. Retrieved from http://treaties.un.org/Pages/ViewDetails.aspx?src=TREATY&mtdsg_no=IV-15-a&chapter=4&lang=en

United States Department of Justice. (2013). *ADA Home Page*. Retrieved from http://www.ada.gov/

Contributing Author

Tyra W. Hilliard, PhD, JD, CMP
Associate Professor, Restaurant, Hotel, and Meeting Management
The University of Alabama
Tuscaloosa, AL, USA
Member of Meeting Professionals International (MPI), Professional Convention Management Association (PCMA)

Reviewer

Paul Cook, CMP
Planet Planit Ltd.
London, UK

Skill 6:
Endpoints

Terminology

Attrition clause

Cancellation clause

Crisis

Disaster

Due diligence

Emergency

Force majeure clause (also, termination of
    performance)

Indemnification clause

Mitigate

Negligence

Phone tree

Reasonable prudent person

Risk

Risk management

Rider

Additional Resources

1. Nonprofit Risk Management Centre. (2009). *Managing special event risks: 10 steps to safety.*
   https://www.nonprofitrisk.org

Skill 6: Review Questions

1. What are the four stages of risk management?
2. Name three aspects or characteristics of a meeting that may create risk or vulnerability.
3. Identify three types of insurance that an event professional might need for a 1,000-person
   conference and exhibition.
4. What are the six types of security that may be used at a meeting or event?

Financial Management

Responsible **financial management** is critical for the success of events. Event professionals need to have a thorough understanding of the financial goals and objectives, which will vary based on the type of event. Event objectives often include a profit, a loss limit, or a break-even scenario.

In this domain we will examine three critical skills for the financial success of an event:

- *Managing event funding and resources.* This includes the management of revenue sources including sponsorship, registration, grants, exhibit sales and miscellaneous items such as merchandise sales.
- *Managing the budget.* This includes developing the budget, establishing pricing, and monitoring and revising the budget as needed.
- *Managing monetary transactions.* This includes establishing and monitoring internal controls and cash-handling procedures.

Sound financial management is based upon clarity in the event's objectives. What are the goals of the meeting sponsors/owners? Is the event expected to be profitable and create revenue that might provide annual funds for the association or go directly to the bottom line? Is the goal for the event to be self-sustaining and to break even, with income matching expenses? Is the event subsidized by the association and planned to provide training that can be applied toward required certification for association members as part of their membership benefits? Corporations may plan events with the goal of providing training, launching products to their suppliers or markets, or motivating sales personnel or their wider organisation. Or they may offer customer events intended to educate and strengthen relationships. Without thoroughly understanding the event objectives, creating a meaningful budget will be difficult.

SKILL 7: MANAGE EVENT FUNDING AND FINANCIAL RESOURCES

Learning Outcomes

- Manage the sponsorship and donor process.
- Direct the grant funding process.
- Establish an effective registration process.
- Oversee the exhibit sales process.
- Manage miscellaneous funding sources.

Many possible sources for event funding will be covered in this section. They include grants, government programme, sponsors, registrations, products, commissions, and exhibits.

Sub Skill 7.01 – Manage Sponsorship and Donor Process

Sponsorship is often a major funding source for events. It not only contributes to the financial bottom line and helps with cash flow but is also an important element of effectively maintaining relationships with suppliers/partners that provide products and services to meeting attendees. Event planners should understand the differences between sponsorship and donations. Sponsorship involves a meaningful exchange of value (such as money, goods, or services) for marketing benefits to the sponsor. Donations involve less direct benefits, such as acknowledgment or expectations of public relations benefits to the donor. Donations to charitable organisations may have tax benefits, depending on the specific jurisdiction.

Developing Sponsorship Goals

When developing your sponsorship goals and targets, begin with an understanding of the value that your event offers potential sponsors, who will be seeking a return for their investment. Elements to consider when developing a value proposition for sponsors include:

- Your audience and their buying habits
- Your marketing reach and frequency (who will see/experience the sponsor's message and how often the message reaches these people)
- Potential for expanding the visibility of the sponsor through channels beyond the meeting
- Depth of exposure that you are able to offer—branding at the meeting or interactions with meeting attendees, virtual elements of your programme, or through social media

Another important factor in setting sponsorship goals are the event's financial needs. This includes identifying the shortfall between the overall financial goal for the event and the revenue from other sources, including registration fees. You'll also need to determine cash flow requirements. For example, if the organisation has to pay deposits six months prior to the event, you'll need to secure sufficient funding by that time to pay those deposits, often through payments from sponsors.

Once you have a sense of the event's appeal to potential sponsors, you'll need to determine the value of that offer and align it with the event's financial needs. From the sponsor's perspective, consider whether the sponsorship benefits will provide measurable value. To the extent possible, benefits that extend beyond the time limits of the event are desirable.

Identifying and Securing Sponsors

Sponsors come from a variety of sources:

- *Previous sponsors.* These should be your first call. Remember that your ability to secure them for multiple years will be based on their experience. Consider negotiating a multi-event agreement with previous sponsors.
- *Current suppliers or exhibitors.* While they may not have provided sponsorship previously, they have an interest in reaching the meeting attendees and may need some explanation of the benefits available in sponsorship.
- *Your stakeholders.* Personal contacts can be the most effective for securing sponsors. Ask your staff members and other contacts if they can introduce you to possible sponsors.
- *Research.* Thorough research into the businesses of prospective sponsors can help you tailor your proposal for a greater likelihood of success. Determine whether their goods and services can benefit your stakeholders and whether their brand aligns with your organisation, event, and theme. Common areas could be sustainability, innovation, building communities, and supporting initiatives for minorities.
- *Referrals.* Ask your sponsors to refer some of their contacts. In some cases, they may be able to reach a higher level of sponsorship by collaborating with one of their own partners.

For some events, certain sponsors should be avoided, as their presence or sponsorship may damage the reputation of the event. Their organisation may simply be out of alignment with the purpose/mission of your organisation. You should identify such industries or specific companies in advance and prepare a response should they contact you to sponsor the event. Excluding competitors of your top sponsors is a well-established practice, as it diminishes the value of a sponsorship if a direct competitor is allowed to sponsor. Your organisation's position on exclusivity should be made clear to prospective sponsors. For example, policies should be established identifying the circumstances under which a sponsor may be denied, and it should be clear on the sponsorship application that the application may be accepted or not.

In some cases, a phone call or e-mail may be sufficient to secure a sponsorship from a well-established relationship; however, you should still produce a sponsor benefit package, also known as a **sponsor prospectus**. This prospectus contains information to assist the prospective sponsor in making a decision. This package may be posted on your Web site or distributed to the companies or organisations you have identified.

Elements to include in a sponsor prospectus are:

- An overview and history of the event
- Return on investment measures and opportunities
- A description of the value for sponsorship
- A letter of proposal
- Audience demographics
- Sponsorship benefits and limitations
- Terms and conditions
- A draft programme of the event content

Types of Sponsorships

Many types of sponsorships can be designed for an event. Event professionals should adopt the types of sponsorships for their event that best accomplish the financial and non-financial goals of the event, and that provide meaningful benefits to the sponsors. These options include:

Title or Main Sponsor. This type of sponsor will underwrite the majority of the event, and its name will be associated with the name of the event; for example, the Waste Management Phoenix

Open, the largest professional golf tournament on the PGA Tour. A title or main sponsor is likely to be involved in the design, planning and execution of the event. The sponsor may also place restrictions on competitors who are allowed to sponsor parts of the event. In these cases, the benefits are customised for the mutual benefit of the sponsor and the event.

Tiered Model of Sponsorship.   Most traditional sponsorship models involve a tiered system; for example, bronze, silver, or gold sponsorship levels, with predetermined benefits for each. This model can also be adapted for sponsorship of specific areas of the event, such as breakfast sponsor or sustainability sponsor.

Credit Model of Sponsorship.   A credit model of sponsorship is a hybrid between a customised model and a tiered model with pre-set benefits. The difficulty with the traditional tiered model is matching the needs of individual partners or sponsors with the benefits offered. A fully customised model involves one-on-one discussions with potential partners or sponsors and a collaborative process for determining benefits. With a credit-based system, sponsors and partners can choose from a list of benefits that are assigned credit values. This allows for equitable benefits across partners and sponsors without giving everyone the same benefits. This model can be easier and faster to administer than a fully customised model.

In-Kind Sponsors.   An in-kind sponsor provides goods or services at no cost to the event. Examples include an audiovisual company providing equipment or a radio station providing advertising spots in exchange for sponsorship recognition. In-kind sponsorship may be valued at the retail value of the goods or services provided, or there may be a predetermined conversion rate. In-kind sponsorship can be very valuable in reducing overall costs; however, care should be taken that these goods and services are relevant to your event and of the quality that your organisation requires.

Moving from Sponsors to Partners

An important aspect to consider with sponsorship models is to look at how you can develop a relationship that expands the value of the event. Having discussions with your sponsors about ways you can collaborate to make the event more successful is to everyone's benefit. Sponsors can make the event more successful—beyond their financial or in-kind contributions—by helping with public relations through their media contacts or with marketing by including information about the event in their communication materials, including social media and their Web site. They may have the ability to connect your event with their educational offerings, such as a high-level keynote speaker. In these cases, you will need clear guidelines regarding acceptable promotional messages. Ensure that your programme committee retains control over the programme itself, even as your organisation takes advantage of your sponsor's influence in the industry.

Managing Sponsor Expectations

Expectations should be clearly outlined in your contract with sponsors. The contract should include details of the event, responsibilities of both parties (e.g., liabilities), personnel, entertainment, financial obligations, release forms and waivers, policy regarding event cancellation, and insurance requirements. When outlining the contributions, be specific about deadlines and what must be done in advance, on-site, and following the event. Pay attention to expectations for receiving copies of the registration list and contact information. Be aware of applicable regulations regarding privacy and distribution of this information, and collect permission from your attendees for use of their personal information.

Assign a staff member to be responsible for working with the sponsors to ensure that your commitments are fulfilled and that donor recognition is done effectively. This person will be the main point of contact and will communicate regularly with the sponsors. Following the event, this person should ask for sponsor feedback. Study the results and evaluations of the event before beginning the process for securing the sponsor for the next event.

Sub Skill 7.02 – Manage Grant Funding Process

In some cases, meetings or events may be eligible for grant funding. Grants are typically money but can be services, facilities use, or products given by an organisation such as a government body, foundation, or corporation for a particular purpose. Most granting agencies have specific eligibility criteria for grants and application deadlines that must be met.

To find grant funding sources, begin your search early and keep a record of application deadlines. Some granting agencies provide grants only once a year, semi-annually, or quarterly. Research on-line grant maker databases or your local library to identify possible grant sources. Other places to check for possible grants include government Web sites, community foundation sites, and corporate Web sites and their affiliated foundations. Remember to determine whether any of your stakeholders, including exhibitors or sponsors, have foundations that may be able to support your event. Be careful not to jeopardize existing commitments by duplicating your requests.

Before submitting a grant application, research the prospective funding agency's profile and read its criteria carefully. Questions to answer include:

- Do they have a history of funding events?
- What types of projects have they funded in the past?
- Does your event align with their criteria?
- Is there a specific aspect of your event that could be eligible for grant funding?

Recommendations for grant writing include:

- Remember to tailor your application to the specific format outlined in the application.
- Answer all questions thoroughly and provide a detailed budget outlining how the grant funds will be utilised.
- Grant applications can be highly competitive, so try to make your application stand out. Include a compelling story and testimonials that support statistics and facts. Use respectable sources for information, and cite those sources.
- If your application is not successful, follow up to find out how you can improve future applications. Make sure that this information is saved for future grant applications.
- Determine whether any successful applications are posted on the grantor's Web site, as these can provide excellent guidance for your application. You might also contact previous grantees to ask for a copy of their application. This is common practice in grant writing. You are more likely to get a positive response if the grantee is ineligible for the current grant process.
- Make reasonable funding requests, with a credible budget rationale.
- Write many grant requests to increase your chances of receiving an award.
- Establish a long-term relationship with potential funding sources. Grantors are more likely to give funds to an organisation they know than an organisation they do not know.
- Be prepared for any grant management requirements, such as the submission of quarterly or annual progress reports.

Subvention

Subvention is a common industry practice in the international meetings market. It is used where competition is high to attract large congresses or events. Subvention is financial support provided by the host destination or government as an incentive to event organisers. Countries and cities have a vested interest in attracting large events for multiple reasons, First, they generate growth in the knowledge economy and advance ideal industries. Second, and most commonly, countries and progressive cities often see major events as generators of direct employment, attendee spending, and tax revenues. Third, national, provincial, and local governments can be motivated by the prestige of certain events (for example, a United Nations meeting or a world-class sporting event like the Olympics or World Cup), as these events are viewed not only for their immediate economic development opportunities but as ways to elevate perceptions of the destination on the world stage and thus attract broader, longer term growth and investment. Subvention agreements often include binding contracts about the number of delegates, attendees or visitors at an event.

Sub Skill 7.03 – Manage Registration Process

In many cases, the first contact your attendees will have with the event is through the registration process. This first experience will influence their perception of the event, so effectively managing the registration process is a very important task for the event professional.

Today, most registration processing is done on-line Issues to keep in mind as you're developing your registration process include:

- Create a registration form with complete information that is easy to navigate.
- Identify all of the information you will need from attendees to track them and ensure that their needs are met at the event; however, don't ask for information you will not utilise effectively.
- Systems can be customised to collect specific data for different types of registrants, such as an exhibitor, a speaker, or an attendee.
- Systems can be integrated with scheduling information that alerts registrants to conflicts with their selections.
- Systems can be edited after the site is live to close options that are full or to make other needed changes.
- Systems can be integrated with secure payment transactions.
- One-stop shopping can be managed by combining registration, housing, and travel in one system.
- Automatic confirmations are usually generated and communication with registered attendees is facilitated. Some application service providers (ASPs) have systems that enable the event professional to filter the message to specific attendees in a session; for example, to send a room change notice.
- Advanced systems can be integrated with the event Web site and mobile applications so updates automatically feed into different components.

Application Service Providers and Full-Service Registration Companies

ASPs are on-line registration companies that offer customizable registration forms, secure sites, credit card transaction processing, and automated confirmations. The transaction fees for these services vary widely, with some based on per-person rates and others based on a percentage of payments processed through the system. When selecting your ASP, compare fees based on volume of attendees with those based on total payments to determine which option is most beneficial. Consider costs for entering complimentary registrations for speakers, board members, or volunteers.

When comparing ASPs, important financial criteria are:

- Financial
  - Does the system protect financial information through the use of a **secure digital certificate,** payment card industry (PCI) compliance, or tokenization?
  - Are the financial reports comprehensive to allow for reconciliation with your accounting and banking systems, and do they allow for cross-event comparisons if needed? Can the data be extracted to import or integrate into other accounting systems used by your organisation?
  - Are you able to issue invoices and payment reminders, and to manually post payments and process refunds? Can these processes be batched for greater efficiency?
  - Are you able to adjust the currency and taxes if needed for international events? This may include setting your fees in the currency of your destination or your company. You may also need to charge in multiple currencies. Is the site available in multiple languages for international delegates?

In addition to financial considerations, other considerations that may apply include the ASP's ability to handle attendee needs such as travel or name badge production, speaker management, marketing and customer relationship management (CRM) functionality or compatability, and features for exhibit sales.

Some event professionals may opt to work with a full-service registration company to handle financial transactions related to registration as well other tasks such as attendee communication, on-site staffing, and housing arrangements. This can be very effective for organisations that do not have expertise in this field or have limited staffing resources. When working with a full-service registration company, it is important to verify their security practices related to financial transaction data, their ability to handle multiple currencies, and their tax management ability.

Sub Skill 7.04 – Manage Exhibit Sales Process

The following section is adapted with permission from *Events Industry Council Manual, 8th ed.*, and the *Events Industry Council International Manual*). Many types of events will need to manage an exhibit sales process. In addition to trade shows, many meetings and conferences include an exhibit aspect. Trade shows and conferences may include elements of each other in their programmes. For example, trade shows may include education sessions on the trade show floor, and conferences may include an exhibit as part of the event. For many event planners, hosting an exhibition results in significant financial support to the organisation. This can be in the form of booth sales, sponsorships, advertising, and registration fees. In addition to their financial contribution to an event, exhibits also provide important educational opportunities, giving attendees opportunities to learn about the latest products, services, and technology relevant to their field. Additionally, exhibits provide an arena for networking, not only with some of the industry's leading suppliers but also with peers.

Market Analysis and Budget Planning

When managing the exhibit sales process, the first step is to determine the feasibility of holding the event. Each year, there are tens of thousands of global exhibitions, and the number is expected to grow. Whatever industry sector you represent, it's certain that trade shows dealing with that sector already exist somewhere in the world. In determining the feasibility, you will need to select the marketplace best suited to the requirements of your constituency—members, exhibitors, attendees and press. These should include the available attendee and exhibitor base, overall demographics, sales/marketing potential of the region, geographic and political considerations, accessibility and transport options, available facilities, support services, hotels, ground transport, and cost of living. You should also take into account the scheduling of similar and therefore competing events, as this could have a significant impact on exhibitor participation as well as attendee registration. The goal of a successful exhibit is to bring together the right attendees with the right exhibitors in order to create a forum of mutual learning, collaboration and, from an exhibitor standpoint, sales. Research what the attendees are collectively interested in and then approach key suppliers in that market or markets. Keep in mind the unique nature of the attendees and the professional purpose of the event to ensure that the exhibitors are right for the group. Answering some basic questions will help in this decision-making process:

- Why would an exhibition be appropriate for the event?
- Are there any reasons why it would be inappropriate (e.g., legal, political, etc.)?
- What products and services are of interest to the demographic audience represented by your attendees?
- Who can be expected to exhibit at the event? Who are the key suppliers among this group?
- What is the reaction of key suppliers in your industry to the idea of exhibiting at the event?
- Can you operate an exhibition profitably?
- Are there existing exhibitions that you would be competing with? If so, develop a list of related exhibitions. Resources may be available through government offices to help you identify other similar events. Remember that competition isn't always bad. Your stakeholders may be seeking a new and more relevant event to help move the industry forward.
- How successful is your event without an exhibit? Keep in mind that if you attract quality attendees, especially those at a decision-making level, organisations are much more likely to exhibit and provide valuable sponsorship revenue.
- What destinations or venue types would be most appealing for your exhibitors or attendees? For example, would hosting the event on an all-inclusive cruise ship or in a non-traditional venue draw a larger audience?

As a practical matter, most event professionals probably will inherit an existing exhibition rather than launch a new one. Even so, some strategic market analysis as described here is a good idea, since competing exhibitions likely exist, and exhibitors may continue to support only those exhibitions that provide them with a sufficient return on investment.

If possible, visit some competitors' events before launching yours, as doing so can provide insight into your marketplace. Both attendees and exhibitors should be observed, as they are the foundation of a successful event. Also, this is an ideal opportunity to develop relationships with staff from other events, as this may lead to future collaboration and cross-promotion. If this is your first exhibition, conduct thorough market research on its viability before making the decision to launch. (Note that in some countries, including China, it is mandatory that you have a local partner to create any new event.)

Develop an Operating Plan and a Budget
Successful exhibitions operate with a plan and a budget that spells out in advance all the details of anticipated income and expenses. Project as accurately as possible what, when, and how money will be spent on exhibitor registration, promotion, on-site operations, etc. The exhibition budget usually will be a subset of the overall event budget. Because of high start-up costs, espe-

cially in attendee marketing, many exhibitions do not produce a profit for their first two to three years, so plan cash flow accordingly.

Setting Prices

In pricing your exhibit booths, consider many factors, including these:

- Prices of past and comparable exhibitions
- Types of available booths (e.g., standard, premium, corner, island)
- How to price (by size of unit, area, etc.)
- Market response
- Event costs
- What you plan to include in the booth area (furnishings, just bare space, material handling fees, or a combination)

As most exhibitions are expected to be profitable, you'll also need to estimate the level of profit. To determine this, you'll need to estimate both your revenues and expenses as they relate to the exhibit portion of the event. In some cases, organisations depend on the exhibit to fund the overall event.

The categories for revenue, at a minimum, likely will be:

- Exhibiting fees
- Registration fees (if not included with exhibiting fees)
- Additional badge fees
- Advertising
- Sponsorships
- Additional revenue items, such as social events and revenue-sharing opportunities with the exhibit's official contractors.

Categories for expenses, at a minimum, likely will be:

- Exhibit hall rental
- Service contractors
- Freight or material handling
- Communications/promotion
- Management fee
- Staff travel/food/accommodations
- Temporary staffing, security
- Registration costs
- Currency exchange
- Cost for hosting buyers, if applicable
- Waste disposal (note that these costs can be minimized through recycling and other waste diversion practices)
- Fees for a high-profile speaker who will draw people to the event
- Contingency fee, which is particularly important should you be planning an international event with possible foreign exchange risk
- Carpeting
- Cleaning
- Electrical
- Internet

- Security
- Signage
- Audiovisual
- Any transport
- Catering
- Pre-exhibition training for exhibitors
- Fire marshall fees
- Paramedic expenses

Keep in mind that, to attract key buyers or attendees, exhibit organisers may pay for the travel and accommodation of VIPs and/or host dinners, golf matches, or social events for them (although in some fields, such as healthcare, this may be prohibited).

A **hosted buyer** programme offers complimentary travel, accommodation and registration for prequalified buyers to attend an exhibit. Typically, there will be expectations on the part of the hosted buyers that they participate in a predetermined number of appointments with the exhibitors. If you will be hosting buyers, this expense must be budgeted for as well, and care must be taken to ensure that the selected buyers meet the criteria in order to deliver the expected return on investment for the exhibitors.

Exhibitors will also have expenses not related to the booth fees, including travel, accommodation, meals, staffing, materials, and client entertainment. When setting your fees, consider the total cost of exhibiting for your prospective exhibitors to ensure that it is appropriate.

Exhibitor Prospectus

It is important that the **exhibitor prospectus** outline all of the benefits for the exhibitors and provide important information about the show, the attendees and the policies. It is the primary promotional material for an exhibit. The exhibitor prospectus should contain:

- Overview and history of the event
- Objectives of the event
- Exhibit floor layout
- Access times and dates for set-up and breakdown
- Fees and costs of participation
- Value for participation
- Any unique issues related to participation
- Letter of solicitation
- Policies relating to sustainability, including recycling before, during, and after the event
- Audience demographics and their buying power
- ROI measures and opportunities
- Pre- and post-event/meeting activity restrictions
- Additional opportunities for sponsorship
- List of past exhibitors
- Testimonials from past exhibitors and attendees

Contracts and Relationship Management

To be considered for participation in an exhibition or trade show, exhibitors should be required to complete an exhibitor application and contract. The application portion of this document is important because it gives the exhibition organiser the opportunity to deny participation to any prospective exhibitor who is not appropriate for the exhibition or who is not allowed to participate, for example, due to some prior infraction of the rules.

The exhibitor application and contract should include the terms and conditions of participation and require prospective exhibitors to verify (by signing) that they have read the terms and conditions and agree to abide by them. Among other things, these terms and conditions will include information about any union requirements at the facility, exhibitor insurance requirements, and due process procedures for addressing any infraction of the rules by an exhibitor. Once an exhibitor is accepted, the exhibition organiser co-signs the document and sends a copy of the fully executed contract to the exhibitor, retaining the original.

The event professional should focus on ensuring positive relations with exhibitors to encourage them to return for future events. This includes pre-event, on-site, and post-event communications. Recognition programmes such as acknowledging exhibitors on anniversary dates (such as the 10th year as an exhibitor) can be beneficial. Soliciting and responding to feedback from exhibitors is also strongly recommended.

Sub Skill 7.05 – Manage Miscellaneous Funding Sources

In addition to registration, grants, sponsors and exhibits, there are many other potential funding sources for events. These additional sources include:

- *Advertising.* Although events are producing fewer printed materials, this does not limit advertising options as a revenue source. Consider the opportunities to include advertising on the event Web site, on the event app, and on digital signage.
- *Merchandise sales.* Types of merchandise that can be sold to generate funds for an event include wearables, such as shirts or hats, promotional items such as water bottles, and content materials such as digital or printed proceedings or recordings of the event.
- *Commissions.* These can be generated from accommodation sales, tours, and other activities. Commission structures must be clearly defined, agreed to, and disclosed in advance.
- *Royalties.* In some cases, events may generate royalties, such as through the sale of published works created by the host. In some cases, content captured at the conference can be made available on-line and on-demand afterward, possibly for a fee.

Contributing Author

Bonnie Wallsh, MA, CMP, CMM
Chief Strategist, Bonnie Wallsh Associates, LLC
Charlotte, NC, USA
Member of Professional Convention Management Association (PCMA)

Reviewers

Paul Cook, CMP
Planet Planit Ltd.
London, UK

Matt DiSalvo, CMP
Chief Sales Officer, SER exposition services
Worcester, MA, USA
Member of Exhibition Services and Contractors Association (ESCA), International Association of Exhibitions and Events (IAEE), Professional Convention Management Association (PCMA)

Skill 7:
Endpoints

Terminology

Application service provider (ASP)
Exhibitor prospectus
Financial management
Hosted buyer
Secure digital certificate
Sponsor prospectus
Subvention

Skill 7: Review Questions

1. What are the different types of event sponsorship?
2. What should you keep in mind when developing your event registration process?
3. What is included in an exhibitor prospectus?
4. What are sources of miscellaneous funding for an event?

SKILL 8: MANAGE BUDGET

Learning Outcomes

- Develop an event budget.
- Establish pricing for sponsors, exhibitors, and attendees.
- Monitor budget performance.
- Revise a budget.

Event professionals are expected to understand the importance of financial management in developing, managing, and implementing events. A comprehensive awareness of all of the factors that impact the financial success of the event is a critical knowledge area for event professionals. The event's goals and objectives are the foundation for financial planning. On a micro level, event professionals must:

- Assess why the event is being held.
- Review previous history.
- Determine the budget.
- Develop the format of the event.
- Identify the profile of anticipated attendees.
- Determine the geographical location attendees will be coming from.
- Appraise the financial value of the business for suppliers.
- Identify "hot buttons" for the event.

On a macro level, event professionals must:

- Analyse the state of the industry, including buyer vs. seller markets, fees, gratuities, access by air, venue charges, and other potential charges.
- Assess the impact of globalisation and risk management.
- Evaluate the economy, with particular emphasis on the cost of labour, petroleum, and food.
- Identify competing events that could impact attendance, event, or sponsorships.
- Research government policies, regulations, and legal issues.
- Understand the impact of exchange rates on the event's budget.

Preliminary research guides the event professional in developing the financial objectives for the event. Determine whether the event must make a profit, can be revenue-neutral, or can be operated as a financial loss.

Sub Skill 8.01 – Develop Budget

The budget is a key piece of event planning information. At its most basic level, the meeting budget is an estimate of anticipated income and expenses for the event and provides financial control and accountability. Creating an event budget begins with understanding the objectives of the host organisation and of the event, the profile of the attendees, and the event's history in order to develop the financial objectives. Developing the budget involves the following steps:

1. Identify the categories of revenues and expenses for your event.
2. Estimate the quantities for each budget item.
3. Research costs for each budget item.
4. Set prices (if applicable) to meet financial goals.

Grouping revenue and expense items into major categories and reviewing the programme from beginning to end to anticipate costs can help to identify all possible expenses.

Sample Budget Items
Revenue
- Registration fees (early, regular, on-site, daily)
- Companion registration
- Miscellaneous income
  - Administrative fees (registration refunds)
  - Advertising in a programme book
  - Conference recordings royalties or webcast income
- Financial or in-kind sponsorships
- Grants or subventions
- Donations
- Any commissions from hotels or tours
- Exhibitor fees

Expenses
- Programme
  - Computer training workshops
  - Audiovisual equipment
  - Signage and registration build
  - Décor
  - Gifts
  - Meeting room rental
  - Speakers (compensation, travel, and accommodation)
  - Special events
- Miscellaneous on-site
  - Coat check
  - Computer resource room
  - Cyber café
  - Fitness centre
  - Housekeeping
  - Gratuities
  - Hospitality room
  - Parking
  - Telephone
  - Transportation
  - Wireless Internet access
- Marketing
  - Creative fees
  - Domain name registration
  - Postage and delivery
  - Printing
  - Signage
- Registration
  - Credit card processing fees
  - Name badges (badges, holders, ribbons, materials, printing, lanyards)
  - Office supplies and equipment
  - Press registration discounts
  - Shipping
  - Registration bags and giveaways
- Production
  - Electrical rigging
  - Staging
- Exhibition
  - Security
  - Exhibit contractor labor
  - Booth installation
  - Carpeting and exhibit hall decor
  - Material handling
- Food and beverage
  - Banquet
  - Entertainment/F&B/speaker/décor
  - Receptions

In creating your budget, distinguish among fixed, variable, and indirect costs.
- **Fixed costs** are those that are incurred regardless of the number of attendees at your event, such as meeting room rental, marketing, insurance, signage, audiovisual costs, and overhead.
- **Variable costs** are those costs that vary according to the number of attendees, such as food and beverage and printed material.
- **Indirect costs** are listed as overhead or administrative line items in a programme budget. These are organisational expenses not directly related to the event, such as staff salaries and wages,

overhead, and equipment repair. Some organisations use programme-based budgeting, which allocates portions of indirect costs to the event budget. You will need to determine whether indirect costs such as administrative costs will be included as an expense in the event budget. Not including indirect costs in your budget can result in an inaccurate assessment of the profitability of your event. As an example of indirect cost allocations, a company with overhead costs of $10,000 that organises one large event and two small events might allocate 50 percent of the overhead costs to the large event, and 25 percent to each of the smaller events.

Note: every segment type in the travel industry has different ideas of what is fixed or variable. A hotel, a resort, a university campus and a cruise ship differ dramatically in what is included, so research is required ahead of time.

The event professional must document the rationale and assumptions underlying how accounting figures were obtained. Calculations used to arrive at each budgeted item can be documented through many types of software, but the most common are spreadsheets, databases, or customised programmes developed by the organisation. Ideally, the event professional can review past history, preferably the last three years, and compare projected and actual figures from previous budgets. This is known as **incremental budgeting.**

Best practices for incremental budgeting include:

- Review the post-event report for guidance.
- Determine whether there have been any changes to the event goals and objectives.
- Update the revenue and expense items with current fees and costs.
- Be aware of any factors that could significantly impact attendance or costs, such as destination selection.

If the event has never been held before, there is no financial history and the budget is created using estimates of anticipated income and expenses. This is known as **zero-based budgeting**. This practice can also be helpful for events with historical budgets to avoid automatically adding expenses that may no longer align with the event's goals and objectives.

Best practices for zero-based budgeting include:

- Conduct careful research regarding the economic and business environment, potential competitors, target market, and pricing.
- Review budgets from similar events, if possible.

As previously mentioned, it is important to understand whether the financial objective of the event is to make a profit, if it can be revenue neutral, or if it can be operated as a financial loss. In some cases, events may be a major source of income for an organisation. In other cases, they may be an expense for the organisation, as in the case of an internal training programme or a product launch.

Budgeting should be tailored to where the event is being held (for example, a convention centre, a university campus, a hotel, a resort, an all-inclusive land programme or on a cruise ship). Venues differ dramatically, so research the potential costs

Avoid the Seven Common Mistakes of Budget Planning

1. Allow contingencies for the unexpected.
2. Include tax and service charges.
3. Include labour costs.
4. Communicate clear policies to speakers and staff.
5. Review master account daily.
6. Rely on history for meal guarantees.
7. Know the value of your business.

before setting the budget for an event that has been held in a completely different destination or venue before, or when the event is new.

Recommendations for developing a budget include:

- Organise your budget by fixed, variable, and indirect costs. This will allow you to make adjustments as the number of attendees is confirmed.
- Include a sensitivity analysis that allows you to track your budget depending on low, medium, or high projections for revenues and costs.
- Build in a formula for exchange rates so you can monitor the budget with exchange rate fluctuations.
- Make sure that you have included all of the costs for your event. Some items can be easily overlooked. Adding them in after the original budget has been accepted and circulated could involve some difficulties. Overlooked budget items often include event insurance, taxes, attrition fees, social media costs, photography charges, inflation, and gratuities.
- Include projected expenses for complimentary attendees, including VIPs, press, volunteers and speakers.
- Include a contingency fund in your budget. Some event planners include a contingency category in their costs and allow around 10 percent of the total overall budget for this category. This provides an element of safety in case you have inadvertently missed some expenses. Ten 10 percent allowance may not be sufficient. Factors that may increase the needed allowance include whether this is a new or repeating event, how far into the future the event will be held, and whether there are exchange rate risks.
- Review all contracts with suppliers and track payment dates.

Budgets and Foreign Exchange Risk

This section is adapted with permission from the *Events Industry Council International Manual*. Budgeting for international events needs to account for currency and tax issues. Failure to manage these issues effectively may result in a serious impact on the event's bottom line, but there are a number of steps that may minimise risk.

Exchange Rates. An important risk to manage for events is from exchange rates—the rate at which one country's currency may be exchanged for another. It represents a financial risk for events if income is earned in one or more currencies and expenses are incurred in another. Should the value of the currencies change relative to each other, the event may face a budget surplus or deficit. Currencies worldwide may float against one another in a market relationship determined by supply and demand (as in the relationship among the U.S. dollar, the euro, and the Japanese yen); may be fixed at a certain level; or may float within fixed limits. Currencies can be fixed for a period but then liable to experience radical adjustments to a new fixed rate if dramatic economic changes occur. On the other hand, positive currency fluctuations can provide income. Options to reduce the risk might be to have registration fees in the local currency or to compensate in pricing slightly for any risk. There is lower exchange rate risk if currencies are fixed, at least in the short term, but there may be dramatic shifts in a floating exchange rate relationship. Cruise ships will typically have a standard currency.

Payments in Foreign Currency. Many international event organisers prefer to deal in the euro or U.S. dollar, as they are almost universally accepted. This often eliminates the need to deal with foreign exchange rates and conversions. However, this convenience comes with hidden costs that may affect the budget and its bottom line. For example, suppliers will often mark up their prices by

10 percent to 15 percent if they know that they have to assume the foreign exchange risk by being paid in a non-local currency. Pay invoices in the local currency whenever practical; in some cases, the host country will require registration fees to be paid in the native currency for tax reasons.

Selecting the Currency. International event professionals often pay the majority of event costs in the currency of the host country but receive event income from attendees (assuming the attendees pay to attend) in their home currencies. If prices for attendees and event costs are in different currencies, any shift in the exchange rate will lower or raise the net of the event. If prices for attendees are fixed in the currency of the country where the event takes place, shifts in the exchange rate will change the real price that attendees pay in their home currency.

Event organisers, therefore, need to make a decision as to whether they or their attendees will carry the risk of exchange rate variations, as shown in Figure 1. Once that decision has been made, clearly communicate the policy to the meeting attendees.

Hedging Currency Risk. One method of hedging currency risk is to "buy forward." This establishes a fixed exchange rate to accurately budget all fixed and variable costs in the home currency. Buying forward is a contract to exchange a certain amount of money on a specified date at a specified exchange rate. Alternatively, a bank account may be designated in a foreign currency to deposit funds and make payments. When registering in a host country for tax purposes, fiscal authorities often specify that you must have a bank account in that country and a certain amount of funds already in that account.

In either case, the risk of negative exchange rate shifts is eliminated (e.g., those that raise costs and/or reduce revenue in the currency being used). However, if exchange rates move in the event's favour, there will be no exchange rate gains. A financial professional can advise on the risk strategy that fits best with the company culture. Corporate, association, and entrepreneurial events may be protected from adverse currency fluctuations in this manner, whether or not attendees pay to attend.

Software. Event organisers need to ensure that their event registration and accounting systems have the capacity to deal with the currencies in which they will be working. If you have a Web-based, secure on-line payment system for delegate registration, ensure that it can receive payments in the currency that best suits your needs; special arrangements will need to be set up with the handling bank, and this may take time.

Tax. International events raise at least two key tax issues that may affect the budgeting for an event:

- Are attendees and/or the organising company liable to pay income or company tax in their home country because the event has been organised abroad? In some cases, the delegate is perceived to have received a taxable benefit from the company, and the company is potentially liable to pay any tax associated with providing that benefit to an employee. This doesn't impact the budget of the event but has a financial implication for the company and for the attendees, potentially affecting the viability of the event from a broader corporate perspective and the desirability of attending from the delegate's perspective. This is a complex and technical area; event organisers who are concerned about liabilities that may be incurred should seek tax advice from their company tax advisers or from specialists in this field.
- Are the organisers and/or attendees liable to pay local tax in the country where the event takes place? In Europe, we are talking primarily of the value added tax (VAT); in the United States and many other countries, this would be local sales tax and hotel/motel taxes.

Figure 1   Example of Exchange Rates for an International Event.

In this example, the event takes place in Europe with 100 attendees from the United States.	
Exchange rate at booking/budgeting stage	euro (€) 1.00 = U.S. dollar ($) 1.25
Exchange rate when attendees are invoiced	euro (€) 1.00 = U.S. dollar ($) 1.40
Cost per delegate = € 100	
Budgeted surplus = 10 percent = € per delegate or €1,000 total	
Scenario 1: Charge delegates in U.S. dollars ($)	
Price budgeted to achieve surplus (set at planning stage)	€110 x 1.25 = $137.50
Total revenue generated	100 attendees x $137.50 = $13,750
Total revenue at exchange rate when delegates are billed	$13,750/1.40 = €9,821.42
Total costs	100 x €100 = €10,000
Event loss	€10,000 - €9,821.42 = €178.57
Scenario 2: Charge delegates in euros (€)	
Price budgeted to achieve surplus (set at planning stage)	€110
Price paid by attendees at invoicing stage	€110
Total revenue generated	€11,000
Total costs	100 x €100 = €10,000
Event surplus	€11,000 - €10,000 = €1,000
Registration per attendee in U.S. dollars	€110 x 1.40 = $154
Price attendee expected to pay at planning stage	€110 x 1.25 = $137.50
Attendee pays $16.50 more than expected when the event was announced.	

Note: In this example, local taxes are not shown. These would need to be added to the fee and remitted to the appropriate authorities.

Value Added Tax (VAT) and Sales Tax.   VAT is a point-of-sale tax that is levied by various countries at different rates for different commodities (e.g., food and beverage or accommodation). It is an extremely complex area, with wide variations worldwide in the level of tax. In Europe, it can vary from a minimum of 6 percent up to 21 percent, depending on the country, the type of services delivered, the location where services are delivered, etc. It is an ongoing matter subject to changes without prior warning and precise rules about what needs to be paid, when, and what can be reclaimed. The impact of VAT is felt directly on the event budget.

As a general rule, companies are entitled to reclaim VAT, but individuals are not. In many countries, there are specialist firms who can advise foreign companies and event organisers about the rules and options for VAT. In many cases, they can help set up legal entities and open bank accounts in the country where the event is taking place to enable the correct charge and reclaiming of VAT. Some can assist with the process of reclaiming VAT from the tax authorities, as well, while retaining a percentage as their fee for taking on what can be a time-consuming process. Start the process of tax registration a year or six months before the start of registration, as you will need to display the VAT registration number on all invoices sent to delegates and provide the same number to local suppliers for their invoices. This way, the fiscal authorities can track the income and expenditures locally through the VAT registration or identification number.

If you are planning to work with local partners in the foreign country (e.g., a DMC or PCO), part of the process of selecting them should include their experience advising clients and/or partners on how to deal with VAT for international events. If mistakes are made, organisers may find themselves liable to pay the tax without having made adequate provision.

Key questions to ask about VAT include:

- How does my company status affect my VAT liability? For example, in Europe, an international company with a subsidiary company anywhere in the European Union (EU) is treated differently from an international company with no EU-based subsidiary.
- Is it desirable/do I need to set up a company in the country where the event takes place?
- What is the level of VAT or sales tax in this country? (Especially on major items such as accommodation and meals.)
- Am I required to register in some way with the tax authorities?
- Am I required to pay VAT on my purchases?
- Am I required to charge VAT to my attendees (if attendees pay a registration fee)?
- May I reclaim VAT? How?
- May my attendees reclaim VAT? How?
- What is the financial/legal risk for making a mistake in these tax matters?
- How far in advance should we start the VAT registration process with the authorities?
- Is there a change in rates predicted between now and the start of my event?
- What are the requirements of my VAT registration number; where do I have to display it or provide it?

When planning an event outside one's own jurisdiction, there will always be added costs and unfamiliar extras (as well as potential savings). Currency and taxes are just two important considerations. The best advice is to seek advice. (The foregoing section was adapted from the *Events Industry Council International Manual* with permission.)

Developing Your Cash Flow Plan

As you schedule all the costs that you have added to your event planning calendar, you will be starting the first part of your cash flow schedule. Cash flow is crucial for any business, especially for events. Having the money in the event's account to pay suppliers so they can provide services is very important.

If you cannot pay a supplier in advance, they could refuse to provide their service, thereby putting your whole event at risk. The best time to negotiate with a supplier is before the event has taken place and before they have provided their services. In the agreement with them, spell out the services to be provided and the costs for those services; also include when payment is to be made. If cash flow doesn't allow you to pay when agreed, it is best to work with the supplier to secure some flexibility for payment.

To manage cash flow, a spreadsheet is helpful to indicate when funds are expected to be received, as well as when expenses will need to be paid. This enables you to determine deadlines for receiving money as well as negotiating payment terms with suppliers.

Many events have short lead times and invoices, especially for deposits, that must be paid "upon receipt," so having some funds available to pay for these before the event will be necessary.

Sub Skill 8.02 – Establish Pricing (for Sponsors, Exhibitors, Attendees)

Establishing appropriate pricing for an event is important for both the financial and marketing success of the event.

Important considerations for establishing pricing include:

- Financial goals of the event—is it expected to generate revenue, allowed to be revenue-neutral, or is a financial loss acceptable?
- What are the expenses for the event?
- Are there any fixed income or other revenue sources for the event, such as a grant or commissions?
- What is the brand image for the event?
- Who will be attending the event, and what is the price they are willing to pay?
- What has been charged by the event in the past?
- What is being charged by successful competitor events, and are your circumstances (such as user profile and reputation) comparable?
- What are the prevailing economic conditions?

Break-Even Analysis and Budgeting for Profit

Many events will base their pricing on breaking even (where income equal expenses). Even events that are profit oriented may use this model to set prices at a point where, based on their projected minimum attendance, the event will not lose money.

Two formulas can be used to calculate the break-even point: the first calculates the number of attendees required for the event to break even, and the other the price that should be set in order to break even, based on the expected number of attendees.

To calculate the number of attendees required to break even, subtract the variable costs from the registration fee to get the contribution margin. Then divide the total fixed costs by the contribution margin.

Break-even attendance example:

- Registration fee is 500
- Variable costs are 300 per person for food and beverage

- Fixed costs are 10,000 for room rental and equipment

- Contribution margin = 500 – 300 = 200
- Fixed costs/contribution margin = 10,000/200 = 50
- The event will break-even with 50 attendees

If you know the number of attendees for an event, you can calculate the break-even registration fee by dividing the total fixed costs by the number of attendees, and then adding the variable costs.

Break-even registration fee example:

- Fixed costs = 10,000
- Estimated attendance = 100
- Variable costs = 200 per person

- Registration fee = 10,000/100 + 200
- Registration fee = 300

Sponsorship

One of the key issues when considering revenue sources is sponsorship. An important first step when developing your sponsorship plan is to understand the expectations of sponsoring organisations. They are most likely interested because of the opportunity to get their message to a target market—the people attending your event or watching the event on-line. They may also be seeking a presence on the Web site and signage at the event, exclusive time with the attendees, or to be positioned as an industry leader by presenting top-rate educational programmes.

Factors to consider when setting prices for sponsorship opportunities include:

- Benefits being offered and fees for comparable marketing opportunities
- Demographics of the attendees to determine the business value of the sponsorship opportunity
- Costs required to service the sponsor's needs (such as signage)
- The brand image of the event
- Past fees
- Prevailing economic conditions

While sponsorships can be a valuable way of generating revenue to help an event be a financial success, sponsors should be chosen carefully to make sure that they are a good match for the event and its reputation.

A similar analysis can be made to calculate the fee required in order to make a specified profit. In this case, the desired profit is added to the fixed costs.

Specified profit registration fee example:

- Specified profit = 20,000
- Fixed costs = 10,000
- Estimated attendance = 100
- Variable costs = 200 per person
- Registration fee = (20,000 +10,000)/100 + 200
- Registration fee = 500

The following example demonstrates how to calculate an event's profitability with multiple income sources.

Example: Will the following event break even, make a profit, or sustain a loss?

- Fixed income = 10,000
- Estimated attendance = 200
- Estimated sponsors = 10
- Estimated booth sales = 20
- Fixed costs = 20,000
- Proposed registration fee = 200
- Proposed sponsorship fee = 500
- Proposed booth fee = 400
- Variable costs = 100/person

- Total income = 10,000 + (200 x 200) + (10 x 500) + (20 x 400)
- Total income = 63,000

- Total expenses = 20,000 + (200 x 100)
- Total expenses = 40,000

Income is greater than expenses, so the event will have a profit of 23,000.

Discounts

Many events offer registration discounts. Examples include early bird rates, group discounts, student or senior rates, and discounts for members. If you are offering an early bird rate, take care to not extend it, as it sends the message that the event is not meeting registration goals. In order to encourage early registration, use incentives such as limited numbers of discounted tickets or special access or benefits for those who register early.

Refunds

Having a registration refund policy clearly stated on your documentation will enable you to clarify the cost in the event an attendee cannot come to your conference. Any applicable administrative fees for cancellations should be communicated in registration information. Refund policies should be established for sponsorship and exhibitor fees if the event doesn't proceed for some reason, especially if that reason is beyond your control. Consider evaluating refunds on an individual basis in case of extenuating circumstances, such as a family death or medical incident.

Sub Skill 8.03 – Monitor Budget Performance

Budgets are used to estimate future numbers; however, actual numbers will almost certainly vary from the projections in the budget. Thus, once the budget is established, it needs to be monitored carefully to ensure that financial goals are on target for the event.

Key performance indicators for revenue targets include volume and pace of sales. From this perspective, you can determine whether your registration numbers or sponsorship numbers are similar to those of previous years. For example, if last year you had 1,500 attendees registered for your event three months prior to the start and this year you have 1,200, you have a good indication that you might need to adjust your marketing practices to meet your targets.

On the expense side, budget control guidelines are needed. Examples include determining who has the authority to make purchases that vary from the budget and the limits that apply. You may require approval from senior management in this case. Forecasted expenses should be regularly updated as the event develops and budget items such as catering needs and event technology requirements are confirmed.

Understanding how variances in the budget occurred is an important aspect of monitoring the budget performance. When this happens, the event professional should determine the cause(s), identify the impact, and respond accordingly. Responses may include revising activities, reallocating funds, and communicating information and decisions to those affected.

Sub Skill 8.04 – Revise Budget

The scale of an event and the corresponding size of the budget are factors in determining the frequency of budget reviews. For small events with few line items in the budget, you will need fewer reviews than for a more complex conference with several thousand delegates.

The budget should be revised as costs are confirmed, as greater certainty of projected revenues is achieved, and as any unforeseen revenues or expenses are identified.

If sales of the income sources are less than anticipated or expenses are higher than expected, decisions will need to be made about how to increase the registration or sponsorship activity, explore other routes to make up for registration income shortfall, or perhaps cut back on other budgeted expenses. The management team should be kept aware of any budget shortfalls. Conversely, if income is higher than anticipated or expenses lower than anticipated, decisions should be made regarding whether the additional funds should be utilised for upgrades to the budget or retained as profit.

The budget will also need to be revised when unforeseen expenses occur. For example, an increase in complimentary guests or VIPs can result in additional catering costs, or you may need to secure additional Wi-Fi bandwidth to meet the needs of attendees. If the costs are considerable, budget approval from the event owner may be required. Dealing with unforeseen costs may mean reducing expenses in other areas or increasing income, or it may be manageable within the contingency fund for the event.

The likelihood of unforeseen costs can be reduced with all-inclusive packages. For example, a cruise ship will often include audiovisual equipment rentals, theme décor or special entertainment, meals and beverages. Some venues or caterers will also include packages that include meals, breaks, equipment and function space. The specifics of what is included may vary regionally or by venue and should be reviewed carefully. These types of packages will typically be listed as:

- Delegate daily rate
- 24-hour rate
- Complete meeting package

Contributing Author

Paul Cook, CMP
Planet Planit Ltd.
London, UK

Reviewer

Bonnie Wallsh, MA, CMP, CMM
Chief Strategist, Bonnie Wallsh Associates, LLC
Charlotte, NC, USA
Member of Professional Convention Management Association (PCMA)

Skill 8:
Endpoints

Terminology

Incremental budgeting
Zero-based budgeting
Fixed costs
Variable costs
Indirect costs
Value added tax (VAT)

Skill 8: Review Questions

1. How can you avoid the seven common mistakes of budget planning?
2. Will the following event break even, make a profit, or sustain a loss?

Fixed income = 5,000
Estimated attendance = 200   proposed registration fee = 100
Estimated sponsors = 10   proposed sponsorship fee = 500
Estimated booth sales = 10   proposed booth fee = 500
Fixed costs = 10,000   variable costs = 100/person

3. How do you monitor budget performance?
4. How do you address unforeseen costs in your budget?

SKILL 9: MANAGE MONETARY TRANSACTIONS

Learning Outcomes

- Establish cash handling procedures.
- Monitor cash handling procedures.

The handling of monetary transactions must be given the same care and attention as every other element of the meeting planning process. Without strict controls, policies, and reporting, the entire infrastructure of the event and the department of those planning the event can be undermined. Whether the reason for financial confusion is due to a lack of experience, a mistake in attribution of a revenue or expense item, or thievery, financial controls enable problems to be spotted quickly and solutions put into place before major damage is done.

While there isn't an expectation that event professionals should also function as trained accountants or bookkeepers, a basic knowledge of financial reporting forms, the ability to read financial reports, and the capacity to identify problem areas are essential skills. Having these skills will help the event professional communicate the success of their events in clear business terms that non-planners will understand and appreciate.

Accounting Basics

The following information has been adapted, with permission, from the *Events Industry Council Manual, 8th ed.*

The two accounting methods most widely used in the events industry and elsewhere are **cash accounting** and **accrual accounting**. A cash accounting system counts income and expenses as they are actually received and paid, whereas an accrual accounting system counts income and expenses when they are earned or incurred.

Cash accounting does not recognise promises to pay (accounts payable) or expectations of revenue (accounts receivable) and generally, does not recognise non-cash expenses such as depreciation. Income and expenses are recorded at the time of each transaction.

Accrual accounting records items as they relate to net worth (assets minus liabilities) when they are incured, regardless of whether cash has changed hands. Accrual accounting provides a more accurate representation of the ebb and flow of an organisation's finances. In the United States, publicly traded companies are required to use accrual accounting, while most small businesses can choose their accounting method. The method to be used for your event will be determined by your chief financial officer (CFO), director of finance, or accountant.

Three important accounting tools that can help an event professional with budgeting and forecasting are **income statements, balance sheets,** and **cash flow statements**.

- An income statement is a statement of revenues and expenses (also known as a profit and loss statement) over a period of time.
- A balance sheet is a statement that indicates overall financial status by subtracting expenses from income. A balance sheet provides the bottom line: the total amount of assets, liabilities and net worth at a particular point in time. Often, your accounting staff can provide these statements, which can be generated automatically (usually monthly or quarterly) through most business accounting programmes.
- The cash flow statement is distinct from the income statement and balance sheet because it does not include the amount of future incoming and outgoing cash that has been recorded on credit. Cash flow is determined through three methods by which cash enters and leaves a company: core operations, investing, and financing.

A chart of accounts is a detailed list of the individual line items that make up the revenue and expense categories in a budget. Consult with your accounting staff to ensure that you understand the numbering system used to identify every line item in your event budget, so income and expenses are posted to the correct master account during the event and then again when they are presented for payment.

To ensure that your master account is handled properly, give clear and comprehensive instructions to the facility. An excellent way to transmit this information is with a master account authorization form. Indicate which charges should be posted on the master account, the limits of financial responsibility that your organisation will accept, and the names of people authorized to sign for master account expense items. Communicate the same instructions to your staff, members of your organisation, and your speakers. This will help to avoid common master account problems or unauthorized charges, such as on-site audiovisual orders placed directly by speakers, mass photocopying charges incurred by staff, and unscheduled coffee breaks ordered by someone in your organisation.

Some event professionals visit each hotel or convention centre department to acquaint themselves with the managers and employees who will contribute to the success of the event. It is helpful to be known and recognised by key individuals in each department, as charges from these departments could flow to the master account. At a minimum, meet the department managers at the pre-event briefing. At this meeting, you should review the billing instructions, the importance of accurate master account maintenance, and what charges you will and will not accept.

Schedule time each day to review the master account with your group billing coordinator to verify all charges. Request that detailed documentation outlining every charge be attached to the statement in chronological order. This will save you a lot of time when you receive the account for payment after your group leaves.

Billing Timetable. The following information was adapted, with permission, from the *Events Industry Council Manual, 8th ed.*

A billing timetable illustrates the budget lifecycle of an event, from its inception to the final payment of the master account, and helps monitor cash flow. It can be based on past events; however, it should be reviewed to consider any changes in suppliers and the lead time for your event. Figure 1 shows suggested timetables for handling billing for events based on 18-month, 12-month, and 4-month lead times.

Sub Skill 9.01 – Establish Cash-Handling Procedures

Establishing internal control policies for cash handling is an important step in ensuring that your financial reports are reliable and making your operations more efficient.

Your cash-handling procedures should establish:

- Who will be responsible for specific tasks?
- How will duties be divided to reduce the risk of errors?
- What are the documentation procedures?
- How will transactions be monitored?

Expectations, policies, and procedures must be clearly communicated to staff and volunteers. This should form part of the training and should be monitored regularly to ensure that the policies are being followed.

Event professionals should take steps to prevent theft, both internal (by a staff member or volunteer) and external. Steps to help prevent theft include:

Figure 1   Timetable for Event Billing Process.

Task	18 months	12 months	4 months
• Establish expense projections and preliminary cash flow schedule. Update regularly as service providers are contracted. • Determine event pricing, and adjust time lines (such as registration deadlines) to align with cash flow needs.	12–18 months before	9–12 months before	4 months before
• Confirm billing instructions and requirements with the facility, including completing a credit application for direct billing (if applicable). • Arrange a confirmation and reporting system for attendees' accommodation reservations.	9–12 months before	6–9 months before	4 months before
• Meet with the venue's representative to review billing instructions, room and master account requirements, and the room confirmation system.	6 months before	6 months before	3 months before
• Verify the master account requirements with the facility's convention services manager (CSM) or sales manager. They will relay the information to the credit manager or group billing coordinator. Request confirmation in writing from the CSM or sales manager. • Make arrangements for the secure handling and deposit of cash and checks received for on-site registration and ticket receipts at the end of each day.	3 months before	3 months before	2 months before
• Review room rates, food and beverage charges, and other charges (note which are acceptable and which are not) and billing procedures. • Confirm who will be authorized to make financial decisions during the event. • Review all non-venue supplier items for terms, price, and settlement issues.	1 month before	1 month before	3 weeks before
• Provide guaranteed numbers for variable cost items such as food and beverage. Request confirmation in writing from the CSM.	3 business days in advance (or as per contract)	3 business days in advance (or as per contract)	3 business days in advance (or as per contract)
• Hold a pre-conference meeting with venue representatives and key suppliers to review the event specifications guide.	1–3 days before	1–3 days before	1–3 days before
• Conduct a daily review of the master account with your accounting representative or CSM.	During the event	During the event	During the event
• Review master account billing and originals or photocopies of attached charges. Approve correct charges and identify disputed, delayed, or missing charges. Attempt to settle the disputed charges. Establish dates for payment of undisputed portions of the bill, for payment of missing or delayed charges, and for the final resolution and payment of disputed charges. At this time, identify and resolve any supplier charges or bills incurred by outside suppliers such as an AV contractor, a general services contractor, or a band. These charges may be identified as either a miscellaneous charge or a "paid out" on the master account. Paid out means that money has been advanced or paid out by the hotel to either the supplier or those authorized to add to the master bill and bill to your account.	Before leaving	Before leaving	Before leaving
• When you receive the complete master account bill, acknowledge the receipt in writing. Upon completion of the master account audit, notify the facility of any disputed charges along with the exact amount of the dispute and the reasons why the charge is in dispute. Send a letter notifying the facility that payment will be made on undisputed charges and that upon proper resolution of the disputed charges, additional payments will be made. Promptly pay the undisputed charges by check, credit card or electronic funds transfer. Some facilities specify that all master accounts must be paid within 30 days of the event's conclusion. Others may offer discounts for payment of the master account at checkout. Be sure to inquire about these policies early in the planning phase.	Post-event	Post-event	Post-event

- Work with trusted staff members or a reputable on-site staffing company.
- Screen candidates who will be handling cash.
- Review the ethics policy during orientation and training.
- Hire security and secure transport for deposits.
- Arrange for a secure on-site location to hold cash, such as a safety deposit box.
- In some jurisdictions, cashiers are bonded, which provides additional protection against loss or theft.
- Use a ticketing system where large volumes of cash are being handled. For example, sell tickets at the entrance that are exchangeable for drinks or catering at the point of serving.

Coordination of money handling is fundamental. This includes setting up a central cash office where deposits are received and reviewed by a separate staff member. Ensure proper record keeping: amounts of cash issued to cashiers as floats; deposits received by type (cash, cheques, credit card transactions, or other forms of payment); copies of receipts and records of cash collection; and deposits. Security and audit systems also need to be pre-arranged. This is important not only to protect financial assets but also for the safety and security of your staff members and attendees.

Cashiers

When working with on-site cashiers, provide each cashier with an appropriate cash bank at the beginning of each sales period. Establish how money will be collected from them during and after the event. The cashiers should acknowledge the amount of cash received and collected at each point during the day. The amount should be agreed upon by the cashier and the person collecting the money.

Do not let cashiers accumulate too much money; they should have just enough to make change. If the event is to take place over a weekend, be well stocked with change, because banks will be closed.

If cheques are to be accepted, policies for receiving cheques should be outlined. Typically, a standard form of identification is noted. If you have an attendee with a history of submitting bad cheques, a policy should be in place to refuse future cheques from that person or organisation.

Accepting major credit cards will reduce the amount of cash that cashiers must handle. It should be made clear with the cashiers which credit cards are accepted and whether or not the credit card company's service charge is to be paid by the organisation or added to the individual's charges. Before developing a policy that could charge back the service fee to the individual, make sure to check local laws regarding this practice.

Establish an accounting procedure to be used after each registration period and at the end of the event. For attendees' convenience, learn about the event facility's policies for cashing personal cheques and establishing credit.

Regardless of the payment type, implement a system for generating receipts so the registrant can have a record of payment. Receipts can cover the spectrum from a handwritten receipt to one sent via text or e-mail.

Sub Skill 9.02 – Monitor Cash-Handling Procedures

Proper security is necessary when money or items of value change hands. You will need a safety deposit box or vault near the registration area. If substantial amounts of money are being handled, consider hiring a security officer whose duties should include accompanying anyone moving large amounts of money through public areas. Arrange for security to escort the cashiers to deposit cash, credit card receipts, and cheques in a secure manner. Deposits should be made on a regular basis. If credit card transactions are being handled electronically, a secure Internet connection and backup are required.

Deposits should be verified by an independent staff member. The duties of this person will be to:

- Review deposits and verify accuracy.
- Count and replenish cash floats (amount of cash provided to make change for cash transactions) as needed.
- Sign in funds.
- Reconcile cashier reports with credit card terminal transactions and bank deposits.

Effective cash handling and monitoring includes the following elements:

- Review security procedures.
- Monitor revenues and expenses.
- Monitor cash-handling procedures.
- Monitor audit documentation.
- Revise procedures as needed. Thoroughly document variations to established procedures.

Contributing Author

Bonnie Wallsh, MA, CMP, CMM
Chief Strategist, Bonnie Wallsh Associates, LLC
Charlotte, NC, USA
Member of Professional Convention Management Association (PCMA)

Reviewer

Paul Cook, CMP
Planet Planit Ltd.
London, UK

Skill 9:
Endpoints

Terminology

Cash accounting
Accrual accounting
Income statement
Balance sheet
Cash flow statements

Skill 9: Review Questions

1. What should your cash-handling procedures establish?
2. What elements are included in effective cash-handling monitoring?

Human Resources

During the evolution of the events industry, we have seen many planners' roles shift from logistics to strategic management, and the level of responsibility has expanded to include advanced knowledge and skills in areas such as technology, legal and regulatory mandates, and international standards. This is true in the human resources domain, where event planners' knowledge now extends to three major areas: recruitment of staff and volunteers, training of staff and volunteers, and management of workforce relations. The scope of the event planner's actual involvement in these three major areas will vary. For some, it may only be minimal involvement, while for others it may be a significant part of their role.

The cyclical nature of meetings means that working in conjunction with suppliers, independent contractors, and other temporary personnel is an area with which the event planner must become acquainted.

The event planner will likely be involved in the hiring of suppliers to provide support services. Because the event planner holds overall responsibility for the meeting or event, he or she should verify that the suppliers are meeting legal requirements regarding hiring practices and training their team members for their roles.

SKILL 10: ACQUIRE STAFF AND VOLUNTEERS

Learning Outcomes

- Learn best practices for developing **selection criteria**.
- Explore how to recruit staff and volunteers.
- Identify best practices in staff and volunteer **recruitment**.

109

When event professionals are involved in recruiting staff, including support services and volunteers, they will need to have an understanding of job descriptions, the outcomes of the roles to be fulfilled, and any policies or procedures that may govern human resources practices. Knowledge of the critical path (see the Project Management Domain) is also valuable in order to identify when, how many, and which type of staff and volunteers will be needed.

Sub Skill 10.01 – Develop Selection Criteria

Creating selection criteria begins with the development of a workforce action plan that takes into consideration staffing needs, recruitment strategies, staff training and retraining, technology enhancements, and outsourcing strategies.

Develop job descriptions for each position, regardless of whether the role is to be filled by staff, filled by a volunteer, or outsourced. The organisation that employs the event planner should have policies and procedures in place that include parameters for the hiring and retention of staff and may include policies on selecting volunteers and working with service providers, including outsourcing to individuals or companies. New job descriptions should follow the policies and procedures of the organisation. Once job descriptions are developed, review them to ensure compliance with applicable local, regional, and national laws. The job descriptions then become the basis for post-event evaluation tools.

Once this information is gathered, development of selection criteria can begin. Workforce requirements planning should be aligned with the organisation's strategic and business plans, and should identify where gaps exist in existing workforce competencies. Gaps can then be filled by use of new staff, volunteers, and outsourced individuals and companies.

Regardless of where an event is held, the event planner must become aware of local employment conditions; local, regional, and national labour laws; skill sets required for specific positions; and, where applicable, local terms and conditions applicable to volunteers. An understanding of the corporate culture and the work environment, combined with an analysis of skills of current employees, can be beneficial when developing selection criteria. Depending on whether the event planner is working domestically or internationally, there are individuals and companies that can act as resources for researching applicable laws, rules, and regulations. Destination marketing organisations (often called convention and visitors bureaus), general services contractors, destination management companies (DMCs), industry peers, and government agencies are just some of the resources available to provide guidelines on hiring and contracting.

If you are conducting on-line research about employment laws, be sure that selected Web sites are legitimate sites providing factual information that is relevant to your specific region. Most important, know when an employment or labour attorney should be consulted. Examples of employment law resources are:

1. European Commission, Employment, Social Affairs & Inclusions, Labour Law at http://ec.europa.eu/social/main.jsp?catId=157&langId=en

2. Federation of European Employers at http://www.fedee.com/employment-law/

3. Labour Laws in Eastern European and Central Asian Countries: Minimum Norms and Practices at http://siteresources.worldbank.org/SOCIALPROTECTION/Resources/SP-Discussion-papers/Labour-Market-DP/0920.pdf

4. United States Department of Labor, Wage and Hour Division, Compliance Assistance - Wages and the Fair Labor Standards Act (FLSA) at http://www.dol.gov/whd/flsa/

When outsourcing to an individual (as opposed to a company), ensure that the agreement specifics are consistent with existing laws and regulations regarding employees (or volunteers) in that jurisdiction.

Working with suppliers often involves the development of a request for proposal (RFP) for specific services. As a best practice, the RFP should be sent to a minimum of three providers. The Events Industry Council's Standards Committee has developed an *RFP Workbook* for some areas of support that covers the basic information, details, and specifications for the most common RFPs and will be regularly updated as requirements change:

- single facility
- citywide/destination
- event technology/audio visual
- DMC and transportation services
- general services contractor

Sub Skill 10.02 – Recruit Staff and Volunteers

Recruitment efforts for staff can take many forms, including job postings on industry Web sites, local media, or through word-of-mouth, which often helps find employees who already fit your organisation's culture. Many members of the Events Industry Council offer job listings or recruitment services that can be used to help recruit staff and volunteers.

Other recruiting methods include use of executive search firms or employment agencies and peer networking. The use of local media, particularly newspaper advertising, may result in a high response rate, but with poorly qualified candidates. Executive search firms and employment agencies are fee-based resources that offer various pricing methods, depending on the services required.

Depending on the job description and responsibilities, background checks may be required. Background checks range from simply checking for driver's license violations to an in-depth investigation into the individual's character and background. The nature of the background check will depend on the expectations for the individual and local regulations. Background checks should be performed for both staff and volunteers, particularly those who may be involved in working with children, driving vehicles, or handling financial transactions. Permission is usually required from the applicant in order to conduct a background check. You should be prepared to offer some assurance of confidentiality regarding information obtained on applications and background checks.

Another factor to consider is population demographics and the development of a diverse workforce. Several elements of diversity should be considered: generation, race, culture, and gender. The workforce should reflect the diversity of the organisation and the people who will be attending the meeting. This ensures that the various interests and needs of the stakeholders aren't overlooked in event planning and execution.

Selecting the right volunteers follows the same processes as selecting employees, with the additional task of ensuring that the roles of volunteers do not conflict with local, regional, or national laws covering employment. Policies and procedures, job descriptions, and evaluation processes should be in place for volunteers, as well as clear organisational and reporting structures. The Volunteer Centre Bedford's *Volunteer Recruitment and Retention* guide provides an excellent overview (see Additional Resources).

When utilising volunteers, remember that they are there for different reasons than paid employees. Identify their reasons for volunteering, and make sure their motivation is a good match for the work to be done and that you are aware of how they hope to be recognised or rewarded.

Sub Skill 10.03 – Select Best Candidates and Offer Positions

The job description serves as the basis for developing evaluation criteria for the selection of candidates. Use application data to answer questions such as:

- Do the candidate's abilities meet the requirements of the job?
- Will the candidate be able to perform the tasks required by the position?
- Does the candidate fit with the culture of the organisation?
- Can the candidate work with the level of supervision needed (i.e., does the person require a lot of direction or do you need someone to take full responsibility for a portion of the project)?
- Can the candidate work with other potential participants, key stakeholders, clients or lead suppliers, and teams?

Many organisations develop a ranking grid/system to evaluate these and other criteria on candidates so the entire process is fair and impartial. Coincident to the development of a ranking system, a timeline or flow chart for the selection process should be created to establish parameters from the job posting through to acceptance and regrets letters. A sample timeline is provided below, and should be adapted to the particular position, needs, and typical requirements for candidates to give notice to a current employer.

Recommended best practices for interviewing candidates include:

- Interview questions
  - Base interview questions on the job criteria.
  - Ask the same questions of all candidates, and take notes of the responses for later comparison.
  - Determine the weighting for each of the questions or skills in advance to minimize the potential for bias in the interviewing process.
  - Use behavioural questions that ask how the candidate previously approached typical employment-related situations.
  - Be aware of questions that do not meet local regulations regarding acceptable interview questions and avoid using them.
- Interview practices
  - Follow the hiring practices outlined in applicable collective agreements.
  - In some cases, selecting times that allow for currently employed candidates to participate discretely in the interviews can be beneficial.
  - Select locations for the interviews that are accessible for all candidates.

Table 1   Sample Selection Process Time Line.

2 months before start date	- Job is posted in relevant places.
6 weeks before start date	- Applications are reviewed and candidates to be interviewed are selected. - In some cases, regrets letters are sent to candidates not selected for an interview.
5 weeks before start date	- First-round interviews are conducted. - Reference and background checks are conducted for top candidates.
4 weeks before start date	- Offers are made and accepted. - In some cases, regrets letters are sent to candidates not selected for the positions.

References

Events Industry Council. (2013). *Accepted Practices Exchange: RFP workbook.* Retrieved from http://www.eventscouncil.org/APEX/RequestsforProposals.aspx

Walker, A. (2009). *Managing an ageing workforce: A guide to good practice.* European Foundation for the Improvement of Living and Working Conditions. Retrieved from http://www.eurofound.europa.eu/pubdocs/1998/65/en/1/ef9865en.pdf

Watanabe, S. (1997, March). *The social security crisis in Japan.* Ministry of Foreign Affairs of Japan, Retrieved from http://www.mofa.go.jp/j_info/japan/socsec/watanabe.html

Contributing Author

MaryAnne P. Bobrow, CAE, CMP, CMM, CHE
President, Bobrow Associates, Inc.
Citrus Heights, CA, USA
Member of American Society of Association Executives (ASAE), International Association of Exhibitions and Events (IAEE), Meeting Professionals International (MPI), Professional Convention Management Association (PCMA)

Reviewers

Shawna McKinley, MAEEC
Director of Sustainability, MeetGreen®
Vancouver, BC, Canada
Member of Green Meeting Industry Council (GMIC)

Chris Prieto, CMP
Regional Director: Africa
ICCA – International Congress & Convention Association
Johannesburg, South Africa
Member of Southern African Association for the Conference Industry (SAACI)

Skill 10:
Endpoints

Terminology

Selection criteria
Recruitment

Additional Resources

1. Events Industry Council, APEX Initiative, RFP Workbook at http://www.eventscouncil.org/APEX/RequestsforProposals.aspx

2. Events Industry Council, Member Organisations at http://www.eventscouncil.org/AboutUs/cic-member-oganizations

3. European Commission, Employment, Social Affairs & Inclusions, Labour Law at http://ec.europa.eu/social/main.jsp?catId=157&langId=en

4. Federation of European Employers (http://www.fedee.com/employment-law/) Labour Laws in Eastern European and Central Asian Countries: Minimum Norms and Practices at http://siteresources.worldbank.org/SOCIALPROTECTION/Resources/SP-Discussion-papers/Labour-Market-DP/0920.pdf

5. United States Department of Labor, Wage and Hour Division, Compliance Assistance - Wages and the Fair Labor Standards Act (FLSA) at http://www.dol.gov/whd/flsa/

6. Volunteer Centre Bedford, Volunteer Recruitment and Retention, a short guide for voluntary organisations at http://www.voluntaryworks.org.uk/volunteeringbedford/documents/Volunteerrecruitmentandretention1.pdf

7. Wall Street Journal's How To Management Guide, How to Manage Different Generations (2009) at http://guides.wsj.com/management/managing-your-people/how-to-manage-different-generations/

Skill 10: Review Questions

1. Why is it important to research local, regional, and national laws and regulations when planning a meeting?

2. What difficulties can arise when managing a diverse workforce?

3. Why are clearly defined policies and procedures required in the management of volunteers?

SKILL 11: TRAIN STAFF AND VOLUNTEERS

Learning Outcomes

- Learn best practices for providing orientation.
- Identify best practices for providing training.

You have a team of staff and volunteers assembled for your event. Now what? Effective orientation and training of human resources plays an important role in planning and running an effective meeting or event. Staff and volunteers are invited onto your team because they bring important skills and perspectives that make them valuable contributors. That does not assume they know important things about your meeting or event, your organisation, or the context of the job they are assigned to do. Orientation and training are required.

Although the words are often used synonymously, orientation and training are different. Orientation suggests a pointing out of one's location relative to the surroundings: co-workers, event attendees, suppliers, clients, customers and other important groups. Orientation is critically important for staff and volunteers so they understand your team and event, how you work, and how they should interact with others.

Training is differentiated by its focus on acquiring skills and improving one's capacity to perform a job. It may happen at the beginning of an employment period and ideally continues as responsibilities expand, tasks change, and the work environment adapts to external forces, such as technology.

Sub Skill 11.01 – Provide Orientation

Orientation provides staff and volunteers with a familiarization tour of your organisation and event. It is typically the first thing new recruits participate in and ensures that they get started with an introduction to the context for their role in the organisation. Orientation is a particularly important process during set-up for an event, when crews of on-site staff and volunteers may need to understand more about your organisation and the event you're hosting in order to help you execute a flawless experience.

Many companies have standard formats for orientation. These may be scheduled as required for individuals when they join the event team or for groups of workers during the event set-up. While standard orientations are important, the commencement of any new event project may require additional orientations as well, even for current staff or volunteers. This is particularly important if you work in an environment where you plan events for clients whose policies, cultures, and event programmes may differ.

The depth of orientation required will vary greatly. Full-time, permanent staff may require a longer, more detailed orientation than a temporary event employee or volunteer. Plan for what is appropriate based on the situation. The following list provides some guidance on details that may be important to cover during orientation:

- mission statement, values, goals, and objectives of the meeting or event and organisation
- meeting or event features and details, including the agenda and venues, and who is attending
- how the meeting fits into the overall organisational goals/objectives
- job descriptions, including roles and responsibilities
- applicable legislation, such as labour laws and statutory rights
- labour agreements, such as union or employment contracts
- workplace health and safety procedures, such as crisis management and emergency response plans, personal protection equipment, first aid, and evacuation plans

- organisational structure
- organisational contact list
- organisational policies, which may touch on sustainability, ethics, accessibility, non-discrimination, harassment, and other topics
- organisational procedures, such as scheduling, payment, and employment reviews
- communication protocols and reporting structures, including clear direction on who is supervising and what staff or volunteers are authorized to do or not do
- available equipment and tools, including how to access technical support
- meeting or event plans, including critical deadlines and deliverables
- workplace incentive or reward programmes that could motivate strong performance
- special organisational or event partnerships or projects, including important collaborators, event sponsors or charity beneficiaries

In preparing to orient staff, it can be helpful to imagine the myriad questions they might ask, some of which may seem obvious to you but all of which are legitimate for new or inexperienced staff or volunteers:

- When do I report to work?
- What are the work hours?
- Where do I work?
- Whom do I report to?
- What if I have a problem or need help?
- What should I wear?
- When is it okay to take a break? Or ask for holidays?
- What if there is a fire? Or an earthquake?
- What if I get sick?
- What do I do when I'm finished?
- When do I get paid?
- What do I do about expenses? What is covered and what isn't? Do I need approval?
- Are there certain things I can do or say, or things I'm not supposed to do or say?
- Will I have need for special work equipment or access to specific technology resources such as social media?

Helpful, plain-language answers to these questions can be prepared as a simple list of frequently asked questions (FAQs) and put at the front of the orientation material. Remember, some people may not be familiar with the jargon used at your event or common terms used by the event industry. Be prepared to define special terms and language they might encounter, perhaps by referring to the APEX Industry Glossary.

Orientation should be a two-way process. While much information may be directed to staff and volunteers, orientation is also a critical time to collect important information about your new team member or members, such as:

- emergency contact information
- current knowledge and skills
- aspirations for training and project work
- any accessibility or personal needs they may want to discuss
- administrative information for compensation and benefits

Absorbing information about a new job can be quite overwhelming for new recruits. Consider learning styles in how the information will be presented (written instructions, diagrams, photos, etc.), and the need for follow-up. Some individuals may absorb information easily by sitting down and reading a manual or listening to it delivered lecture-style. Others may need more creative formats that could include role-playing, scenarios, and hands-on mentorship. Orientation may be a brief affair of a few hours or involve several weeks of working alongside another employee. Various formats can be effective. Find the method that ensures a strong foundation for your staff and volunteers to perform at their best and be confident in their job.

Supervisors should plan for the inevitability that volunteers may not show up or cancel at the last minute. One way to compensate is by recruiting more volunteers than you need. Having a pool of standby volunteers will ensure that you can fill a position on the fly when a team member does not show up. Remember, these fill-in volunteers may not have received any special orientation for their new task until it is assigned, so be prepared to brief them on what they need to know.

Do not assume that all shared information will be remembered. Anticipate that staff and volunteers will be uncertain on many points in their first few hours, days, or months of work. Keep an eye on them. Positively reinforce what they are doing well, and correct undesirable behaviour as soon as it is noted. If appropriate, plan to check in again following the formal orientation to see if they have questions or feedback, or require coaching. Don't overlook the fact that new staff and volunteers are often a great source of fresh ideas to improve your organisation or event! Responding to their feedback, especially at an early point in their employment, reinforces the fact that you value their contribution.

Sub Skill 11.02 – Provide Training

Every job has core skills that will be required and assessed during the recruitment process and may require further training once the volunteer or employee is engaged. Volunteers and employees often require different training depending on their roles and responsibilities. Job-specific training will be required. As well, the rapid rate of technological change in the industry requires constant expansion of skills using software, interacting through social media, and utilising advanced production equipment. The global movement toward sustainability requires a heightened awareness of opportunities to not only deliver exceptional experiences, but reduce environmental impacts and provide social good at the same time. All of these issues require meeting and event professionals to provide their teams with opportunities to upgrade and develop skills.

Training may take place in response to an individual's request or be developed for a group of new employees. Developing a policy for ongoing professional development can help ensure improvement and sustained motivation. With a policy like this in place, employees can be encouraged and guided to shape their own learning and explore areas that are of interest to them and useful to the organisation. As an example, a staff member, on his or her own, may ask to attend a conference, register for a course, or apply for a credential, such as the Certified Meeting Professional (CMP) designation. It is helpful to communicate this policy during orientation and to continue with regular reminders. Adopting and communicating consistent criteria to evaluate personal training requests is important, especially if professional development budgets are limited and not every applicant will be approved.

As part of the professional development policy, staff or volunteers may be provided with training as a group, such as your planning department, suppliers or on-site registration team. This is advisable for teams that need a common skill set, such as learning to operate a registration or badge-scanning system. First-aid training and responsible alcohol service are other common skills event planners are trained to accomplish appropriately. Employee or volunteer groups may need to improve their capacity to address a specific subject, such as hybrid events, sustainability, accessibility, or crisis management.

Whether for an individual or a group, ensure that the training subject matter is relevant. Questions to help evaluate the value of potential training programmes might include the following:

- Is the training required by law on a recurring basis to ensure that personnel are up-to-date on regulations?
- Does the topic of training fit within the employee's area of responsibility—now or in the future?
- Does the training ensure that staff or volunteers can perform a necessary task?
- Does the topic have value to your customer or meeting/event stakeholders?
- Could this training help differentiate your organisation in the marketplace?
- Does the training experience contribute to organisational objectives?
- Does the training content help fill an identified knowledge gap?
- Does the training contribute to a professional credential?
- Does the training experience prepare a team member to train others?
- Does your budget support the training?

Training may be provided by a you or a third party. For example, associations may designate subject matter or task experts within their membership to train staff and volunteers to provide special services at an event, such as delegate voting, recycling, or local information. Third parties, such as temporary staffing agencies, may also be involved in on-site aspects such as coordinating registration, information and wayfinding. If you will be working with a third party, you will want to research their training credentials prior to committing to work with them. Do they have a professional certificate? Are they a member of or affiliated with a recognised training body? It is also helpful to ask for and interview references.

If you are developing your own training, give careful thought to how you design your instruction programme. Learning objectives are a critical first step to ensure that your programme is designed around what you want your audience to get out of it. Think, too, about the knowledge that may be needed as a prerequisite for the training and about readings or assignments that may be necessary in advance.

Method of delivery is also an important consideration. Many of us picture training as a classroom-style exercise, where a teacher tells us what to do. While some learners respond well to this kind of directed learning, it is not the only option. Give some thought to how to include different learning styles. Some people learn better by listening to a lecture. Others prefer discussion or direct, hands-on activities. Some learners need solo reflection, through activities such as journaling, while others want to be involved in a team. Advance questionnaires for your audience may help you determine what kind of instruction they prefer, or you may be familiar enough with your team to know what is best.

If you don't have the opportunity to use different methods of training, use the following questions to help identify the most appropriate approach:

- How much time do you have for training?
- What are the two or three most important points you need trainees to learn or apply?
- What is the culture of your audience? Are they used to learning in a certain way? Or in a different language?
- Will you be getting together in person or delivering the training remotely through a webcast?
- Where will the training be conducted, and is this space limited or flexible to accommodate certain kinds of activities and interaction?
- What technology do you have or need—projectors, flip charts, etc.?

The Unitarian Universalist Association (UUA) uses diverse training formats to prepare their "green team" for their annual General Assembly. This team plays an essential role in educating attendees about how to recycle and compost their event waste, contributing to UUA's goal of keeping as much event material from landfill as possible. Volunteers are first briefed about recycling practices via an e-mail pre-event, using written instructions that include text, diagrams, and pictures. This information is reiterated in a classroom-style orientation with an opportunity for discussion, questions, and answers. A third type of training is held when the volunteers show up for their first shift; it involves them in role-playing with event attendees. Here supervisors can provide one-on-one coaching using actual event materials to ensure that they are disposed of properly.

Think about how to get the most mileage out of training. Some training is best conducted in person. Other topics may require regular review sessions. For example, annual first-aid and disaster response training may be required by insurance carriers. Efficiency and flexibility could be improved by recording sessions so users can receive training on-demand via the Web. Reinforcing key take-aways (important information to remember) and procedures through posted signage can keep lessons at the forefront of activities on a daily basis.

The training process does not stop when a course or demonstration is over. Evaluate the effectiveness of training against the objectives you set. This may be done in a variety of ways. Formal assessment of skills and knowledge may require testing or completion of an assignment. Evaluation of training outcomes may also be integrated into regular employment reviews. Event professionals who conduct regular trainings should also consider polling staff and volunteers about the effectiveness of their training. This is a great way to make trainings more user-friendly and may be done through written evaluations, questionnaires, informal conversation or formal exit interviews.

Don't forget that training can lead to evolved responsibility and more specialised skills that can have an impact on staff workload. This may have repercussions for compensation and advancement. It is therefore important to regularly review the impact of training and ensure that job descriptions and employment agreements are updated to reflect new roles and realities that result from training.

Training needs to evolve over time. This can cause an organisation to amass a wealth of presentations, guides, and webinars that could be included as resources for new staff and volunteers. So don't forget to go back and update your orientation to include training opportunities that might be relevant to communicate.

Contributing Author

Shawna McKinley, MAEEC
Director of Sustainability, MeetGreen®
Vancouver, BC, Canada
Member of Green Meeting Industry Council (GMIC)

Reviewers

MaryAnne P. Bobrow, CAE, CMP, CMM, CHE
President, Bobrow Associates, Inc.
Citrus Heights, CA, USA
Member of American Society of Association Executives (ASAE), International Association of Exhibitions and Events (IAEE), Meeting Professionals International (MPI), Professional Convention Management Association (PCMA)

Chris Prieto, CMP
Regional Director: Africa
ICCA – International Congress & Convention Association
Johannesburg, South Africa
Member of Southern African Association for the Conference Industry (SAACI)

Skill 11:
Endpoints

Terminology

Labour agreements
Training
Orientation

Skill 11: Review Questions

1. How does orientation differ from training?
2. What kinds of information are important to include in an orientation?
3. How might you determine whether a training programme is relevant to or needed for your event?
4. What kind of styles, tools, and methods may be helpful to use to deliver training?

SKILL 12: MANAGE WORKFORCE RELATIONS

Learning Outcomes

- Learn how to supervise staff and volunteers.
- Review best practices for managing teams.

No event is ever produced alone: It requires a well-trained team that works well together. From modeling expectations to conducting effective reviews, resolving conflict, and communicating well with groups, management of workforce relations is a core competency for any event professional. Important resources for managing workforce relations are job descriptions and performance expectations, organisational structure, policies and procedures, and applicable labour legislation and agreements.

Sub Skill 12.01 – Supervise Staff and Volunteers

Just communicating expectations through orientation and training is insufficient. Managers must reinforce norms of acceptable behaviour by employees and volunteers on a day-to-day basis. This requires event leaders to set a good example by modeling respectful and appropriate behaviour with co-workers, management, subordinates, supplier partners, and meeting attendees. It also calls for quickly acknowledging appropriate behaviour and correcting inappropriate behaviour.

All organisations and events should institute regular feedback systems for staff and volunteers. These reviews, which are both formal and informal, are an important part of ensuring that staff get the support they need and receive information about how well they are performing against the roles and responsibilities outlined in their job descriptions. Reviews can be very stressful for staff members, so it helps to outline the structure and time line for reviews up front. Be sure to inform employees and volunteers in advance about opportunities they will have to provide their own comments and feedback.

Supervisors can and should provide two separate kinds of feedback: coaching sessions and formal evaluations. Coaching sessions focus on personal growth and help employees and employers stay in good, regular communication. Don't forget volunteers, who also need regular affirmation of good performance and feedback on behaviours that need to be corrected. Coaching sessions may be held fairly frequently, especially for new employees. These meetings are a good time to mentor staff and discuss daily challenges and opportunities to improve, without the added stress of how compensation might be affected.

In addition to coaching, structured and formal performance reviews should be held. These reviews should be conducted on a recurring basis and documented. They should cover overall performance, highlight areas of strength and success, and draw on improvements from previous coaching sessions. Annual reviews may also set performance goals which can be brought forward during the next review cycle. These evaluations might also revisit and possibly adjust pay, benefits, and other important aspects of employee agreements.

In spite of managers' best efforts to coach, review, and improve, workplace conflict is inevitable, especially in the fast-paced, on-site environment at an event. Conflict resolution skills and systems can assist in steering disagreements and problems to productive, respectful dialogue and, hopefully, an agreeable resolution. While not always possible, it is best to resolve ongoing conflict before going on-site for your meeting. This helps ensure that the on-site process goes more smoothly, and lessens the chance of a disruptive interpersonal conflict during the meeting. The following tips can help when workplace conflict affects your team:

- Model and affirm respectful communication.
- Acknowledge the problem and attempt to clearly define it.
- Ensure that all sides are provided with an opportunity to share their perspectives and desired resolutions.
- Acknowledge the validity of feelings that resulted from the problem and move quickly to focus on the facts of the situation.
- Involve conflicting parties in suggesting possible solutions.
- Discuss what is ideal and fair, and encourage each party to give and take.
- Agree to a solution.
- Have each involved person articulate what he/she believes the agreement is and that he/she is willing to abide by the agreement.
- Thank involved parties for their commitment to resolve the conflict.
- Commit to follow up and review the outcome within a reasonable timeframe.

Some conflicts are impossible to resolve, in spite of best attempts. Still, meeting and event organisers have a responsibility to staff, volunteers, attendees and other stakeholders to listen and attempt to reconcile problems to the best of their ability. Make sure that you have a way to determine when a problem needs to be referred to a higher level or an outside party brought in to help resolve it.

Many staff and volunteers are stellar contributors to your event and organisation. Recognition programmes can provide these individuals with the positive reinforcement they require to feel rewarded and appreciated for what they do, which can encourage them to excel further and may improve retention rates. The type of recognition should be tailored to local customs as well as organisational and local policies regarding gifts and gift limits. Examples of recognition ideas for staff include:

- Public acknowledgement of their contributions
- Certificate of accomplishment for their employee file
- Handwritten letter or thank you card

Examples of recognition for volunteers include:

- Public acknowledgement of their contributions
- Letters of recommendation
- Certificates of participation
- Eligibility for an incentive prize
- Complimentary registration for the event
- Handwritten letter, thank you card, or phone call

For example, large events may rely on temporary event staff or volunteers to serve as information ambassadors, welcoming people to your event, helping them on their way, and answering questions. These individuals play an essential customer service role and might be rewarded by a supervisor who catches them in an act of service that goes above and beyond what is expected of them. These ambassadors might receive a write-up or employment reference for future work or perhaps be eligible for an incentive prize.

While it is important to reward all workers who do a good job, volunteer appreciation may require special effort. Volunteers are unpaid; therefore, opportunities to reward them through refreshments, food, gifts, and personal gratitude are essential. Often volunteers participate in an event because it provides them with free or discounted access to sessions, expositions or entertainment. Don't forget to clarify expectations about on-duty responsibilities and off-duty benefits. As volunteers are being recruited and oriented, find out from them what kind of acknowledgment or reward they would appreciate, and to the extent possible, provide that.

Sub Skill 12.02 – Manage Teams

Teams serve a critical role in the event industry. Many hands help ensure that essential tasks get done that could never be completed alone, and different perspectives create innovative and inspired experiences. Effective teams need a clear mandate so that all members are focused on achieving the same outcome, even when they are working on different tasks and aspects of planning. Successful teams are also aided by good orientation and direction from leaders, who assign and clarify roles and responsibilities.

Diversity within teams can promote success. Few things in our integrated, global world are mono-cultural these days, including events. They serve varied stakeholder groups, the members of which have unique needs and perspectives, from dietary considerations to translation equipment and mobility needs. Ensuring that the event planning team, on-site staff, and volunteers respond to this diversity is important. Also ensure civil discourse between staff members and other stakeholders. Diversity may come in the form of demographic characteristics or expertise. Different aspects of diversity to consider may include:

- Gender
- Age
- Languages
- Ethnicity
- Race
- Sexual orientation
- Physical ability
- Technological ability
- Learning styles

The role of the leader is to align staff and volunteers behind the vision for the meeting. Leaders delegate tasks, monitor progress, provide course correction, lead by example, and model good judgment. They recognise and respond well to the stages of growth that teams and individuals within the team often exhibit. They step in to provide structure and clarity when the event team forms or a new member joins. They exercise confidence, focus, objectivity, and patience when there is conflict or uncertainty during pre-planning or when the final meeting or event plan may still be taking shape. Effective managers delegate, encourage, and then step back to foster the creative team process and growing responsibility of team members as they settle into a norm of behaviour. They applaud, motivate and reward their team when they perform, giving credit to those who helped realize the event vision. It is important to note that these stages of growth may happen simultaneously for different individuals on the same team, making empathy, agility and flexibility essential leadership traits in the event industry.

Clear communication and fairness are important conditions for maintaining a healthy, well-functioning workforce. These are not a default precondition of events or event organisations, which are typically fast-moving, high-pressure environments. Hours may be long and pay at times lower than in other careers. Recognition, reward and effective reviews are important to provide adequate compensation and healthy conditions for staff and volunteers to excel and contribute their best efforts to a successful event.

Contributing Author

Shawna McKinley, MAEEC
Director of Sustainability, MeetGreen®
Vancouver, BC, Canada
Member of Green Meeting Industry Council (GMIC)

Reviewers

MaryAnne P. Bobrow, CAE, CMP, CMM, CHE
President, Bobrow Associates, Inc.
Citrus Heights, CA, USA
Member of American Society of Association Executives (ASAE), International Association of Exhibitions and Events (IAEE), Meeting Professionals International (MPI), Professional Convention Management Association (PCMA)

Chris Prieto, CMP
Regional Director: Africa
ICCA – International Congress & Convention Association
Johannesburg, South Africa
Member of Southern African Association for the Conference Industry (SAACI)

Skill 12:
Endpoints

Terminology

Performance reviews
Conflict resolution

Additional Resources

1. UK Health and Safety at Work Act at http://www.hse.gov.uk/legislation/hswa.htm
2. Canada – Information on Duty to Accommodate at http://www.chrc-ccdp.ca/preventing_ discrimination/duty_obligation-eng.aspx

Skill 12: Review Questions

1. Describe different kinds of staff or volunteer feedback.
2. List steps you can take to resolve conflict on your event team.
3. What benefits are gained by building a diverse team?
4. What different styles do team leaders need to demonstrate to ensure that event teams work well together?

Stakeholder Management

All organisations affect, and are affected by, the environment within which they operate and the people within that environment. This also applies to events: The many organisations and individuals with whom the event interacts—including attendees, workers, suppliers, and the broader community—have an impact and are affected by the decisions made in planning and delivering the event. These individuals and organisations are the event's stakeholders. Effectively managing relationships with stakeholders means incorporating their perspectives during the event planning process. By taking the time to understand stakeholder perspectives, the event organiser is more likely to align the event's goals and objectives with stakeholder requirements and goals.

SKILL 13: MANAGE STAKEHOLDER RELATIONSHIPS

Learning Outcomes

- Identify, assess, and categorize stakeholders for an event.
- Describe how to manage stakeholder activities.
- Determine how to manage stakeholder relationships.

Sub Skill 13.01 – Identify, Assess, and Categorize Stakeholders

Define "Stakeholder"

Every event professional comes into contact with a wide range of event **stakeholders**—people who can have an impact on the success of the event or who can be affected by the event. As mentioned in the project management domain, stakeholders are the "persons or organisations who are actively involved in the project or whose interests may be positively or negatively affected by the performance or completion of the project" (*PMBOK Guide*, 2008, p. 23). Stakeholders can be internal or external to the event host organisation. Individuals and groups of people such as employees, managers, suppliers, customers and sponsors may be classified as stakeholders because of their close relationship with the organisation, and specifically with the projects being planned.

Stakeholders include those who have an economic interest in the organisation's future as well as those who are affected by the actions of the organisation, such as the local community, businesses, and those who have an interest in the natural environment that is impacted by the event. Each stakeholder or group of stakeholders will have their own objectives, which are dictated by their specific role(s) and how their performance is measured. They will need access to different types of information that will vary depending on their role and their needs.

In an effective **stakeholder approach,** event professionals take into account their responsibilities to others and adopt a consultative demeanor, including stakeholders in the event's decision-making process. The organisation as a whole can significantly benefit from co-operation and inclusion of the various stakeholders' needs in decision making. Because stakeholders' needs may sometimes conflict, event professionals should anticipate and be prepared to address any contradictory requests.

A stakeholder approach can lead to many benefits for an organisation, including attracting and retaining employees, suppliers and customers, which can support a strong organisational image and enhanced ability to meet core purpose and business objectives. Strong stakeholder involvement can also result in support for the budget and other resources needed to produce the project.

All event professionals should allocate time and resources to identifying stakeholders, assessing their objectives, planning communication activities, and managing relationships to ensure the successful achievement of the specific event objectives. This chapter focuses on best practices in these key skill areas.

Identifying Stakeholders

Identify the internal and external stakeholders of the event. **Internal stakeholders** include the owner of the project and the owner of the budget; **external stakeholders** include attendees, sponsors, and the community where the event is taking place.

The first priority in managing stakeholder activities is to clearly identify the **event owner.** The owner is the person who has requested the event and is responsible for defining its overall objectives and measurable outcomes. The event owner has a critical role and should be in a position to allocate resources, engage with other stakeholders, influence change, and remove barriers to ensure the event's success.

The **budget owner** is also a key stakeholder and, in some cases, may be the same person as the owner of the event. This stakeholder has the overall responsibility for the income and expenditures related to the event. He or she will focus on the organisation's business objectives and be accountable for financial costs and liabilities.

Event attendees/participants and their managers (or equivalent person who authorises involvement) are the next main groups of stakeholders. These are the people whose participation is required to achieve the designated event objectives. The source of this group will vary depending on the desired outcomes of the meeting. They can come from both internal and external areas of the organisation and could be employees, customers, suppliers, partners, or a combination of various groups.

Internal Stakeholders. Internal stakeholders (see Table 1) in organisations are typically business owners, other departments, managers, employees, and internal customers or consumers.

For each event, the list of stakeholders will vary depending on the organisation, the type of event to be planned, the business objectives, the culture of the organisation, and the extent to which services and support have been outsourced. The event professional needs to review the organisation and identify relevant stakeholders.

Some organisations will have all of the departments listed in Table 1, while others will use different titles or not have a department dedicated to this function. If the organisation does not have one of

Example of Stakeholder Terminology Applied to a Corporate Event

Event = Meeting for all national store managers for a major retail company to launch a seasonal range of products.

Objective = Maximise sales of the new range of products during a limited period.

Event owner = Most senior person in the sales and marketing function at the board level.

Budget owner = National sales and marketing manager.

Attendees = Regional managers, store managers, and vendor representatives.

these departments, its role(s) will need to be fulfilled by another department or by the event professional.

The key departments or roles for the majority of events are considered in more detail below. Depending on the size of the organisation, these roles may be fulfilled by the event planner, a separate individual or department within the organisation, or an outside organisation.

- **Finance.** Every event's finances need to be carefully monitored and managed. The finance team should be engaged as stakeholders early in the planning process to agree on the measures required, including the data to be collected, processes to be used, and the systems available for use. The proper use and management of financial processes and systems will provide reassurance to all stakeholders that the financial data being provided is credible and accurate. The event professional is responsible for the expenditures associated with the event and will focus on ways to achieve the event owners' goals, while ensuring that financial liabilities are minimised through the careful negotiation and management of venue and supplier contracts. Working closely with the person(s) or department responsible for finance and informing them about any important considerations for supplier selection can ensure their support in the budgeting process.

- **Procurement.** Procurement is responsible for sourcing, contracting, and paying for goods and services. This department also has a key role in auditing to ensure appropriate use of an organisation's funds. Increasingly, its mandates include working with sustainable supply chains that share the same environmental and social values as the organisation. In some organisations, procurement is referred to as the "purchasing department." The procurement departments of larger organisations often set the standards and processes for purchasing within events and may be involved in the management of suppliers, identification of preferred partners, budget approval, payment processing and reconciliation, negotiation of standardised contracts, and reporting. Event professionals should ideally meet with the procurement department to discuss specific processes. The event professional can bring value by offering industry-specific insights on suppliers' roles, suppliers' value to an event, and how those suppliers will support the event objectives and enhance the attendees' experience.

■ **Technology.** The technology department or outsourced technology provider will be a key stakeholder if specialised meeting technology needs to be incorporated into an event. Its role is to ensure that technology decisions are compatible with organisational policies and

Table 1.   Internal stakeholders Typically Associated with Events.

Stakeholders	Key area of focus
Organisation owner E.g., CEO, board of directors, members, shareholders	Organisational growth and sustainability, finance, relationships and brand
Event owner E.g., marketing manager, sales manager, meetings manager, travel manager, product manager, organising committee, membership chairperson	Performance targets and meeting objectives, cost and resource management or return on investment (ROI)
Finance E.g., budget owner, treasurer, finance director or manager, accounts department	Budget, compliance, process, costs, savings, credit authorisation, legal and financial risk mitigation, audit, event ROI
Procurement	Compliance, process, savings, sustainability, legal and financial risk mitigation
Participants' decision-makers	Cost and resource management, performance targets
Travel department E.g., corporate travel	Compliance, process, savings, legal and financial risk mitigation
Sales and marketing	Organisational growth, finance, relationships and brand management
Technology	Application, security, impact on existing technology, training, cost and resource management
Legal and risk management	Compliance, process, minimising legal liability, minimising all risks associated with event processes
Security	Physical safety and security of all stakeholders
Ethics and compliance	Transparency, minimising legal liability, corporate responsibility and ethics
Sustainability department	Ensuring compliance with applicable sustainability standards and organisational mandates, reporting
Human resources	Employee engagement, retention, and motivation; safety, security, and wellness of all employees
Training and development	Continuing professional development (CPD)
Facilities management	Effective and efficient use of on-site facilities and equipment, safety and security, cost and resource management, sustainability
Employees and labour unions	Compensation, organisational stability, job satisfaction and security, future opportunities, public image of organisation, health and safety

existing systems. This stakeholder should be involved during the planning stages and assist with the selection of any meetings-related technology—for example, request for proposal (RFP) tools, attendee registration, on-line accommodation booking tools, abstract management, exhibition management, social media tools, on-site attendee networking systems, audience response systems, and measurement tools. Internal technology departments may have specialised knowledge that can be beneficial to the event professional in areas such as data security or industry-specific technology needs. The information technology (IT) department will also focus on how internal systems will cope with an increased load, particularly if lots of attendees will be logging in to access agenda and session information, register for sessions, or book their accommodations and travel. Additional aspects for consideration will be how users will access meetings-related technology tools, who will own the data, confidentiality issues, and security and maintenance concerns.

- **Legal and risk management.** Event professionals have a responsibility to their corporate owners/shareholders or non-profit membership to ensure that the organisation is protected from the risks associated with events. By working with their legal department or counsel, event professionals demonstrate to all stakeholders that the organisation is diligent about reducing its legal and financial risks. Legal and risk management advisors (including in-house departments where applicable) are stakeholders who should be engaged prior to contracting or creating a contract addendum, so that the legal and financial risks to the organisation can be minimised. See Domain B. Project Management for more information on contracts and Domain C. Risk Management for more information about this topic and other event-related risks, including liability and natural disasters.

External Stakeholders. Table 2 shows the range of external stakeholders with whom an event professional might work.

Sub Skill 13.02 – Manage Stakeholder Activities

Having identified the internal and external stakeholders who may have an impact on or be affected by an event, the event organiser should begin collaborating with those stakeholders at the appropriate stage in planning. Stakeholders will have different degrees of interest in the event, and their specific priorities will affect their level of engagement and the extent to which they need to be kept informed.

To start to uncover the interests, issues, and priorities for each stakeholder, schedule a series of **stakeholder interviews**. Stakeholders who will be included in these interviews should be prioritized, as this can be a time-consuming process. The stakeholders who will have the greatest influence on the success of the event should be interviewed. When the stakeholder is a group of people, the interviews should be arranged with a number of representatives from that stakeholder group, to establish an overview of their particular interests, issues, and priorities. The interviews should be conducted face-to-face where possible; this provides the best opportunity to understand and influence the stakeholder. The information collected from the interview should be used to develop a **stakeholder profile** to inform the event professional on strategy and implementation for the event. Suggested information to incorporate into the stakeholder profile includes:

- Stakeholder details – name, job title, role within the organisation
- Connection – why this event is important to the stakeholder
- Key values – what elements the stakeholder considers important; define, prioritise, and determine key performance indicators (KPIs)

- Sphere of influence – which relevant individuals/groups the stakeholder can potentially influence
- Preferred communication channels
- Information required – format and frequency; how information might be used
- Key stakeholder objectives for event
- Measures of success based on previously defined KPIs

One of the major benefits of conducting the stakeholder interviews is that the event professional has a greater opportunity to engage those stakeholders early in the success of the event and to gain wider understanding and acceptance of the event. In addition, the information gained will drive the development of the event plan so that it is more relevant and customised to the organisation's culture, structure, and internal processes.

When conducting the interviews with stakeholders, agree on a convenient time and place and allow enough time beforehand for the stakeholder to prepare for the interview by providing information about the purpose of the interview and the types of questions that will be covered. The interview should be structured as follows:

- Introductions
- Define event and event professional's role
- Set context – event owner, organisation's objectives, and desired outcomes

Table 2. List of Potential External Stakeholders for Events.

Stakeholders	Key area of focus
Participants/attendees	Value, benefits and return for their attendance; time allocation; cost and/or ease of participation; performance targets; meeting objectives
Suppliers Selected hotels and venue(s), event management company (EMC) or professional conference organiser (PCO), destination management company (DMC), site selection and contract negotiation companies, attendee registration and management specialist, caterer, freight forwarder, transport companies, sponsorship sales and support, technology company, production company, audio visual or staging company, exhibition build and management specialists	Sales of goods and services, long-term client relationships, client satisfaction
Media	Identifying news worthy stories
Partners and contributors Exhibitors, sponsors, advertisers, education content providers (speakers, trainers, and facilitators)	Organisational growth, relationships and brand management
Local community organisations and businesses Destination marketing organisation (DMO) or convention and visitors bureau (CVB), surrounding businesses, community groups and non-governmental organisations (NGO), and local government(s)	Impact on the community, revenues for local businesses, tax revenues, reputation of the destination

- Outline why stakeholder's support is needed
- Identify possible conflicts with other stakeholder groups
- Complete stakeholder profile
- Answer questions
- Confirm level of engagement
- Agree on next steps

After the interview, follow up on actions suggested at the interview, monitor the stakeholder's level of engagement, and write a summary. Use the stakeholder profile for future decision making and when any processes are being implemented; for example, the event communication plan. The engagement of all stakeholders will ensure that varied interests and goals are considered, and this approach will reduce the potential for conflict at a later date.

Stakeholder Categories.   Stakeholders can be categorized based on their level of interest and the degree to which their day-to-day work will be affected by the event. Using a grid, the stakeholders can be placed into four different categories, which can form the basis for making decisions about how to interact with each of them:

		Interest	
		Low	**High**
Influence	**Low**	**Low Interest and Low Influence** This group should be monitored, but does not require extensive communication. This group might include local businesses in the area around where the event will take place.	**High Interest and Low Influence** These stakeholders might be very interested in the event, but have little direct influence upon it. This group should be kept informed of event plans. This group might include volunteers who are not actively involved in the planning, but may fill an important role in marketing the event.
	High	**Low Interest and High Influence** These stakeholders should be kept updated and involved in the planning process with a goal of keeping them satisfied and interested. This group will often include, as an example, the budget owner.	**High Interest and High Influence** These are stakeholders who will be heavily affected by and who are also very interested in the event. Significant time should be allocated to managing the relationships with this group, and they should be kept engaged and updated. This group will often include, as an example, the event owner.

Stakeholder Concerns.   The event professional may need to modify the event plan to accommodate any potential obstacles or challenges that have been exposed and to demonstrate to stakeholders that their issues and concerns have been addressed. Stakeholders have different interests and goals, and therefore different expectations. Any objections and obstacles to the event should have been identified and made visible to guide the event plans. If those objections are not addressed, they may jeopardise the success of the event. The first approach is to address the objections raised as part of the event plan. However, not all objections raised can be fully addressed. Changes required could damage the likelihood of achieving the event objectives. In these cases, the event professional will need to communicate effectively with the stakeholder (using verifiable data) about why the event supports the strategic interests of the organisation. Supporting statements and case studies from other stakeholders will add weight to the discussion.

Gaining Stakeholder Support.   At times, event professionals may need to gain support from one or more stakeholders, whether it is their support of the event, the timing, or the budget. The most likely reason for lack of support is the lack of a clear and mutual understanding of the event's purpose. The objectives and the expected outcomes need to be clearly explained from the start so that stakeholders can see the value of the event to the organisation and why their support is needed. The support required may vary; for example, it may require a stakeholder to attend an event, follow a new process, or speak to and influence relevant people. However, all stakeholders will have different perspectives and needs and will not always receive, interpret, and react to the information provided in the same way. Clear communication skills, active listening, and questioning skills (to check understanding) are critical to avoid the problem of stakeholders interpreting information in different ways. In some cases, the event professional may need to leverage the assistance of other stakeholders, such as the event owner, in order to clarify expectations, goals, and objectives.

Stakeholder Communication Plan.   The content, purpose, frequency, and format of communication with stakeholders needs to be tailored specifically to the recipients and should be culturally sensitive. Depending on their level of involvement, many stakeholders should receive regular written communications to update them on progress toward event objectives and measurable outcomes, highlighting issues and concerns as well as proposed solutions.

Depending on the complexity of the event and the number and geographical spread of the stakeholders, customised electronic communication tools can be utilised. An event-specific Web site, an intranet designed for the organisation's strategic meetings management programme (SMMP), social media tools, on-line sharing and working groups, and electronic newsletters and reports are potential electronic communication tools that are useful for event professionals.

If face-to-face meetings are an essential part of the event plan, schedules for these meetings should be confirmed and circulated to all relevant stakeholders well in advance. Attendees should include team members, internal and external stakeholders, and representatives of stakeholder groups. The purpose of such meetings is to review progress against event objectives and outcomes, create project plans, contribute toward project recommendations and deliverables, and support the event through appropriate activities, such as communications, marketing campaigns, and stakeholder training. A specific agenda and set of topics designed to allow each participant to provide opinions and prospective solutions should be included.

Feedback from meetings or conference calls should be communicated regularly to all relevant stakeholders. Three factors that most frequently affect the success of event are:

1. Failure to identify key processes and assign ownership.
2. Failure to apply a robust improvement approach that builds an understanding of fundamental root causes of problems.
3. Failure to measure the right things.

After every meeting or conference call, an executive summary should be provided to stakeholders as part of the overall communication strategy.

Whatever communication method is selected, the opportunity for stakeholders to be a part of the event is a valuable tool for the success of the overall initiative.

Sub Skill 13.03 – Manage Stakeholder Relationships

There are four aspects that event professionals will be involved with in order to maintain positive long-term relationships with event stakeholders:

- Communication
- Recognition
- Conflict resolution
- Legal considerations

Communication.   The event professional will frequently work on events with a team of support staff and volunteers who will carry out many of the day-to-day tasks. Communication within the team is essential—it is their performance that will determine the successful delivery of any event against its measurable outcomes. Effective communication will satisfy numerous objectives for stakeholder management, including these:

- To inform team members of their roles and responsibilities.
- To track those responsibilities and encourage accomplishment of objectives.
- To motivate and inspire stakeholders to be fully engaged with the event.
- To share the organisation's values and match them with stakeholder behaviours.
- To empower stakeholders to meet their responsibilities and expectations.

The type, amount, timing and method of sharing information depend upon the complexity of the event and the event professional's objectives. Typical information that needs to be shared with team members includes:

- the purpose of the event and why it is important to the organisation;
- what the organisation expects to achieve through the event;
- a list of the stakeholders and their reasons for having an interest in the event;
- the expectations of the stakeholders;
- potential obstacles and how to overcome them; and
- team members' individual roles and responsibilities for meeting stakeholder expectations.

Recognition.   Stakeholder relationships will benefit from a focus on recognizing the contributions of stakeholders, including staff, suppliers, attendees and others. In some cases, this may take the form of a reward or recognition strategy, or it may be as simple as written letters of thanks. An effective reward and recognition strategy will motivate team members to perform better and engage more readily. It can also reinforce behaviours that are needed to achieve the event objectives. When developing a reward and recognition strategy, identify the incentives that motivate the stakeholders within the organisation. Rewards may be intangible and do not have to be monetary. Many organisations have internal policies that should be followed regarding giving and receiving funds or gifts. The strategy utilised to reward and recognise preferred actions should support the event's objectives and measurable outcomes, and comply with company values and policies. A reward and recognition programme should:

- be part of the overall strategy to improve performance;
- be applied visibly and fairly across the organisation;
- be appropriate to the culture of the organisation;
- be adaptable to different regions; and
- encourage teamwork by creating a culture in which individual and team success is identified and people value the contributions of others.

In many cases, recognition must be geared toward the team or its superiors. Individual recognition is not always valued or understood.

Table 3. Suggested Methods for Team Communication.

Format	Advantage	Disadvantage
Individual meetings	Personalised and can cover confidential questions and concerns	Others may feel excluded; no standardised message to everyone; different interpretations of key messages
Written communication	Key messages easily communicated	Too much information may not be read; reduced opportunity to ask questions/seek clarification; different interpretations of key messages
Team meeting	Save time by explaining key messages once; clarify interpretation and issues/concerns through questions and discussion; peer pressure to conform; create team atmosphere from the start	Not everyone can attend; larger group to manage; written information also needed for key messages

Conflict Resolution Processes.   Event professionals should attempt to anticipate and resolve conflicts between stakeholders to make sure that everyone is working together toward the same result. The quicker a conflict is noticed, the better, because conflict that is ignored can often escalate. Noticing conflict at an early stage provides the opportunity to identify the underlying causes, reach a sustainable agreement, and resolve the conflict. A clear and effective process should be in place to investigate and resolve recurring problems.

Legal Considerations.   The law may already address issues that may arise from internal stakeholder relationships. For example, the legal doctrine (in the United States) governing works made for hire (intellectual property) clearly delineates who owns intellectual property created in the process of developing an event; worker's compensation legislation addresses injury sustained by an internal stakeholder acting in the scope of employment; and company policies may govern other issues.

The relationships with external stakeholders have to be handled more directly. For example, contracts can be used to clarify the details of the role of external stakeholders, including reasonable expectations, performance obligations (if any), and limitations on authority. Insurance requirements can be set forth and enforced. Good Samaritan Laws or the Volunteer Protection Act (U.S.) can limit the liability of those who act in a risky situation. Other issues regarding the relationship with external stakeholders can be found in the requirements for permits and licenses.

Reference

Project Management Institute. (2008). *A Guide to the Project Management Body of Knowledge (PMBOK Guide)*, 4th ed. Newtown Square, PA: Project Management Institute, Inc.

Contributing Authors

Carole McKellar, MA, CMM, FCIPD
Executive Director, Europe, HelmsBriscoe
Stockport, United Kingdom
Member of Meeting Professionals International (MPI)

Stakeholder Management and Culture

When working with other cultures and customs, many differences may need to be considered, including business ethics, approaches to work, the conduct of business, meeting protocol, language differences, and political and legal requirements. Failure to follow appropriate protocols can damage a relationship with a stakeholder from the start. Event professionals should research, plan, and prepare before every interaction, whether in person or electronic, to ensure that they are sensitive to the protocols followed by the other party. Specific areas to research prior to the event include:

- Expectations about relationship building before trust can be built and a business can be established
- Who provides the agenda for the meeting and conducts the meeting
- Proper protocol of seating and hierarchy for the meeting
- Cultural meanings of body gestures (for example, nodding up and down does not always mean agreement)
- Adherence to time schedule for a meeting
- Formality of written materials
- Conclusion and follow-up to the meeting

Lack of prior research and understanding of each culture can lead to tremendous damage to a relationship. When planning a meeting where multiple cultures will be present, the CultureActive© tool from Meeting Professionals International (MPI) can provide excellent background information and preparation recommendations.

Michael Lynn, CEM, CME, CMM, CMP, CPC, CPECP
Director, Exhibitions, Events & Protocol
L-3 Communications, Integrated Systems Group
Rockwall, TX, USA
Member of International Association of Exhibitions and Events (IAEE), Trade Show Exhibitor Association (TSEA)

Colleen A. Rickenbacher, CMP, CSEP, CPC, CTA, CPECP
President, Colleen Rickenbacher, Inc.
Dallas, TX, USA
Member of Meeting Professionals International (MPI), Religious Conference Management Association (RCMA), International Special Events Society (ISES)

Reviewer

Joanne H. Joham, CMP, CMM
Regional Director, North America, International Congress and Convention Association (ICCA)
Freehold, NJ, USA
Member of Meeting Professionals International (MPI), Professional Convention Management Association (PCMA), Society of Incentive Travel Executives (Site)

Skill 13:
Endpoints

Terminology

Budget owner
Event attendees/participants
Event owner
External stakeholder
Internal stakeholder
Stakeholder
Stakeholder approach

Additional Resources

MPI CultureActive© tool

Skill 13: Review Questions

1. What is a stakeholder?
2. What is a stakeholder approach? Why is it valuable for event professionals?

Meeting or Event Design

E**vent design** is a process that starts with the development of event objectives that align with the overall objectives of the sponsoring organisation. Those objectives drive all decisions about programme, content, venue, theme, décor, food, and marketing. Everything about the event should focus on delivering the greatest value to the attendees and the event owner(s), to make sure that they are fully engaged in every element of the event and to ensure that the event is a good use of their investment of time and/or money.

This domain covers a broad range of topics, from designing the elements of the programme and content of an event through logistics. The domain includes the following areas of event design:

- Developing the programme
- Engaging speakers and performers
- Coordinating food and beverage services
- Designing the event environment
- Managing technical production
- Developing the plan for managing the movement of attendees

What is design thinking and how is it applied to events?

According to Tim Brown, CEO and president of the international design firm and innovation consultancy IDEO, **design thinking** is "a discipline that uses the designer's sensibility and methods to match people's needs with what is technologically feasible and what a viable business strategy can convert into customer value and market opportunity" (Brown, 2008, p. 86). When this theory is applied to meetings and events, the event professional's expertise and creativity are powerfully directed at achieving

139

organisational goals and objectives through the event. There are three distinct phases, or spaces, as described by Brown, in the design thinking process: inspiration, ideation, and implementation.

Figure 1   Design Thinking Phases.

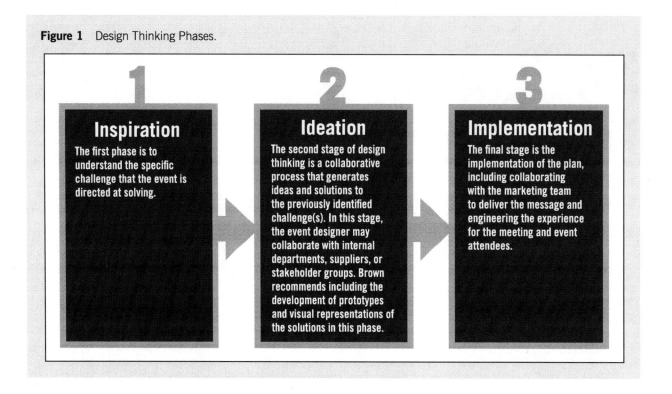

SKILL 14: DEVELOP PROGRAMME (CONTENT AND ACTIVITIES OF EVENT)

Learning Outcomes

- Determine programme components.
- Select programme content and delivery formats.
- Structure and sequence programme components.
- Identify frameworks for measuring event success.

Developing the programme for an event begins with establishing the goals and objectives of the programme and the needs of the stakeholders. This will provide the basis for the decisions that will follow with respect to the components of the event.

While there are many formats for event design, Meeting Professionals International (MPI) has identified five principles (Nawn, 2013) that should be used to guide the decision process. These are summarized below, along with a description of how they align with Brown's design thinking phases.

1. **Principle of assessment and evaluation.** This aspect emphasizes the importance of clear, measurable objectives for the purpose of determining the event's return on investment. This principle aligns with elements of the inspiration stage, where the event designer asks: Why is this event needed? What are we hoping to achieve from this event? What do we want the attendees to do as a result of their attendance?

2. **Principle of meaningful engagement.** This refers to designing the event to connect with the audience physically, intellectually, and emotionally. This principle also aligns with elements of the inspiration stage, where the needs of stakeholders are identified.

3. **Principle of distributed learning.** This principle considers determining the optimal scheduling of distribution of learning, including formal and informal elements, and what should occur before, during, and after the event. This aligns with the ideation stage, where the event designer asks: What programme components and formats are best suited to meeting the needs of the attendees? What is the attendees' experience, and how do we design it for their optimal benefit?

4. **Principle of collaboration.** This principle links understanding the needs of the audience through direct consultation and collaboration on the design of the event. This principle is directly aligned with the collaboration aspect of the ideation stage, where the event designer consults with stakeholders in the development of the event programme.

5. **Principle of experience.** This last principle highlights the importance of considering the event experience from the attendee perspective and designing it to be meaningful and memorable. This principle is considered within the ideation phase, where the event designer visualizes the event experience, and is realized during the implementation stage.

Focus on Meeting Architecture

Meeting architecture is a methodology for designing the content of an event. It focuses on the top meeting objectives, the meeting formats and designs, and the conceptual and practical building blocks to construct a meeting for better learning, networking, and motivation for the attendees (Vanneste, 2007). The meeting architect process includes four phases (IDEA):

- Identifying meeting objectives
- Designing the meeting to support these objectives
- Executing and guiding the meeting toward its objectives
- Assessing the meeting results against the objectives

Figure 2   Meeting Architecture IDEA Phases.

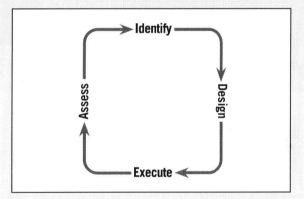

Sub Skill 14.01 – Determine Programme Components

Determining programme components involves selecting, structuring, and sequencing potential elements. The types of components will depend on the nature of the event, but some of these may include educational or team-building sessions, entertainment, food and beverage functions, exhibitions, or community service programmes.

Factors to consider when determining the programme components—in addition to the goals and objectives of the event—include the budget for the event, the goals of event stakeholders including sponsors and exhibitors, available technology resources, and the profile of the attendees.

Evaluations from past events provide excellent information on how to structure and improve future ones. Some of the most valuable information from past programme evaluations that relate specifically to event design include:

- Preferred session design formats for the attendees
- Preferred method for interacting with specific attendee segments (customers, media, exhibitors, sponsors, public officials, students, contestants)
- Types of programme components that are meaningful for the attendees

- Success of past programme elements, including networking events, team-building exercises, entertainment functions, and education sessions
- Preferred flow of the event
- Any elements from previous programmes that should be added or eliminated

Sub Skill 14.02 – Select Programme Content and Delivery Formats

In this section, we will focus on content-related considerations, notably for education, training, and networking events.

The content of an event will be determined by the objectives. To choose the proper format for the delivery of this content, consider first the needs of the audience, the issues they face, and their preferred method(s) of learning. This can be determined through a combination of past evaluations, surveys of past and potential future attendees, and feedback from a programme or planning committee. Many times this information is readily available and can help you make a more informed formatting decision. Avoid repeating programme elements simply because they've always been a part of an event.

One key consideration should be the amount of time spent on passive versus active involvement of the audience in the cultural context. For example, in many cultures, audiences want to interact, ask questions, and process the information. For other cultures, a quieter approach is preferable. Speakers, presenters, or facilitators should be instructed on expectations regarding the level of interactivity and be prepared to adjust their format to align with local customs.

Speaker selection is explored more in Skill 15; here we note that event stakeholder objectives should be a key criteria in speaker selection. The planner must ensure that the speakers understand the desired outcomes, the group profile, the room set-up, and the technology that will be available to them, and that the deliverables and expectations of the speaker are clear.

Leveraging technology is a great tool to drive learning and engagement. We are evolving in many event sectors to use technology in various mediums to connect with attendees before, during, and after the event. Technology such as event mobile applications (apps) can be customised to each event and can be used to replace much of the paper traditionally produced by meetings. Delegates can now access the information they require electronically. If you are planning to record content during the event to offer to a hybrid or virtual audience, or for editing for future broadcasts, it is best to consider this early in the planning process. Content distribution beyond the meeting room requires approval from the speaker for the recording and distribution of his or her intellectual property.

Focus on Gamification

Gamification is defined as "the process of game-thinking and game mechanics to engage users and solve problems" (Zichermann & Cunningham, 2011, p. xiv). It is being used in programme design for many meetings and events as a way of engaging attendees, promoting behaviour such as engagement with social functions or networking, and encouraging the application of the event's educational content. Examples of how gamification can be applied to events include:

- Incorporation of game elements in the event's mobile application, with features such as leaderboards, badges for achieving specific goals, and missions/quests for attendees to complete
- Inclusion of an optional game activity for attendees, such as a photo scavenger hunt or a sustainable actions challenge

Gamification can be very effective for engagement; however, it should be undertaken only with a strong awareness of the stakeholders—not all events will be suited for this type of approach. If gamification is undertaken, the development process should begin with a clear understanding of the goals and objectives of the event, so that the game elements can be designed accordingly.

Types of delivery formats

A variety of formats exists for events. Event design must always be considered in partnership with the event stakeholders, although the event professional has the opportunity to suggest formats, along with the reasons they are appropriate. The following list provides a summary of commonly used formats. Not all of these terms may be used in all countries; differences in terminology should be identified at the outset to avoid misunderstandings between stakeholders.

- **Audience reaction team.** Four or five attendees query the main speaker from the stage with questions from the audience and follow-up questions.

- **BarCamp.** These are participant-led conferences where everyone who attends contributes a demonstration or session, or otherwise volunteers in a way to contribute to the event.

- **Breakout or concurrent sessions.** These sessions typically include a speaker or facilitator and provide in-depth discussion on a focused topic.

- **Buzz sessions.** A method to increase audience participation by dividing attendees into discussion groups, each of which reports the group's findings and opinions during a following plenary session.

- **Colloquium.** An informal meeting for the purpose of discussion, usually of an academic or research nature, to ascertain areas of mutual interest through the exchange of ideas. Generally conducted when deemed convenient and useful, with little regularity.

- **Debate.** Two teams are composed of two or three people each, arguing the opposite sides of an issue.

- **Fishbowl.** An interchange between an inner circle debating an issue and an outer circle of observers. Individuals occasionally move from one circle to the other.

- **Keynote sessions.** Keynote sessions are designed to bring everyone together and may include a high-profile speaker or a panel presentation.

- **Interview.** A moderator, on behalf of the audience, asks the presenter questions.

- **Open space technology.** This is an approach to hosting meetings where the agenda is determined on arrival by the participants. A facilitator helps the participants organize parallel working sessions along the event theme.

- **PechaKucha.** This design format originated in Japan and refers to sessions that include a series of short presentations of 20 slides lasting 20 seconds each. Other similar formats include "ignite presentations" of 20 slides lasting 15 seconds each.

- **Seminar.** A lecture and/or dialogue, usually involving a small group of attendees—usually 10 to 50—led by a specialist who meet to share observations or experiences on a particular subject.

- **Symposium.** A meeting of experts in a particular field, at which papers are presented and discussed by specialists on particular subjects with a view to making recommendations concerning problems under discussion.

- **Unconference.** This is a participant-led event. The agenda is typically created by the attendees on arrival and includes open discussions rather than formal presentations.

- **Workshop.** An intense, often hands-on, learning experience in which a limited number of attendees participate directly in learning a new skill or tackling an issue.

Sub Skill 14.03 – Structure and Sequence Programme Components

Structuring and sequencing the programme components is a critical task for the event professional. The event professional should balance the historical structure of a programme with introduction of new learning formats or elements. The objectives and needs of event stakeholders must be considered when determining which particular sequence of events is most appropriate. A logical starting place is to develop a programme grid that shows all major components in a clearly laid out fashion. This grid includes pre-event functions through final departures. It should be a clear, one- or two-page document that shows the event's flow, including meal functions, trade show/exhibition elements, and educational sessions, as well as ancillary and group activities.

A **programme flow** outlines the timing of each element and helps provide a realistic time frame that identifies where the schedule may be too crowded or where gaps appear in the programme. It enables the planner to insert appropriate breaks and to schedule the movement of people from one room to another, creating a flow that allows people to intermingle—at general sessions, meal functions, and smaller sessions—while noting the consecutive and concurrent times for elements in the schedule. Equally important is to consider the flow between sessions, the time that can be spent in an exhibition, going to and spending time at meal functions, and time and place for the "hallway moments" to happen throughout the day. It is often these unstructured times that become the most important and memorable networking opportunities at an event.

The programme flow should be outlined in on-site management documents that are customised for particular roles. These documents include:

- **The Event Specifications Guide (ESG).** The ESG will become your final working document that is shared with key staff, supplier partners, and venue representatives. It is rarely shared with executives, as it contains every detail that is required to make an event happen. This document should be in progress for weeks before your event and should be shared as a draft for input at least 14-30 days before the event, depending on the venue and event complexity. The ESG ensures that everyone is on the same page and is a critical tool for success.
- **Detailed agenda.** A detailed agenda will provide a key overview for your front-line or registration staff and key hosts. You may want to prepare a special VIP/host agenda that highlights where they need to be, including any rehearsals.
- **Scripts for the master of ceremonies or host (live and/or virtual).** Scripts for your master of ceremonies (MC) and hosts who are making announcements may be useful. If a full script isn't necessary, at least have a list of key points. The amount of information needed will be dictated by the programme needs and the skills of the MC.
- **Attendee agenda.** This is often called a "programme" and might be in print or electronic form. A full programme typically includes room information and a venue floor plan if the facility is a large convention centre or a complex of several buildings.

Programme planning should be done with consideration of religious or cultural activities or requirements. For example, if the event is taking place in a predominantly Islamic country, schedule breaks to coincide with times for daily prayers. During Ramadan, when Muslims may not eat or drink between sunrise and sunset, the schedule should be adjusted accordingly. Consider whether local cultural practices include rest times after lunch, as well as regular times for starting and finishing work, meals, and refreshment breaks.

Protocols and Ceremonies

Often when a conference rotates through a country or around the globe, a traditional welcome is included as a courtesy to the host country and a welcome to the international guests. This may involve an indigenous or traditional cultural performance, or local religious or ceremonial elements. It includes protocols beginning with the invitation process; often an honorarium, gift, or fee for the presenter; placement at an appropriate time in the programme; and allowing enough time for the ceremony or ritual to be completed without rushing. It is best to have an open discussion with a local expert about what will take place, the timing, and expectations on both sides.

Many events also include a political component, whether it is having local or national government representatives speaking or introducing important guests, or the focus of a meeting, dinner, or session. This will require knowledge of protocol (see the Site Management Domain) and may involve added security, specific seating requirements, and specific timing.

Often, having attendees together is a time for recognition, celebration, and identifying key individuals or organisations that have been integral in the planning or support of initiatives. These activities should be factored into the appropriate time, which may be at the opening session, at a general session on another day, or at a gala dinner, with adequate time allowed, and including key attendees as determined by the hosting organisation.

Sub Skill 14.04 – Measure Event Success

Event measurement methodology helps the event professional demonstrate the value of the event. As detailed in the Strategic Management Domain, the Phillips ROI methodology considers inputs and indicators for events at six levels (zero through five) of evaluation. These levels increase in complexity and meaning for determining return on investment for an event, as illustrated below in figure 3. In addition to these elements, intangibles are also measured as part of the methodology (Phillips, Breining, Phillips, 2008).

Figure 3   Event Return on Investment (ROI) Pyramid.

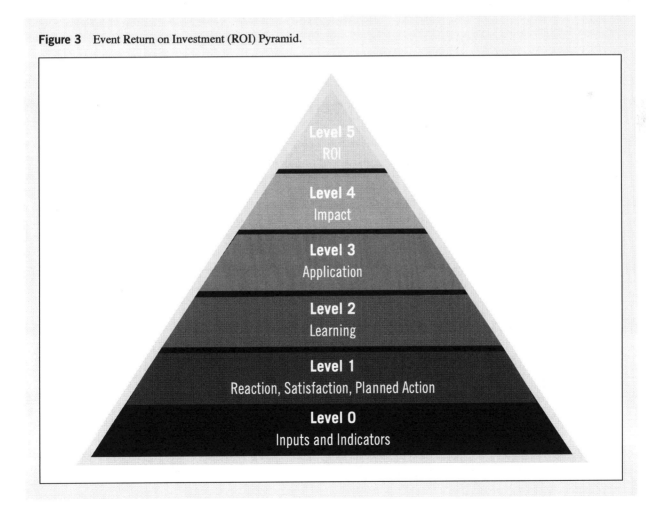

While only about 5 percent of an organisation's meeting portfolio should be measured at Level 5 (ROI), because of the time and cost involved in securing the necessary data, every meeting should be measured on the basis of the value it brings to the organisation, not just what it costs or how much is saved because of skillful negotiation.

The first step in credible measurement of an event is to determine appropriate objectives. This is a constant theme throughout this book, but its importance cannot be overstated. We have to be very clear about why the event is to be held and what we hope to accomplish as a result. Whether the meeting costs a thousand dollars or a million euros, we must be able to articulate the value it brings to the organisation.

While most planners aren't responsible for determining the objectives of an event, they can take responsibility to ask the right questions of the planning committee or organisation's leadership to ensure that the objectives are clear, easily understood, and measurable. The following questions are examples:

- What kind of business impact do we want as a result of this meeting (more sales, reduction in expense, greater employee retention)?
- In order to achieve that impact, what is it we need people to do (sell more of a particular product, work more efficiently, reduce costly waste, utilise a different management technique)?
- In order to have people change their behaviour as needed, what is it they need to learn (the benefits of the new product, more efficient scheduling of personnel, different ways of handling conflict)?
- In order to have people learn effectively, how do we want them to feel as they leave the meeting (enthusiasm for the company and pride in their work, knowledge that they have the support of management, confidence that they have the tools to do their job right)?

All of these elements may not be measurable; for example, you may not have the data or the time to measure the extent to which expenses are reduced in a particular department and/or how much that reduction is attributed to your meeting. However, by asking these questions—in this order—you can determine what *is* measurable; for example, the extent to which attendees learned the process of more efficient personnel scheduling. This information provides a more compelling argument for the value of a meeting than a mere satisfaction survey that indicates that attendees had a good time at the event.

References

Brown, T. (2008, June, pp. 84-92). Design Thinking. *Harvard Business Review*.

Nawn, J. (2013). *Meeting design: The what, why and how*. Meeting Professionals International. Retrieved from http://www.mpiweb.org.

Phillips, J. J., Breining, M. T., & Phillips, P. P. (2008). *Return on investment in meetings and events*. Oxford: Elsevier.

Vanneste, M. (2007). *Meeting architecture, a manifesto*. Meeting Support Institute. Retrieved from http://www.meetingsupport.org/.

Zichermann, G., and Cunningham, C. (2011). *Gamification by design*. Sebastopol, CA: O'Reilly Media.

Contributing Authors

Richard Aaron, MFA, CMP, CSEP
President, BizBash Media
New York, USA
Member of Green Meeting Industry Council (CMIC), Society of Incentive & Travel Executives (Site)

Tahira Endean, CMP
Director, Creative and Production, Cantrav Services Inc.
Vancouver, Canada
Member of International Special Events Society (ISES), Green Meeting Industry Council (GMIC)

Glenn Thayer
Conference Moderator, The Voice of Meetings and Events
Denver, CO, USA
Member of American Society of Association Executives (ASAE) and National Speakers Association (NSA)

Maarten Vanneste, CMM
President, Meeting Support Institute
Antwerp, Belgium
Member of Meeting Professionals International (MPI)

Reviewer

Jon Trask, CMP, CMM
Co-Founder, AVforPlanners
Oakland, CA, USA
Member of Meeting Professionals International (MPI)

Jeff Hurt
Executive Vice President, Education & Engagement, Velvet Chainsaw Consulting
Dallas, TX, USA
Member of Professional Convention Management Association (PCMA)

Skill 14:
Endpoints

Terminology

Design thinking
Event design
Gamification
Programme flow

Skill 14: Review Questions

1. What are the five principles of meeting design?
2. How does cultural context affect decisions regarding programme scheduling and formats?
3. What is programme flow?
4. How is return on investment calculated for events?

SKILL 15: ENGAGE SPEAKERS AND PERFORMERS

Learning Outcomes

- Determine event requirements for speakers and performers.
- Develop selection criteria for speakers and performers.
- Select candidates.
- Secure contracts and communicate expectations with speakers and performers.

The right speakers and performers contribute to the success of an event. They should be chosen based on the overall event objectives and considering the best fit for the format and level of audience interaction and engagement. Event professionals must identify and secure the speakers and performers who will help achieve the event's goals within the allowed budget.

Sub Skill 15.01 – Determine Meeting or Event Requirements for Speakers and Performers

Before engaging speakers and performers, the first step is to determine the objectives and learning outcomes, if any, and your event requirements. Would the event benefit from having a professional speaker, an expert facilitator, or an entertainer? The type of event you are planning—such as a networking event, an educational event, or an entertainment event—will in part determine this. You will also need to consider your audience and whether it will be a live event or partially or entirely virtual. Choosing the right speakers or performers could enhance your event if your choice is the correct fit for your audience. Determine whether what this person offers will meet the event's learning outcomes or objectives. If you are considering a celebrity, make sure the hiring decision is based on the intended outcomes, not having a celebrity for celebrity's sake. In some cases, the presence of a celebrity speaker can add credibility and visibility to an organisation, which may be one of the event goals. A celebrity could also attract attendees who are undecided about attending, thereby helping to achieve attendance objectives.

For any given event, you may need professional speakers, moderators or facilitators, industry experts, panelists, live and/or virtual hosts, and performers. Each could provide distinct benefits for your programme. With each serving a different function at the event, there will be different considerations for how they are engaged and prepared.

Content-based Speakers, Facilitators, Moderators, and Hosts

Determining the requirements for content-based speakers, facilitators, moderators, and hosts requires a thorough understanding of the audience's needs, from a content perspective and a learning-style perspective. The following section is adapted, with permission, from the *Events Industry Council Manual, 8th edition* (2008), and the National Speakers Association resources.

Selecting the right speakers, panelists, and other programme attendees is key to an event's success. When selecting possible candidates, a number of factors should be considered. This begins with the needs of the attendees and the educational goals of the event. The type of speaker should also be considered—in some cases, an expert presenter is needed, while in others, a skilled facilitator may be more appropriate. Other factors to consider are the event budget and the availability of the speaker (many professional speakers book engagements a year or more in advance). Diversity of the speakers should also be considered.

You can find professional speakers and entertainers in many ways, from a recommendation from within an organisation to contacting a speakers bureau that represents hundreds of potential speakers. The speakers bureau works for a fee that is usually included with the quoted price, but confirm this arrangement, since it could be different in some regions. Many reputable speakers

Table 1 Engagement and Preparation Considerations for Speakers, Facilitators and Entertainers.

	Role	Engagement Considerations	Preparation Considerations
Professional Speakers	▪ Often keynote speakers.	▪ May be represented by one or more speakers bureaus. Some non-professional speakers can be booked directly.	▪ Will need to be briefed on the audience background and demographics, along with the desired outcomes and desired learner.
Moderators and Facilitators	▪ May be internal to the organisation or an external expert familiar with the industry; lead a panel or similar discussion.	▪ Must prepare ahead of time with any other panel or session attendees. ▪ Professional speakers may also have the skills to serve as a moderator and/or facilitator.	▪ May need special training on facilitation and moderating. These skills are very different from regular public speaking, although an ability to speak in front of a group confidently is important.
Industry Experts	▪ These may be identified through a call for proposals and are typically used in break-out sessions. ▪ In the corporate world, experts are often selected from internal staff.	▪ Peer reviews may be used to determine expertise. ▪ For corporations, a demonstrated knowledge of the subject and the ability to speak in front of a group are required.	▪ May require presentation skills coaching.
Academic Speakers	▪ Includes professors, researchers, and administrators; may include graduate students to present a paper or poster.	▪ Peer reviews are often conducted using an on-line abstract management system.	▪ May present with others; need to be briefed on sticking to time allotments; may require protection for intellectual property.
Live Event Hosts/MCs	▪ Keep the event on track; link between events.	▪ If you do not have a strong internal candidate, hire a professional. ▪ Some professional speakers can also serve in this role.	▪ Must be articulate, focused, and able to tie links together across the programme.
Virtual Hosts	▪ Engage remote audience; link between live and remote events.	▪ Practice makes perfect. Hire someone who has the skills to do this.	▪ Must be able to use the technology, aid guests, and fill in gaps.
Performers, Musicians, and Entertainers	▪ Entertain appropriately for the audience.	▪ Determine whether this is a feature act or a background act and hire as needed.	▪ Will need to be briefed with audience background, demographics and interest in interactivity.

bureaus and entertainment agents represent a myriad of artists and can provide suggestions based on your group's needs, objectives, and audience demographics, as well as your specifications and budget. The speakers bureau will naturally direct you to people they represent, so if you have specific people in mind, it is worth doing the research to find their booking agents. If there is a bureau that you prefer to work with, they will be happy to book a speaker on your behalf, even they do not represent that speaker. Once a speakers bureau has been contacted and has provided recommendations, do not contact the speaker directly to avoid paying the bureau's fee; this is considered unethical by many professional speakers and event professionals.

The bureau will be able to provide you with information about the speaker, including the speaker's professional history and qualifications, usually in formats that are easy to share with

Special Considerations for Virtual and Hybrid Meetings

Virtual and Hybrid Hosts

With the popularity of virtual (on-line exclusively) and hybrid (live and on-line) events growing every day, the need for hosts who specialise in on-line audience engagement is increasing. Ideal candidates for virtual hosting include news presenters and people with on-camera experience who are used to delivering into a camera, good at improvising, and proficient at using a teleprompter and interruptible foldback (IFB) (earpiece for the director to speak to the person on-air during the broadcast). This is very different than delivering to an in-person audience. Many professional speakers have experience in front of the camera as well. These people should be considered before assigning someone from inside the organisation to handle these duties. Virtual hosts are the link between the virtual audience and the content. Ask to see demo footage of them performing for a virtual audience before you make a hiring decision. Remember, just because they can speak in front of an audience does not make them a great presenter in front of a camera. This person may be summarizing what happened in the sessions earlier in the day, conducting interviews of speakers and executives, and giving commentary on what you missed. Great care should be given to producing these segments. Remember, this is a broadcast, and it must be produced in advance with your broadcast producer.

Broadcast Producer

If you are hiring a virtual host, you will also want to hire a broadcast producer. This person oversees the broadcast and typically has a background in live sports or live news broadcasts. He or she will work with you on the content for the broadcast so the audience has a meaningful and engaging experience. A broadcast producer can format a 60-minute programme that will keep the virtual audience watching. A series of attendee testimonials will never take the place of great content delivered by engaging guests and formatted for viewing in a broadcast.

your stakeholders or those who will make the final selection. Personal referrals and recommendations from colleagues are other sources for identifying speakers and performers. Many bureaus specialise in particular types of speakers—such as celebrities, athletes, or authors—and can save you time and effort in locating the right professional speaker to complement your programme.

When you've identified a possible speaker, secure a biography, testimonials, and references. Request videos of presentations, preferably those given before live audiences. Most professional speakers have their own Web sites, many of which have streaming videos of presentations. If a candidate is speaking in your area, ask if you may attend the programme.

Ensure that potential speakers have addressed groups similar to yours. Find out what books or articles they have published, whether they belong to professional organisations, and what awards or certifications they have earned.

After you have decided which professional speaker or entertainer to hire for your event, be sure to let any others who were under consideration know that someone has been chosen. This will allow them to remove the hold on the dates from their calendar.

Sub Skill 15.02 – Develop Selection Criteria/Strategies

Developing the selection criteria for speakers and events begins with understanding what skills will best help achieve the event objectives. In addition, an understanding of the audience and the organisation's culture and of the political culture of the country where the event is being held should also be considered.

An event may have the need for various types of performers or speakers, and criteria will need to be developed for each of these. For example, there would be different criteria for the keynote speaker, the concurrent session speakers, the lunchtime entertainment, and workshop facilitators. For each type of speaker or performer, criteria should be established in advance and weighted to allow for easy comparison when some criteria are more important than others. In some cases, there may also be a criterion that automatically excludes an individual. For example, an organisation might stipulate that a keynote speaker not be utilised again for five years.

The criteria should be developed in consultation with event stakeholders and after reviewing evaluations from past events. Many stakeholders in your event will also attend numerous other events and will have input on their expectations and preferences for speakers, which must be weighed against the organisation's culture and the meeting objectives. You will often work with a planning or programme committee—a small and committed group of people who will ideally share their expertise and experience by suggesting speakers. If you conduct a call for proposals or presentations, the committee will also review the proposals and help you develop the criteria for selecting the best ones.

Table 2 is an example of a weighted speaker selection criteria sheet.

Table 2   Sample Weighted Speaker Selection Criteria Sheet.

Criteria	Criteria Weight	Speaker 1	Speaker 2	Speaker 3	Speaker 1 (Weighted)	Speaker 2 (Weighted)	Speaker 3 (Weighted)
Relevant topic	10	8	10	9	80	100	90
Willing to adapt topic to audience	8	5	10	9	40	80	72
References	10	10	5	9	100	50	90
Has a bestselling book	3	0	10	0	0	30	0
Active on social media	3	10	10	8	30	30	24
Engaging speaker (as determined by video)	10	10	2	8	100	20	80
Required Criteria							
Available on date		Yes	Yes	Yes	Yes	Yes	Yes
Has not spoken at the event previously		Yes	Yes	Yes	Yes	Yes	Yes
Weighted Score					**350**	**310**	**356**

The selection criteria should be communicated in advance to prospective speakers or performers so they can customise their proposals to best meet the event's needs. As with any RFP, you must be clear about your requirements and your expected outcomes and objectives. Without this, a speaker will not know whether he/she is a good fit for your event. This may be done in a formal RFP or in an e-mail with all the information given to a booking agent or speaker or performer representative, or posted on your Web site for on-line submissions. Include information on the type of performer or speaker required, duration and location of performance or programme, compensation and/or benefits, and time commitment, including any pre-event commitment.

In addition to determining your criteria, you will also need to determine your selection strategies. These may include working with a speakers bureau or a programme committee, or distributing an on-line RFP. In some cases, you will use multiple selection strategies for the same event, such as working with a speakers bureau to select a keynote speaker, an entertainment services company for the performers, and a programme committee for concurrent sessions.

Sub Skill 15.03 – Select Candidates

With your programme or planning committee, or in consultation with the stakeholders, you will evaluate the options and make decisions that will get you closest to your objectives. Ensure that speakers are clear on your objectives and are aligned with your overall learning outcomes and any actions you hope to attain from attendees.

If you are paying for a speaker through a fee-plus-expenses or expenses only agreement, be certain to clearly outline your expectations.

As part of the selection process, your selection committee or person(s) will need access to the selection criteria, speaker biographies, and topic proposals(s). Ideally, candidates should be observed in either a live setting or through a recorded session. When observing their performance, monitor not only the candidate but also the audience response and the interaction with the audience (if applicable). Try to determine whether the presentation has been tailored for that particular audience to gauge how it could be adapted for your event.

Comparing several speakers is more efficient if you use a spreadsheet to track ratings and comments. The ratings can be weighted according to your priorities.

Ensure that your desired presenter can work in the country or region you have selected for the event. You might have to help expedite the visa process.

Ensure that the material being presented is theirs to use, or that appropriate licensing has been secured, and that you do not break any laws in the country serving as the event's location.

Selection of Speakers for Academic Conferences

Academic conferences usually have a call for papers through which academics and researchers are invited to submit abstracts (written summaries of speeches or papers, generally between 200-500 words) for consideration as either presentations or posters. The abstracts are assessed and selected by a review committee. Most academic conferences accept and review abstracts using an on-line system. These systems should allow for:

- Submission of author names (including the ability to prioritize principal authors) and contact information.
- Ability to enter specific programme information. In the case of many scientific conferences, the ability to upload documents that may contain special characters, formulas, or formatting, or be in other languages is essential for reviewing the material.
- A review and feedback mechanism for the reviewers to communicate, possibly confidentially, to those submitting an abstract. This may include a scoring mechanism to allow sorting of abstracts.

This kind of system will allow you to schedule your programme and make it available both on-line and in print.

Sub Skill 15.04 – Secure Contracts and Communicate Expectations

(This section is adapted, with permission, from the *Events Industry Council Manual, 8th edition* (2008) and various materials published by the National Speakers Association (NSA), with permission from the NSA.

Once you have selected speakers and/or facilitators, create a letter of agreement or contract that clearly outlines the expectations of both you and your speaker. Be clear whether the contract is with the speaker or with the speakers bureau. Understand that many speakers do not consider the speaking engagement definite until the contract is signed by both parties. The contract should include:

- Travel arrangements for both air and ground transportation
- Date, time, place, and duration of presentation
- Information on accommodations and meals
- Fees, reimbursements, and payment terms
- Whether you want the speaker to attend social events and other sessions
- Whether the speaker may promote products at the event and, if so, how this will be handled
- Procedures on handouts and materials
- An agreement on any audio, photo, or video recordings of the presentation
- Cancellation policies
- Audiovisual requirements
- Legal implications, if any
- Agreement on action to rectify non-compliance and deal with breaches of contract within acceptable time frame
- Speaker's agreement to utilise some form of social media before, during, and/or after the event

Before making the booking, secure the speaker's written agreement that he or she will send you an outline of the presentation at a certain time. This is vital to promote attendance and hold the speaker accountable for delivering as promised.

Furnish Background Information

Share information on your organisation and audience to help the speaker create a customised presentation. Send publications or anything that includes profiles of key people, buzzwords, key themes of the event, or insider news and views. Be specific about the size and demographics of the audience. Also, let speakers know about other speakers on the programme, so they can build on, not duplicate, what the others are presenting. Consider sharing what has worked and not worked at past events, along with the objectives and expected outcomes of this event. If expectations change after a speaker has been booked, be sure to share that information.

Set the Stage

Make sure the room is set up for optimum effect. Consider the number of chairs and how they are arranged. Speakers may have input into how they would like the room set up in order to meet your learning objectives. These conversations should happen before the room diagrams are finalized with the venue. Also consider room temperature and lighting. Ensure that the audiovisual equipment is in place and working properly. Stay on schedule. Speakers should provide you with a short introduction to themselves and their topics.

Evaluate the Results

Have the audience complete evaluations of speakers and their presentations. This will help you plan future programmes. Send copies of the evaluations to the speaker.

Contracts and Marketing Responsibilities

How are you reaching out to your attendees before the event? There is a great opportunity to collaborate with speakers and performers in advance of the event with respect to marketing and promotion. Consider adding some of the following marketing responsibilities to your contracts:

- **Video**. Many professional speakers will create a custom video for your event. This not only gives your audience a sneak peek of what to expect, it creates an additional touch point for marketing your event.
- **Social Media and Web-based Marketing**. Ask speakers and performers to promote your event through their social media channels and to include a link on their Web site to your event.

Music Licensing

When playing music at an event, whether as background music or as the primary focus, determine whether you require a music license and how to obtain one. Licensing societies will change depending on the country where you are holding your event. In some regions, the license must be obtained in advance of the event to avoid fines, while in other areas, reporting and paying licensing fees afterwards is acceptable. If your event is being broadcast virtually, inform the licensing society when the license is obtained. Most countries have a licensing society that represents songwriters, composers, and music publishers, which avoids the need to contact each copyright owner. Many of these societies have reciprocal agreements that allow them to license the works of all the societies. Sample licensing organisations include:

Argentina	Sociedad Argentina de Autores y Compositores de Música (SADAIC)
Australia	Phonographic Performance Company of Australia Limited (PPCA)
Canada	The Society of Composers, Authors and Music Publishers of Canada (SOCAN)
France	Société des auteurs, compositeurs et éditeurs de musique (SACEM). (Note: SACEM has offices in several countries)
India	The Indian Performing Right Society Limited (IPRS)
United Kingdom	PRS for Music (trading name for the Performing Rights Society Ltd.)
United States	The American Society of Composers, Authors and Publishers (ASCAP) and Broadcast Music, Inc. (BMI)

Make sure that you understand whether you will pay the society directly; whether it is part of a DMC contract with a local organisation you have hired; or if it comes directly from your venue. The event organiser will be held liable for failure to have a music license if it is required, regardless of who was contracted to secure the license and who requested that license agreement. This is why an indemnification clause in a contract between the event organiser and whoever is responsible for securing the license is important. It protects the event organiser by requiring the indemnifying party to hold harmless the event organiser for failure to secure the license.

Contributing Authors

Tahira Endean, CMP
Director, Creative and Production, Cantrav Services Inc.
Vancouver, Canada
Member of International Special Event Society (ISES), Green Meeting Industry Council (GMIC)

Glenn Thayer
Conference Moderator, The Voice of Meetings and Events
Denver, CO, USA
Member of American Society of Association Executives (ASAE) and National Speakers Association (NSA)

Reviewer

Cara Tracy, CMP, CMM
Scottsdale, AZ, USA
Member of Meeting Professionals International (MPI), Professional Convention Management Association (PCMA)

Skill 15:
Endpoints

Terminology

Speakers bureau
Virtual host
Broadcast producer
Music license

Skill 15: Review Questions

1. How do the engagement and preparation considerations differ for professional speakers, moderators and facilitators, industry experts, academic speakers, live event hosts, virtual hosts and performers?
2. What should be considered when selecting speakers and performers for virtual or hybrid events?
3. What are the best practices for speaker selection?
4. What should be included in a speaker's contract?

SKILL 16: COORDINATE FOOD AND BEVERAGE SERVICES

Learning Outcomes

- Determine food and beverage requirements.
- Identify and select appropriate service styles.
- Identify and select appropriate food and beverage providers.
- Manage alcohol service.
- Select an appropriate menu, based on preferred outcomes.

The food and beverage programme, often referred to as F&B, included in an event is a significant area of responsibility for the event planner. Planning decisions, including those related to menu choices and service styles, should be based on delivering on the event objectives. In many cases, it is a primary area of spending and may be the largest event budget item. Even when the cost isn't significant, food and beverage can play a major role in the perceived success of an event. This chapter covers key areas to be considered during event planning to create the optimal experience.

Sub Skill 16.01 – Determine Food and Beverage Service Requirements

When beginning the process of determining the food and beverage requirements for an event, the event planner needs a thorough understanding of the event goals, the budget, the profile of the attendees, and the event specifications (programme schedule, dates, times, and expected number of attendees).

The event goals will set the parameters for the food functions, including type and style. For example, many multi-day events begin with an opening reception designed to encourage networking. In this case, food stations set around a room will encourage attendees to move around and meet more people.

When determining the food and beverage requirements, begin by outlining the programme schedule and determining when meal functions are needed and from there, the style best suited to the event goals and within the event budget. Examples of standard food functions are listed below:

- Breakfast: A good breakfast starts the day on a positive note. The three standard options are:
  - **Full-service breakfast:** Attendees are seated at one time, with a combination of pre-set and plated service. This option is best when there is a speaker or programme planned.
  - **Continental breakfast:** This option balances variety and budget. Most continental breakfasts are served on a buffet, often set in the meeting room, with a variety of choices, including pastries, juice, and coffee. They may be expanded (depending on local customs and budget) to include other items such as fresh fruit, cereals, meats and cheeses, and yogurt. When planning a continental breakfast, try to meet the dietary requirements of all participants.
  - **Full buffet breakfast:** This is usually the most expensive option and includes the greatest variety of food selections, which should be customised for the profile of the attendees.
- Refreshment breaks: Many events offer mid-morning and/or mid-afternoon refreshment breaks. Menu selections, duration, and set-up should be designed to boost attendees' energy levels and increase their networking opportunities.
- Luncheons: When determining menus and service styles for luncheons, consider the activities that will be held at the same time as the food service, as well as the amount of time available, attendee preferences, and cultural norms. If a presentation is scheduled and time is limited, a

plated lunch may be preferable. If attendees are likely to use the lunch period to stay in touch with their offices, buffets or take-away may be better options. Luncheons may include chilled or hot entrées. Some events may also choose to have attendees purchase lunches from local restaurants or concessions, in which case, sufficient time should be provided and restaurants notified.

* Receptions: Many multi-day events begin with a welcome or opening reception. These are excellent networking opportunities and may have a theme or feature local specialties. Generally, entertainment is not the main attraction but may be used to enhance the event while still allowing networking to take place. Receptions often feature hot and/or cold hors d'oeuvres set at a buffet table. Hors d'oeuvres may also be passed, which can be less costly. While seating is typically minimal, there should be enough seats to meet accessibility needs of attendees.

* Banquets: Often a highlight of an event, the banquets may be served plated at tables or offered as a buffet. Banquet menus often highlight local specialties and the event may include entertainment, dancing, or a special programme such as an awards ceremony. If the banquet will be a formal event, attendees should be advised in advance of expected attire. If a buffet is offered, consider allowing service from both sides of the buffet table to reduce wait times.

Sustainability   Sustainability practices should be a consideration when booking either a venue or food services provider. **Consider asking food services providers how they incorporate sustainability** in their food and beverage service. This may include such strategies as:

* Using fresh, local, and seasonal ingredients raised either organically or sustainably.
* Following recommendations from sustainable seafood organisations such as OceanWise® (Canada), the Monterey Bay Aquarium Seafood Watch (United States), or the Marine Stewardship Council (United Kingdom).
* Managing food waste appropriately, including composting and donating unused food (following local regulations and safety standards).
* Limiting the use of individually packaged items and disposable serviceware.
* Recycling glass and aluminum at a minimum, and ideally all elements that can be recycled or composted.
* Offering vegetarian options, which typically have a lower environmental impact.

For additional information on sustainable food and beverage planning, see Sub Skill 2.02 – Demonstrate Environmental Responsibility.

Attendee Profile   While every location in the world has a food profile—dictating some menu selections, guest expectations, and times for meal availability—the event planner must also consider the demographics of event attendees to select the appropriate menu and food service options. Historical information may be available in post-event reports that can be helpful in determining the attendee profile and attendee food and beverage preferences. Examine historical records for the following information:

* Average age range(s)
* Gender mix
* Economic levels
* Travel familiarity
* Religious requirements relative to food (e.g., kosher, halal).
* Preferences related to the type of event.

- Time zone guests are traveling from—especially important for the opening reception or first evening meal.
- Event design—what the attendee will do during and following the meal.
- Cultural differences in meal times with respect to the audience and/or the meeting location.

In addition to historical information, specific requirements for attendees should be collected through registration information, including:

- Allergies and stated dietary requirements.
- Medical conditions that require special menus (e.g., diabetes, celiac disease, Crohn's disease).

Dietary Needs or Concerns   There are many specific dietary needs or concerns that affect event participants, and an awareness of how these personal requests impact event planning is critical. Requests can vary from no salt to vegan selections only, and from no peanuts or shellfish to low-calorie meals. Guests may experience slight discomfort to a life-threatening reaction to certain foods or beverages. Information about food and beverage needs and preferences is easily collected at registration and can be reviewed and shared with the catering representatives in a timely fashion.

The most common dietary concerns are:

- Allergies, including relatively common nut and shellfish reactions
- Celiac disease, or a requirement for gluten-free foods
- Lactose intolerance
- Vegetarian or vegan preferences
- Religious requirements
- Low-salt/sodium, low-fat, and low-calorie requests

Each of these requires knowledge of ingredients and specific preparation of foods. In most cases, the chef or caterer will be able to make these accommodations, but in some cases the request may require bringing in special meals for specific guests.

With plated meals, communication is critical among the event planner, the convention services manager (CSM), and the kitchen and service staff. All of these stakeholders must ensure that guests with special meal requirements obtain the correct meals. Strategies to facilitate meal accommodations may include colour-coded place cards, tickets, or another system to readily identify guests with special needs. For buffet service, clearly labeling all items is critical. Items such as eggs, wheat byproducts, butter, and ground nuts may not be easy to spot, and simple labels can ensure guest safety. Appropriate signage may also promote wise food choices and portion sizes.

Specific recommendations for managing dietary requirements are listed below (adapted and summarized, with permission, from A Meeting Planner's Dietary Requirements Check List, Thrive Meetings):

- **Site and/or caterer selection:** Ask the venue or caterer how they manage dietary needs of guests, including specific information on avoiding cross-contamination, training, and labeling of food items and buffets.
- **Event registration:** Collect dietary needs and medical action plans, with emergency contact information, as part of the registration process.
- **Menu selection:** Distribute dietary needs to all caterers in advance of the event, and update this information regularly. If possible, depending on the nature of the requirements, ask if the chef can prepare a single menu that meets the dietary needs or all or most attendees. Ensure that all menus are included in the banquet event orders (BEOs).

- **Pre-conference meetings:** Confirm that all catering parties have plans for meeting all dietary needs, that all buffets will be labeled, and that staff know what is being served (including ingredients). Also confirm processes for serving attendees with dietary needs, including how cross-contamination will be avoided, whether they will be served at the same time as other attendees, and how they will be identified.
- **On-site registration:** Provide attendees with meal tickets and explain processes. Confirm emergency contact information.
- **During the event:** Confirm that all items are labeled and that staff members know the ingredients of each item and how to identify attendees with dietary needs.

Food, Culture, and Religion   (The following section is adapted, with permission, from the *Events Industry Council International Manual, 8th edition* (2008).)

Food is closely linked to the traditions and culture of an area. However, globalisation increasingly blurs differences. Religious or spiritual beliefs can heavily influence the food of a region and the manner in which it is eaten. Religions, while often associated with a region, do roam with people.

For example, most people in India are vegetarian because their religion requires it, while across the border in Pakistan, the meat of animals is eaten, but they must be slaughtered according to set religious rituals. The United States and other western countries are not perceived as being governed by such religious constraints and their food choices are mainly influenced by lifestyle and culture. However, the United States is increasingly diverse in cultures and religions. The prudent event planner will profile potential event attendees, ask pertinent questions on registration sites, and make menu selections based on awareness of those attendees and their needs and preferences. As a general rule for international meetings, have an alternative if pork or shellfish is being served.

Since food and beverage has special significance during holidays, special occasions, and seasons, knowledge of these occurrences can guide menu selection. With the influence of globalisation, we see an increasing tendency to serve fusion cuisine, which combines different regional approaches to food and ingredients.

Programme Schedule   Timing of meals or breaks during the programme will have an impact on what you choose to serve and how it is served. A meal can enhance a program or the entire meeting experience. Examples include hosting events on a trade show floor to draw traffic or hosting a roundtable breakfast where topic experts can meet and share knowledge.

You may also choose to serve no meals or only certain ones during your event. This might be done to save money, or to provide opportunities for networking to self-formed groups, or to offer free time for all attendees. In destinations known for great cuisine, attendees may appreciate a few unscheduled meals so they can patronize local restaurants. If you are not providing meal service, consider whether restaurants in-house or nearby can handle the number of guests in the time allowed. Keep in mind that while the event budget benefits from having few or no food and beverage charges, the attendees will absorb those costs, and that may factor into their decision to attend the event.

The timing of meals should be based in part on cultural context. For example, in North America, meals usually take place earlier in the day than they would in Europe or South America. Attendees with long travel times may need options other than set times for meals. Providing alternatives for these attendees may improve their event experience.

Compliance with Legislation and Regulations

Liquor licensing. Every country (or specific state/province) will have its own laws related to alcohol service and the event planner must be aware of these laws. Laws on alcohol service are designed with public safety in mind and must be followed to avoid fines and unnecessary risk exposure.

In many licensed establishments and when people may be driving after the function, the establishment will offer driving guests non-alcoholic refreshments at a reduced rate or on a complimentary basis. Providing alcohol could open the venue and the provider to risk exposure should the attendee suffer or cause damages as a result of alcohol consumption. Solid public relations strategy suggests that the organisation should not only follow the applicable laws at a destination but, where possible, should provide the most responsible service possible. The care and safety of attendees and others with whom they come into contact is the primary concern.

Food safety. Countries around the world have various regulations related to food production, delivery, cooking temperatures, and allowable service times on buffets. These rules are designed to ensure that food pathogens are eliminated and the food is safe for consumption. Become familiar with the destination's laws or work with a local destination management company or professional congress organiser who is familiar with them.

In some countries, for example, food being served outside requires a service area that is covered to protect it from elements such as direct sunlight and birds. Other countries have more relaxed standards for outdoor food service. Understanding the risks associated with a global destination is part of the research during site selection and selection of food and beverage providers. Event planners may rely on the local knowledge of a DMC partner or caterer, but should still research the local requirements as a risk management strategy to limit the organisation's liability and protect attendees.

Public health. Each jurisdiction will have laws that apply to public health, and these will need to be followed, whether the event is held in a convention centre, hotel, restaurant, or other location. These laws will vary by area and may include a much more comprehensive inventory of requirements than the list below. At any time, the venue can be audited by a certified public health inspector, who can shut down the kitchen if compliance is lacking and the venue is not meeting all the conditions conducive to safe service to the public. Laws for public health include:

- The amount of time food can be left on a buffet and the specific temperatures the food must be held at until service.
- Temperatures that meat and seafood must reach internally when heated during the cooking process.
- Temperatures that must be maintained for freezers, refrigerators, and dishwashing equipment.
- Location, number, and temperature of water at handwashing stations.
- Surfaces and types of materials acceptable for walls, floors, and counters.
- Ground faults for electrical outlets.
- Plumbing specifications.
- Mats and surfaces for areas where water might splash or accumulate.
- Sanitation practices for garbage, compostable materials, and recycling.
- Sanitation practices to limit vermin and rodents.

Trends in Food and Beverage   Being aware of worldwide trends in food and beverage is important in planning a successful event. However, your attendee profile may suggest whether a trend is applicable or not to your audience. One example is the trend to small plate or tapas service, which can offer your guests an opportunity to try a variety of local flavours to mingle with other guests. This trend might suit your audience very well, but if they prefer sitdown meals and long networking sessions, the small plate service could be a distraction. Your chef, catering company, or convention services manager are excellent resources on trends, including local specialties and seasonal items.

Another example is the global trend of micro-climate production, which may allow you to introduce local, fresh, and seasonal products to your group. This could be produce, a specialty fruit or chocolate, a wine or beer made in the region, and cheeses or other artisanal products. Local cuisine provides an opportunity to connect with the local culture, and it generates conversations.

Confirm Expectations   Include the date, time, location, and expectations of food and beverage services in all contracts and in the **event specifications guide (ESG).** You must receive a contract or **banquet event order (BEO)** from the food service provider that clearly outlines all elements you have discussed. Communication through standard and unique forms must be clear to both the event planner and the supplier partner.

Quantity calculations. Calculating appropriate quantities for food and beverage and for staffing is important for budget management, to ensure sufficient provisions for the event, and to avoid unnecessary waste from careless overordering. See Figure 1 for guidelines on calculating beverage amounts.

Figure 1   Beverage Calculations Guidelines.

How Much Should You Order?			
For a Morning Break			
Drinks	**All Male**	**All Female**	**50/50**
Regular Coffee	Attendance x 60%	x 50%	x 55%
Decaf Coffee	Attendance x 20%	x 25%	x 25%
Tea	Attendance x 10%	x 15%	x 10%
Soda	Attendance x 25%	x 25%	x 25%
For an Afternoon Break			
Drinks	**All Male**	**All Female**	**50/50**
Regular Coffee	Attendance x 35%	x 30%	x 35%
Decaf Coffee	Attendance x 20%	x 20%	x 20%
Tea	Attendance x 10%	x 15%	x 10%
Soda	Attendance x 70%	x 70%	x 70%

How to use these charts: Locate the percentage associated with the makeup of your group and multiply that percentage by your overall attendance. If calculating in litres, divide the resulting number by 6 (167 ml cups per litre) to determine the number of litres required. If calculating in gallons, divide the resulting number by 20 (six-ounce cups per gallon) to determine the number of gallons needed. Round each partial litre or gallon to the next highest litre or half-gallon. For example, beverages for a morning break at a conference that has an audience of 500 predominantly male attendees should be calculated as follows:

Regular coffee = 500 x 60% = 300 cups = 50 litres or 15 gallons
Decaf coffee = 500 x 20% = 100 cups = 17 litres or 5 gallons
Tea = 500 x 10% = 50 cups = 9 litres or 2.5 gallons
Soda = 500 x 25% = 125 sodas

Note that the conversion from litres to gallons is not exact due to variations in the cup sizes and rounding. These numbers should be adjusted for larger size cups or disposable cups that may hold larger volumes. Cultural preferences should also be considered. For example, in some countries, tea is more popular than coffee.

Determine Supplies and Equipment Required   When numbers can be based on registration or ticket sales, ask the venue or caterer to set one additional table beyond expectations. This allows guests to move around and connect with small groups and allows for overflow. For additional information on set-ups, see Sub Skill 17 – Design Environment.

Supply ordering falls to the food services provider or venue, but this task requires the event planner to supply timely and accurate estimates, and knowledge of the group's history. In addition to providing guaranteed numbers, the event planner should share information such as whether or not the group needs more plates for a buffet than usual, large coffee mugs instead of smaller coffee cups, and other preferences, such as particular condiments to accompany meals. Supplies are ordered based on final numbers, a detailed floor plan, and an allowance for extras. The final numbers must be received in time to order and receive supplies, prepare décor and some food items, and comply with guarantee deadlines required by the caterer or venue. However, supplies often need to be ordered well in advance of when final numbers are known, so the event planner must be prepared to make realistic predictions on attendance and the special accommodations that may be necessary, based on history with this event or this audience. In lieu of a historical perspective, an accurate attendee profile may be all the event planner has available to make predictions.

Set-up   Generally, the facilities used by the caterer are under the purview of the venue rather than the event planner. However, when the event planner has to provide a tent for food service or other temporary shelter arrangements, the event planner must have an understanding of the principles of safe food service operations. The event planner will need to include at least some of these positions:

- a person or a caterer in charge of monitoring supplies, and their delivery and storage of supplies;
- a manager responsible for bar service, including determining the methods and control procedures needed for alcohol service;
- a supervisor who ensures the recruitment and scheduling of service-trained staff;
- another supervisor to manage the security of cash on-site (if all food and beverage is not part of the registration or entry fee), including storage or removal of excess cash at the end of the day or event.

For detailed information on set-up arrangements, see Sub Skill 17 – Design Environment.

Staffing   Staffing is typically arranged by the food services provider or venue. The ratio of staff to attendees (including waiters, bussers, and bartenders) will depend upon many variables. Considerations will include:

- The number of guests
- The style and formality of the event
- The chosen menu
- The style of service expected
- The amount of space available

If you are using an off-site venue and the caterer is not familiar with that venue, a thorough site inspection is conducted. The catering representative walks through all aspects of the event, from food delivery to storage and preparation areas, plating space, how and where the pickup will be, flow from the service areas to the guest areas, bussing station options, handwashing and changing areas for the service staff, and available power and cooking implements.

Ratios for front-of-house staff will vary based on the level of service expected. For average service, the ratio will be 1 server to 20 guests. This allows for clearing, running replacement food to the buffets, and assisting with guest requests, such as special meal requirements or beverage service. For a high-level dinner or when there is a short amount of time for service, the ratio may be as high as 1 server to 10 guests. This allows for a degree of service where guests feel valued by the service staff. White-glove service is usually reserved for a gala or formal dinner. If the service staff are hired from an external staffing company by the caterer or venue, ask how they will be trained and ensure that they will be familiar with the menus and ingredients, and that they will comply with applicable regulations.

One bartender usually will suffice for every 75–100 people if they will be arriving at intervals. If guests will arrive in one group or closely spaced together, one bartender for every 50 guests is more appropriate.

Sub Skill 16.02 – Select Menu(s)

Event professionals often receive a large package that includes menu options to choose from. If pre-existing menus are not suitable for the group's needs or expectations, many venues and food services providers can customise menus in consultation with the event planner. Engage your CSM or chef in seeking alternatives for your meeting.

Attendee Profile – Additional Considerations

The following are some potential considerations in connection with menu selection:

- In North America, a gala dinner may begin at 18:30 with a reception, but that would seem very early to attendees from South America or Europe, where 20:00 is a more typical time for a reception with dinner to follow.
- Fish and rice would be a typical breakfast in parts of Asia; many Europeans would prefer pastries, bread, cheese, and even meat, while North Americans typically prefer eggs, fruit, or cereal.
- Men typically eat larger portions than women, so a buffet offers patron control for quantity; plated meals are served one size for all. Consider attendee demographics when planning portion sizes.
- The nature of the event will affect nutritional expectations. As an example, a group of elite athletes in training will have different requirements than a typical business meeting.
- Most North Americans would not eat a three-course lunch, whereas people in other parts of the world would have three courses for lunch and expect wine to be served with this mid-day meal.

Fresh and Brain-Friendly Food

Advances in neuroscience studies related to learning and performance offer many specific ways you could plan your meals with healthier, "brain-friendly" options, including the following:

- Limit high glycemic foods—anything made primarily with white flour and white sugar that provides instant gratification but leads quickly to a blood sugar rush and as quickly to a crash as the blood sugars become unstable. Be attentive to hidden sugars in otherwise healthy menu offerings.
- Fresh, regional, local ingredients tend to be more nutrient-rich.

- Limiting salt and processed food is a health-conscious decision in menu planning. Communicate clearly and work with your catering partners to provide fresh and healthy menu alternatives.
- Include nutritional information about key ingredients (e.g., protein, carbohydrates, fat content, calories, sodium).

Venue and Location

Let your location and the specific venue guide your menu selections. What are the regional specialties, and what does the chef love to prepare, based on experience and locally available ingredients? You may be pleasantly surprised when you open your group menus to suggestions.

Most event meals are offered in a hotel or convention centre, but some can be held at unique off-site locations. You might try tying the food to a theme to enhance both. For example, a dinner could be served at long feast tables with family-style platters in a castle-like or historical venue. A welcome reception on a beach could lend itself to a giant paella and buffet service of local specialties. Do consider the ambience of the meal—where you will be eating, the overall event experience and how it might be enhanced with food and beverages. The venue itself may suggest a menu: Try fish or seafood on a yacht, a hearty Midwestern (U.S.) breakfast on a farm, or haute cuisine at a French chalet.

Finalizing Details

Ensure that each food and beverage function is clearly defined and that you share detailed information for the successful execution with the partners responsible for each meal. You must in turn ensure that you are adhering to the contract policies requested by the venue or caterer.

Menu Details

There are many factors to consider in itemizing the details of your menus, including the time of day/meal being served as well as the dietary needs of the group. In addition, you need to know the organisation's policies regarding nutrition, food service, sustainability, and selection of food service providers. Menu selection and service options need to fit within a set budget. Transparency with your catering coordinator about needs and budget constraints will provide you with the best alternatives.

At the event, servers must be aware of what ingredients are in each of the dishes being served, particularly those ingredients that may cause sensitive or allergic reactions. This should be part of the service briefing, so you must have a clear list of ingredients from the food preparer. Be certain that you communicate this need to your venue representative or caterer.

Guarantees

Provide an estimated number of guests for planning purposes to the caterer and venue for every food and beverage function. Based on your contract (but typically 48–72 business hours in advance), you must provide the **guaranteed number** of guests. You will pay for either the guaranteed number (whether or not the food is consumed) or the actual number served, whichever is higher. Once a guarantee is given, it cannot be reduced; however, guarantees can be increased, if the venue/caterer permits. Typically, the maximum additional number of seats that a venue or hotel will overset is 5 to 10 percent of the guarantee number, to allow for people to move to tables with their friends. Oversetting policies should be reviewed with the venue or caterer in advance, as they may be more or less than 5 to 10 percent. Oversetting provides additional seating but does not provide additional food.

Typically, caterers will prepare 5 percent above the guaranteed number of meals, so you must be as accurate as possible with your guarantee numbers, using your knowledge of the group and its history to provide the best possible information. When history isn't available, guarantee numbers are based on registrations or the attendee profile. This implies that the registration system requests information about intent to participate in meal functions, and that the attendee profile includes information about meal preferences (e.g., "Do you prefer breakfast service?").

Sub Skill 16.03 – Plan Service Style(s)

Service styles include how food is served. It depends on numbers, desired traffic flow, programme intent, and the theme of the event. A buffet might seem out of place for a formal meal and awards program, whereas it would complement a meal of ethnic flavors and a networking session. The event's objectives, program schedule, and attendee profile are key to determining how, what, where, and when food service should occur.

Service Styles

When you have a formal meal such as a gala dinner or a meal function with presentations to be made, a plated meal allows better control of timing and traffic flow. Attendees who will receive awards or deliver a presentation should be close to the stage in reserved seating. Other guests can sit either at tables pre-selected by the event planner or where they choose, which encourages networking and discussion. A disadvantage of plated meal service style is a limited choice of food, as the menu is usually pre-selected, with accommodations for special requests made in advance, such as vegetarian or gluten-free meals. Plated meals require more service staff and ample space around tables for staff to maneuver appropriately with plates and trays.

With a less formal meal, a standard buffet offers your guests a greater selection of food and portion sizes. The disadvantage of buffet service is the space requirement to hold the buffet stations and the ability to move the attendees through tables and maintain queues at the buffet areas. Generally, a buffet service plan will limit food access areas to one or two for small gatherings and more for larger numbers of attendees.

When you want to encourage mingling or play off a theme, such as "international flavours," a set-up with multiple action stations may be ideal. Multiple stations also allow you to separate various courses; for example, one or more stations handle appetizers, other areas handle the entrée, and one or more offer dessert. Additional stations may be set up for beverage service.

The following are the most common service styles used in meetings and events:

- **Butler service**. When trays of bite-sized items are passed around by serving staff, the system is called butler service. One type of item per tray is recommended; trays may contain food or beverages.
- **Plated service**. Serving two or more courses at tables is called plated service. Plates may be filled in the kitchen and delivered (usually with covers) or filled tableside by staff. Salad and/or dessert can be pre-set to save service time; however, this may result in food waste.
- **Buffet**. A line or multiple lines of attendees take plates past the buffet set-up (single- or double-sided) and select their own food. When the buffet is set up with one side for attendees and the other side for servers, who place food on the guest's plate, it is known as **cafeteria service**.
- **Food stations**. Attendees may be directed to multiple areas, which may be themed to a specific food type or style of preparation. An **action station** is one where the chef cooks, slices, or otherwise prepares the food at the time of service.
- **Concessions** may be used for a pay-on-your-own set-up and are often seen at larger conferences or trade shows. This type of food service is typically provided by the venue rather than through a caterer, at no cost to the event host.

Other service styles that are less often used at events include:

- **Family-style (or English) service,** where each table receives platters of food, and the guests serve themselves. This format can be very effective for networking.
- **French service,** where specific items are prepared and served tableside. The specially trained staff and service carts required, along with the time needed for cooking do not make this particularly suitable for large group service.
- **Russian service,** where each item is placed by a server onto the guest's plate at the table, instead of filling plates in the kitchen. This is an elegant style that requires training and is more often seen in restaurants than at group banquets. The service is slower, so it requires additional staff to be successful.

Selection of service styles is based on numerous considerations and should be determined in cooperation among the event planner, the venue, and the caterer. Factors to consider include menu, costs, available staff, and the event programme. In partnership with the food services provider, walk through the entire meal plan, select the location and timing of each part of the plan, the service staff ratio, and the equipment required to provide the selected service. Equipment can include items such as the size of the plates to the location of the utensils (i.e., will guests pick these up at the buffet or will they be set on tables?). Questions such as location of bars and how guests will manage both plates and glassware should be addressed as part of this overall discussion. When a reception is held and networking is encouraged, the event planner may prefer to limit the number of banquet tables and chairs, instead using reception tables (guests stand and place their plates and glasses on the tables as they converse).

When a room is quite tight due to the number of attendees and the size of tables, a service style should be selected that minimizes the amount of room required to serve food and beverages. When food should be served hot but the serving staff is relatively small relative to the number of guests, traffic flow is critical to avoid unnecessary delays. Pre-setting part of the meal can help reduce delays and luke-warm food. When the meal is served during a programme, timing of the various courses is an important consideration and should be carefully orchestrated. Should the meal be concluded (in which case some guests may leave) before the presentations begin? Will diners be enjoying the meal during presentations (which could cause difficulty for servers who are given special requests)? Discuss how tables will be replenished with beverages as the meal progresses and how guests will request special items (such as replacing a dropped fork).

The event planner should also discuss authority and the process by which changes might be made. All partners in food and beverage service should be clear about who can make changes and who will be responsible for paying for those changes. Limitations on changes may be considered, as well as timing for changes. Costs associated with changes should be clearly delineated in food and beverage contracts.

Event professionals typically supply confirmation of details to suppliers via the ESG. This document should include floor plans, a timeline for the event (including all elements from set-up to strike), and clearly outlined service expectations. Suppliers should acknowledge receipt of the ESG; pre-conference meetings are useful for checking these arrangements before the event begins. Venues often supply their confirmation of details through the BEO, which must be reviewed and acknowledged by the event planner. Caterers may use a similar document.

Sub Skill 16.04 – Select Food and Beverage Provider(s)

Event professionals must carefully consider who will provide the food and beverage service. Most hotels, convention centres, restaurants, and many off-site venues have exclusive catering providers, with an on-site kitchen and their own china, cutlery, glassware, and trained serving staff. However, some facilities may have a list of providers to suggest, and the event planner has an opportunity to select a provider, based on organisational policies or guidelines. In rare circumstances, you may have your own preferred provider and will have to negotiate with the facility could ensue, to gain approval for your provider's service at that site.

Exclusive providers for food service include chefs, kitchen staff, service staff, and food and beverage choices. The venue may allow some exceptions, but these would need to be negotiated on a case-by-case basis. The negotiations should occur before contracting with the venue if having this exception is an important to the success of your event. Exceptions relate particularly to events such as food and beverage expos, events planned by a food and beverage-based organisation, or when the theme of the event is clearly connected to food and beverage; for example,

- A poultry-producer council hosts an outdoor exhibition with multiple poultry options on the menu.
- A religious-based organisation hosts an event that requires specific food preparation techniques, or a historical re-enactment group specifies certain ingredients and preparation techniques for a historically precise meal.
- A conference is held with a theme of responsible food consumption, including low-calorie variations for common meals.

In some cases, the venue may not have exclusive providers but may suggest a small group of **preferred** or **approved providers** who have been chosen by the venue for the quality of their food, their experience, and their familiarity with the venue and its specific rules and regulations.

A venue that has its own equipment and staff will often have indoor and outdoor locations for food and beverage service. Typically, if you book outdoor space, you will have an indoor backup. Request this option in case bad weather forces your event inside.

When venues do not have catering facilities on-site, the caterer and event planner must provide all necessary items, potentially including service structures, washrooms, tables, chairs, linens, décor, and service items. For elaborate set-ups, the caterer and event planner may need to provide a temporary kitchen with power and utilities, as well as necessary public safety elements such as sinks for handwashing.

Should you find yourself in the position of needing off-site catering, seek qualified food and beverage providers. Having a clear list of criteria for this service will be essential to selecting the best provider; this requires development of a detailed request for proposals (RFP). There is quite a difference in providing food and beverage service in a location that has a kitchen everyone is familiar with, compared to providing service in a location with no kitchen, questionable power sources, and uncertain access to basics such as running hot water. Working with a catering organisation experienced in off-site locations will lead to a greater chance of success.

Requests for Proposals (RFPs) and Contracts

Many organisations have procurement and RFP policies that guide the selection of suppliers, including caterers. For instance, some organisations require proposals from at least three potential suppliers. Write the RFP to specify both required and preferred criteria for selection. Organisational policies could dictate a low-bid approach or a value approach to selection. The low-bid approach focuses on who will get the job done for the lowest price, whereas the value approach considers who will provide the best value in terms of food quality, experience, adequate numbers of trained staff, provision of other specific needs, and the budget. When the low-bid approach is utilised (costs must be tightly controlled) the decision is usually made on the basis of required criteria only. However, when the bids are very close, the selection may be based on which supplier provides more value (preferred criteria) for the cost.

Obtaining recommendations and checking references is strongly advised when selecting a caterer or food service professional. Complete proposals will allow you to make an informed decision that should meet the needs of your event.

From the contract with your caterer or venue to the BEO, carefully review the paperwork sent to you from service providers. Pay special attention to details, then sign and return the documents as requested. When a deposit schedule is provided, be sure to share this with internal sources responsible for accounts payable, and follow up on this process to ensure that the payment schedule is met.

After the event, carefully review the master account to make sure nothing appears on this document that was not included in the service contract and that all services were rendered as indicated by the contract. For more information on contracts, see Sub Skill 5.02 – Manage Contracts.

Inevitably during the planning process, changes will occur as new information comes to light about the group, the client's wishes, the venue, or the availability of menu items. Throughout the process, maintain open communication with the venue and caterer, as they are key partners in the event's success.

Sub Skill 16.05 – Manage Alcohol Service

Alcohol service at events can be simple or quite complex. The event planner must consider attendee expectations, local laws, provider capabilities, cost, and, in some situations, liability exposure.

Beverage Service Options

If you are not providing a host bar, guests will pay for their drinks as they order them, at prices set and posted on a menu, table card, or signage. Payment may be through cash or credit at the bar. The venue may require your guests to purchase a ticket at a cashier station, or you may have a sponsor who provides one or two drink tickets per guest. The ticket is taken to the bar as a form of payment. You may also host one or two tickets for each guest, and consumption beyond this limit would be at the guest's own cost. Note that in some jurisdictions, provision of a drink ticket may expose the sponsor (or event) to liability if the guest suffers or causes damages.

When your event offers a hosted bar that will be charged by consumption post-event (costs are determined by the drink, bottle, or per person/per hour), you may wish to implement controls ahead of the event to limit consumption and perhaps liability. This strategy may include having someone assigned to ensure that product is not opened unnecessarily (such as wine that is opened but not served). You may want to count the empty bottles at the end of the meal and ensure that there is agreement before you leave as to the appropriate charges.

A number of options exist to provide bar service at an event. You should take into consideration the following issues:

1. What you are serving?
   a. Serving beer and wine typically includes red and white wine and beer. It may also include sparkling wine and minimal or no garnishes (such as fruit).
   b. A full bar with spirits requires several different types of glassware, as well as mixers— including sodas and juices—and garnishes.
   c. Non-alcoholic options may also be served at the bar.
2. Is this an **open (host) bar** or a **cash bar**?
   a. Fully hosted = event pays all costs; cash bar = patron pays individual costs; sponsored bar = sponsor pays all costs; ticketed = event or sponsor pays for tickets and tickets are controlled (e.g., one or two per patron).

b. Are you paying by the hour (an option only available in some countries or states), by the drink, or by the bottle? What are the service charges (gratuity) and taxes? Will guests be able to use cash, credit, or charge to an in-house guest room, or will they need to go through a cashier to purchase a ticket? The venue may levy additional charges for cashiers and/or bartenders.

3. Is this a **combination bar**, with open bar and cash bar components? For example, the event begins with a limited number of hosted tickets, followed by a cash bar. (Drink prices might be different from one component to the other.)

Refer to your contracts to determine the fees that will be charged, should alcohol consumption not meet predetermined amounts.

Alcohol Controls

To address the liabilities and requirements of responsible service, research the laws of the event's destination, then plan your service in compliance with those requirements. Consider the following issues as you develop your beverage plan:

- Age limit for alcohol service
- License requirements
- Time that service can be provided, and the time that guests have to leave the venue following final beverage service
- Off-site/non-licensed venues may have laws that require a special permit and may stipulate where service is permitted, fencing or barrier requirements, what may be served, quantities that may be served, and prices that may be charged.

It is incumbent upon the event planner to understand the applicable legislation (e.g., legal drinking age) and ensure that these rules are followed. For example, your guests may come from a country where the legal drinking age is 18, but if your event is in a state where the law requires 21, alcohol should not be served to anyone who cannot provide a photo identification and proof of appropriate age. Additionally, controls should be in place to limit alcohol consumption by children who are given a drink by a guest. In the United States, for instance, some states allow parents to give their children an alcoholic beverage in a public setting, but other states do not allow this.

Responsible Beverage Service Training

In some locations, service staff must study a guide on responsible service and pass a short exam in order to receive a certificate. Examples include "Serving It Right" in British Columbia, Canada, and "Training for Intervention Procedures (TIPS)" in the United States. Responsible Hospitality Guides are also available from the International Centre for Alcohol Policies.

Similar certifications exist around the world, and you must be aware of who may serve alcohol at your events. For example, you might find yourself in the position of having an executive host who wishes to pour wine for the guests at the gala dinner, but by law the server needs to be certified through a relevant training programme. A responsible venue that holds the license to serve alcohol should advise you of this. The event planner must know if the country (state/province) has such requirements and training options in place, and ensure that the serving staff are trained or certified. Hiring a trained bartender is strongly advised.

Monitor alcohol service

Often alcohol is used to enhance an event experience. During the event, the consumption of alcohol must be monitored to avoid overconsumption and potential problems. Limit service to responsible levels and only to those who meet the legal age requirement.

While the licensee must ensure that guests maintain a reasonable level of consumption, the responsible event planner is also concerned with public safety. In many places, the licensee is allowed by law to stop service at either a hosted or cash-based function to any or all guests.

Additionally, monitor alcohol service to determine that the contract arrangements are met fully. Cost is one factor, as is the use of authority to change arrangements based on conditions at the time of delivery.

Reference

Thrive Meetings, A Meeting Planner's Dietary Requirements Check List, www.thrivemeetings.com

---

Contributing Author

Tahira Endean, CMP
Director, Creative and Production, Cantrav Services Inc.
Vancouver, BC, Canada
Member of International Special Event Society (ISES), Green Meeting Industry Council (GMIC)

Reviewers

Dale Hudson
Knowledge and Events Director, IMEX Group
London, UK
Member of Green Meeting Industry Council (GMIC), Meeting Professionals International (MPI)

Arlene Sheff, CMP
Strategic Meeting Consulting
Orange County, CA, USA
Member of Meeting Professionals International (MPI)

Andrea Sullivan, MA
BrainStrength Systems
Philadelphia, PA, USA
Member of National Speakers Association (NSA)

Tracy Stuckrath, CSEP, CMM, CHC
Founder and Chief Connecting Officer, Thrive! Meetings & Events
Atlanta, GA, USA
Member of International Special Events Society (ISES), Meeting Professionals International (MPI), National Association of Catering Executives (NACE)

Skill 16:
Endpoints

Terminology

Action station

Banquet event order (BEO)

Buffet

Butler service

Cafeteria service

Cash bar

Combination bar

Concession

Continental breakfast

Exclusive provider

Event specifications guide (ESG)

Family-style (or English) service

French service

Food safety

Food stations

Full buffet breakfast

Full-service breakfast

Guaranteed number

Liquor licensing

Open (host) bar

Plated service

Preferred or approved provider

Public health

Russian service

Skill 16: Review Questions

1. Why is responsible alcohol service important in planning your meeting?

2. What are four key considerations in planning your menus?

3. What service style is best suited to a welcome reception at a multi-day event?

SKILL 17: DESIGN ENVIRONMENT

Learner Outcomes

- Establish functional requirements for an event, including selecting appropriate set-ups.
- Select décor and furnishings appropriate for the event.
- Identify and design event signage.

The environment design refers to the spaces available for an event and how those spaces are intentionally arranged, furnished, decorated, and equipped to set the tone and purpose, and to connect with the event's theme. This section focuses on the rationale behind the decisions to be made about the event environment and why some selections help achieve event objectives.

Sub Skill 17.01 – Establish Functional Requirements

When designing the event environment, you should establish the functional requirements based on event goals and objectives, as well as event type. Planning for these requirements should focus on what attendees will be doing and the desired behaviours you expect from them, such as networking, listening, or discussing. Determine the types of attendee areas that may be needed, such as meeting or function rooms, exhibition areas, registration, security and credentialing areas, and networking or entertainment areas. Additional functional requirements may include areas for designated attendees (staff, speakers, etc.) and storage areas. For each function area, the desired atmosphere will also need to be selected. This will be determined by two primary factors: your audience and the objectives of the event. While your key stakeholders may have very clear ideas about what they want, it will be incumbent upon you to prepare the floor plans, signage guide, and an effective environment design plan to ensure that the event objectives are met, on budget, and within the allotted time.

Ask questions that will provide a clear profile of the audience as well as branding guidelines, and develop a theme to fit. Work through the schedule of functions room by room, following logical traffic flow, to determine where the theme might be applied through décor. Also consider room changes: You might have a lunch and a gala dinner in the same room, but how you create the two environments may be quite different.

Throughout environment design planning, consider what the attendees expect, what they will experience, and what they might be doing at the function.

Set-ups Based on Audience Interaction

For many events, education is a major objective. For example, an association event might include a series of industry experts, each tasked with raising awareness about a key topic; whereas a corporate event might share its new products for the year with staff, customers, or partners. Depending on the nature and topic of the event, attendees' expectations, cultural considerations, and the event's goals, the function rooms may be designed with a presenter-focused set-up, a partially interactive set-up, or a highly interactive set-up. In some cases, a mix of set-ups in the same function room may be appropriate.

Presenter-Focused Set-up   Presenter-focused set-ups can be characterized as prioritizing the speaker and the speaker's message. They also prioritize maximum capacity over interactivity and are typically used for general sessions and keynote presentations. Attendees in these formats tend to be passive—they are not actively involved in discussion and are focused on the speaker. In these cases, a highly skilled speaker is necessary to maintain audience engagement with the content. Examples of presenter-focused set-ups are shown in Figure 1.

Figure 1 Presenter-Focused Room Set-ups.

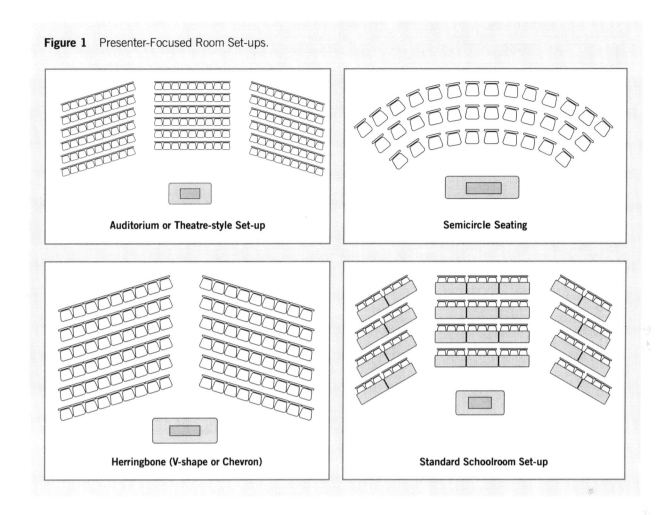

Partially Interactive Set-up Partially interactive set-ups encourage group discussion to coincide with a speaker's presentation. The audience will typically face the stage or speaker but will also need space to engage in group discussions. When this type of environment is provided, the attendees' expectation is that the session will allow them opportunities to interact with each other. Examples of partially interactive formats are shown in Figure 2. When these kinds of set-ups are used for meetings without a speaker but with visuals (such as a board meeting with a screen showing an agenda or participants who are connected virtually), they can also be highly interactive.

Highly Interactive Set-up Highly interactive set-ups are designed for attendees who will be actively involved in session discussion. Although there may be a facilitator or even a chairperson for the meeting, the highly interactive orientation promotes face-to-face communication and equality in group dynamics. These room set-ups can be quite challenging if audiovisual presentations are planned. Some highly interactive set-ups are shown in Figure 3.

Best Practices for Function Space Configurations

There are a number of best practices for function space configurations, including these:

- Set up staging on the long side of the room when reasonable. Although this is more space-intensive than setting to the short side, it will bring the audience closer to the speaker or stage.

Figure 2   Partially Interactive Room Set-ups.

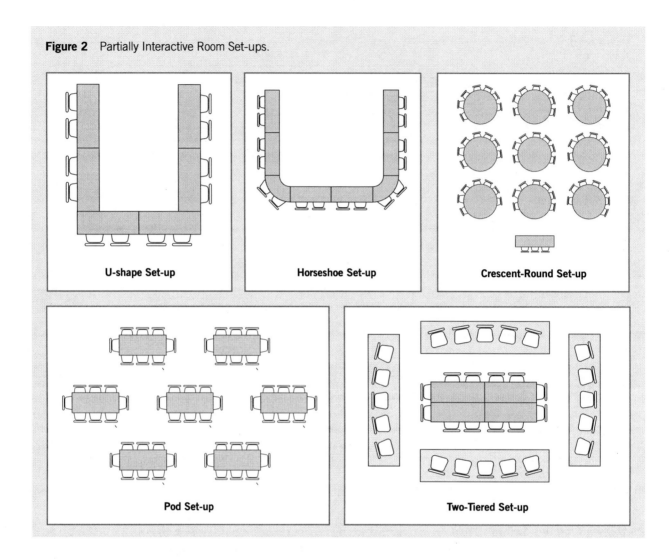

- Adjust the floor plan for audiovisual needs. If you are using rear-screen projection, you will need to reserve additional floor space behind the screen. For wide rooms, multiple screens may be needed for audiovisual presentations.
- Plan for attendee electrical needs for laptops and mobile devices. Furnishing the seating area with adequate electrical outlets will be appreciated and will reduce tripping hazards.
- Minimize straight-row seating. If needed, include straight row seating in the centre of the room with herringbone seating on the ends to improve sight lines. When straight-row seating is required, the presenters or entertainers should be on a stage or risers, so all audience members can see them.
- Avoid centre aisles whenever possible. The centre area provides the best viewing and should be reserved for seating.
- Many venues have relatively narrow chairs to enable them to set the room for high attendee numbers. These chairs are often set touching each other; however, this can be uncomfortable if the attendees are adults and strangers to each other, and if cultural norms dictate ample personal space. Set the room with at least a few inches between chairs.
- Plan for quick sets. A "quick set" refers to how quickly the function space can be set up and rearranged. For example, a general session set at crescent rounds can be more quickly converted

Figure 3   Highly Interactive Room Set-ups.

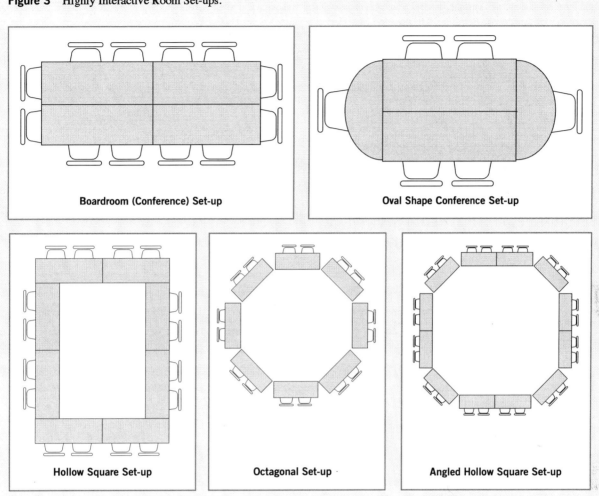

into banquet-style seating than a general session set to theatre style. A centre aisle is advisable if that helps split a room quickly after a general session to form two breakout rooms. Ensure adequate time in the schedule for the venue's staff to reset the room.

- With consecutive workshops or sessions, plan the sessions in coordination with the room set-ups. For example, all highly interactive sessions would be scheduled in room A, while presenter-focused sessions would be in room B. This will minimize room set-up changes for venue staff and long breaks (to accommodate those changes) between sessions, and may reduce costs.

- Consider accessibility requirements and ensure adequate access and seating for all attendees.

- Allow adequate space in aisles if the audience will be allowed to ask questions. Microphones can be placed in wide aisles, allowing audience members with questions to start a queue to approach the microphone, if needed. If hand-held microphones are used, the persons holding the microphones will need multiple aisles to reach all audience members. Coordinate these room arrangements with the audiovisual provider.

- An essential part of hybrid event design is looking for new ways to group attendees, focus dialogue, and integrate comments from remote attendees. Theatre and classroom-style arrangements, while good choices for traditional meetings, work less well for hybrid events, especially when the conversation is among multiple groups in multiple venues. Living room style groupings—with comfortable furniture, TVs, and even focused cameras—promote comfortable levels of engagement. Living room style furniture may reduce alertness levels because attendees are in relaxed seating positions.

Exhibition Set-ups

If your event is, or includes, an exhibition, offering different types of booth layouts can help broaden options for your exhibitors. Various exhibition set-ups are shown in Figure 4.

Banquet and Reception Set-ups

Traditional banquet layouts use round tables that are 60, 66, and 72 inches (152, 168, and 183 cm) in diameter. Interaction is typically localized at the individual tables. In some cases, a head table, speaker, or audiovisual presentation may be featured. In these cases, a platform of 18 inches (46 cm) or higher may be required, depending on the size of the audience. For small banquets with a speaker, a T-shape set-up may be suitable, but is not ideal for audiovisual presentations unless the screen is at the bottom of the T. Banquet and reception room set-ups are shown in Figure 5.

Sub Skill 17.02 – Select Décor and Furnishings

During the site selection process, you will likely consider many destinations and venues. You may be able to choose a beautiful venue with furniture and décor that will enhance your meeting experience. However, some venues need additional touches to create ambiance for the function rooms. Consider what you need to enhance the function space and what is available to you to use from the venue. From meal functions to meetings and other activities, what attendees are sitting on and what they are surrounded by will have an immediate impact on their impression of the event.

Standard descriptions and dimensions for event furnishings are shown below (adapted with permission from the *Events Industry Council Manual, 8th edition*):

Chairs

- The footprint of most conference chairs measures 17.5 to 18.5 inches (44 to 47 cm) wide by 20 inches (51 cm) deep and 17 inches (43 cm) tall.
- The stacking type of padded armchair generally has a 15.5 by 17.5 inch (39 by 44 cm) seat and is 17 inches (43 cm) tall.
- Interlocking chairs vary in how far apart they will be after they are locked. The spacing can be as little as 1 inch (2.5 cm) and as much as 3 inches (7.5 cm). The farther apart they are placed, the better.

Tables

- Most schoolroom and banquet tables are 30 inches (76 cm) high.
- Rectangular tables that are 6 six or 8 feet (1.8 or 2.4 m) long by 30 inches (76 cm) wide are used for head tables, U-shaped schoolroom set-ups, boardroom or conference-style set-ups, buffets, registration tables, and displays.
- Rectangular tables that are 6 or 8 feet (1.8 or 2.4 m) long by 18 inches (46 cm) wide are used mostly for schoolroom set-ups in order to save space.
- Half-rounds are 30 or 60 inches (76 or 152 cm) and are used to build oval, cloverleaf, and buffet tables.
- Quarter-rounds and serpentines are for the construction of horseshoes, rounded hollow squares, and buffet tables.

Figure 4   Exhibition Set-ups. (Adapted with permission from the International Association of Expositions and Events' *Guidelines for Display Rules & Regulations*, 2011 update.)

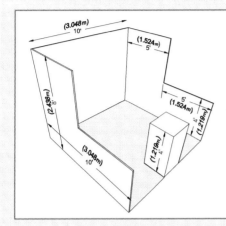

Linear booths. Also called "in-line" booths, linear booths are generally arranged in a straight line and have neighboring exhibitors on the immediate right and left, leaving only one side exposed to the aisle. Linear booths are most commonly 10 ft. (3.05 m) wide and 10 ft (3.05 m) deep. A maximum back wall height limitation of 8 ft. (2.44 m) is generally specified.

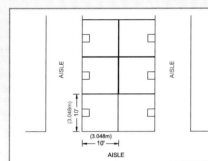

Corner booth. A corner booth is formed in a linear booth layout, at the end of the row of in-line booths, offering exposure to intersecting aisles on two sides. All other guidelines for linear booths apply.

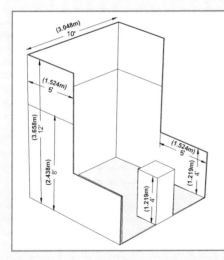

Perimeter booths. A perimeter booth is part of a linear booth layout that backs to an outside wall of the exhibition space rather than the back of another exhibition booth.

End-cap booth. An end-cap booth is exposed to aisles on three sides and is comprised of two booths.

continued

Figure 4 Exhibition Set-ups, con'd.

A

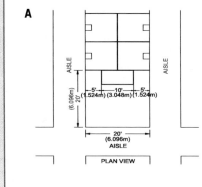

Peninsula and split-island booths. A peninsula booth is exposed to aisles on three sides and is comprised of at least four booths. There are two types of peninsula booths: (1) it backs to a row of linear booths, and (2) it backs to another peninsula booth and is referred to as a "split-island booth."

B

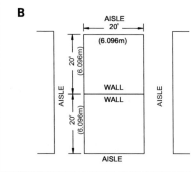

Island booth. An island booth is any size booth exposed to aisles on all four sides. An island booth is typically 20 ft by 20 ft (6.10 m by 6.10 m) or larger, although it may be configured differently.

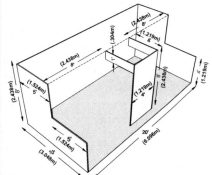

Extended header booth. An extended header booth is a linear booth that is 20 ft (6.10 m) or longer with a centre extended header.

Figure 5 Banquet and Reception Room Set-ups.

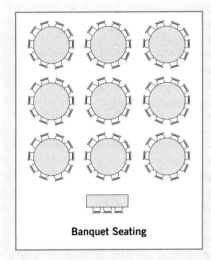
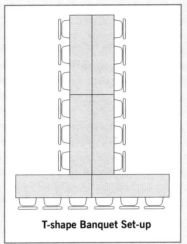
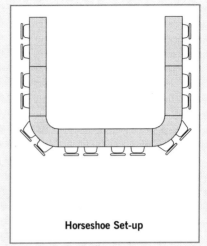

| Banquet Seating | T-shape Banquet Set-up | Horseshoe Set-up |

Lecterns, podiums, and platforms

- **Lecterns** are speaker-support furniture. They are slant-topped reading stands, either tabletop or freestanding, and should be equipped with a reading light and extension cord. Be sure to request these options.
- A **podium** is a raised speaker's platform. Freestanding lecterns are often placed on podiums.
- A **dais** is a raised platform for a head table.
- **Platforms** (also known as **risers**) can be 6, 12, 16, 24, or 32 inches (15, 30, 41, 61 or 81 cm) high and are usually in 4 by 8 ft. (1.2 by 2.4 m) or 6 by 8 ft. (1.8 by 2.4 m) sizes. Dimensions and construction vary from place to place, so check local regulations on their assembly.
- **Handrails** on stairs will help ensure safety when using raised platforms. If there is a gap between the back of the platform and the wall, have handrails placed there as well. Not all facilities carry rails for the backs of platforms, but most do have stairs with handrails.

Décor for Functional and Experiential Events

The event environment should be considered a critical element in supporting the stated objectives. The term "experiential" refers to designing an event where the guests are engaged by the environment, décor, performance, food and beverage, and overall ambience.

The function of the space should influence the room set-up and décor. On another level, the décor may enhance the experience, whether the primary focus is learning, connecting, interacting, or just enjoying a special event. When you are creating a stimulating environment that will keep your attendees energized or offering a presentation and a memorable dining experience, knowing what you want to achieve should guide the design.

Even colour choices can influence event outcomes. Neutral colours (whites, greys) provide less stimulating environments that tend to result in less engagement and consequent learning, while warm colours (reds, oranges, yellows) are more stimulating, and cool colours (blues, greens) are more calming (BrainStrength Systems, 2011, pp. 15–16). Cool colours also stimulate creativity and innovative thinking. Rooms that are starkly neutral provide the least stimulating environments. Neutrals can be both relaxing and stimulating as long as there are some splashes of colour in the room (plants, paintings.)

A third influence on the choice of décor elements is the need to create a strong brand presence. There are many ways to enhance the environment, the event experience, and the brand presence, creating a positive connection for the attendees between the host organisation, the brand, and the experience.

Another aspect of décor design is that a change in the environment from what is "normal" or "expected" by attendees can alter their perceptions and invite them to change how they react and interact throughout the event. Heightened awareness created by a novel or unexpected design element will enhance the engagement experience as perceptions shift with the décor's positive influence.

Room Capacities

(The following section is adapted, with permission, from the *Events Industry Council Manual, 8th edition*.)

Unfortunately, many facilities suggest room capacities that would maximize the audience size but would be impractical with AV and other design elements. The event professional is responsible for alloting the right amount of space. To determine how much area is needed for a function, refer to Table 1 Function Room Space Requirements and Table 2 Banquet Seating Space Requirements. The guidelines in Table 1 are for the amount of space needed for seating and a standard front-screen presentation.

Design Trends

Design trends are extremely subjective and require the event designer to stay up to date on current styles and how these might be integrated in creating appealing environments. Guidance and inspiration can be obtained from Web sites, social media, and being in tune with popular culture.

Develop relationships with a variety of suppliers who provide the elements that may come into your overall design: furniture, staging, signage/graphics, floral arrangements and other centrepieces, décor mediums, and technology. These experts will help you stay current with what is possible and what is available in the marketplace. Many suppliers rent furniture and décor; these items must have multiple applications over a number of years to be affordable for the provider. Using them is an excellent sustainable choice to make for your event. Talk with your suppliers about what can be re-used or repurposed versus a new build or purchase. This is often a more budget-friendly option. When working with florists, ask about items that are in season at the time of your event and what can be sourced regionally to meet the sustainable vision of the event. Like food, floral arrangements should be considered and ordered from a FLOSS (fresh, local, organic, seasonal, and sustainable) perspective whenever possible.

Props, Scenery, and Decorations

To create a meaningful environment, the event professional must consider the space from the first entrance to the final exit, and all spaces in-between. How you use the venue and enhance the space with props, scenery, and decorations is part art and part science.

Props refer to any pieces added to a room that are for decorative or branding value. They are typically large pieces that draw the eye. Scenery applies to elements on a stage or a room periphery that create a visual background. Decorations are typically the smaller elements in a design, from centrepieces on a dining table to small elements in lounge groupings or reception settings. Each has its place and can be used in conjunction with the overall room set to build out an event's theme and the host's brand.

While your theme may dictate unique and new scenery or props, and the budget may allow this expenditure, at most destinations, abundant rental scenery and props are available. Re-using

Table 1 Function Room Space Requirements.

Set-up style	Space per person	Notes
Reception	9 to 10 sq. ft. (.84 to .93 sq. m)	If you have a reception with entertainment, décor, and many food stations, or if you wish to have seating at your reception, calculate the square footage those items will take and add them to the total needed. The space shown per person is for a standard bar with light hors d'oeuvres (not dinner).
Theatre: Less than 60 people	12 to 13 sq. ft. (1.1 to 1.2 sq. m)	Allows at least 24 in. (61 cm) of space between rows and 4 in. (10 cm) side to side between seats. Most facilities provide only 20 in (51 cm) between rows, which is insufficient. Don't allow your chairs to touch.
Theatre: 60 to 300 people	11 to 12 sq. ft. (1.0 to 1.1 sq. m)	Same set-up rules
Theatre: More than 300 people	10 to 11 sq. ft. (.93 to 1.0 sq. m)	Same set-up rules
Schoolroom: General	17 to 22 sq. ft. (1.6 to 2.0 sq. m)	Allows for use of rectangular tables that are 6 or 8 ft (1.8 or 2.4 m) long and 18 in (46 cm) wide, with 2 ft (.61 m) per person and 3.5 ft (1.1 m) between tables as the minimum for a comfortable set. Beware of sets with 3 ft (.91 m) or less between tables—that is too tight. When using 30-in (76 cm) tables, add 1 square ft (0.1 square m) per person to these figures. Always use the larger area per person when the speaker is on the long wall, since this set is less efficient.
Schoolroom: Less than 60 people	22 to 23 sq. ft. (2.0 to 2.1 sq. m)	Same set-up rules
Schoolroom: 60 to 300 people	20 to 21 sq. ft. (1.9 to 1.95 sq. m)	Same set-up rules
Schoolroom: More than 300 people	17 to 18 sq. ft. (1.6 to 1.7 sq. m)	Same set-up rules

Table 2 Banquet Seating Space Requirements.

Table Diameter	Number of People per Table		
	Comfortable	Maximum	Too Tight*
60 in. (152 cm)	8 people 13.5 sq. ft. per person (1.25 sq. m)	9 people 12.5 sq. ft. per person (1.16 sq. m)	10 people 11.5 sq. ft. per person (1.07 sq. m)
66 in. (168 cm)	9 people 13.5 sq. ft. per person (1.25 sq. m)	10 people 12.5 sq. ft. per person (1.16 sq. m)	11 people 11.5 sq. ft. per person (1.07 sq. m)
72 in. (183 cm)	10 people 13.5 sq. ft. per person (1.25 sq. m)	11 people 12.5 sq. ft. per person (1.16 sq. m)	12 people 11.5 sq. ft. per person (1.07 sq. m)

* There are two problems when you put this many people at one table: The chairs touch each other (side to side) before they are fully under the table, and each guest gets only 18 inches (46 cm) of table space, which is too little for comfort. If wine service is planned, the area available per person gets even more crowded.

existing items is one part of sustainable planning and, where possible, should be considered. Look for props or scenery that can be used in a new way rather than duplicating precise layouts from previous events. For instance, a prop that was used to create a gateway to the on-site registration and check-in areas could be re-used, with slight modification, as the background for an entertainer or presenter. Potted plants once used to decorate a stage could be re-used, with minimal maintenance, as table decorations, as long as the size of the plants does not interfere with face-to-face discussions.

Identify Venue Assets and Limitations

When a destination selection is made, part of the process is to identify venues within the destination to suit the event(s) that will take place over the course of a multiple-day programme. Whether you are choosing an on-site location (i.e., hotel or convention centre) or an off-site specialty venue, or even creating an event in a temporary structure, you will have to talk through it from the first entrance to the final exit to assess its appropriateness to your specific objectives.

Once this has been finalized, the key considerations to selecting décor and furnishings will include:

- **Available square footage.** This requires a detailed floor plan that identifies all components to be included and will allow you to identify the space available for furnishings and other décor elements.

- **Ceiling height and ceiling structure.** Are you working around chandeliers or trying to hide beams in an exhibition hall? Consider ceiling height when selecting décor and furnishings, such as stages.

- **Existing environment.** Fixtures, furnishings, and equipment (FF&E), walls, flooring, natural and electrical lighting, pillars or obstructions, style, and colours—all of these elements make up the environment with which you must contend. Your décor selections should complement, not contradict, the style of the rooms you are decorating.

- **Access to the room.** Include the loading bay, loading elevator, and load-in door access when planning decorations, as this may limit what comes in or require items to be built to certain sizes. When doors are doublewide, check for removable dividers between the two doors.

- **Time.** How much time is available for decoration builds? Also include the time available for set-up and strike if your decorations are elaborate.

- **Walls and rigging points.** When décor has to be fixed to the venue's structure, coordination with the venue is critical. Check on rigging points and equipment. Also check on staff, if any are required, to install your decoration selections. Some venues and cities have local regulations that dictate who can install decorative items, particularly signage. Regulations are also common on how the decorative items are to be installed.

- **Power accessibility.** Adequate power and access can be critical for signs and other decorative elements. Don't assume it is available or that access will be an easy part of the décor set-up. Power is frequently available in perimeter walls but not in the centre of a room, where you may want to have a feature such as a lighted table with an ice sculpture.

- **Décor maintenance.** Particularly for multiple-day events, some décor may require refreshing or daily maintenance. This is typically an additional cost and should be considered when making selections for decorative items such as live plants, flowers, and balloons. Outdoor decorations in particular may need daily maintenance due to weather conditions.

Elements in the Environment Design Plan

The complete environment design plan is complex and depends on clear details. Key elements include the following:

- **Begin with a floor plan and indicate**
  - Entrances and exits, delineating which will be used by guests, entertainers, and service staff, and any that will be blocked (Ensure that blockages are approved by safety officials, such as a fire marshal.)
  - Existing obstructions, such as pillars
  - Staging, including dimensions, height, wings, and staircases for front-of-house and backstage entrance needs
  - Backstage area, which may include technical working space
  - Dance floor, if required
  - Buffets and bars, if required
  - Tables and chairs in the styles and configurations you choose
- **Include technical elements**
  - Technical areas, including the front-of-house position where your technical crew will sit and operate the show, truss towers, and camera risers, if applicable
  - Case storage for empty technical cases and back-of-house areas such as video production space
  - Location of power drops and planned cable runs
  - Lighting plan, including colours and gobos to be included
- **Conform with branding requirements**
  - Organisational branding, as well as branding of sponsors
  - Organisation's colours versus a unique colour scheme for event
  - Décor location—foyer or reception spaces, function spaces, outdoor spaces, walkways, etc. Outline locations for décor elements, including linens and florals.
  - Signage—see Sub Skill 17.03.
- **Include other details as necessary**
  - Style and size of all tables
  - Colour and style of chairs and/or chair covers
  - Colour and size of any linen being used
  - Tabletop items, such as decorations
- **Meet safety requirements**
  - Draping has been treated with fire retardants.
  - Freestanding items are anchored for stability; for example, with concrete blocks or sandbags.
  - Aisles and walkways are not blocked.
  - Venue rules are followed; for example, no lit candles or indoor pyrotechnics.

Submit Draft Plan for Approval

For some events, approval of the environment design plan will come from key stakeholders such as a board of directors, clients, and the venue, and from authorities such as a fire marshal. If you can clearly show how the design plan will effectively support objectives, it will be easier to present persuasive suggestions to the key stakeholders. It may be useful to emphasise different aspects of the plan when addressing different stakeholder groups.

Client. Whether the client is internal or external, an individual or a committee, you must prepare documents that clarify the general plan. The client is typically more interested in the budget and that all branding requirements and safety regulations are met. At a minimum, include a floor plan that details seating arrangements and is set to scale. For atmosphere, provide photos of the venue and potential props or scenery selections. Make a clear connection, through the event theme, to all selections.

Venue. Any event that will bring in a group of suppliers to create a new environment requires a plan to be submitted to the venue. Typically a responsible party will review this plan to ensure that you are within room capacities and are not blocking any entrances or exits, and that all materials are suitable for public use (e.g., fire-retardant materials have been used, weight limits have been observed, and appropriate rigging has been provided by a reputable supplier). The venue will want the event specifications guide (see the Events Industry Council Web site for the APEX standards and documents such as the event specifications guide), as well as the floor plan details.

Fire marshal/other authorities. If you will be hosting a public event, an event in a non-traditional venue, or one that takes place in a tent, your plans will need to be more detailed. In the case of a tent, many countries require architectural drawings and local government approval. The event professional must ensure that all requirements have been met in the timeframe dictated by the relevant authorities in the selected city, state, or other jurisdiction. This will vary by location and also by the level of event; for example, creating an environment for an Olympic hospitality venue will have more entities with jurisdiction than the same environment for an event that is not a world-class activity.

Communicate Plan to Appropriate Parties

With approval of the environment design plan, ensure that the venue team and your team clearly understand who is bringing in what elements and when. This will require that you supply at minimum a clear floor plan/site plan and a production schedule that delineates the exact order of set-up and strike for all décor elements going in and out of a room, and who is responsible for these. You will also need to review all your supplier contracts and venue banquet event orders to ensure consistency.

Additionally, you will typically move in as another group departs, and there will be another group moving in right after your event. Each of you is likely to need a combination of venue FF&E, as well as supplier-provided equipment and décor elements. If you clearly communicate all your requirements, you will greatly increase your chances of having a successful experience.

Source Décor and Furnishing Suppliers

You may be fortunate to have a naturally beautiful venue that needs little enhancement, but the typical meeting room does require some thoughtful enhancements. In some cases you will be able to work with your venue to provide the enhancements you seek, and it is important to begin this discussion at the beginning of the planning process to identify what is available to your event and how your meeting can benefit. It is equally important to understand what is not available and when you will need to rely on other suppliers. Never assume that what you see is available or included.

To begin the supplier selection process, ask the venue representative if the venue has preferred providers. You may decide to use that list or contact your industry connections to find suppliers active in the area of the event. Larger city centres offer more potential for selections. If you are working with a local destination management company or professional congress organizer, ask for their recommendations.

The next step is to prepare the request for proposals, in which you detail what you want for décor, furnishings, etc., and the criteria by which you will make the supplier selection. Provide a clear deadline for proposals and any format requirements, if any. When you receive the proposals, you may need to form a team to review them and make decisions which will be based in part on qualifications, recommendations, specific equipment to be provided, and staffing. See the Events Industry Council APEX *RFP Workbook* for more information.

When the decision is made, contract negotiation ensues. The contract may specify a deposit; when that requirement has been met, work on the event schedule and details with the venue and decorations supplier to plan shipping and delivery of supplies, placement within the venue, maintenance, and strike.

Sub Skill 17.03 – Coordinate Meeting or Event Signage

When attendees are to be in an unfamiliar environment, often in an unfamiliar city, create signage that ensures that they can get where they need to go with comfort and ease. Poor wayfinding can create unnecessary stress and delay the arrival of attendees, so it is important that planners provide clearly marked routes.

Signage is a constant element of large meetings and events; however, materials continue to evolve. Many materials and types are available; the choices will vary based on each sign's purpose and location. For examples of signage materials and types, see Table : Signage Materials and Table 4 Types of Signs

Signage Restrictions and Requirements

In using signage to provide branding, recognition, and direction to a meeting, there may be many restrictions. Many buildings have sponsor agreements in place that involve naming rights of buildings or rooms with restrictions on what you cannot cover up. You will find that some hotels and other venues will not allow any signage at all in their lobbies. Hanging of items may be restricted

Table 3 Signage Materials.

Corrugated plastic/ alligator board	This plastic surface is durable, light, and, in some countries, recyclable if printed. Good when you are shipping signage great distances and need it to arrive intact. It is inexpensive, and you will often see it used in trade shows or at hospitality desks for booth headers.
Closed-cell polyvinyl chloride (PVC) sheet	This hard plastic is also recyclable in some locales. It is thick, durable, and fits well into many hard sets, such as existing exhibition stand construction systems. It is heavy and not the most suitable for shipping in large quantities, but is very durable and stores well.
Showcard	Moderately durable. When printed with soy-based inks, it is easily recyclable.
Foamcore	A light material best suited for décor elements, creating 3D-look banners, or other temporary uses. Does not transport well and is easily damaged.
Vinyl, synthetic non-woven, or similar banner materials	When you are producing a banner, talk to your suppliers about options and be honest about how it will be used—indoors or out, once or for years, etc. Ask for recommendations, as many systems are available for various uses. Avoid PVC banners where possible to protect the environment.
Roll up	Printed vinyl assembled from a small carrier to a large banner, normally over 2 metres (about 7 ft.) tall.

Table 4 Types of Signs.

Modular reusable signs	This term applies to a board that can be used for one or multiple meetings and has space to attach or insert smaller, specific signage. For example, it may have your organisation's logo, but the same mother board could be used to identify breakfast, lunch, shuttle locations, etc., throughout a meeting and can be moved around as needed rather than printing multiple non-reusable signs.
Digital signage	Many venues offer digital signage. This signage may have a cost associated with it, which is generally much less than preparing and printing signage. Options are worth exploring at the initial site inspection. The benefits include the ability to incorporate branding for your organisation or sponsors, use full colour, make changes up until the last minute, add features, and avoid storage and shipping costs.
Hand-held signs	Friendly, knowledgeable staff or volunteers who are recognizable by a uniform or hand-held sign and help attendees get where they need to go can be very valuable for an event. They are especially important at outdoor events, such as walks or runs, to make sure attendees stay on course.

by either policies or a lack of rigging points. Safety is a concern, and signage should not cause a hazard in walkways or at access points. If you have particular requirements or requests, it is best to outline these at the beginning of your planning process—there is nothing more frustrating than showing up with a sign only to be told you are not allowed to use it!

Signage can direct traffic flow, provide information, and support the brand message. Specific purposes and locations for signage will include:

- Transportation signage (airport, coaches/shuttles, staff meet and greet areas, etc.)
- Welcome signage in the host hotel(s)
- Exterior of the building—electronic, static-cling vinyl on glass, banners (water- and windproofed)
- Flags
- Registration/hospitality area
- Trade show or exhibition area
- Floor signage (directional or sponsor)
- Stairway signage
- Food and beverage areas
- Sponsor identification signage
- Room identifiers before or at the entrance
- Staging—backdrop and front riser elements
- Screen styles and surrounds
- Banners or similar hard or soft branded elements
- Podium signage
- Lectern signs
- Name tents
- Set elements
- Bar signage
- Buffet signage (may be supplied by food supplier)
- Recycling bins

Signage may be produced in only one language or multiple languages, depending on the policies of the host organisation, the destination, and the attendees. International symbols for signage are common in public facilities throughout the world and can be added to event-specific signage as needed. They can be downloaded free of charge from the American Institute for Graphic Arts (AIGA), the professional association for design.

At minimum, your sign should include a recognizable logo or graphic and information relevant to the function. Text should be large and minimal, as attendees will generally be reading and walking, or seeking information from a distance. Occasionally you will prepare signs that contain a lot of content, such as an agenda for a day or the week; in this case, use a large sign (8 ft. x 3 ft./2.5 m x 1 m, commonly called a meter board, would be a standard).

Making accommodations for people with disabilities suggests numerous adjustments or additions to standard signage. For instance, some people have trouble distinguishing certain colours (red and green), so black and white signs or signs with high contrast are important. Signage in braille may be necessary. Signage used in the United States does not have to comply with the Americans with Disabilities Act (ADA) as long as it is temporary. However, preparing signs that meet or exceed ADA guidelines could be a strong public relations gesture for all attendees.

Involve other stakeholders—such as sponsors, exhibitors, transportation providers, registration providers, and the venue—to create and proofread signage orders before they are sent to avoid mistakes. Designers are not hired for their grammar and spelling expertise, so be sure to check designs submitted for approval before they are forwarded to the printer.

Attendees, for the most part, will take the shortest or easiest route available; the route that has the most noticeable signage is generally the one they will follow. Consider the most desirable routes to facilitate traffic flow through your event's venue.

Select Suppliers and Coordinate Signage Installation

Often for an event, your signage plan will dictate more than one supplier. For example, the venue may work with your graphic designer to prepare the look and content of the digital signage, while your printed signage materials will require a separate supplier. Banners may or may not be produced by your hard signage supplier.

Effective management of signage includes coordinating the following so you can follow a suitable event schedule:

- **Signage that requires rigging, who will rig it, and when.** For safety reasons, the majority of venues have exclusive suppliers who must be contracted to rig anything that is over people's heads.
- **Structures that require signage.** Exhibition booths, registration kiosks, custom bar fronts, and similar areas often require signage; determine who installs these and when.
- **Signage that goes on easels.** Who provides the easels or roll-up banners, and who assembles them?
- **Exterior signage guidelines.** The venue, local government agency, or other entity may have control over what signs may be posted, how, when, and by whom. Ensure that the appropriate representatives are involved in your signage plans.
- **Signage responsibilities.** For daily signage changes, have one person assigned to manage the signage, and supply adequate team members for this task at a set time based on the complexity involved.

Signage Sustainability

With forethought and good planning, you can impart the information you need through signage that limits waste and harmful materials, and still saves your organisation money. Signage sustainability includes the following best practices:

- **Use digital options.** Many venues offer this as an alternative, both for general information and for specific room information, with a sign at each door

- **Select sustainable substrate materials.** A static-cling vinyl sign that adheres to any shiny surface (e.g., window or plexiglass) might be used only for your event, but its carbon footprint is relatively small. It is possible to re-use vinyl signs for many meetings, depending on the information you include on them. Determine whether the signage material is made from recycled or partially recycled materials, and if the substrate itself can be recycled. Showcard is easy to recycle, whereas plastic gatorboard requires a local facility to manage its recycling. Find out ahead of time what the venue or city can recycle, and plan your signage accordingly.

- **Select sustainable inks.** Many options exist for soy or vegetable-based inks versus more harmful solvent-based inks; ask your printers to recommend sustainable inks.

- **Design re-usable signs.** Can you design generic signage that can be used year-to-year or event-to-event? Perhaps you can coordinate signage with an event occurring just before yours or just after yours at the same venue. This might eliminate duplication and unnecessary efforts.

- **Use materials that can be donated and re-used.** If printed signage is a must, used vinyl can be donated to community groups; some suppliers are turning these materials into delegate bags.

A cautionary note about signage: Even if you have noted Do Not Post on your ESG or BEO, function names often make their way onto venue reader boards. You should assign one team member to check these on a daily basis to ensure accuracy and work with the venue for any changes that need to be made before your attendees begin to arrive for the day.

References

BrainStrength Systems. 2011. *Audio Visual Technologies and Adult Learning in Meetings.* PSAV. Retrieved from http://www.brainstrength.net/images/uploads/av-tech-adult-learning.pdf.

IAEE Guidelines for Display Rules & Regulations. 2011. International Association of Exhibitions and Events. Retrieved from http://www.tradeshowstore.com/.

Contributing Authors

Tahira Endean, CMP
Director, Creative and Production, Cantrav Services Inc.
Vancouver, BC, Canada
Member of International Special Event Society (ISES), Green Meeting Industry Council (GMIC)

Reviewers

Andrea Sullivan, MA
BrainStrength Systems
Philadelphia, PA, USA
Member of National Speakers Association (NSA)

Jeff Hurt
Executive Vice President, Education & Engagement, Velvet Chainsaw Consulting
Dallas, TX, USA
Member of Professional Convention Management Association (PCMA)

Skill 17:
Endpoints

Terminology

Angled hollow-square set-up
Auditorium or theatre-style set-up
Banquet seating
Boardroom (conference) set-up
Corner booth
Crescent-round set-up
Dais
Decorations
Décor
End-cap booth
Extended-header booth
Herringbone (V-shape or chevron) set-up
Hollow-square set-up
Horseshoe set-up
Island booth
Lectern

Linear booth
Octagonal set-up
Oval-shape conference set-up
Peninsula booth
Perimeter booth
Platform
Pod set-up
Podium
Props
Riser
Semicircle seating
Split-island booth
Standard schoolroom set-up
T-shape banquet set-up
Two-tiered set-up
U-shape set-up

Additional Resources

1. The American Institute of Graphic Arts (AIGA), the Professional Association for Design, Symbol Signs at http://www.aiga.org/symbol-signs/.
2. Events Industry Council, Accepted Practices Exchange (APEX). Event Specifications Guide at http://www.eventscouncil.org/APEX/AcceptedPractices.aspx.
3. International Association of Exhibitions and Events (IAEE), *The Art of the Show, An Introduction to the Study of Exhibition Management*, 4th edition, 2013.

Skill 17: Review Questions

1. For a meeting in which one person will answer questions posed by several others, which room set-up would be appropriate?
2. For a session that encourages audience participation and group interaction, which room set-up would be most advantageous?
3. Besides wayfinding, what other purposes does event signage serve?
4. In what ways might a venue help the event professional prepare sustainable signage?

SKILL 18: MANAGE TECHNICAL PRODUCTION

Learning Outcomes

- Determine the staging and technical equipment requirements for an event.
- Develop the RFP for event staging and technical equipment suppliers.
- Define basic concepts regarding installation of staging and technical equipment.
- Identify how to oversee a technical production for an event.

Technical production at an event is one of the most rapidly changing areas that any event professional can master; it can also be a significant portion of an event's budget. Without appropriate audio and visual support at an event, the audience can miss much of the message and content presented.

Despite the rapid pace of change in technology, the basics remain somewhat constant, as well as the guiding principles for effective sound, projected images, lighting, and visibility. Once those basics are established, the event professional can discuss ways to add unique technologies or upgrades that will enhance and support the event's objectives.

Sub Skill 18.01 – Determine Requirements for Staging and Technical Equipment

A vital element in event design is determining the audiovisual (AV) equipment and support that are required to inform and engage the audience. Because the technology can change so rapidly, ensuring that the proper equipment and labour are provided can be challenging. The event professional should determine that each potential attendee will be able to clearly see and hear the presenter or entertainers. This means that audio reinforcement should be intelligible and at appropriate volume for the size of the audience. Visual support elements presented on screens should be visible and large enough to be clearly read or viewed by each audience member.

Quite often, venue limitations can interfere with these elements. Therefore, the event professional should approach each event by first defining in basic terms what is to be presented at the event and then determining the general types of event technology needed. Next, the event professional will examine the proposed space to make sure that it is suitable to contain the equipment identified to meet the event's needs effectively.

Once the event professional has determined the needs of the programme, as well as the limitations and advantages of the selected venue, he or she can focus on the categories of support needed to meet the event's objectives. The event professional must be aware of any venue rules, labour contracts, fire permits, and any other legal or safety-related issues that will impact the venue and potential choices for technology and production equipment.

Venue Considerations

When looking at a venue, the event professional should understand how the room configuration would either allow or hinder event technology support. Elements to consider and document regarding the venue (subject to production design) include:

- **Room capacity charts**. Note exact room dimensions, not just room capacities. Many venue room capacity charts are written to listed legal maximums and do not account for the space needed to add staging, screens, and technology to a meeting.
- **Ceiling heights**. Note any changes in height or soffits (lowered part of a ceiling), and verify the height of each. Note also the height and width of doorways and critical access points for delivery of technical and production equipment.
- **Availability of power**. Note the location, type, and capacity of all room electrical power.

- **Room lighting and control**. Note the type of lighting in the space. Determine whether this lighting will need to be augmented for the planned production. Note the location of lighting controls.
- **Loading dock**. Note the location, size, and height of the loading dock, and whether a lift gate will be needed.
- **House sound system**. The venue-provided sound system should be tested, as some sound systems are unsuitable for a variety of reasons, depending on event design.
- **Walls**. Note the thickness and composition of walls, as noise can often travel through thin partition walls. Hollow-core walls and doors conduct more noise than thick, solid wood or fibrous materials.

Room dimensions provided by the venue should be verified for accuracy. If possible, ask the venue for an architectural or scale drawing. If you have the appropriate software, ask for a **computer assisted design (CAD)** file that allows you or your technology supplier to position all items in the room, and submit the plan for fire marshal (or equivalent) approval when required.

Often the highest point of a room will be listed on a capacity chart, but elements in the room can cause the effective height to be lower. Chandeliers can impede screens and projection. Low soffits can prevent draping from being raised to its full height. A ceiling that is too low can mean that projection screens cannot be raised high enough for the entire audience to see the presentation.

To an event professional, electrical power means much more than simple wall outlets. When evaluating a venue and a room, document the location of the closest power panel that the engineers can connect to for the higher power needs of modern technology equipment. Note the type of power outlets available (varies by country). On occasion, more than one panel may be required for a large event. When the venue's power is not suitable or even available for the event's needs, a generator can be brought in at additional cost, and long cables can be run to bring necessary power into a room. If you are supporting a trade event with exhibitors, you will likely need to work with the venue's engineering staff or your production team to ensure that ample power can be distributed to the exhibitors and to confirm applicable costs.

In addition to power, many exhibitors and attendees may have Internet access requirements. The APEX Event Bandwidth Estimator on the Events Industry Council's Web site is a free tool to help event professionals determine bandwidth requirements.

Look at the venue lighting and note how it is adjusted. Venues can be lit in myriad ways, some of them not very flattering or suitable to the type of event that is being planned. Evaluate whether the lighting can be set at the intensity needed for the event, or if additional lighting will be required to satisfy the recommendations of the audiovisual provider. Some venues may be equipped only with non-dimmable lights like fluorescent or sodium-vapor lights; these may need to be augmented at additional cost. Some types of lights can take a long time to come back on after being turned off; this may not be suitable for the event's needs. The control of room lighting is vital for many events, to set a desired intensity level. Make sure the room controls are easily accessible. Since lighting can have such a profound impact on the way people feel in a room, working with a lighting professional is a good investment for more elaborate events.

Other physical aspects of the venue should be noted as well. The location of the loading dock and its arrangements can have an impact on your move in/out time; costs may also be affected due to the dock's distance from or availability to the space where the event will be held. Some facilities will charge for equipment transfer service from the dock to the location within the venue where that equipment will be put to use; this fee should be included in the budget.

Mirrors, columns, windows, and other room architectural features can impact your technology choices. Mirrors can cause unwanted reflections, columns can interfere with the audience's ability to see presenters or screens, and windows may need to be draped or covered at additional cost. Think about how each feature of the room can impact your technology needs, and try to minimize the challenges and added costs by avoiding decisions that will have a major negative impact. For example, consider adding multiple smaller screens in a room with low ceiling heights to allow for better visibility if a large screen cannot be raised to an appropriate height.

Listen to the installed house sound system (if there is one). Some systems may be new and state-of-the-art, but others may be old and unsuitable for your event. Your ears will be your best guide to deciding whether the sound system is acceptable or if other equipment should be brought in.

Technology Considerations

Event professionals should look at each recommended piece of technology and evaluate how it supports the event's goals and objectives. Costs must also be considered. Often cost savings can be made by selecting older equipment or technology that can deliver similar or equivalent results.

Cultivate contacts among event technology suppliers; ask them questions about their quotes to learn their rationale and reasons why they chose a piece of equipment for your event. Over time, you will develop some trusted advisors who can keep you informed about new technologies that might fit your event and to whom you can turn when designing the specifications to support an upcoming event.

While technology is constantly changing, some constant basics fit the needs of most events. To start the process, the event professional sends an RFP to potential AV providers. In response, the suppliers will design a system to maximize the use of the space, meet the audience needs, and provide the equipment and labour required. Some items may be priced line by line, and others may be quoted as a system price. Proposals will break down equipment and labour costs to the following basic categories:

- Audio
- Visual
- Digital
- Lighting
- Scenic or staging
- Labour
- Transportation and expenses

Audio   A well-designed audio system will create even sound dispersion and an audible and comfortable level throughout the audience. This can be accomplished via a house-installed audio system or an external system supplied by the selected AV company. The basic parts of any audio system will be:

- An input source, such as a microphone or a playback device.
- A mixer and any items used to change the properties of the sound or switch between microphones.
- Speakers or other output devices that amplify and carry the sound waves to the audience.

Event technology suppliers carry a large volume and selection of microphones; they will attempt to match the use of the microphone, the presenter's preferences, and the situation, according to a specific type from their selection. Most types of microphones are available as either wireless or wired versions.

Additional expenses can occur when numerous wireless microphones are called for at an event, so make sure you discuss this topic in detail with your potential supplier. Ask about any venue-specific concerns that can affect wireless reception. These concerns can involve nearby external situations, such military or municipal public safety traffic, or even multiple competing events at the venue that could be on similar frequencies.

Anytime you have more than one source to be amplified, you will need a **mixer**, which takes all the signals from microphones and any other devices that need to be played audibly for the audience. It allows the technician to combine and balance all of those sources and send them along to the amplification system. Once the sound is sent from the mixer, it travels to an **amplifier**, which then increases the sound levels of the signal to be sent out of the speakers and into the room.

Processing and effects are additional tools used by your technician to alter the properties of the sound in myriad ways. One of the most common is an **equalizer**, which allows the technician to boost or decrease specific bands of the audio spectrum. In this way, the technician can alter the properties of the sound to be more natural and decrease the potential for feedback.

Numerous ways exist to design a speaker system, many of which will depend on the venue, the selected room in that venue, and content. Every system will have one or more main speakers that will carry the majority of the sound levels. These can be placed on stands, on staging, on the ground, or hung in the air. These choices will depend on many factors, including room features and audience size.

Depending on the event's needs and the system design chosen by the supplier, the audio system may also use:

- **Subwoofers** (a non-directional speaker used to increase the very lowest frequencies of things like music or video playback).
- **Delay, centre**, and other **fill-type speakers** (mostly small speakers used to cover areas out of the range of the main speakers' projection areas).
- **Monitor or fold-back speakers** (speakers used to let presenters or musicians hear themselves and other sources—like questions from the audience—without straining to hear the main system, which is directed away from them and toward the audience).

Visual In such a rapidly changing landscape, it makes little sense to write too much about specific technologies. We can, though, examine the objectives that should be met by a well-designed visual system. The basic system will include:

- A source or sources of input to be visually presented to the audience.
- Switching or other processing, in most cases, to alter or combine input sources.
- A viewing medium for the audience to see the images clearly.

The most common source now is a computer or tablet, but other sources can be video players or cameras to enlarge or magnify a presenter or items on stage. Ask your presenters what format and type of presentation they use, and communicate this to your supplier so the proper devices will be provided. Some presenters will want to control their own slides or material from the stage, while others may want to have someone offstage, like a technician, to handle the slide show via a cue system. Other devices, such as a laser pointer, may be needed.

As with playback devices, a wide variety of cameras are available for an event. Define the purpose first, then select the technology needed to fulfill that purpose. Will the images only be sent to the screens for viewing in the room or via a stream outside the room? Will they be recorded and preserved for future use or documentation? With this information, your supplier will be able to match the type of camera or cameras needed to your purpose.

If you are documenting the presentation, one key decision is what you want preserved. This can require a single camera, multiple cameras and angles, or a recording of the feed sent to a screen that includes all graphics exactly as presented. These decisions have ramifications and should be discussed with your supplier to make the best choices to achieve the event's goals.

Mixing and processing video signals are in some ways very similar to mixing and processing audio. The supplier will combine the various devices sending visual signals into a single balanced feed that is sent to the screens for the audience. Many technologies are available, including hi-definition (HD), 3D images, mapping onto a variety of surfaces, and multiple outputs of different feeds. Make the event's needs clear to the supplier, then ask if any technologies fit those needs. Don't add something just because it's new. Complex technologies can have a great impact on your meeting, but your event may not realize that value if technologies are added unnecessarily or inappropriately.

The viewing medium will typically be some type of screen, but it can involve technologies such as **light emitting diode (LED)** walls, monitors, blended screens, personal devices, or even projection onto buildings, water, or smoke. When determining screen placement, it can be helpful to create a floor plan detailing any obstructions and desired sight lines. The following section on screen placement is adapted, with permission, from the *Events Industry Council Manual, 8th edition.*

- The screen should be at least 5 ft. (1.52 m) off the floor.
- The distance from the projector to the screen should be at least 1.5 times the width of the screen.
- The projection platform must be placed at 90 degrees to the screen.
- The projection platform must elevate the projector to at least the bottom of the screen.
- One other factor that may drive screen placement is how the audience is seated. Follow these guidelines when you decide how and where to place the screens:
  - The first row of seating should be no closer than twice the height of the screen.
  - The back row of the audience should be no more than eight times the height of the screen. Naturally, there are always exceptions, but visibility of the screens is important for all concerned.

Lighting   The lighting category includes obvious sources of light as well as other elements, such as power distribution, cables, and special effects. Adding lighting can be one of the best ways to change a drab venue into something vibrant and exciting. Generally, one or more instruments providing light should be available, as well as dimming and control units.

The basic tools of lighting have improved in efficiency and quality, but have changed much less than audio or video. These basic tools include:

- An **ellipsoidal** (or **Leko**) **light** source, which is a focused beam of light that can be shaped and controlled. A fabricated insert called a **"gobo"** can be inserted to further shape the light into graphics or scenery or to project a logo for branding purposes.
- A **par** is a less focused or shaped light used to wash a broader area with an even light.
- A **fresnel** is a softer, beam-focusing light.

In the past, light could be coloured by placing a frame with a coloured gel in front of the beam. In recent years, though, higher quality LED lights have entered the market, and they allow nearly any colour to be created by adjusting to the light itself (either remotely or at the lamp). These energy-efficient units allow even more creativity and simpler changes during the event to alter the mood or energy of the room, while using less energy than conventional alternatives.

A variety of "intelligent" and moving lights are available, and they can be programmed to perform multiple functions during the event. They can perform all the functions of the basic light types listed above but are not fixed and can change position, focus, colour, gobo, and even be used as a scenic or special-effect element aimed onto different surfaces at the venue.

The supplier may suggest other specialty lights. These can be used for situations like a room with non-dimming lights that needs adjustable lighting levels during the event. Lights can flash or provide other special effects to support a presenter or musical group. These items should be discussed with your supplier, as your choices depend greatly on the venue and on any requests from your presenters or talent.

Most lighting quotes will include dimmers to allow the lights' intensity to be raised and lowered via a system controller. The size and complexity of dimmers will be specific to the overall lighting system needs. They can range from a simple slider to raise and lower the levels to a complex computer-controlled system programmed to match the movement of presenters or to highlight elements across the stage as needed. Items such as hazers, confetti cannons, or other special effects might be requested to support a presenter or performing act; they are often included in a contract rider.

Trusses, ground-supported lighting trees, ladders, and lifts to support the lighting system may also be detailed in the proposal and contract. As with the other parts of the system, this equipment can vary widely. When equipment must be suspended in the air, the event professional should use the services of a trained and bonded (where applicable) **rigger**. There are significant risks to each element of rigging, and only a trained rigger can provide assurance that the work is done safely and correctly. For this reason, some venues require that clients use a specific rigger to attach anything to the venue. This is done to protect the attendees and to ensure that the riggers are trained, insured, and meet the venue's standards.

Staging Area or Scenic Equipment

Equipment for staging a production may be combined with the audiovisual proposal. If it is included, the supplier will often detail scenic backdrops, draping, and other elements used to dress or enhance the stage. The equipment might even include the stage itself.

Draping comes in a wide variety of colours and types of material. The most commonly used in meetings is a heavy velour fabric in a basic colour (black is most common, then blue or grey). The draping will be measured by section width (often 10 ft. or 3 m) or priced per foot or per meter. It is available in a variety of heights; most ground-supported draping is adjustable to various heights, which should be stated in the proposal. Generally, 5 m (16 ft.) is the maximum height for ground-supported draping. If it must be higher, it should be suspended from the ceiling.

Scenic elements can range from simple strips of fabric to elaborate backdrops built for the event. Draping and other scenic elements can be highlighted with lighting to allow subtle changes to the appearance of the room or just the staging area.

A temporary stage can be provided by the venue or brought in by a supplier. The primary concern should be safety. Any raised structure should be constructed properly and anchored. All national and local regulations for markings, handrails, and accessibility must be followed. When a stage is required, consider the height of the ceiling and any obstructions that could endanger the presenters or entertainers on stage, such as low ceiling beams, decorative elements, or lighting that protrudes from the ceiling surface. Stage height is often determined by the size of the audience, so that people in the back row can see the presentation or performance over the heads of people in front of them. The venue or supplier will be prepared to determine optimal stage height.

Regardless of who provides the stage for your event, inspect it to ensure that its surface is even, clean, and free of any gaps or hazards. The edges should be marked so they are clearly visible to someone on stage. Handrails on stairs or ramps should be sturdy and at the appropriate height. Stages over a certain height will require a rear railing, stairs or ramps, and handrails on the steps. Check local regulations carefully. The venue, supplier, or local DMO should be able to provide a copy of local regulations regarding staging.

Labour   The labour for an event can range from the very basic delivery and pick-up of the equipment to the full operation and programming of a complex show. Depending on the complexity, you may be provided with general technicians or with specialists for each type of equipment required for the show.

If your event is to be held in a country where unions are involved with labour, check union jurisdiction and other labour rules that apply to the venue; the venue should be well-informed on these regulations. Union rules can have an impact on who you hire to support the event and what duties may be carried out by specific technicians. Union rules and jurisdictions in some cities can overlap and may require you to staff with certain minimum levels from multiple agencies. A trusted advisor can help you understand, navigate, and =adhere to these rules.

Understand the local rules and customs regarding how many hours are worked before a technician is paid a premium such as overtime or doubletime. Also, be aware of the time between set-up and start of the event. In many cases, if a technician is not allowed a certain number of hours between shifts, he or she will be paid a premium on the second day for the entire workday.

Some venues may require that you use one of their on-property staff when bringing in an outside supplier to ensure that all rules are followed and there is no damage to the venue. This is usually specified in the venue contract and should be discussed and understood clearly before signing that contract.

Transportation and Other Expenses   You should be aware of and discuss any charges related to delivering, storing, and removing equipment to and from the venue. Additionally, supplier proposals may include charges for parking, meals, taxis, hotels for the crew, and other expenses related to the event. These charges may be significant, so be clear on what is necessary for the success of your event. Compare budget estimates from more than one supplier carefully before making a selection.

The venue may have restrictions in its contract that limit outside suppliers. These types of clauses can add to the expenses if the event professional is not aware of them and they are not discussed in advance. There may be service charges, taxes, and other expenses that add to the final bill. Be specific with your venue and suppliers to eliminate any surprises at or after the show relating to charges, contracts, rules, and regulations you need to meet.

Hybrid and Virtual Productions   A well-planned **hybrid event** allows the audience to reach beyond the confines of the meeting room and join with people from around the world. Because of the appeal and, in some cases, necessity for globalisation, on-line attendees are a potential addition to any meeting or conference.

Some confusion exists regarding terminology used for hybrid or **virtual productions**. The hybrid event has two components at least: one component is face-to-face and the other is from a distance. This distant component may be on-line or may use digital technologies to include speakers, entertainers, or audience members from anywhere in the world where the technology requirements can be met. The virtual event is wholly on-line; the majority of event participants are not meeting face-to-face. **Webinars** are a good example of virtual meetings.

An important speaker may be feasible only if viewed on-line via a remote link. In other cases, significant cost savings may be realized by having the speakers meet in one place, while the audience is present at a variety of remote destinations. From the speakers' location, which may be known as a **speakers' lounge**, **den**, or **ready room**, the speakers offer all their presentations or demonstrations. In the space of a few hours, these speakers can reach groups of attendees in nearly every time zone around the world.

For a hybrid production, an event professional should realize the potential for adding a second project that could take as much time to design and produce as the on-site, face-to-face meeting. You may have to do some testing before you can decide whether a hybrid component will create enough value for the time and money you will invest to plan it.

Virtual attendees may gain less from your meeting than the on-site audience; certainly, networking is less available in the virtual environment. However, many interesting methods are available to make the on-line attendee experience worthwhile. Consider whether your on-line attendees will pay for unique content or if they will pay the same registration fee as the on-site attendees. Pricing considerations may impact how many people participate at a distance or on-site at a hybrid event.

Other considerations for the event professional who is charged with a hybrid or virtual event include:

- **Physical constraints of the site.** For the on-line attendees, the venue usually is of less direct impact and importance. The most direct influence is the availability of Internet bandwidth for incoming and outgoing visual and sound signals (two-way video or more).
- **Programme objectives.** The objectives of the programme should be defined and the design of the event shaped to support those objectives. The task of the **production team** is limited to executing that plan. The production team will consist of key stakeholders, including the event professional or designee, the supplier, and the venue representatives. Distant sites may also need a representative on the production team. This technical and creative crew translates objectives into highly effective tools and services.
- **Audiovisual fundamentals.** The on-line attendees or speakers need technology equipment known as "**CCC**": capturing, composition, and Webcasting. See below for more information about CCC.

Capturing Event Content   In capturing, the main driver of quality and cost is the number of cameras and operators used. Usually a minimum of three to four cameras, with an operator behind each, creates a nice set-up for capturing content. This set-up will result in a natural, close, and intense production view. This is because the production is filmed, as it would be in a television studio, where a technician switches between cameras, creating a professional and broadcast-like experience. For many events, the cost of multiple cameras and operators will be beyond the budget. The simplest and most affordable way to create a Webcast is by using one camera on a stand without an operator. In this case, the image remains the same, and the recording may be less engaging.

Composing Event Delivery   Depending on the length and the kind of session, you may decide to choose a **one-box Web-cast** solution. This device makes a composition of two images: the camera image with sound and presentation slides. The output of this box is not like a TV programme, where we switch between camera image and slides, but a composition of these two images: for example, a large slide and a smaller camera image positioned side-by-side on the screen. As a viewer, you might also see a **pictogram** (a postage-stamp-size copy of all of the slides in a row) at the bottom of the screen. You can scroll through the slides and click on the one you want to see, when you want to see it. The Webcast system will jump to that section of the presentation, keeping the video in sync with the slides. In most cases, such a Webcast box allows you to choose full-screen video or full-screen slides. These tools are flexible and effective for on-line learning programmes. Many systems also have a **mobile app** for use on tablets or mobile devices, as well as chat or social media integration.

Webcasting the Event   The options for live Webcasting vary in their degree of complexity. Just recording for later on-demand use can be straightforward. Arranging for live viewing can call for an entire and separate production to create a quality on-line experience. Webcasting can be demanding on bandwidth at the event site, but if you have hundreds of remote people watching the distribution, images and sound become very important. Specialised suppliers who can arrange for these multiple connections and even interactive abilities should be consulted.

Webcasting has become reasonably reliable and affordable. On-line services may be offered with a **"freemium"** model (limited free services with paid additional services available). When you already have cameras in the event's production, sessions can be recorded for post-event/on-demand viewing, but they can also be available during the event via live Webcasting. Live streaming an event can be costly and is best when it is complemented with opportunities for remote attendees to interact with the audience. Alternatively, recording and broadcasting sessions at a later time allows for editing and for scheduling for optimal viewing in the time zones where the remote attendees are located.

Figure 1   One-box Web-cast.

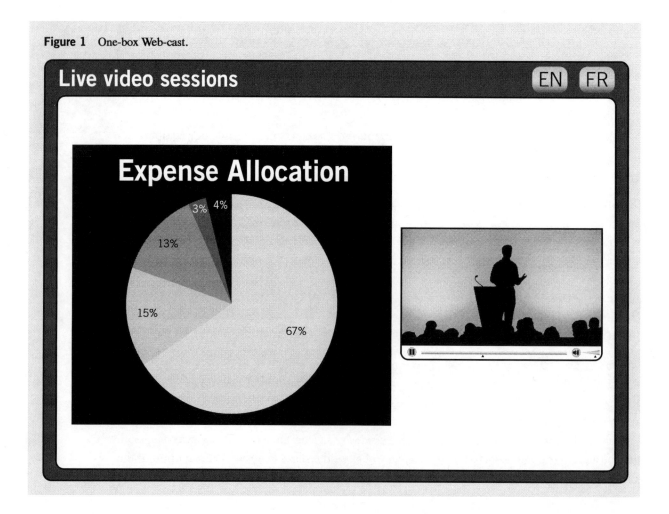

Sub Skill 18.02 – Acquire Staging and Technical Equipment

Most technology is chosen via the request for proposals (RFP); this document communicates the needs of the event from the event professional to potential suppliers. To create an effective RFP, the event professional should anticipate the information a supplier will need to offer the best solutions for the event at the most reasonable cost. The APEX *RFP Workbook*, available on the Events Industry Council Web site includes a section on Event Technology, that covers contact information, the event profile, agenda, history, exhibition information, other requirements, future event dates, and the RFP process.

In the RFP, the event professional should provide contact information and preferred method of contact, as well as any deadlines that should be met by the supplier. Provide information about the venue with as many specifics as you can offer. Room dimensions, ceiling heights, and other information gathered during your site inspection are critical data for suppliers. If possible, provide a room diagram (for larger events, provide a CAD shell if available). Describe the purpose of the event and any relevant details about attendees that might affect the event. Note whether any attendees who might require visual or listening assistance, or access to raised areas such as stages.

The event professional should include at least a preliminary schedule so that the suppliers can estimate the labour needed. Also detail the seating arrangements and any changes during the event that might have an impact on equipment or crew selections. Give as much detail as you are comfortable with about each system you'll require for the event.

Audio Requirements in the RFP

In the audio area, list the items that need amplification (computer, mp3 player, etc.) and the maximum number of presenters who will be on stage at one time; include your preference for wired or wireless microphones. List any additional microphone needs (e.g., audience microphones for questions). List performers and include, if possible, any contract riders that detail specific event needs.

Video Requirements in the RFP

Much of the same information from the audio area will be relevant to the visual systems. Audience size, seating arrangements, and any set-up changes throughout the event will need to be considered by the supplier. Note the intended viewing sources for the audience (computers, video players, tablets, etc.). Discuss whether you'd like presenters to control their own presentations, or you'd prefer offstage control. Consider whether you will need a monitor so the presenter can see the presentation as it is being displayed to the audience.

With numerous projection and display options, you may want to discuss this area directly with a supplier. From audience size, room layout and seating, and other data you've provided, the supplier should have good suggestions on how many displays are needed and their suggested placement. You can also address the question of cameras to record or magnify the presentation onto the displays.

Lighting Requirements in the RFP

Lighting can be addressed by much of the same data about the venue and event. You may want to simply list the areas you'd like to make sure are lit as well as the décor you want to highlight, and discuss with suppliers their suggestions for accomplishing these goals.

Labour Requirements in the RFP

Labour will be defined by the same information. You should be clear about whether you'd like the equipment set up and/or removed or operated. Note any places that your staff might be performing these functions. You should also detail any rehearsals or other needs that will require labour to be present. In this area, you can inquire about union and other labour rules that could affect the set up, removal, or operation of the equipment. Finally, ask for details about any other items that will impact the final price (hours for move-in and move-out, travel, shipping, service fees, taxes, etc.).

Other Supplier Selection Considerations

There are literally thousands of suppliers who provide audiovisual and event technology support. When considering a possible supplier, you should seek recommendations from trusted advisors such as fellow event professionals or staff members. Companies can range from a single person to thousands in an organisation.

The key is to develop a level of trust and understanding about your specific needs for the event. There are no one-size answers. For some events, a large supplier may provide terrific hands-on service; in other cases, a single person can step in and handle the needs of the event flawlessly. You might request references in the RFP; if you do, check with these references before you make your selection decision.

When talking to potential suppliers, begin by asking questions and listening to the questions they ask you. Look at their photo gallery or portfolio to see recent work. When looking at samples of the work, ask specific questions about how much of it they performed (sometimes a supplier may have done only a small portion of a larger event). From these conversations, you will begin to build a relationship with suppliers who can fulfill the specific needs of your event, regardless of the size or complexity.

Hybrid and Virtual Event Requirements in the RFP

On-line attendees and on-line speakers require additional equipment and technicians. If you already have all the cameras and camera operators you need for a group of significant size, you also ideally have:

- A separate sound-mixing technician who focuses on the sound that the on-line attendees receive.
- A separate image switcher who can select images that are independent from what is seen on the on-site screen in the meeting room.
- A separate video recording/Web-cast technician who checks what goes out via image and sound.

You can make the on-line experience more engaging by adding (optionally):

- A hybrid moderator talking to on-line attendees conducting interviews with the on-site speakers, etc.
- An on-line moderator who sits in with the on-line breakout group (a group video call); this moderator can be on-site or anywhere that allows access to the Internet.
- A social media moderator who monitors and replies to tweets, etc.

From an equipment perspective, you may already have microphones, cameras, and a switcher for your on-site production. In that case, you may need to add a few laptops and/or tablets, all connected to the Internet. Individual devices are required for each of the following functions:

- On-line speakers or moderators
- Social media stream
- Webcast monitoring
- On-line breakout groups
- Enabling the on-site attendees to talk to on-line attendees in the on-line breakout group area or pod.

All this on-line equipment, connectivity, and activity may need to be connected to s display monitor, but even in a simpler form, it will require a separate production or crew leader with the right skills. The entire hybrid (on-site and on-line) event needs to be well-coordinated, since increased complexity creates more opportunities for things to go wrong. One reason to have a separate team is that the on-line function should not hinder the on-site function or the other way around. The complexity of event production increases when you turn a normal on-site production into a hybrid one.

Sub Skill 18.03 – Install Staging and Technical Equipment

When looking at your event schedule, ensure that you have allowed ample time for set-up, rehearsal, and any other checks of the systems. Short load-in times can cause stress, delays, and mistakes. Giving your team enough time to install and check equipment and set-ups will eliminate many of the potential issues that can arise well before your first attendee enters the room. Schedule ample time for removal of equipment as well. Equipment generally takes less time to remove than to install, but you should still account for both, as they can cause hidden costs for additional labour.

Speak with your suppliers and make sure they bring or have arranged for all of the tools needed to install the equipment. Ladders, man lifts, wrenches, floor mats, etc., should be in the room and ready so the set-up crew is not delayed in doing their work. Also confirm whether additional fees will be incurred for the use of this equipment.

Air-conditioning or heating requirements may be lower on move-in and move-out dates, because fewer people will be in the meeting space; make sure they are adjusted accordingly to conserve energy. This should be done with consideration for working conditions, however.

Include time to bring the equipment to the room from its storage area or truck. This time can be determined when the supplier specifies the labour required. If the equipment and labour is being brought to the show site, make sure that parking and dock space (when needed) have been arranged in advance. The same applies for any tools needed to unload a vehicle, such as a forklift.

Make sure your suppliers have appropriate storage space; this is where they will place empty cases and spare equipment. This could be done by using a separate room, or having equipment hidden in the room (behind draping) or even removed to a vehicle and brought back when the show ends. You should make sure that, whatever area is used for storage, it meets all fire codes and venue rules and regulations.

During the move-in and move-out processes, you will be in contact with your production team manager, who can provide you with progress updates and answer any questions that may have arisen. Near the end of the set-up time, you should contact this person again and inspect all areas to ensure that they are ready for your audience to enter the room.

When inspecting the room, look at the visual displays, listen to the audio system, verify that the lighting is set and working, check that the stage is placed correctly with no hazards, check that room exits are visible and marked according to fire codes, and make sure all cables are taped or covered with mats that meet venue and safety standards. A walk-through of the area will be essential. Follow the traffic-flow patterns you have identified for participants.

Sub Skill 18.04 – Oversee Technical Production Operation

Depending on the size and complexity of the needs at the event, a wide variety of positions may be filled for operation of the show. A department or specialty will generally define most of these, but for some events positions or departments may be combined or handled by a technician with general skills.

The lead technician or head of a department can be identified as an "engineer." This is an accepted term, although it normally will refer to a level of experience and skill rather than a degreed title. There are not any universally agreed upon definitions, so you will find many variations between suppliers or geographic areas. If you are ever unclear on the duties of anyone listed as labour, take the time to clarify what the roles and duties are for the event. Beyond the audio, video, and lighting areas, you may have positions for carpentry or scenic construction, truck loading and unloading, electrical, riggers (tasked with suspending items), and various show-management roles.

Many shows will be assigned a **project manager** by the supplier to oversee the crew and directly liaise with the event professional. On the largest shows, you may also have a **producer** who oversees all of the details of the technical production and all technical suppliers, including videos and graphics created for the event. A **technical director** who functions with the project manager to oversee the production schedule, drawings, permits, and any other technical details of the show may be required. A **stage manager** who will work with all of the presenters and instruct the crew via cues when each presenter or element is to be started may be necessary. Many of these roles may be combined or eliminated depending on the scale of the event and supplier practices.

Providing ample rehearsal time for the crew and presenters allows them to become familiar with the materials and to work out timings and cues. Even if the presenters are not available, the crew will often hold a **tech rehearsal** where they run through, in order, each element of the show. Elimination of rehearsal time can lead to stress, missed cues, and sloppy performances. Rehearsals also help anticipate any trouble areas of the presentations and make sure that all of the material is correct and the proper version of the digital file is in use.

No matter how prepared you and the crew are, however, challenges often arise due to unforeseen issues. When these challenges happen, speak with your main contacts and let them instruct the crew; often these contacts will have information they can impart to you to explain the issue and the possible solutions. Allow your team to do their jobs and resist the urge to panic; even the serious issues can be solved in moments, and a professional crew will be working on solutions from the moment an issue becomes apparent. Once you have information from your main contacts, you can jointly decide on a course of action.

Contributing Authors

Jon Trask, CMP, CMM
Co-Founder, AV for Event Professionals
Oakland, CA, USA
Member of Meeting Professionals International (MPI)

Maarten Vanneste, CMM
President, Meeting Support Institute
Antwerp, Belgium
Member of Meeting Professionals International (MPI)

Reviewer

Tahira Endean, CMP
Director, Creative and Production, Cantrav Services Inc.
Vancouver, Canada
Member of International Special Event Society, (ISES) Green Meeting Industry Council (GMIC)

Skill 18:
Endpoints

Terminology

Amplifier

Capturing

CCC

Composing

Computer assisted drawing (CAD)

Ellipsoidal (Leko) light

Delay, centre, and fill-type speakers

Freemium (model)

Fresnel

Gobo

Hybrid event

Information and communication technology (ICT)

Light-emitting diode (LED)

Mixer

Mobile app

Monitor or fold-back speakers

On-line production

One-box Webcast

Par

Pictogram

Producer

Production team

Project manager

Request for proposals (RFP)

Rigger

Speakers' lounge, den, or ready room

Stage manager

Subwoofers

Tech rehearsal

Technical director

Webcast

Virtual event

Skill 18: Review Questions

1. What should be considered with respect to venue features that may affect technical production?
2. What is the best way to eliminate feedback in a room?
3. How tall would the top edge of a 10-foot tall screen be if positioned at the minimum recommended height off the floor?
4. What should be included in an event technology RFP?

SKILL 19: DEVELOP PLAN FOR MANAGING MOVEMENT OF ATTENDEES

Learning Outcomes

- Develop an admittance credential system.
- Identify crowd management techniques.
- Coordinate accommodations.
- Establish a transportation plan for an event.
- Explain protocol requirements.

The event professional is regularly involved with managing the movement of attendees from admittance to transportation to accommodations. Observance of protocol will have some influence over transportation, accommodation, and crowd movement plans, so knowledge of international protocol is encouraged for all event professionals.

Sub Skill 19.01 – Develop Admittance Credential Systems

Many events have strict admittance requirements that require the development of a credential system. Other events may be open to the public but still require practices to ensure that payment has been made before admitting the attendee. In either case, there is typically a pre-event registration process or ticket sales followed by on-site verification. In some cases, on-site registration or ticket sales may also take place.

Pre-Event Registration

In many cases, the admittance credential system begins with registration. You may begin the process by controlling who can register; for example, people who work for your organisation or those who are invited to attend. For such events, you may provide a unique registration code that allows access to the registration system. Once the attendee is approved, a name badge (card or photo) is prepared for the registered person and identification would be requested at the pick-up point.

Depending on the nature of the event, different types of **admittance-verification systems** may be needed as part of pre-event registration. Examples are shown below.

- **Private, hosted event.** A corporate meeting may be closed to the public and may require a registration system to confirm employment with the company. The registration system would allow the company to collect other important information, such as dietary requirements.
- **Paid public event.** A verification process may be required for a paid event to confirm eligibility for discounted rates, such as student or member rates; to restrict access to certain groups, such as buyers, and to limit registration based on maximum capacities.
- **Credentialed event.** Some events, such as sporting events or voting sessions, may require further credentialing and verification to register an attendee.

On-site Verification

When attendees arrive on-site, a verification process may be required for admittance. Depending on the nature of the event, the formality or depth of this verification will vary. It may be as simple as presenting a ticket (paper or electronic) or may require the presentation of photo identification. Personnel at a registration or admittance area will manage this verification system, or attendees can scan their own tickets at a self-serve station.

Once attendees have been verified for admittance, they are often given a ticket, name badge, or wristband to proceed to the event. For some events, these name badges are equipped with **radio**

frequency identification (RFID) technology or a simple bar code that can be scanned for lead retrieval at trade shows or for tracking attendance when issuing **continuing education units (CEUs)** is a promoted service. Tickets are suitable for one-time-only access to a venue or specific event. Where you have controlled seating, a ticket that is in two parts is ideal; with this kind of ticket, the guest keeps his or her seating information on the ticket stub to find the appropriate seat. Name badges are helpful for introductions and can be colour-coded to represent different attendee groups, such as speakers, members, or media. Wristbands are excellent for multiple-day events where a name badge is not required but a confirmation of payment and access has to be shown.

High-security events, such as international government or sporting events, will require a credential system, which often includes photo identification for the attendees at a variety of levels. Using the Olympics as an example, this would include athletes and their entire support teams, venue staff, agency staff that will be bringing groups into the venues, officials, transportation, logistics and technical staff, programme staff, sponsors, media, volunteers, host committee members, and families of dignitaries who will have access to specific venues. This complex identification system requires pre-planning and may include extensive information from each attendee, including passport details and proposed itinerary. This type of system will include specific details for each person, as well as the role and level of access permitted. For example, during the Beijing Olympics, photo accreditation also functioned as the visa for all non-nationals, and it was expected that each person would have the identification documents in hand at all times, whether the person was working or not.

A written plan for admittance to an event should be prepared and shared with the security team, registration team, and venue personnel. The plan should clearly outline the following information:

- Criteria for attendance (ticket, invitation, payment, qualification, or other)
- Levels and categories of registration (general admission, VIPs, exhibitors, sponsors, etc.)
- Methods of registration and accepted payment
- On-site identification requirements (badges, tickets, other)
- Requested accommodations, including mobility options, hearing assistance, vision assistance, language translation, etc.
- Exceptions to the standard registration process

Sub Skill 19.02 – Select Crowd Management Techniques

If you are planning an event where the crowds are large and risk exists for crowds to surge, rush a stage, push as a group, or otherwise pose a hazard, you need to be vigilant about planning and assign a team for on-site crowd management, which includes who is watching the crowd, from where, and what they should do if danger is imminent.

A communication plan needs to clearly outline the reporting structure in the event of an emergency. Each person needs to know the chain of command and to whom they report. Access control methods should be established and followed in accordance with local regulations. Some jurisdictions will have regulations related to ingress and egress, capacity limitations, fire safety, and other situations. Depending on the nature of the event, you may require specialist assistance from local law enforcement, a private security team, and venue personnel. Your team, the venue representatives, and every other person responsible for checking access at any point must understand their responsibility and should not allow unregistered guests to enter areas for which they are not designated.

Queues at one or several points at an event are inevitable with large groups. To direct queues and group movement, provide tools that establish direction and order. Where appropriate, keep people entertained as they wait in line. Amusement parks around the world have utilised this strategy to excellent effect; long wait times in queues seem much less troublesome when the crowd is engaged with reading information, listening to music, or observing entertaining activities.

Technology and equipment on-site, such as security cameras, may be available to assist in crowd management and to monitor bottlenecks and other traffic-flow limitations. If cameras are being used, a monitoring plan should be established, along with a communication plan, should a response be required when a troubling situation is observed. A crowd-related crisis may be averted if the event professional is aware that a problem exists and is able to respond quickly. Maintaining a visual account of the crowd, communicating with key personnel, and making appropriate decisions about developing situations can effectively mitigate risks associated with crowd movement.

A crowd may behave in a manner that is not safe. This is commonly known as **crowd mentality**. If people at the back of a crowd begin pushing, it ripples through, and soon everyone is pushing. Part of crowd management is empowering and training key personnel—ushers, security personnel, and law enforcement—to know their role and what they can do to head off or relieve potential problems before the crowd surges out of control.

When developing a crowd management plan, event professionals should incorporate:

- **Floor plans**. Venue floor plans that incorporate set-up information and capacities are necessary for crowd management. In many cases, the plan may need to be approved by the venue and/or a fire marshal. Floor plans include the basics of seating to provide good line-of-sight, the staging and technical areas, appropriate aisles, and any obstructions to crowd movement, such as camera risers, dance floors, and bussing stations. This plan will give clear evidence that the space is suitable for the number of attendees expected.

- **Ingress and egress**. This plan will need to include front-of-house entrances and access control. For example, you have a breakout session set for 170, and you expect it to be at capacity based on early interest or registration. So you have ticketed the event. To collect tickets, you need to have one access point for entrance. If the expected count is 1,700, you will need multiple access points and the human resources to manage access in a timely fashion. Depending on your final capacity, you will need to have all exits from the room clearly marked and readily available to guests in the event of an emergency. If you are draping any part of a room, you may need to add lit exit signs on the drape, if you if it covers any existing safety signage or blocks a clear view of the egress point.

- **Screening systems**. For large-scale events with high security, you might require guests to go through an electronic and/or physical screening system. This will include a bag check, using either an X-ray machine or a visual search by trained personnel.

- **Site plan**. When you move to an off-site venue, you will need to manage additional considerations, including fencing that keeps your attendees in and the public out. In this barricade or fencing plan, you need to allow for adequate, staffed exits should evacuation be necessary. In an outdoor scenario, you will have additional considerations for public safety, such as parking locations, supplier management, maintaining a secure border, and dealing with the obstructions created by power generators and portable restrooms.

- **Signage**. Appropriate signage should be used that advises attendees what to expect from the organizers and how they are expected to behave. This can be done in a fun and interesting way that fits the theme of the event, while still clearly outlining any restrictions on movement.

- **Attendee behaviour and response mechanisms**. A crowd may lose control of safe behavior for many reasons, including a presentation that incites negative emotions or violent behavior. Drugs or alcohol may have a negative effect on the crowd. (Please refer to the food and beverage chapter for additional information on licensing and responsible service.)

An effective response to an eruption in a crowd will be impossible unless your team is trained in appropriate crowd management techniques. Communicate your expectations to your staff and security personnel for watching crowd behavior, for changes in that behavior beyond pre-set thresholds, and for reacting to these situations. Alerts should be utilised following designated protocol, which includes a description of the situation, a call for action, and a direct report to appropriate, designated personnel. Follow-up is critical as well, to review the process of observing the crowd, identifying problems, communication to key people, response, and resolution. This debriefing allows you and your staff to evaluate your plan and its implementation, and to recommend improvements for future events.

Sub Skill 19.03 – Coordinate Accommodations

Accommodation may be required for any type of event—large or small, corporate, association, or incentive. The type and cost of accommodation will vary widely depending on the venue, your group, and the type of event you are planning. Below is a list of accommodation types that are most commonly used for events.

- **Five-star deluxe properties and resorts.** Most often used for corporate incentive events, these properties are designed to impress attendees, and the function space often includes outdoor spaces or views that feel like a reward. Due to the distracting scenery and rates, these properties are seldom used for work or informational meetings, unless they are held as part of a larger or even citywide block of rooms.

- **Conference centres with housing.** A facility that provides a dedicated environment for events, especially small events. May be certified by the International Association of Conference Centres.

- **Meeting properties, typically four-star rated.** These properties are designed to appeal to event professionals, with a good ratio of sleeping rooms to meeting space relative to the destination (i.e., a hotel in Las Vegas may have 4,000 rooms and meeting space for thousands, whereas a smaller city will have hotels with 400 rooms and meeting space to comfortably fit a group of that size). These properties are designed to be comfortable for the typical adult traveler and have amenities frequent travelers expect. Cost will vary by destination, time of year, and demand on the space.

- **Three-star hotels.** Some of these properties have meeting space integrated into their design, and are suitable and used for many types of work-focused meetings by corporations and associations. Typically, the meeting space is relatively small and conducive to small working sessions. Often the services—from food and beverage to parking—are less expensive than those at larger properties, making these hotels a viable alternative for many reasons.

- **Two-star, hostels, etc.** For large international meetings that will draw people from many economic sectors in many countries, having options available and on hold in a lower price range is good practice. Most destinations will have a range of properties within walking or easy shuttle distance that allow you to offer options as needed.

- **Premium/luxury cruise lines.** Often used for corporate incentives, cruise ships are designed to impress like high-end hotel and resorts. The ships have excellent amenities, inclusive rates for function space, AV, food and beverage, and entertainment. The service, dining, staterooms, and public spaces give the feeling that guests are being served richly. Although meeting space is usually available, the events on these ships tend to be more incentive-focused rather than informational or training-oriented. These cruise ships tend to have an adult atmosphere.

- **Contemporary brand cruise lines.** Most of these ships have more meeting space integrated with their design and are suitable for many types of work-related meetings. The rates include function space, AV, food, and entertainment. Usually larger in size, the ships have many activities and events on board for a more active client. These ships have a family or multigenerational atmosphere.

- **College and university campuses.** These properties are most often used during the summer or during breaks between semesters as an affordable option for large meetings to small gatherings; however, some have conference centres that are available year-round. The campus may offer a variety of accommodation options to match the meeting experience—from traditional dorm rooms to state-of-the-art apartments and on-campus hotels. Universities and colleges may offer full-service conference offices that can assist event professionals with logistics, registration, marketing, and other tasks. Most campuses offer several service levels at a variety of price points, so event professionals can take advantage of the most economical plans with few guest services or opt for service upgrades to increase guest comfort, such as daily housekeeping, in-room amenities, televisions and Internet service, and access to campus resources (e.g., swimming pools, fitness and recreation facilities, libraries, and shuttle services).

- **Convention centre hotels.** Many large association meetings and trade show or exhibition-focused events will use a convention centre. As the planner, you will provide room block options in nearby hotels, often utilising 3- to 5-star properties, depending on what is available in the vicinity.

Accommodation by Room Type

Reserving a hotel room is very similar around the world, but what is a little different is the exact terminology. Be clear when you are blocking rooms to secure the room type(s) needed: a single room, twin room, or double room. Generally you will be receiving one single bed in a single room, two single beds in a twin room, and one double bed in a double room, but this can vary in different countries. You will also see terms such as double-double, double-queen, etc.

Be sure that terminology in the contract is clear regarding room blocks, cut-off dates, and review dates.

Many changes have been made in recent years due to the Internet, the modernization of front desk systems, and more brand-name hotels throughout the world. However, there are still a lot of privately owned and family-owned hotels that stand on old traditions.

Reservation Procedures and Policies

Once a room block has been reserved, individual reservations will need to be made via a number of methods, including the following:

- **Rooming list.** The event professional provides one list to the hotel with all attendees included. This approach is typical for corporate meetings, where all travel and housing is routed through one planner and specific internal cost centres. Some associations or small fraternal groups might also use this method to control costs.

- **Individual reservations.** This method is used by groups that have a designated housing block tied to specific meeting room allocations in that hotel. The event professional relies on the guests to select the hotel (if options are provided) on their own before the specified cut-off date and to identify themselves as being connected to the meeting or event. The guests typically pay for their own overnight accommodations. In this case, clear communication is needed to ensure that attendees know how and by when to make their room reservations.

- **Combination.** For some events, a combination system will serve the event professional, in which attendees are responsible for their own reservations, but the event professional makes arrangements for VIPs and staff. Since the hotel may negotiate complimentary ("comp") rooms based on the number of rooms that are used, the event professional may use the comp rooms for VIPs and staff. In this case, the event professional must determine what type of room is included in the comp room package, to ensure that the appropriate types of rooms are available for assignment to VIPs and staff.

- **Housing bureau.** A centralized system for booking rooms, which offers large conventions and their attendees a one-call option. Many cities and their destination marketing organisations offer this service based on the size of the event and the number of hotel rooms in the room block. Attendees are generally able to book through either a Web site or a phone call, and the event professional is able to stay up-to-date with reports on the progression of bookings. There are commercial options as well, such as online group reservation technology providers.

Contracting and Payment Policies

In reserving accommodations, event professionals should be familiar with contracting policies, including cancellation, attrition, deposits, and payments. For more information on contracting policies, see Sub Skill 5.02 – Manage Contracts.

A room block contract will almost always require a deposit, as well as partial and full payment of the anticipated final billing during specific windows leading up to the event. The event professional should monitor the dates and payment amounts and ensure that these payments are made in a timely fashion. For an association conference, where you are relying on a number of revenue streams including sponsorship and registrations, complete a cash-flow projection to ensure that your organisation is able to meet payment deadlines. Many event professionals are able to negotiate payment dates to match registration milestones, such as early-bird deadlines, or they can match revenue milestones to the event's deposit requirements.

When appropriate, attendees secure their accommodation reservation using a credit card, or the organisation pays for the event's commitments. For room blocks and other contracts you are paying for directly, the contract will specify the acceptable currency and payment method: wire transfer, credit card, or certified (or bank) cheque being the most common. It is not uncommon for a hotel to require a credit check in order to establish a master billing account.

Accommodation Requirements

Room blocks are typically based on the event's historical use of hotel rooms. Keeping accurate historical information about room blocks and actual pick-up is crucial to negotiate contracts for a future event. Request a post-event report from each hotel with which you block rooms, and outline the revenue-generating statistics of your event when you negotiate contracts. In some cases, industry associations such as the Destination Marketing Association International (DMAI) keep records of event histories.

In addition to historical information, event professionals need to record special circumstances that affect room block requirements. These records will include:

- Number of local attendees
- Flight patterns in relation to attendee travel (e.g., will most attendees need to stay an additional night, since evening departures are limited?)

- Special programme features that influence attendance
- Proximity of other hotels that may be reserved by attendees
- Likelihood that attendees will have corporate travel policies that require them to stay in other accommodations or at a specified rate (such as a government per diem)
- Pre- and post-event activities, such as tours, that encourage reservations for extra room nights

Sub Skill 19.04 – Coordinate Transportation

Transportation is a basic requirement for many events. From flights to ground transportation—arrival at, travel within, and travel from the destination—transportation requires planning. When you are moving hundreds or thousands of attendees, the details of the transportation plan can enhance the event or leave attendees stranded and frustrated. Each destination will have transportation-related regulations with which the event professional must comply; the country and industry will have regulations; and the vagaries of weather may have a significant impact on even the best transportation arrangements.

Some event professionals rely on a destination management company (DMC) or professional congress organizer (PCO) to plan transportation, using their knowledge of local issues to ensure the smoothest possible travel experience. Many types of transportation are available to event attendees, and they vary by destination. Transportation options include:

- **Air travel** for group and individual arrivals is common.
- **Motor coach** for large group movements is also common; this option requires more than 40 but can efficiently move thousands of attendees. Motor coaches range from 47 to 65 passengers, and the quantity will vary by supplier. Most coaches have undercarriage space for luggage, although supplemental luggage transport may be needed (see below). During the event, you might use motor coaches to move guests from host hotels to a convention centre and back, or between multiple venues for city-wide programmes.
- **Trains**, depending on the location of your event, may work well to transport guests.
- **Luxury trains** may be appropriate for transfers at incentive programmes; many trains of note exist in destinations around the world and add highly perceived value to the event experience.
- **Shuttle services** provided by airlines, the destination, or venues may be used by event attendees. This can be done by giving registered guests a link to book the transport on their own or by arranging a reservation or voucher system for them.
- **Mini-coaches** typically seat 20 to 24 guests and have limited or no luggage storage space, so they are not recommended for airport traffic but work well to supply or augment group movements between venues.
- **Party bus** transportation is rarely used for business meetings but would be typical for events such as graduations.
- **Boats** can be used in multiple ways during an event, including activities such as regattas, rallies, or races. A multiple-day event might be held on a cruise ship. From a transportation perspective, boats can take guests on a dinner or reception cruise, thus becoming the event, or they can provide a unique transfer to the event location. Occasionally you may find that the destination you are using is accessible only by boat or ferry, which can add a unique element to the experience.
- **Limousines** are often used for celebrity or VIP transfers.
- **Sedans and other vehicles** may be used for VIP transfers, and they are often chartered on standby status for the use of VIPs over the course of a programme.

- **Taxis** are typically used for individual, not group, travel. Where available, taxi vouchers are commonly seen at corporate and hosted events to ensure that everyone gets to their destination safely.
- **Luggage transport** may be required for guests who will have an abundance of luggage. For this service, you may need a separate luggage truck with ground support.
- **Float planes** or **ferries** may be used in harbor cities to move guests between locations, as a unique small-group transfer system, or for sightseeing. Float plans range in size from 4 seats to 30 and may be limited in availability. Ferries can generally hold many more people but will have some restrictions.

The transportation plan, like many event elements, begins by determining attendee needs. Include travel to/from the destination as well as transportation at the destination and between event venues. For some events, a transportation plan should be developed that will include arrival and departure points and times, expected number of attendees, preferred method of transportation, and arrangements for attendees with accessibility requirements.

You will want to make sure that all transportation options provided are suitable for anyone who attends the event. Check ramp access at boat docks for grade, for example, if you are hosting an event that utilises a boat, and ensure that guests can easily access that boat and ramp.

To improve the environmental impact of the event, consider the following transportation options and practices: using public transit, walking, use of hybrid vehicles, selecting venues in close proximity (may be referred to as a walkable convention package), implementing a no-idling policy (turning off engines) when appropriate, and operating vehicles at capacity.

Once the needs are determined, securing transportation may include issuing an RFP to transportation companies or working with a preferred supplier. Rates may fluctuate by time of day or night, with very early or late calls incurring additional fees. Rates are also based on demand or business season at the destination. When selecting the transportation provider, consider capacity, experience, personnel training, condition of the equipment to be supplied, and service, as well as rates.

Once you have chosen the supplier, contract negotiation begins, and the contract issued should outline the service requirements known at the time of booking, with a process to make changes as needed in the service plan. As with all contracts, transportation contracts will outline cancellation and change policies, deposit requirements, and payment procedures.

Safety Notes

Some organisations have a global requirement for travel with seatbelts, so finding out if the selected destination has coaches with seatbelts may be a priority. Safe drivers are paramount, and working with professional, licensed transportation agencies is of benefit. Confirm that the transportation provider has valid certificates of insurance. Some organisations do not permit specific transportation options, such as hot air balloons, ATVs, and speedboats. At all times, safety regulations—such as providing life preservers, helmets, or seatbelts—should be followed.

Travel to the Destination

An event professional must identify attendee travel requirements. For many corporate meetings, company travel policies will dictate some of the arrangements, such as using an exclusive provider to coordinate air and ground transportation. The meeting budget should include transportation for all attendees at corporate meetings.

For association meetings, the majority of travel to the event will be coordinated by attendees at their own expense. This may affect the level of participation, depending on the origin of the attendees and the destination chosen. A typical part of the site selection process will be an analysis of average air fares based on the origin of the majority of attendees and the destination; it may also include an analysis of the carbon emissions related to travel to that destination. Rates and the number of available seats to the destination in a given time frame should be considered to confirm that the destination is viable for the budget and the majority of attendees. If alternative transportation methods—driving, train, ferry, etc.—are available to reach the destination, an analysis of those methods must be completed. Include rates, services offered, timing, and capacity in this assessment.

You may also need to note which countries will require a passport, visa, or other documentation to attend the meeting. Ample planning time will be required to help attendees work through the process of obtaining appropriate credentials to travel to your chosen event destination.

For association meetings, include information on transportation and access as part of the registration packet and on the promotion Web site. For internal or corporate meetings, this information should be distributed using the appropriate medium—Web site, intranet, e-mail, etc. If your meeting has a mobile app, ensure that transportation information is easily accessible through that app.

Crossing national borders for a meeting is an added factor for both the planning committee and the attendee. Information and documents attendees will need to register for your event—whether they are traveling by air, ship, coach or rail—might include:

- Up-to-date passport
- Visa
- Health certificate
- Inoculations
- Laws pertaining to import and exports
- Currency
- Travel insurance guidelines
- Shipping information
- Proof of a return and/or an onward travel ticket in order to gain entry to some countries

If the attendees are arriving by air, the following needs to be part of your information checklist:

- Complete name as it appears on their passport
- Mobile number
- Name of departure airport
- Name or number of departure terminal
- Flight number(s) and departure time(s)
- Class in which they are traveling
- Checked or carry-on bags
- Pre-arranged meeting location at airport or within the city upon arrival
- Earliest and latest reporting or check-in times
- Parking arrangements
- Special travel arrangements made to pick up the attendees when returning to the airport
- Train and bus connections to the airport
- Baggage, baggage allowances, and any other labeling that may be necessary
- Weight and size limits on baggage (varies by carrier)
- Name and contact information for the person or company that will be meeting them at the airport upon arrival

- Emergency travel contact information (including contact's mobile number)
- Special security procedures
- Attendee recognition such as a name badge, pin, or luggage tag
- Fees that could occur when departing a country at the airport

Prior to their international trip, advise attendees of the following details (some of this information will only be necessary if the event professional makes the travel arrangements):

- Flight duration
- Type of aircraft
- Any stopping points
- What meals or snacks will be served
- Baggage procedure at the arriving airport
- Customs allowances
- Security or immigration controls in force
- Money exchange information and the currency for that country
- Name, address, and phone number for the hotel(s)
- Name of company that or person who will be greeting them upon arrival
- Transportation options at the destination, with costs and location
- Time of arrival
- Time difference at the final destination

Once they arrive at the airport, the person meeting them should provide information regarding:

- Money exchange areas at that airport or in the city
- An agenda for the upcoming events for that day or evening
- Distance and time to their hotel
- Arrangements for snacks or first meal

Destination Transportation

After arriving at the event destination, attendees will need on-site assistance to get to and between the event venues. In some cases, staff or volunteers may be stationed at airports, train stations, and other transportation centres. They should be identifiable with an appropriate sign, using the event or company logo, or a uniform. These greeters help answer questions guests have and direct them to either provided or public transport, as needed.

For group movements of any size, the capacity of your departure venue and destination venue must be determined. Most hotels and even convention centres have limited capacity for coaches. A realistic plan will be necessary to control the movement of the crowd and transport vehicles, as well as to maximize capacity and minimize the time required to move the people. For instance, if you have 400 people to transport but can only have two coaches at the loading area at one time, you will move 80 to 100 guests comfortably; make sure that the next coaches are nearby and can replace the first coaches quickly as they depart. When you have multiple host hotels, you need to know how many guests are in each hotel and dispatch coaches accordingly. A scheduled shuttle system for multiple venues may be necessary to get everyone to where they need to be in a timely fashion. Work with the transportation provider to achieve a shuttle schedule that minimizes wait times while maximizing fuel efficiencies.

If you are moving guests by air, most countries will have federal regulations in place that require a check-in or manifest procedure for private charters, so they know exactly who is on what conveyance and when; this procedure must be pre-planned and followed meticulously.

In some cases, VIPs may require special transportation, timing, and routing. You may plan this additional transportation in conjunction with the VIP's staff or security team member, who will advise you of the specific needs for this dignitary. Special transportation can range from having a standby vehicle at all times to unique entrance and exit points at the venues being used. You may be given arrival and departure information only. This is perhaps one of the most challenging areas for which to budget and plan, as VIP travel is often conducted with limited advance notice and may be subject to change at any time.

Each method of transportation and orchestrated crowd movement will have unique challenges. Work closely with your venues and DMC/PCO partners to ensure that you have planned crowd movement, timing, routing, and appropriate access points. For large or complex meetings, a transportation manager on the planning team should take care of these details and keep the event professional advised as to progress, challenges, and changes.

Sub Skill 19.05 – Manage Protocol Requirements

The rules of protocol and etiquette encompass a body of knowledge and a set of international rules for courtesy and civility. The basics of event protocol include:

- **Order of precedence**. The hierarchical order of precedence of guests is an important etiquette guideline, as improper recognition of someone's rank is tantamount to an insult to the individual's position or the country he or she represents. When envoys of equal rank are on the guest list, they are ranked according to the date/hour they presented their "letters of credentials." Order of precedence is not based on the size or influence of the nations the official represents.

- **Titles and styles of address**. When writing to and addressing correspondence to an individual, proper formatting should be followed. Etiquette resources are provided at the end of this chapter. The event professional should contact the dignitary's embassy for guidance on appropriate protocol with regard to that person's rank. Some dignitaries will have a protocol officer on staff who can be contacted for guidance.

- **Invitations**. The proper salutation is very important when addressing an invitation to a head of state, ambassador, mayor, or member of congress or parliament. The salutation could be Mr., Mrs., Ms., The Honorable, or His/Her Excellency. Invitation style should complement the event by expressing appropriate formality or informality. Even today, many less formal invitations are sent electronically. More formal invitations are engraved on white or ecru heavy stock, high-quality paper with black ink. The invitation is a large card or a double-fold invitation. A formal invitation is hand-addressed in black ink. For a dignitary, three lines are used to address the envelope:

    His/Her Excellency
    Full name (with no prefix)
    The Ambassador of (name of Country)

- **Flags**. Follow local and national flag codes to demonstrate respect. While codes may vary, generally applicable guidelines include:
    1. When two or more nation's flags are displayed, they should be of approximately equal size and flown at the same height on separate staffs (the flag of one nation is never placed above that of another nation in time of peace).

2. When displaying flags on crossed staffs, the host nation's flag is in front.

3. Flags should not be used for advertising purposes or embroidered, printed, or otherwise impressed on anything that is for temporary use, and they should be kept free of any markings, insignias, letters, words, figures, designs, pictures, or drawings.

4. Advertising signs should not be attached to the staff or halyard.

5. When the national anthem of any nation is played, the audience should stand at attention and face the flag (or the music if the flag not visible) and render a salute if appropriate by the nation's citizens.

6. At an event, the visitors' national anthem is played first and may or may not be followed by the host's national anthem.

7. The United Nations uses alphabetical order in its presentation of national flags so that no country has precedence over another.

- **Religious, cultural, and ritual observations.** Religion, culture, and local rituals will influence how meetings are conducted regarding dates and times, food selections, and even the manner in which food is prepared, served, and eaten. Some attendees will be vegetarian, while others will consume meat at each meal; some meat eaters will only eat certain kinds of meat, prepared in a specific way. More information can be found in Sub Skill 16.01 – Determine Food and Beverage Service Requirements.

Introductions

Introductions are a bit more complex than the basics of protocol. While introductions can be quite informal within a business culture or among friends and colleagues, many international events follow a more formal introduction protocol. Formality is important when introducing a person for the first time or meeting a person for the first time. The first rule in a formal introduction is that only one person should be speaking at a time.

The highest ranking or honored person's name is stated first, followed by the name of the person who is being introduced. In high-ranking situations, the phrase "May I present" is used instead of "May I introduce." Stand to make and receive introductions. Use titles or the appropriate salutation, such as Mr., Mrs., or Ms. Only after given special permission by that person, or in a long-standing relationship or friendship, would you address a highly ranked person by his or her first name, even in private.

A younger person is introduced to an older person. Example: "Ms. Robert, I would like to introduce, Shaeffer Lott, my grandson."

A man is introduced to a woman. Example: "Ms. Albert, may I introduce Mr. Jones. Mr. Jones is the CEO of ABC Company. Ms. Albert is the event planner of this event." Exception: International diplomatic protocol states that women are presented to ambassadors, ministers in charge of delegations, chiefs of state, royalty and dignitaries of the church.

An easy way to remember introduction policy is by the acronym **"HOW"** (higher, older, and women). In the case of rank, the higher or honored person is introduced first. In formal introductions, age (older) and gender (woman first) are considered next.

Seating Arrangements

An event can be well planned, but when seating the attendees, protocol may suffer without appropriate measures. Seating by rank is the preferred arrangement and allows the host to meet the guests. However, other factors may play a role, including language barriers and congeniality.

Seating charts may be placed outside the room, in addition to seating cards that can be distributed to the guests as they arrive. Your staff may personally seat special guests. Once guests reach their seats, the table host should be responsible for introductions and should ensure that everyone is served appropriately.

Placecards will help avoid confusion about seating arrangements and will also help identify people at the table. The placecards are usually written in black ink (by a calligrapher) on both sides of the card and placed just above the place setting. Titles and surnames are spelled out in full, except for senior dignitaries; in that case, only the title is necessary.

Menu cards may also be placed at a more formal table setting. This should appear in black ink on a card matching the style and formality of the placecard, either above the dessert fork and spoon or between two place settings. Your guests may want to keep the menu card as a souvenir of the evening. If this is the case, make sure you date these menu cards and include the year.

Consider the formality of your event when you are engaged in site selection. Highly formal events will run more smoothly if the venue's service staff are well trained and prepared for the dignitaries you invite to the event.

Contributing Authors

Tahira Endean, CMP
Director, Creative and Production, Cantrav Services Inc.
Vancouver, BC, Canada
Member of International Special Event Society (ISES), Green Meeting Industry Council (GMIC)

Michael Lynn, CEM, CME, CMM, CMP, CPC, CPECP
Director, Exhibitions, Events & Protocol
L-3 Communications, Integrated Systems Group
Rockwall, Texas, USA
Member of International Association of Exhibitions and Events (IAEE), Trade Show Exhibitor Association (TSEA)

Colleen A. Rickenbacher, CMP, CSEP, CPC, CTA, CPECP
President, Colleen Rickenbacher, Inc
Dallas, Texas, USA
Member of Meeting Professionals International (MPI), Religious Conference Management Association (RCMA), International Special Events Society (ISES)

Reviewer

Marilee Sonneman, CMP, DMCP
Founder and CEO, Spotlight Events Consulting
Member of Association of Destination Management Executives International (ADME International), Meeting Professionals International (MPI), Society of Incentive & Travel Executives (Site)

Skill 19:
Endpoints

Terminology

Admittance-verification systems
Continuing education unit (CEU)
Crowd mentality
Egress
Ingress
Order of precedence
Radio frequency identification (RFID)

Additional Resources

1. French, M. (2010). United States protocol: The guide to official diplomatic etiquette. Lanham, MD: Rowman & Littlefield Publishers, Inc.
2. Hickey, R. (2008). Honor & respect: The official guide to names, titles, and forms of address. Columbia, South Carolina: Protocol School of Washington.

Skill 19: Review Questions

1. How would the admittance system differ for a private, hosted event; a paid, public event; and a credentialed event?
2. What should be incorporated in a crowd management plan?
3. Describe the different accommodation types that are most commonly used for events.
4. What options are available to event planners for individual reservation procedures?
5. What should be included in a transportation plan?
6. What is order of precedence, and why is it important?

Site Management

Site management refers to all of the details that the event manager must supervise at the venue, area, location, property, or specific facility to be used for an event. The site management process begins with **site selection** and encompasses designing the event's layout, managing the event on-site, and managing event communications.

SKILL 20: SELECT SITE

Learning Objectives

- Determine site specifications.
- Identify and inspect sites for an event.

Site selection is an essential component of any successful meeting or event. An event professional must first determine the goals and objectives of the event prior to selecting a destination or venue. Preparing the event profile, determining the features of an event, and putting together the budget must all be complete before the site selection process.

Sub Skill 20.01 – Determine Site Specifications

An event's location can contribute to the achievement of the event's goals and objectives. In order to effectively select a site, event professionals need to determine their site specifications. Criteria to consider include:

- Goals and objectives of the event
- Expected event activities such as meetings, exhibitions, and food and beverage events
- Physical requirements, including accommodation and event spaces
- Expected and historical attendance for the event
- Financial criteria, including the event and attendee budgets
- Preferred geographic region
- Attendee preferences
- Preferred dates
- Availability of services such as event technology or interpreters
- Sustainability considerations

Site selection includes selection of the destination, as well as the venues used for the event. Resources for destination selection are outlined in Table 1.

Table 1 Resources for Destination Selection Information.

Destination marketing organisation (DMO)	A **destination marketing organisation (DMO)** is often referred to as a convention bureau, **a convention and visitors bureau (CVB)**, or a **tourism office**. DMOs are a resource for all suppliers in and around a specific destination. They are usually supported by government funding, membership dues, and/or hotel occupancy taxes. They can provide you with information on their city or area, including hotels and event venues, transportation, and local entertainers and speakers, and they can arrange site visits. Many DMOs are members of the Destination Marketing Association International (DMAI); you can find information on cities, regions, and resources on their Web site at www.destinationmarketing.org. An alternative is to seek information from local government agencies or the larger venues and hotels in an area.
Publications	Many event publications are available in printed and electronic formats to qualified event professionals free of charge that highlight different destinations each month. Most of these publications also have Web sites and weekly or daily e-mail newsletters where you can access this information.
Event industry trade shows	Many annual international trade shows bring together representatives from destinations around the world to exhibit and share all they have to offer for events. Many include a hosted buyer programme through which attendance by qualified event planners is sponsored.
Association membership and meetings	Industry association publications, Web sites, and events highlight locations that excel in hosting events. You can network with destination representatives through industry associations to learn more about these locations. The Events Industry Council's Web site, for instance, includes a list of member organisations.
Professional congress organisers (PCOs)	**Professional congress organisers (PCOs)** can assist with destination selection and even execute events. There are stand-alone agencies that specialise in site selection only.
Destination management companies (DMCs)	**Destination management companies (DMCs)** possess extensive local knowledge, expertise and resources, specializing in the design and implementation of events, activities, tours, transportation and programme logistics, and can assist in selecting sites at a destination.

Types of Venues

When choosing the **venue** for your next event, consider what type of venue is best suited to your needs. Different facilities to consider are convention and exhibition centres, conference centres, hotels, resorts, cruise ships, college or university campuses, and other non-traditional venues (see Table 2).

Security and Special Needs for VIPs

When considering sites for your event, you will need to take into account any specific security and access requirements for VIPs. For example, a private, secure entrance or **green room** may be required. The venue should also be advised of any privacy requirements, such as excluding the meeting room or event name from public listings. If demonstrations or protests are possible, cooperation with local authorities and venue security teams to develop a security strategy is recommended.

Building the RFP

An event organiser will develop the site selection criteria and will communicate these criteria to potential venues via a request for proposal (RFP). An RFP will cover the following:

- Contact information of the event organiser or person submitting the RFP
- Event profile, including detailed information on the group, attendees, event theme, history, and preferred dates
- Requirements for guest room block and housing pattern, function space, food and beverage, event technology, accessibility and insurance

Table 2 Types of Event Venues.

Convention centres	A **convention centre** is a venue built to host trade shows, conventions, and other large functions. It combines exhibition space with a substantial number of smaller event spaces.
Conference centres	**Conference centres** provide a dedicated environment for events and may be certified by the International Association of Conference Centres (IACC). You may choose a conference centre that offers of a complete meeting package to keep within a set budget.
Hotels	Hotels may have a large amount of meeting space, but usually less than convention centres. This varies by destination. Hotels are attractive venues if you can fit all of your attendees under one roof and have enough sleeping rooms and event space to accommodate the group.
Resorts	A resort offers or is located near facilities for recreational activities such as tennis, swimming, golf, etc. If your meeting attendees expect resort amenities when they attend a meeting, you may need to host your event at a resort in order to encourage their attendance.
Cruise ships	Cruise ships can be chartered solely for your group or you may use a portion of the cruise ship. Outdoor areas and arenas can be used for exhibits or demonstrations.
College and university campuses	On-campus venues are most often used during the summer and student breaks; however, many campuses have conference centres that are available year-round. On-campus facilities include dormitories, cafeterias, classrooms (often with built-in event technology), computer labs and recreational activities.
Non-traditional venues	**Non-traditional venues** for events include historical facilities such as palaces or castles, restaurants, museums, outdoor areas, and arenas.

- Proposal specifications, such as outline of the decision-making process, timeline of the decision process, key decision factors, required attachments, and instructions for responding
- Proposal content, specifying what is needed in the proposal, such as references from the destination leadership or site(s) participating in the proposal

DMOs, PCOs, hotel chains, and specific venues should be selected to receive the RFP. Those organisations will review your RFP and return a proposal in the requested time frame. Their proposals should outline all of the criteria you listed in the RFP, explain whether or not they can meet your event's needs, and provide available dates and rates.

The Events Industry Council's APEX initiative has developed the *APEX RFP Workbook* to help streamline the process. The workbook can be found at www.eventscouncil.org. Additional information on RFPs can be found in Domain B. Project Management.

Accessibility

Accessibility is a fundamental consideration in site selection. Many attendees have specific site requirements related to accessibility, including structural requirements, programme requirements, and the availability of services. Many countries, states, and provinces have specific regulations related to accessibility. Examples include the Americans with Disabilities Act of 1990 (ADA), Australia's Disability Discrimination Act 1992 (DDA), and Costa Rica's Law 7600 Equal Opportunities for Persons with Disabilities (1996). In some cases, venues built before the regulations were enacted may not be required to meet newer laws. These venues should be inspected carefully to ensure that they meet the event's needs. Accessibility should not be viewed as only a legal requirement. It is also an important customer service consideration (Park, 2003, p. 10)—failure to provide adequate accommodations related to accessibility can affect attendance, participation, and the organisation's reputation.

The United Nations Convention on the Rights of Persons with Disabilities provides valuable definitions for accessibility considerations:

- **"Reasonable accommodation"** means necessary and appropriate modification and adjustments that do not impose a disproportionate or undue burden, where needed in a particular case, to ensure to persons with disabilities the enjoyment or exercise on an equal basis with others of all human rights and fundamental freedoms;

- **"Universal design"** means the design of products, environments, programmes, and services to be usable by all people, to the greatest extent possible, without the need for adaptation or specialised design. Universal design shall not exclude assistive devices for particular groups of persons with disabilities where this is needed.

The following lists of accessibility-related considerations provide examples of structural, programme, and service requirements that should be inspected as part of the site-selection process. These lists may not cover all possible accessibility requirements; event organisers should research the specific requirements for their attendees and allocate budgets accordingly.

Structural Considerations

- Ramps and elevators that are wide enough to accommodate a wheelchair or electric scooter
- Easy-to-open doors with levers, automatic door openers, or key cards
- Access routes to the event spaces that are close, well lit, and well indicated with curb cuts, handrails, and audible signs where needed
- Availability, size, and location of toilet facilities
- Egress routes and procedures in case of emergencies
- Meeting room and function space layouts
- Designated parking spaces within proximity of the venue

Sub Skill 20.02 – Identify and Inspect Sites

Selection Criteria

In reviewing proposals, sites should be prioritized for further inspection based on your selection criteria; for example, determining whether the dates of the event are more critical than the precise destination or whether sleeping accommodations are more critical to stakeholders than the potential for unique venues at a destination. You may have narrowed the options to only major European business hubs, cities on the East Coast of the United States, or a leading financial capital in Asia. Whatever your criteria are, you will now focus your search on specific destinations and look into specific sites.

The RFP should be adapted to the types of venues and their norms. However, this could make comparing proposals and selecting one venue difficult. If assumptions are being made by the event professional, these should be listed in the RFP to be confirmed by the venue. For example, when booking an event in university classroom facilities, confirm whether built-in equipment is included

Accessibility, (cont'd)

- Availability of accessible hotel accommodations and dining facilities
- Availability of grass areas for service animals

Programme and Services Considerations

- Distance and routes between locations being used for the event programme
- Availability of accessible transportation options
- Availability of sign language interpreters and assistive listening devices from an event technology provider
- Availability of service providers that may be required by attendees, such as wheelchair repair and veterinarians

Sign language interpretation

When working with a sign language interpreter, many factors should be considered. The first is the specific sign language used by the deaf attendee(s). For international meetings, this is particularly important, since each country tends to have its own preferred sign language. In some cases, multiple languages may exist in the same country. For example, within the United States, individuals use a wide range of languages from true form American Sign Language (ASL) to SEE (Signed Exact English). Placement of the interpreter also needs to be considered. According to David Wagner, the meetings manager at the Registry of Interpreters for the Deaf, in a 2013 interview, a number of factors influence effective placement of the interpreter on a podium or platform. These include:

- *The location of the consumer.* The interpreter should be placed in such a way that the attendee can shift his or her gaze easily from the presenter to the interpreter.
- *The use of screens.* If the presentation will be displayed on a screen, the interpreter should be positioned for the consumer to easily shift his or her gaze between them. If the event is being held in a large venue, a dedicated screen for the interpreter or the use of PIP (picture in picture) technology may be advisable.
- *Lighting in the room.* If there is dim lighting, a separate follow spotlight will be required for the interpreter, or the interpreter should be positioned in the main lighting of the stage. Be cautious of busy stage sets/backlit stages. These can be distracting for the consumer.

Other considerations include making sure that the interpreter is fully prepared for the assignment. This includes receiving supporting materials a few days before the assignment. It's important to remember that sign language interpreters are not experts on the event's content, so providing the appropriate background information is key for a successful interaction. Finally, interpreters are humans as well and require breaks at regular intervals. There isn't a specific formula for the number of interpreters required for a specific assignment; however, generally speaking, one interpreter can interpret for up to an hour alone—beyond that, have a team to relieve the stress and strain of sign language interpreting.

in the rental or there will be an additional fee and whether the university's technical support will be available to assist during the event. When comparing different venue types, such as a cruise ship to a hotel, review all of the services included onboard the ship to understand the equivalent costs in a hotel.

Site Infrastructure

When concentrating on a specific destination, evaluate it for the facilities and services available. You may consider the following:

- Availability of technology resources
- Environmental conditions at destination (climate, etc.)
- Range and distance of satellite event venues for additional functions
- Safety and security
- Ease of shipping and freight deliveries
- Accessibility for travel and proximity to attendees
- Natural and cultural attributes

When you have narrowed down your choices, conduct a site inspection of the venues at that destination. If possible, you should travel to the location to personally inspect the properties to ensure that they meet your needs. Use a checklist to verify the capability of the facilities and determine the availability of services. Bring executives with you to the site inspection if they will be the final decision makers. Include your suppliers to be sure that the facility has the space or access they may need to complete their work. You may also want to include key exhibitors or sponsors in the site inspection to be sure that their needs are met.

In the site inspection, you may consider evaluating the location based on proximity to hotels, availability of parking in the area, public transportation, and airlift. You may rate the venues based on dates, rates, space, guest rooms, and other capabilities or constraints.

Consider sustainability-related initiatives and features at the venue. You might want to include the recycling facilities, kitchen and composting practices, and talk about working conditions and charity partnerships. While sustainability questions should be listed in the RFP, seeing the venue's efforts in person may lead to more precise questions and information than provided in the proposal.

Customizing the Site Inspection

The site inspection should always be adapted to the specific type of venue being used for the event. For example, cruise ships and historic venues will have specific considerations. Site inspection considerations for a cruise ship will include terminal facilities, embarkation and disembarkation procedures, public areas and event facilities, guest accommodations, and dining and recreation activities. For historic venues, the site inspection should include suitability of toilet facilities, heating and cooling, and accessibility at the venue.

Risk Management Factors

When considering a site for a future event, you should consider risk management factors. You should ask about safety issues, including venue condition, anticipated construction, environmental factors, emergency exits, elevator inspections, fire sprinklers and number of extinguishers, room keys and issuance protocol, guestroom floor access, lighting, and health department rating (if applicable). You should ask about contingency planning such as backup generators, evacuation plan, first-aid capabilities, weather emergencies, and the nearest medical facility. With regard to security, you should inquire about security cameras, event-specific security requirements, crime rates, and the venue's safety record. Risk management factors should be included in the site inspection checklist, and the site inspection should include meeting with the venue's director of security (or equivalent) to address these issues.

Making a Decision

Once you have determined the best site based on your thorough research and inspection, you may need to communicate information to colleagues and key stakeholders to secure their approval. A decision matrix that outlines the pros and cons of each destination and venue can help to identify the most suitable choices and can be used to present your case for why you have chosen the selected site. Negotiate and contract with the facility and make sure the contract outlines the responsibilities of each party. Once you obtain a contract, maintain and develop an effective working relationship with the venue personnel.

References

Park, C. (2003). *Accessible Meetings and Conventions*. Association on Higher Education and Disability. Waltham, MA.

United Nations. (2006). *Convention on the Rights of Persons with Disabilities*. Retrieved from http://www.un.org/disabilities/convention/conventionfull.shtml

Contributing Author

Erin Tench, CMM, CMP
Associate Director of Events, The Pennsylvania State University
University Park, Pennsylvania, USA
Member of Meeting Professionals International (MPI)

Reviewer

Karen M. Gonzales, CMP
Senior Vice President, Membership & Operations, Destination Marketing Association International (DMAI)
Washington, DC, USA
Member of American Society of Association Executives (ASAE), Professional Convention Management Association (PCMA)

Skill 20:
Endpoints

Terminology

Conference centres
Convention and visitors bureau (CVB)
Destination
Green room
Non-traditional venues
Professional congress organiser (PCO)

Reasonable accommodation
Site management
Site selection
Tourism office
Universal design
Venue

Additional Resources

1. APEX RFP Workbook and Templates from the Events Industry Council, www.eventscouncil.org
2. APEX Meeting and Site Profiles from the Events Industry Council, www.eventscouncil.org

Skill 20: Review Questions

1. What criteria should be considered when selecting a site for an event?
2. What types of resources are available for destination selection information?
3. What different types of venues are available for events?
4. What should event professionals consider with respect to the accessibility of a site?

SKILL 21: DESIGN SITE LAYOUT

Learning Objectives

■ Design the event layout at a specific venue.

A well designed site layout enhances an event. If you played a large role in the site selection process, you may already be quite familiar with the site. This section will help you determine the information that should be captured before you begin designing the event layout and how to incorporate your event details into that site design to make the best use of the venue. Investing the proper amount of time in site design will increase the likelihood of a successful event and ultimately lead to satisfied stakeholders.

Consider the event's goals and objectives, **event profile**, budget, and historical data as you work on the layout. Historical data usually remains static while designing an event layout; however, other components of the event may change slightly as the event approaches, so it is necessary to review the event requirements again before any substantial designing begins.

Sub Skill 21.01 – Design Site Layout

Determining Site Needs

First and foremost, consider the event's goals and objectives. Other aspects that are especially important to consider when designing an event's layout are the existing site infrastructure, attendee profile, event concept, and programme design.

Site Infrastructure.   The existing site infrastructure will form an outline of the site layout. Obtain detailed **floor plans** that provide sizes of rooms, locations of partitions, and other structural elements, as well as locations where temporary structures can be added if needed. These floor plans should be shared with suppliers who may be involved in designing the site layout, including general services contractors and event technology suppliers. Additional information on site infrastructure is provided below under Site Inspection.

Attendee Profile.   The **attendee profile** is important to consider for a number of reasons. In some cases, accommodating your attendees' needs on-site is required, and in other cases it is optional; however, it plays a large role in determining the success of an event. Several countries have laws governing accommodation requirements for persons with disabilities, including the (U.K.) Equality Act 2010 and the (U.S.) Americans with Disabilities Act (ADA). For example, Title III of the ADA provides guidelines for public accommodations to prevent discrimination and ensure equal opportunity for people with disabilities. In countries that have a law addressing persons with disabilities, it is required that appropriate steps be taken to ensure that persons with disabilities are accommodated so they can fully participate. Event professionals should familiarize themselves with local regulations in advance of the event. Even in the absence of a legal requirement, appropriate steps to accommodate all persons at an event should be taken.

An example of an optional accommodation is interpretation services. If you are expecting a significant number of international attendees at the event, you may offer **simultaneous interpretation** services that often require a designated area for equipment and translators. Although interpretation services may not be required by law, they could have a significant impact on the success of the event.

Other important considerations that may affect the site layout include the following:

- What are the attendees' expectations? Do they typically expect certain areas and services to be available, such as an Internet café or mobile device charging station?

- Are most of the attendees familiar with the site? If not, how much signage will be required and where should the signage be placed throughout the site?

- How will most attendees travel to the event? Is there enough space at the entrance of the facility for taxi or tour bus dropoffs? Are there enough parking spaces available near the facility?

- Will most attendees arrive early or on time every morning? Some events may have attendees who always arrive 15-30 minutes in advance of when registration opens or when the event begins. The site design should include sufficient space for areas that may have a lot of traffic with minimal furnishings or obstructions.

Event Concept and Programme Design.   The **event concept** and **programme design** have significant influence on site design. For example, if an event is mainly focused on networking or peer-to-peer interaction, the site design may include multiple lounge areas for attendees to meet between sessions. If an exhibit hall is included in the programme, the site design would include the configuration and layout of the exhibit space. Also remember that people have a tendency to repeat actions that have positive effects and discontinue actions that have unpleasant effects. An example of how this may apply to your site design is in the exhibition. If your exhibition space design is difficult to manoeuvre and attendees do not find it enjoyable, they may choose to skip their visit the following day. However, if the design is intuitive and the attendee experience positive, they may choose to return to the exhibition the following day. The following are a few additional considerations:

- Are any social functions scheduled?

- Are staff offices needed? How about a speaker ready room or press room?

- Will there be any equipment on-site that requires a locked storage room?

- What are your event technology requirements at each function? How will that affect the room set and capacity?

- How much time is allocated to breaks between sessions? Where will the attendees go during their breaks, and how can the break area be incorporated into the site design?

Needs vs. Wants.   While working on the site layout, remember the difference between needs and wants. A great design idea for the exhibition may prove to be too costly and you may have to decide whether the idea will contribute to the goal and objectives of the event or if it will only enhance the space aesthetically. A good procedure to follow is to list all the design components that must be incorporated into your site, then split them into two lists: components that are required and components that would useful but are not required.

Site Inspection

If you are unfamiliar with the site, a **site inspection** is recommended. A second site inspection may be required with suppliers to confirm that the site layout can be implemented. If you are not able to make a site visit, your venue should be able to provide you with diagrams and photos of the space. Some venues may be able to provide you with a virtual tour that can be helpful if you are unable to see the site in person prior to your event. Cruise ships within a class typically have the same layout, so visiting a similar ship is often adequate for a site inspection, although conducting the inspection on the ship that will be used for the event is preferable.

Site Infrastructure and Capacity.   The following information should be captured and noted if it was not part of the site selection process:

- Floor plan of meeting rooms that show permanent structures (e.g., walls, posts and columns), temporary structures (e.g., tents and stages), and furnishings (e.g., chairs and coffee tables in the lobby and foyers)
- Floor plan of venue that shows the location of toilets, entrance/exit doors, loading area/dock, windows, escalators/elevators, gathering points in case of evacuation, etc.
- Sustainability features of the venue, including energy, waste and water management equipment and practices
- Accessibility considerations
- Services available at the venue such as a prayer room, reservation desk, bell stations, concierge desk, business centre, gift shop, and dining areas
- Areas near the meeting space where there may be poor wireless accessibility
- Capacity chart with room dimensions, including ceiling height
- Floor load capacity
- Any obstructions that may negatively impact the attendee experience (e.g., low chandeliers in meeting room, columns or pillars, or floral decorations)
- Floral decorations or scents that may trigger allergies
- Any areas under construction or any plans to begin construction
- Utilities, such as the location of water fountains, electrical outlets, and Internet hard lines
- Location of any permanent signage and areas for temporary signage
- Number of accessible and available parking spaces and any valet services

Fire Codes.   Be sure that your site plan is in compliance with the local fire regulations, such as the number of individuals allowed in a room and the placement of temporary structures. These guidelines are in place for attendee safety. If you do not follow them, it is possible that your organisation may face legal action or be forced to cancel the event. If you are working with an exhibition contractor or **general services contractor (GSC),** they should obtain a permit from the local fire authorities in order to build temporary structures. They will also be able to assist you should you have any questions about placement of temporary structures or fire codes.

Site Design and Planning

An integral part of planning your conference is to create a document detailing meeting room assignments and the placement of permanent and temporary structures within your venue. This document is the **site plan,** and its main purpose is to show a visual and written representation of your on-site conference layout and actual venue space. Your general services contractor or event technology provider may be able to help you by preparing a computer-assisted drawing (CAD) or scale diagram. If you choose not to request this service from a supplier, there are other applications available to help with floor plans and room diagrams. Programmes that assist with room diagramming allow the planner to take a floor plan that is to scale and place items such as tables, chairs, stages, screens and other equipment. Some applications provide an option to download the floor plan directly from a facility. Because exhibition halls usually are more extensive than a meeting room set-up, some applications are specialised for exhibit hall design.

The Convention Services Manager (CSM) can offer support in creating a site plan, as he or she is usually familiar with the site and has a great deal of experience working with different types of groups. Share your site plan with your CSM prior to sharing it with your stakeholders to ensure that it meets all regulations and to see if there are any areas of concern from the venue's perspective.

Establishing Space Assignments and Set-Up Configurations

Establish your space assignments based on the projected attendance for each programme element or session. Use your capacity charts to ensure that meeting rooms have adequate space for each session. Remember to use all the information you have collected thus far—including goals and objectives, meeting profile, budget, historical data, event concept and programme design, and site infrastructure and capacity—when establishing the placement of meeting rooms. Be sure to take into account exits and entrances, stage placement and AV equipment, as they impact your room set and may take away from your seating space. Depending on estimated attendance, your equipment needs may require you to place a session in a larger room than you originally anticipated. Some examples of space-intensive equipment include rear projection, riser, image magnification (I-MAG) equipment, and rigging.

Begin by placing the events or sessions with the largest number of attendees in the appropriate rooms or spaces. For some events, the programme is exactly the same as it was when the site was selected, while other events continue to make slight changes to their programme as the event approaches. If the meeting rooms have not yet been assigned, begin with the general session, exhibition space, and any social functions. These functions are typically easiest to place, as the rooms dedicated for them most likely played a large role in deciding which venue to choose during the site selection process. Then begin assigning any functions that take place in common open areas, such as registration or coat check. Think about where most attendees will enter the facility and what they will do first. Ask yourself, is the registration desk easy to find when attendees enter the facility, is it on the way to the main function area, and does it have enough space to accommodate the largest number of people likely to be registering at one time? Once the large functions have been assigned to appropriate areas, begin assigning space for the smaller functions. These functions may include:

- Break-out rooms
- Speaker/artist ready room
- VIP room
- Press room
- Offices
- Storage rooms
- First-aid room (unless the facility provides a first-aid station in a fixed location)

The function itself plays a large role in room assignments. For example, some events may choose to place staff offices away from high-traffic areas, so that the office space serves as a staff lounge area during the event. Others may choose to place staff offices in areas that are easily accessible by attendees, such as near the registration desk, to help troubleshoot issues and answer questions. Also, if you consider the function of a speaker ready room, it might be best to assign a space near the meeting rooms, so it can be easily accessed just before and in between sessions. However, a VIP room might be best placed away from high-traffic areas in a quiet and private part of the facility.

The exhibition hall usually requires a plan and design of its own, as it typically includes many components and structures, such as booths, food and beverage stations, exhibition hall office, Internet café, and signage. The design should include aisle locations and widths.

Traffic Flow.   **Traffic flow** will help determine the best use of your space. For example, a foyer area near the general session may initially seem like the best area for registration. It is close to the venue entrance and attendees pass through the foyer area to enter the general session room every morning. However, upon taking a closer look, if even a short queue were to build at the registration desk, it could potentially block some of the doors to the general session, which would prevent attendees from entering and exiting freely. Rope and stanchion (decorative cord and upright posts to direct where the queue forms) are important to make sure that lines flow easily and to help direct crowd movement. Also consider multiple registration areas. Should there be separate registration desks for speakers and general attendees? Where should exhibitors register?

Signage.   Once the site layout is complete, signage will play an important role in making sure attendees are able to find their way around the facility. It is often helpful to walk the space just as an attendee would and find crossroads that may require some clarity. Make use of any digital signage the venue has in place, and any easels and stands they have in-house. Design and order whatever else you need. Consider signage that can be used event after event to avoid waste and save costs. Place signage outside of each room so attendees are able to find their destination quickly. Signage in multiple languages may be needed, depending on the participants and local signage regulations. For more information on signage, see Sub Skill 17.03 – Coordinate Meeting or Event Signage.

Review Site Plan and Execute

Visualising a design or layout is difficult without actually walking through the venue, so another site visit is highly recommended before the event. While on-site, make sure the design is accurate. Are all temporary and permanent structures noted? Are there any concerns about traffic flow after walking through the space? For example, maybe a break-out session was placed in a room and you forgot to take into account a large column located in the centre of the room. What adjustments do you need to make to the room's layout?

Take a draft of your site plan as you walk through the facility and note any changes on the draft. If possible, ask your AV provider and GSC to attend as well. They need to familiarise themselves with the space and it will provide an opportunity for them to request any changes that pertain to them. Update key stakeholders if you make any edits to your plan.

Build in Flexibility for Adjustments.   When adding your room set and assignments into your site plan, be sure to account for changes and make sure that it allows for flexibility in case any requirements for changes occur. If there is a possibility that you will have a popular session and more attendees will attend than expected, consider an overflow room. If a general session room is not in use during break-out sessions, it may be a good candidate for an overflow room. You may also want to place chairs along the back of a room to provide extra seating. Have a contingency plan for room layouts, so it will be easier to adapt should any changes be necessary.

Review Site Plan with Stakeholders.   After the site design is completed, it should be shared with the event stakeholders. This includes the planning committee, clients, facility personnel, and members of your staff. Make sure the site design is reviewed in detail, and ask questions along the way. Someone may be able to contribute new ideas or share some thoughts that you did not consider that could enhance the event.

Separate meetings should be scheduled for each of the suppliers that are associated with your site plan, specifically your AV provider and GSC. During this time, the site plan should be reviewed in greater detail and any questions regarding set-up should be discussed. They will know if any changes need to be made to the site design from their unique perspectives to ensure a smooth and successful event.

On-site Changes.   Changes to the site plan can occur while working on-site during the actual event. If a change is made, a good communication plan is of utmost importance. Who needs to know about the change? Who will be affected by this change? How will changes be communicated? For example, have a mechanism in place to inform attendees in case a room change needs to be made. You may need to change signs or make an announcement during other sessions to inform attendees. Mobile applications will allow room changes to be made directly into a live programme and immediately communicated to attendees.

Site Design Changes and Budget.   Do you need to change the room set while on-site at a venue? Do you need to build an extra stage? If so, have you considered the additional labour charges? Changes can be extremely costly, and additional coordination with your suppliers and stakeholders will be required. Likewise, if you need to remove a temporary structure from your site plan, this could potentially lower costs. Communicate last minute changes to the site plan to key stakeholders, especially if they affect the budget. Finally, make sure the facility and all suppliers know exactly who has the authorization to request changes on-site. Only a few people on-site should have the authority to request changes so additional services can be easily tracked and additional costs can be avoided where possible.

Contributing Authors

Linda Dhawan, CMP
Government Event Manager
Experient, a Maritz Travel Company
Arlington, VA, USA
Member of Professional Convention Management Association (PCMA)

Nicole Schray
Government Event Manager
Experient, a Maritz Travel Company
Arlington, VA, USA
Member of Society of Government Meeting Professionals (SGMP)

Reviewer

Karen M. Gonzales, CMP
Senior Vice President, Membership & Operations, Destination Marketing Association International (DMAI)
Washington, DC, USA
Member of American Society of Association Executives (ASAE), Professional Convention Management Association (PCMA)

Skill 21:
Endpoints

Terminology

Attendee profile

Convention services manager (CSM)

Event profile

Floor plan

General services contractor (GSC)

Programme design

Simultaneous interpretation

Site inspection

Site plan

Traffic flow

Additional Resources

1. Events Industry Council (www.eventscouncil.org), downloadable templates and the APEX Industry Toolbox

Skill 21: Review Questions

1. How do the goals and objectives of your event impact the design of your site layout?
2. What are some attendee expectations to consider with regard to your site layout?
3. How do the event programme and event concept impact your site layout?
4. Give four examples of how to incorporate the event's needs into your site design.
5. What kind of implications does traffic flow have on your site design?
6. What is a site plan?
7. What are three items that need to be taken into account when drafting your site plan?
8. If you are unable to make a site visit, what type of documents can be used to assist with development of your site plan?
9. What are some temporary structures that need to be taken into account when assigning sessions to meeting rooms?
10. What are some ways to ensure that you allow for flexibility in your site plan?
11. How do fire codes impact your site plan?
12. What are some types of changes to your site plan that can impact your budget?

SKILL 22: MANAGE MEETING OR EVENT SITE

Learning Objectives

- Develop a logistics action plan for venue set-up and take-down.
- Describe the steps necessary to set up the event.
- Explain how an event professional monitors a venue during an event.
- Define the steps necessary to dismantle the venue.

The managing of an event on-site requires the event professional to wear many hats and to solve many problems that arise in the course of executing the event.

An experienced event professional begins far in advance of the event, working to minimize potential problems, anticipate the things that could go wrong, and address each in advance. He or she carefully analyses all of the pieces that need to be present to make the event a success and then fits those pieces into a plan that allows the event to flow perfectly.

Sub Skill 22.01 – Create Logistics Action Plan for Site Set-Up and Take-Down

The first vital piece of information to organise a good **logistics action plan** is the exact dates and times your group will have access to the venue. This is the contracted amount of time that you have to complete on-site logistics and activities required for the event. If not enough time has been allowed, either before or after the event, you will need to arrange the additional time or add resources to make sure that you can complete everything within the allotted time. Other groups will likely have contracted the space both before and after your event. So, unless this is handled early in the process, you can find yourself hemmed in and unable to meet the outlined goals and needs of the event.

Once the available time is confirmed, begin to build an **event specifications guide (ESG)**— sometimes referred to as a production schedule—of each significant function and activity that needs to happen before, during, and after your event. Like a large puzzle, a properly planned ESG contains all the pieces of your event, organised in the correct order so that each part happens smoothly and in logical progression.

Unlike an event agenda that you distribute to your attendees, the ESG need not contain details about information being presented in sessions, but it should capture the specific details that make the session happen as planned. Supplemental materials may be included with the ESG to communicate additional information. These can include detailed floor plans of the rooms, room set-up information, exhibit floor layouts, personnel lists with areas of responsibilities, commitment to sustainability, and your objectives and security procedures.

As you build the ESG, you'll need to account for all of the places where different suppliers or parts of your team must interact. For example, if your event technology supplier needs to hang items from the ceiling, you'll want to make sure their time is planned so that the space they need to work in is empty of any obstructions. You can incur additional expenses and duplicate work if, for example, all of the tables are set and in place, then you learn that they all need to be moved to hang trusses. Be sure to specify recycling facilities in the build-up and breakdown of the event, as well as during it, since most waste is produced on either side of the event. You do not want your linen supplier to arrive to place table covers on the tables before they are delivered and set in place.

You'll need to rely on all the members of your team and your suppliers to provide approximate times for each deliverable. Then you'll need to fit each department's needs into the overall time line, making sure that all the necessary work can be performed in the time allotted.

The delivery of items from outside the venue can affect the schedule in significant ways. You should discuss with each department or supplier all items that might be arriving from another location and then make the necessary arrangements for loading dock space with access to the rooms at the proper time.

Items that are shipped too early can incur additional handling or storage charges to be kept until needed by your group, while items sent too late can incur rush charges or may not arrive in time. Each delivery should be fit into the ESG and be clearly communicated. Because of the interrelated nature of all items brought in to support an event, timeliness should be stressed and adhered to by all of the parties involved. Consider using a freight forwarder to handle some of the stress and to reduce the carbon emissions caused by separate deliveries. Offer the service to exhibitors, sponsors, and presenters.

Clarify when the space is contractually yours to use. Make sure that nothing required from any supplier is scheduled to arrive before that time. Items that arrive early may result in storage charges, and people who arrive early will likely cost you for wasted labour hours.

Once the set-up (or load-in) schedule is completed, the details of the actual event should follow on the ESG. Note things like times each course should be served, speakers and the lengths of their presentations, and breaks for crew or other staff. Additionally, rehearsal times should be scheduled well in advance, since they often involve many different people and much equipment. When working with a unionized facility, you should be aware of and adhere to all mandated rules regarding working hours, breaks, and meals.

You should note and detail security needs and procedures so that everyone is aware of the times the room(s) will be guarded and the procedures for anyone to access the space outside of event hours.

Each part of the ESG will be a balance among time, availability, and costs to make sure that everything and everyone flows into and out of the room without undue stress to time pressures. Once the ESG is written, you should distribute it to all department leads for any comments and input they can offer. This gives them an opportunity to fine-tune the needs of their areas against the overall needs of the event and look for time or financial savings. Any changes to the ESG should be made through you, so they can be communicated as necessary to other department leads.

Sub Skill 22.02 – Set Up Site

When properly planned, setting up an event on-site is a well-orchestrated dance among your team, multiple suppliers, and venue personnel. When all of these groups are working together and have a clear plan or timeline to follow, event set-up will flow smoothly right up to the event's opening.

A well-thought-out ESG accounts for suppliers, team members, and venue personnel and their responsibilities. Many of these will interrelate, so you'll need to make sure that at each step the necessary actions have been performed so no one is delayed waiting for another department to complete its responsibilities. For example, you may need to ensure that the event technology is partially in place before allowing the tables to be set in place, and the tables must be set up before linens and service items can be put in place. Complex events have literally hundreds of necessary activities that interlock. The ESG should list each step that needs to be completed and estimates for the time needed along the set-up timeline.

Discuss the arrival of suppliers and their loading/unloading requirements (such as forklifts or other equipment) with the facility and security department. You may need to schedule specific times for your suppliers' trucks to arrive or arrange for items such as forklifts or other equipment to unload. There may be other rules that govern the loading dock area, so make sure you understand and communicate those rules and how they might impact your arrival. For example, deliveries may not be allowed at certain times due to neighbourhood or venue restrictions. If your team needs to unload equipment to begin working at a certain time, and the dock is closed, you can cause yourself undue stress, trigger financial issues, and even have difficulty starting the event on time in extreme cases.

Learn the rules and costs for items received by the venue. Many larger facilities, like convention centres, will charge a **material handling fee** to receive and handle the items, and if the materials arrive early, there may be storage charges as well.

Once materials begin arriving on-site, the schedule will direct personnel in the most efficient way to install and set up each necessary item for the event. The schedule should also account for ample time to test and verify that everything is correct. Your presenters may not ask for a rehearsal, but it is wise to allow time for that anyway. This time can be used by the technical crew to rehearse and to make sure that their systems are functioning properly.

Sub Skill 22.03 – Monitor Site During Meeting or Event

Once the event opens, continue to monitor the ESG and make sure the event is running on time and according to plan. Try to interact with a single member of each supplier's team, and allow them to communicate with their staff members to carry out your requests.

Your event specifications guide should contain a sheet of names, phone numbers, and other emergency contact information for every supplier and department involved in the event and should be updated if new suppliers or on-site phone numbers are obtained. Knowing how to reach the correct person in a timely and efficient manner can reduce much of the stress of any unplanned occurrences and will help you get the event back on track quickly.

The event professional will be called upon to make many decisions as the event happens, so be prepared and make sure you have a good sense of the ESG and the flow of events.

Sub Skill 22.04 – Dismantle Site

In many ways, the dismantling of an event simply reverses the steps taken to set the event up. You'll need to continue monitoring the ESG through the time that the last person and box of equipment leaves the venue. You'll need to ensure that loading dock space is available and scheduled if necessary and that recycling of waste materials is managed well.

Often during the dismantling phase, the staff and crew will be tired; this can lead to unsafe practices and a rush to finish. You should make sure that all safety precautions are adhered to throughout dismantling. You should also make sure that you have allocated ample time.

You will also need to ensure that any items used during the event that are not being returned are disposed of in a safe and environmentally friendly way by your team and your suppliers. Advance research can often find groups that will accept donations of various materials. Any hazardous wastes generated by the event will need to be disposed of in a legal and safe manner. Leftover food should be accounted for and either disposed of or donated, depending on local regulations and safe practices.

Shipping. The following information has been adapted from the *Events Industry Council International Manual* and used with permission.

You may have to ship some items; make sure that all the paperwork is filled out correctly and the items are handed off to the party responsible for their shipping.

Expert assistance is recommended for international events. Shipping products, exhibits, gifts, and literature to overseas destinations is a complex process requiring expert knowledge, as well as detailed planning. As there are often no official, on-site service contractors at the venue, booth installation and freight handling become the responsibility of the exhibitor and exhibition organiser.

All freight travelling between countries must have descriptive documentation as to the contents, dimensions, weight, and value of each item (think of this document as a passport for goods). There are fees and assessments to be paid and import/export taxes from each nation (by providing proper paperwork, many of these can be avoided). Finally, the nature of the goods being shipped may fall under strict security guidelines (hazardous materials, armaments, etc.), and there are global procedures that must be followed carefully.

Professional Assistance.   Since international shipping and exhibition freight handling are quite complicated, a specialist is required to make the process proceed smoothly and successfully. Retain a **freight forwarding company** that is also a **customs broker** (surprisingly, not all forwarders are both). The Exhibition Contractors Association has lists of such companies. Work with freight forwarders and customs brokers that have experience in events.

This company should have bona fide global event experience within your particular industry sector. It is also beneficial if this company has experience in the country or countries where you will be exhibiting and has contact offices both in your country and abroad, as this indicates that their on-site support will meet your needs. They should be able to advise about local holidays when offices or collection points might be closed. Their Web site should be user-friendly so that you can monitor and, if necessary, download key information. If you're choosing among several companies, ask for cost estimates and be sure to understand every item specified before making your decision. Do not make assumptions; it is best to ask for clarification in advance.

After you select a freight forwarder, work with them to choose the transport mode most appropriate for your shipment. Your choices are air, ocean, courier service, hand-carry, or a combination of these. Factors to consider when selecting your transport mode include the following:

- Air freight is definitely quicker and usually safer, in that goods are handled fewer times, but it's more expensive and has both weight and size limitations.
- Ocean freight is less expensive, by 30 percent to 50 percent, but much slower, requiring a three- to seven-week transit time.
- Major courier services may be appropriate for shipping packages; however, their delivery services on weekends or holidays, if needed, should be confirmed.
- Hand-carrying goods with a simple government commercial invoice form is generally acceptable for the European Union and for the United States/Canada/Mexico since the North American Free Trade Agreement (NAFTA) came into force. Allow two days for on-site clearance. Check in advance about all other territories.
- Overland carriage may sometimes be the only available means in certain places (China, for example), and long-distance rail and truck freighting will be common.
- Freight forwarders are a powerful tool to reduce your shipping emissions if you can funnel your exhibitors, sponsors, and your organisation's needs to a single supplier. This may reduce the volume of flights and 40 or so local truck journeys to just a handful. Transportation emissions are often the largest component of event impact when delegate and freight mileage is calculated.

Packing.   Packing event materials requires careful handling:

- Fragile materials should be packed to withstand rough handling.
- Materials can be opened by official inspectors; make sure they can be inspected without permanently damaging the packaging or enclosed materials.
- Valuable materials should be packed securely so they cannot be tampered with or stolen easily.
- Packaging itself should be reusable or, at the very least, not made with unsustainable materials, such as polystyrene.

Banned Material. Some countries will confiscate or delay material that they consider offensive or corrupting. This may include things like fashion plates that are considered innocuous in western societies. Material that could be construed to criticise governments may be refused entry as well. Advice should be sought from local officials, the PCO, if you contract with one, or the local DMO if you have any doubt about the appropriateness of materials you want to ship to a destination.

Paperwork. Government regulations will dictate which forms are necessary, usually determined by the materials to be shipped. All freight travelling between countries must have descriptive documentation. This should include their destination, and how long the materials will be out of the country of origin or in the destination country. Your freight forwarder should guide you through this important process. You will have several copies of the documentation. One copy of everything should be in the possession of the first staff person to arrive on-site and another copy should be in the hands of the person who will receive the goods at their final destination.

Some Useful Terms

- **Pro forma invoice** – a packing list on which you describe what you're shipping, the quantity, the value, the weight, and dimensions (in metric). Note: Prepare separate invoices for materials (a) returning home, (b) to be sold overseas, and (c) to be distributed free of charge at the show (promotional items).

- **Temporary import license** – in some countries, you will need to find out (through your broker, preferably) how tax exemption regarding the temporary imports works. Within NAFTA or other free trade agreements (in the European Union, for example), a variety of incentives and privileges are available to assist organisers.

- **U.S. export license** – government document that permits the licensee to engage in the export of designated goods to certain destinations. Check with the U.S. Department of Commerce or State Department to determine whether licensing is needed for any of your goods.

- **ATA carnet** – an international customs document that permits duty-free and tax-free temporary import of goods for up to one year. The initials "ATA" are an acronym of the French and English words "admission temporaire/temporary admission." ATA carnets cover commercial samples, professional equipment, and goods for presentation or use at trade fairs, shows, exhibitions, etc. It is accepted by 75 countries and greatly simplifies customs procedures. It eliminates or reduces VAT charges, customs fees, and bond fees as well. The only items not covered are consumable or disposable goods, which will not be returned home.

- **Value-added tax (VAT)** – applies to all EU countries, Switzerland, and other countries such as China, India, Mexico, and New Zealand. VAT is a tax on the estimated market value added to any product at each stage of its manufacture or distribution, ultimately passed on to the consumer. The percentage applies to cost, insurance, and freight value and duties; the percentage differs from one country to another. Local VAT on forwarding/handling services is not charged between EU companies with a registered VAT number or to non-EU exhibitors on condition the local forwarder executes customs clearance and transport.

- **Cost, insurance, freight (CIF)** – a pricing term indicating that these costs are included in the quoted price. Cost + insurance + freight = CIF value.

- **Temporary import bond (TIB)** – when materials are not for sale and are admitted on a temporary basis without paying any duty. Exhibition material with temporary import status exempts the owner from payment of duties and taxes.

Valuation.   A word of caution when determining the value of materials for customs purposes, as charges are levied according to their stated value: To save money, list the product replacement value instead of the sales value. Be conservative in estimating the value of giveaways and literature as well, since you might pay up to 33 percent of full value in duty or VAT. Rely on the advice of your freight forwarder in these matters.

Ex Gratia Payments.   In certain countries, it is customary to pay officials for the unhindered passage of goods. Known as "ex gratia payments," these payments might be described by some as bribes; they are commonly reflected in the accounts under euphemisms such as "easements" or "subventions." Before paying, consider the following:

- The policy of your organisation in relation to this practice
- The law in your country of origin regarding such payments
- The laws and customs in the destination regarding this practice
- Alternatives, such as donations to official charities

In every event, consult with your immediate supervisor; you might also examine your organisation's code of ethics and written policies for international business.

Responsibilities of a Freight Forwarder.   Your freight forwarder should perform the following functions to facilitate your exhibition or event:

- Pick up all materials going to the exhibition; in some jurisdictions they may be able to set up on-site customs clearance at the event venue.
- Provide the proper shipping paperwork (forms, etc.) and instructions.
- Offer the best selection between air and ocean shipments.
- Provide insurance cover for the shipment.
- Assist in the preparation and handling of all customs formalities (especially carnets) for goods exiting the home country and entering a foreign country.
- Provide transport from the point of entry to the show site
- Provide show site supervision and services (this is important for your peace of mind), including customs clearance, delivery of freight, storage, return of empty containers, and freight loading and removal after the show.
- Provide transport from the show back to the home location (or next trade show), and offer competitive rates to accomplish this.

Contributing Author

Jon Trask, CMP, CMM
Co-Founder, AVforPlanners
Oakland, CA, USA
Member of Meeting Professionals International (MPI)

Reviewer

Karen M. Gonzales, CMP
Senior Vice President, Membership & Operations, Destination Marketing Association International (DMAI)
Washington, DC, USA
Member of American Society of Association Executives (ASAE), Professional Convention Management Association (PCMA)

Skill 22:
Endpoints

Terminology

ATA carnet

Cost, insurance, freight (CIF)

Customs broker

Event specifications guide (ESG)

Ex gratia payment

Freight forwarding company

Logistics action plan

Material handling fee

Pro forma invoice

Temporary import bond

Temporary import license

U.S. export license

Value-added tax (VAT)

Skill 22: Review Questions

1. What is an event specifications guide, and what should it include?

2. What information should be included on your on-site contact sheet?

3. What are the responsibilities of a freight forwarder?

SKILL 23: MANAGE ON-SITE COMMUNICATIONS

Learning Objectives

* Establish a communications framework.
* Determine required communication equipment and resources.
* Specify event communication procedures and protocols.

The ability to effectively communicate with your staff, **outside suppliers**, clients, attendees, and other stakeholders while on-site is very important for executing a successful event. An on-site communication plan can help you manage on-site operations more effectively. It allows you to easily communicate last minute room set changes to your convention services manager (CSM) or communicate to your on-site team that a speaker is running late for a particular session. Develop a communication plan for emergencies so proper steps can be shared quickly and effectively to ensure everyone's safety. As you begin to draft a plan, think about what communication tools might be appropriate for the event and what the protocol is for each type of device.

Sub Skill 23.01 – Establish Communications Framework

Defining the Communication Matrix.   In order to ensure that you have created the proper flow of communication, you need to first define the specific communication needs of your event. Who are your points of contact for each aspect of the event? If anything needs to be communicated regarding the event venue, you most likely will need to contact your CSM. If you are having technical difficulties with the event technology equipment, you most likely will need to contact your event technology provider. Some communication may not be directed to your staff or just one individual, but to a group. For example, last-minute programme changes and updates may need to be communicated to all of the attendees. What type of communication tools will you need on-site not only to communicate with your team internally but to make announcements externally? A **communication matrix** is a chart that depicts what messages need to be communicated, by whom, to whom, through which delivery method, and when. This is a valuable tool for project managers and event professionals. A sample communication matrix can be found in Sub Skill 4.06 – Develop Integrated Communication Plan.

Types of Messages.   Before you finalize your communication matrix, consider the types of messages that may need to be communicated on-site. Messages may be in the form of an announcement to a group of individuals, or private conversations with your righthand person on-site, or an urgent alert to all the attendees at the facility. Some messages may be informal and some messages may need to be more formalized. Some messages may be communicated with the use of technology, like mobile applications, and other messages may be communicated in person. It is also important to think about who is responsible and who approves certain types of communication. For example, informal messages to the internal team may not need approval, but formal announcements may need to be reviewed by key stakeholders.

Communication Hierarchy.   A flowchart of communication responsibilities is important to share with meeting stakeholders before an event and to have available during the event. The flowchart should outline the distribution structure and identify the approval hierarchy that will be in place for quick decision making. It may also be helpful to create an outline of messages beforehand. For example, if you frequently have at least one speaker cancel at an annual event, it may be helpful to not only develop a process to address this cancellation, but also create a slide that can be displayed on the screen communicating the cancelled session.

A flowchart should be accompanied by a list of all stakeholders and contact information. The flowchart as well as the contact list can be included in your ESG so it is easily accessible at all times. A list of emergency contacts—including local law enforcement, hospitals, and fire and rescue—should be incorporated into your contact list and communication plan as well.

Sub Skill 23.02 – Determine and Acquire Required Communication Equipment and Resources

Analysing Event Needs.   To determine what type of communication equipment you will need on-site, analyse the needs of your event. Things to consider include the type and size of the facility, as well as the individuals who will be using the equipment. If you have a small meeting with only a couple of sessions, it may not be necessary to use radios or push-to-talk phones. Some planners or groups may prefer to use such equipment to contact individuals quickly; however, most equipment requires a rental fee. If your event will be taking place at a fairly large facility with a considerable amount of staff and suppliers, equipment such as radios or push-to-talk phones may be very helpful additions to your event.

Types of Equipment.   Determine which type of technology is appropriate for your communication needs. Table 3 is a list of some of the technology available today; however, new technology is always being developed.

Table 3   Equipment for Event Communication.

Equipment	Description	Advantages	Disadvantages
Walkie-Talkie or Radio	Handheld, two-way radio transceiver	▪ Not associated with a service provider, so data fees do not apply ▪ Good in emergency situations when cell phone lines are busy ▪ Frequencies can be adjusted so communication can be both private and heard by all	▪ Outdated technology ▪ Limited by distance between radios in use ▪ Only one person may access a frequency at a time
Push-to-Talk Phone	Cellular or mobile phone that also functions as a two-way radio	▪ Allows typical phone communication (e.g., longer conversations) ▪ Can communicate with individual or group ▪ Not limited by number of frequencies	▪ Not as advanced as cellular phone (e.g., no Internet capability)
Mobile Phone	Mobile phone that can make and receive calls and (usually) send messages by text	▪ Not typically limited by distance between phones ▪ Ideal for long conversations ▪ Able to leave voice messages ▪ Able to send text messages, so immediate response is not required ▪ Smartphones include Internet service	▪ Requires a provider for service and an area with good reception ▪ Can encounter challenges with busy networks in emergencies
PA System	Electronic sound amplification and distribution system	▪ Ideal for announcements to large groups	▪ One-way communication only
Web-based Tablets	Mobile-friendly computer that focuses on Internet use	▪ Great for communication requiring Internet, such as e-mails and cloud storage	▪ Not ideal for quick phone communication ▪ Requires a provider for service and an area with good reception for Internet use ▪ Requires compatible apps across mobile devices

If you are unsure as to which piece of equipment you would prefer to use on-site, talk to your information technology department and/or event technology provider. They should be able to discuss which is best for your event, as well as the pros and cons of each. Some facilities are also able to provide this equipment. If a venue provides the equipment, the individual contacts within the venue are usually already programmed into the device.

As you will notice in Table 3, some communication devices are used to communicate to one person and others are used to communicate to a group. Communication can take on many forms in addition to the options listed in the table. Signage is by far the most popular and common example. Most meetings have signage to communicate how an area is assigned (e.g., registration area), to communicate directions, and to make announcements during the event. Signage can be printed or electronic, located throughout a facility, or provided through mobile devices, so an attendee can explore who is in the exhibit hall or view a map of the facility. All forms of communication should be considered while a plan is being developed.

Issuing Equipment. If you are planning to use communication devices on-site, develop guidelines and procedures for all equipment. To keep track of your equipment, develop a sign-in/sign-out log. A sign-in/sign-out log usually includes a numbered table with an area for each individual to print his or her name. Each number corresponds to a specific piece of equipment that is being checked out. Have people sign in and out every day in order to check all inventory and recharge equipment for the following day. One individual should be assigned to issue and collect walkie-talkies and recharge them at the end of the day. If you choose to collect all the equipment at the end of each day, make sure to have an area or room that can be locked when unattended. Another option is to use a locked charging dock, which is becoming increasingly popular for items such as tablets. Taking these precautions will help to mitigate risk of theft, as you will be responsible for paying for any rental equipment that is not returned.

Local Infrastructure. Local infrastructure can play a large role in determining which equipment is appropriate for your event. Most communication devices require at least standard electricity for charging. Many communication devices also require a service provider for network phone use or Internet. Most facilities are aware of all the technical needs of an event and are usually fully prepared to provide the necessary tools for any on-site communication devices. If they are unable to provide assistance, they usually can recommend a provider that can assist you. Be aware that to efficiently use mobile applications on-site, you will likely need a strong Wi-Fi signal.

Sub Skill 23.03 – Specify Communication Procedures and Protocols

Determining a Plan

Communication Ideas. If you need to make an announcement to your on-site team, it might be best to do it during a scheduled daily on-site planning meeting. If the message is an emergency, it may need to be communicated to either the group or an individual over a radio. It may also be beneficial to discuss options for getting mass messages out to all attendees on-site via your audiovisual company in case of last-minute meeting cancellations or room changes. If your event has a speaker ready room, it may be possible to push messages out to meeting rooms so that a message is displayed on the projection screen or on the speaker's computer, requesting the speaker to make an announcement to the group. Another option is to have a responsible individual in each room pass messages to the speaker, who then makes an announcement to the attendees. For a small conference, this method may work, but it might not be conducive to effective communication at a large event. Event communication plans vary greatly, and it is nearly impossible to predict every communication scenario. Having a plan is always the first step; usually it will transform into a revised plan that includes lessons learned from previous events or best practices offered by others in the industry.

Communication Protocol.   Discuss protocol and best practices with personnel for each piece of equipment before it is distributed, such as appropriate volume and what type of conversation is acceptable. While communication equipment is very useful, interrupting a session with a loud walkie-talkie is distracting and unacceptable. Some personnel may need to use a headset or earpiece. Also, not everyone on-site may be familiar with the equipment. Communicate instructions when distributing the equipment.

All team members and suppliers who are scheduled to staff the event should have their communication device with them at all times. Communicate this necessity when distributing the equipment. Also, event staff should be reminded to avoid private conversations that can be overheard by attendees or other personnel. As always, it should be expected that all communication is professional.

Briefing and Debriefing Meetings.   Schedule briefing and debriefing meetings for all events. A briefing or pre-conference meeting is an introduction to the on-site portion of the event. During this meeting you may want to review the agenda, roles and responsibilities, expectations, and the communication plan and equipment usage. Invite key stakeholders to this meeting to ensure that you are able to communicate a uniform plan prior to the start of the event. Briefing meetings are also a great time to answer or address any last-minute questions or concerns people may have.

A debriefing or post-conference meeting allows stakeholders to discuss the outcomes of the event and any lessons learned that can be applied to the next day or future events. Daily on-site meetings with your staff are helpful as well. They provide an opportunity for everyone to discuss the expectations for each day of the event and any changes that may have been made so that everyone is aware and up to date on all facets of the meeting. Debriefing meetings are also a great time to discuss whether anything should be improved for the following day of the event. Although not all lessons learned can be applied immediately, some changes can be made fairly quickly.

Final Steps.   As you decide which equipment may be best, think about whether everyone on your team requires a communication device. Can equipment be limited to key decision makers? Having too many people involved in all communication may inhibit the communication and decision-making process on-site. If you plan on using walkie-talkies, think about how the different frequencies can be utilised. For example, one frequency can be assigned to your event technology contact, while another can be assigned to just you and your CSM.

Finally, a plan that includes communication equipment is not complete without instructions on what to do should all the equipment fail. For example, what would you do if you were relying on cellular phone usage to communicate with all your staff, but you could not connect to a line due to a national emergency? Establish a communication plan that includes steps to take should everyone be separated with no method of communicating. One example is to establish a meeting area, one indoors and one outdoors, just in case everyone is evacuated from the building. If part of the event is abruptly cancelled due to an emergency, what type of message will you send to your attendees? Would it make sense to have all the staff at the hotel communicate a message as attendees go back to their rooms? Would you be able to e-mail all the attendees overnight to provide a plan for the following day? All emergencies cannot be predicted; however, consider what everyone would do in an emergency and establish the best plan possible beforehand.

Contributing Authors

Linda Dhawan, CMP
Government Event Manager
Experient, a Maritz Travel Company
Arlington, VA, USA
Member of Professional Convention Management Association (PCMA)

Nicole Schray
Project Manager
Experient, a Maritz Travel Company
Arlington, VA, USA
Member of Society of Government Meeting Professionals (SGMP)

Reviewer

Karen M. Gonzales, CMP
Senior Vice President, Membership & Operations, Destination Marketing Association International (DMAI)
Washington, DC, USA
Member of American Society of Association Executives (ASAE), Professional Convention Management Association (PCMA)

Skill 23:
Endpoints

Terminology

Outside suppliers

Stakeholders

Convention services manager (CSM)

Event specifications guide (ESG)

Speaker ready room

Skill 23: Review Questions

1. What are three examples of communication equipment? What are some pros and cons of each?

2. How does the type of message impact the type of equipment that may be necessary on-site?

3. What is a communication flowchart?

4. Why does local infrastructure impact on-site communication?

5. Why are debriefing meetings important?

Marketing

In the field of event marketing, the following skills need to be mastered:

* create and manage a marketing plan
* manage marketing materials
* manage event merchandise
* promote event
* contribute to public relations activities
* manage meeting-related sales activities

The term "event marketing" can have two meanings: marketing an event or using an event as a marketing tool. This is where crossover and integration occur between the organisation's marketing department and the event professional. When the event's goals are to teach attendees about new products and potentially prompt them to make a purchase, event marketing is used because the event is a marketing initiative. The additional value for potential customers depends on what might be of interest to them: the opportunity to network with peers and other customers, or professional development provided alongside the education about the organisation's products and services. At a certain level, all events are public relations (PR) tools, even if they are meant for an internal audience, because they provide a networking experience for the participants. Those stakeholders will tie that experience to their feelings about the brand or organisation hosting or sponsoring the event.

If either strategic or tactical integration with an organisation's marketing department is common for a particular activity, it will be discussed in this chapter. However, the goal of the chapter is to focus on the skills required to promote a event, and that definition of event marketing will be used.

Event professionals have developed the habit of asking themselves the following questions:

- Are we delivering on the organisation's and/or event's objectives?
- What can we measure?
- How are we going to measure that?
- What will we do with that information?

The return on investment (ROI) to the meeting/organisation should be considered with every decision that is made.

SKILL 24: MANAGE MARKETING PLAN

Learning Outcomes

- Collect market information—current and historical.
- Analyse target market demographic and psychographic research.
- Recognise available marketing distribution channels.
- Identify the strengths and weaknesses of different types of media.
- Identify preferences for types of media.

A marketing plan is a written document outlining the situational analysis, audience, and distribution channels, that will support the goals and objectives of the event. A Web site for entrepreneurs stated, "Developing the plan is the 'heavy lifting' of marketing. While executing the plan has its challenges, deciding what to do and how to do it is marketing's greatest challenge" (How to create, 2013, para. 3).

Marketing plans are as critical as event specifications guides (ESGs) to the success of a event. Many parts of the marketing plan will rely on the ESG and vice versa. The marketing plan can be created and implemented by either the marketing department or the meeting logistics team, or a combination of the two. A strategic event professional will understand the implications of a change to the marketing plan on the ESG and vice versa. Analysing what does and does not help achieve the organisation's or event's goals and objectives is just as crucial for the marketing plan as it is for the ESG.

While many marketing plans for meetings focus on increasing attendance, attaining large numbers of participants is not always the goal. Often, the quality of participants, overall financial impact, or amplification of the organisation's branding are more appropriate measures of success. If attendance at the event is mandatory for those who are invited, certain components of the marketing plan are still critical to the attainment of goals and objectives. To achieve success, the event marketing plan must be aligned with the organisation's overall marketing strategy and brand values.

Various types of meetings and events have striking differences in the technology and human resources required to implement a successful marketing plan. This is why strategy becomes so important. Deciding what needs to be done will guide the execution process. If new technologies and additional staff or contractors are needed, the marketing plan will paint a clear picture of how the results of these decisions will be measured.

Event features act as anchors in marketing materials. The "who, what, when, where, why, and how" details provide the basic information that must be communicated, whereas the marketing message should feel like an extension of the organisation's brand. Any communication about the event should not have a brand message or theme that is so different from the organisation's brand message or theme that a connection cannot be made to the organisation hosting the event.

While meetings and events once existed primarily as solitary events, not necessarily connected to the broader brand messages of the organisation, today they must be a part of continuing the message. Event professionals need a thorough understanding of the objectives and messaging of the marketing department and must be able to integrate those into the event.

Several marketing concepts—traditional and modern—are useful to comprehend the function and application of marketing to an event. The "marketing mix" (also known as the Four Ps: product, price, place, and promotion) doesn't directly apply to meetings and events in an obvious way because it was created for traditional product marketing. However, "price" could refer to the cost for a participant to attend the event. "Place" could reference the position of the event in the marketplace and among competitors, or to where the event is being held; it also connects with distribution of products and services. "Product" in this case is the event, and "promotion" is the media and other tools used to market the event. A more modern mix is known as the Five Cs: customer, company, competition, collaborators, and context (Master Class Management, 2013).

Marketing is a rapidly changing field of communication. Until very recently, communication from the organisation toward a customer was the extent of marketing. Now, communication from the customer to the organisation and customer to customer via social media are considered an important part of the marketing equation, as well as customers advocating on behalf of the organisation. Today's success comes from adopting a culture that promotes positive customer interaction at every point of contact and the implementation of new technologies such as social media to allow and encourage customers to communicate with the organisation before, during, and after the event.

Marketing channels are becoming more integrated, and one of the most important marketing concepts is integrated marketing communication. Clow and Baack (2006), said that marketing efforts should not only be integrated, but should feel inseparable from the culture of the organisation (p. 108). Knowing the marketplace and being able to tie attendee buying behaviours to the event experience are integral components of integrated marketing. The logo and branding style need to be consistent across all modes of advertising and promotion. Technology such as customer relationship management (CRM) and marketing automation software enable the tracking of customer behaviour and campaign effectiveness.

Sub Skill 24.01 – Conduct Situational Analysis

Before starting a list of action items or tasks, conduct research on a variety of factors to help guide marketing efforts. A situational analysis requires an assessment of the perception of the event by all stakeholders involved. Both internal and external factors should be studied to provide a clear picture of the position of the event. The sources for this data will not only be internal and external but also current and historical.

If the organisation has a current marketing plan or business plan that includes items such as a situational analysis, refer to this plan instead of duplicating efforts. Differentiate, where necessary, the position of the organisation and the position of the event. For example, Company X sells the same types of products that your company sells. Company X also hosts a user conference (common in the information technology field). You might think that Company X's meeting is a competitor to your meeting; however, dig deep to determine if the same target audience is appropriate for both events. A competitor of your organisation may not always be a competitor of your event; collaboration is increasingly common.

Surveys from previous events will help identify the participants who were a good fit for different types of events the organisation has hosted in the past, if demographic information was collected along with those surveys. In addition to the formal surveys that were given to previous participants, information that was shared via social networks and other public or private on-line media should be considered. Insight from stakeholders will provide a different perspective than insight from other sources. Advances in technology make crowd-sourcing easier than ever, and many stakeholders will appreciate being part of the research phase of the event. Many organisations use such methods to engage and create loyalty in potential participants. Information can be gathered by sending out surveys via mail or e-mail. Conversations should be initiated and monitored via on-line platforms and communities as well. Creating buzz early by including potential participants in the planning phase is a great way to keep the event "top of mind" and encourage a sense of ownership. Start with your product, which may be the event itself or the products or services your organisation sells and which the event is helping market. How is the event fulfilling the client's and/or attendee's needs? What are the features that support the goals and objectives of the event? Why would your potential participants choose your event over other methods of achieving their goals and objectives?

Research the competition, taking into consideration that your competition may be another event (possibly another event that your organisation is hosting) or it may be the products or services of your competition. Associations are facing a myriad of competition these days, not limited to the other traditional associations they were competing against for members in the past. The competition may also be conducting a situational analysis, so in addition to incorporating the current position of competitors, anticipate moves by competitors in the future.

A SWOT analysis examines factors that are internal to an organisation (strengths and weaknesses) as well as external to the organisation (opportunities and threats). Complete a SWOT analysis to further distinguish your event's position.

Examples:

Strengths	Weaknesses
■ Support of stakeholders ■ Repeat of a successful event ■ Experienced team ■ High motivation level ■ Strong community support	■ Lack of funds ■ Undefined roles or decentralised planning committee ■ Volunteers responsible for critical tasks ■ Disconnect with potential participants
Opportunities	**Threats**
■ Little competition ■ Favourable economic/political/social conditions ■ Availability of state-of-the-art infrastructure ■ Strong relationships with suppliers/sponsors/external stakeholders ■ Position to implement sustainability initiatives ■ Expansion into new markets	■ Lack of knowledge about new technologies or formats ■ High labour rate or restrictions ■ Government regulations ■ Unfocused priorities ■ Public perception

As you analyse your event using SWOT and other research techniques, a road map will start to form that will help guide the decision-making process for both the marketing and logistics of the event. Summarising this data into a format that is efficient and persuasive will be the key to sharing information with stakeholders. The same data may be presented in different formats to make it clear and accessible to various stakeholder groups. Make recommendations and conclusions, considering budget and resources, based on this information.

Sub Skill 24.02 – Define Target Market Segments

Market segmentation is a marketing strategy that starts with a broad target market and divides it into groups of potential participants who have commonalities. Design the event to satisfy their needs and desires, and use messaging and channels that reach them.

Companies in the industrial age used to create a product that would sell because it was innovative ("If you build it, they will come"). As more and more products entered the marketplace, companies needed to promote their products to the masses in order to sell them. Then products became more specialised and the concept of market segmentation was born. A company would define the audience first and then create a product that a specific audience would want to buy.

In addition to defining the ideal audience, digging deeper to determine the current and future needs and expectations of the ideal audience will help the event professional create the event a participant wants to attend. This would suggest that target market research should take place before any logistics are planned for the event. However, this may not be feasible. Regardless of the timeline of target market research versus the planning phase, this research should be incorporated into the design of the event.

Start first with the broadest possible community of potential participants, then narrow the description based on the psychographics and demographics of participants. Psychographics is the study of personality, values, attitudes, interests, lifestyles, preferences, activities, tastes, likes, dislikes, and complaints. Demographics, on the other hand, has to do with specific data that is used to profile individuals, such as age, gender, race, education, qualification(s), marital status, income, profession, level in an organisation, and seniority in the industry.

Geography is no longer an important demographic for many organisations because people from afar can be reached through virtual platforms. If it is important to reach an audience in a particular geographic location, an event could be located in a convenient location for that audience. This will have the added benefit of reducing travel-related carbon emissions for your event if shorter and more direct flights are possible. If it is more important to focus on other demographics and the potential audience is located on a national or global scale, virtual technologies can assist with extending the reach of the event. If this is the case, consider optimal timing to enable multiple time-zone participation. Another option for a geographically diverse audience is to create a "road show" that enables the personal connections that are one of the essential elements of meetings.

One of the demographics to consider is whether or not the potential participants have decision-making authority within their organisation. If the event is a business-to-consumer (B2C) event, it will be more likely that the attendee will make the choice or decision to buy. If the event is a business-to-business (B2B) event, there may be a process involving several people to determine whether or not to purchase. It is also possible to face a mix of both. Participants are usually categorised as customers, while exhibitors and sponsors are most likely businesses that want to appeal to those customers.

Creating tools to help potential participants convince their organisations to let them attend the event is an important service provided by experienced event promoters. One way to provide this service is by producing a "why attend" document or video for potential participants who need to get budget approval.

In addition to the various influencers identified by the economic buyer model, social media have created a word-of-mouth amplification system. Word-of-mouth has always been a powerful marketing tool; however, providing a quality product (event) and hoping potential participants would spread the word was all that marketers could hope to achieve. Now people influence the decision made by potential participants—and those people may not be part of your target market. Consider the influencers throughout the marketing plan, regardless of whether or not they are likely to attend the event themselves, and equip your key sponsors and event partners with the tools and knowledge to support your social media campaign.

After narrowing down the demographic and psychographic profiles of various participants, sponsors, and other stakeholders, the next step is determining their current and future needs and expectations. One method of obtaining this information is to survey people who have already been identified as fitting into select categories. Ask questions that relate to their personal or professional goals and objectives and not specifically about the event.

- How do the buyers and sellers prefer to meet, connect, and develop relationships and do business?
- Where are they currently connecting?
- Who are they currently buying from?
- Who do they hope to sell to?
- What challenges are participants having at work and at home?
- Where do they receive their professional development?
- How are they using on-line tools?
- When do they plan to make a purchase from a supplier in the community?
- Why do they attend meetings or events?
- Who influences their decision to attend meetings or events?
- What position do they want to hold five years from now?
- What are their current three main concerns?
- What do they expect to achieve by attending?
- What are their criteria to measure successful attendance?

Sub Skill 24.03 – Select Marketing Distribution Channels

The term "**marketing distribution channel**" refers to how a business gets its products to the customers. Marketing channels and distribution channels are also used when referring to the activities necessary to transfer the ownership of goods from the point of production to the point of consumption. The definition of channels has transitioned from traditional methods such as warehouse or retail through mail order catalogues or direct personal communications to more modern on-line methods such as a Web site, e-mail marketing, and social media campaigns. This transition saw the use of the terms "channel marketing" and "marketing channels" expand to cover the ways in which products were advertised.

There are many different media and tools to consider. It is tempting to try a lot of different methods and hope that something works. However, a better approach is to choose two media that have worked in the past, and experiment with a new medium, while measuring the return on investment for each medium to guide future decisions. This section focuses on the messaging considerations for various media.

Advertising

Advertising should encourage action. In fact, marketers differentiate advertising efforts from public relations efforts on this key point: Does the advertisement encourage action? If it does not, the piece is probably a public relations tool. An advertisement should gain the potential customer's attention, provide some information, call for action, and declare the benefits of completing that action. The following checklist for what should be included in advertising is adapted, with permission, from the *Events Industry Council Manual, 8th edition.*

- Include a call to action (e.g., request more information, register, or visit a Web site).
- Use event colours and logo.
- Keep message consistent with other promotional messages for that audience.
- Write copy that is short and to the point.
- Include full contact information.
- Work trade-outs with industry publications.

Print advertising is typically run in newspapers and magazines. Broadcast advertising is typically run on television or radio. The lines are starting to blur between traditional advertising and on-line advertising, now that newspapers and magazines offer on-line versions of their publications. By the same token, radio and television programmes are starting to utilise on-line platforms. Advertising on one of these channels may also open the opportunity to run that advertisement on-line.

Billboards are a form of outdoor advertising. Outdoor signs are not restricted to traditional roadside billboards but can also include wraps on vehicles, trucks, and buses, as well as sports arena advertising. Outdoor advertising can include signs hanging from lampposts and banners hanging on buildings or across roadways. Outdoor signs are a common method to welcome meeting and event participants to the destination, as well as to encourage public attendance. Other forms of advertising might include transit advertising (in buildings, subway terminals, buses, etc.), point-of-purchase advertising (includes shopping cart ads, signs on roadside vendor carts, etc.), and indoor advertising. Advertising is also placed in mass media outlets, direct or business-to-person (B2P) outlets, and on-line.

Direct Marketing

Direct marketing is any direct personal communication from the organisation to potential customers by printed medium or electronic communication, such as e-mail, social media, phone call, or text message.

Printed messages mailed directly to potential participants can arrive in several different formats: with or without envelopes, including attention-grabbing graphics, specialty items, even smells and sound. With the prevalence of electronic communication, the impact of a piece of mail has actually increased. Letters, invitations, brochures, postcards, and programmes are commonly used by meeting and event professionals to market their events. Mailing lists can be generated from the organisation's existing lists of members or customers, or may be purchased from research firms based on target market demographics.

Telemarketing can be conducted by individual sales staff or by machine robo-calling. If goals for registration numbers are not being met four to eight weeks in advance of the event, staff or telemarketers should call potential attendees. A script might include the deadline for pre-registration or hotel cut-off dates and questions about why the prospect has not yet registered.

Text messaging can be a simple yet effective way to market, inform, or alert stakeholders. Services are available that allow your clients to opt in to your service via a keyword they text to a specified number. They receive a default message (including a disclaimer about the costs they may incur from their wireless providers) and are then placed in your database. You can send different messages to this database at any time, and anyone in the database will receive the new message. Promote the code and keyword on other marketing media to increase adoption. Send messages to your database with event information. Text messages can have a high response rate, making them one of the most effective marketing media in this mobile society.

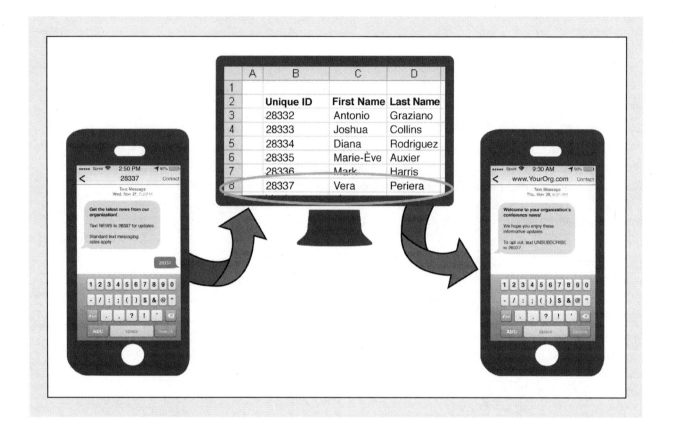

On-line Communication

E-mail marketing is a great combination of direct marketing and on-line communication. The capabilities have quickly advanced from text-only to very rich interactive messages. The branding and messaging that needs to be conveyed is much easier to achieve, and content, such as video, can be delivered directly in the body of the e-mail without the recipient needing to click on a link. However, the goal of the e-mail should be to get recipients to click on a link that takes them to the organisation or event Web site, where more information is available, including registration forms.

The better the data (current e-mail addresses) an organisation starts with, the more successful an e-mail campaign will be. Efforts to personalise these messages by including the recipient's name in the subject line or the body increase the chances of the recipient opening that message. One way of gathering quality data is to use a data collection form on the organisation's Web site. Offering an incentive in exchange for providing an e-mail address and other contact information typically works well. Examples include white papers, case studies, discounts, and promotional items. The more information that is collected, the more market segmentation can be utilised when sending promotional pieces.

Laws concerning whom an organisation may contact via e-mail or telemarketing change periodically to protect consumers. They are stricter in Europe than in the United States. Research the laws for any country where promotion is conducted. Refer to the resource section of this chapter for a starting point on the U.S. CAN-SPAM Act and EU Opt-In Directive.

The number of e-mails to send for any particular programme will vary widely; however, a minimum of one per month and a maximum of one per week is recommended (Internet Marketing Blog, 2011). Unfortunately, this medium is becoming more and more crowded, and most inboxes and spam filters are overflowing with unread messages. Carefully crafted messages and designs for this medium take time, practice, and testing. Make each marketing piece different, though thematic to the event's brand, and test the result in various e-mail platforms and Internet browsers.

Web sites or on-line registration sites act as the hub for all marketing efforts for the event. Any medium that is used should have the goal of directing the recipient to visit the Web site and then register for the event. The secondary purpose is directing the recipient to share the message with others, assisting with word-of-mouth efforts and driving additional traffic to the Web site or on-line registration site.

These sites can be as simple as a blog platform that is free to set up and can be as advanced as a fully customised platform with many features and capabilities. This medium is the most important part of the potential attendee's experience, so most of the marketing efforts should be focused on making the user's experience a positive one. The user's experience starts when he or she first visits the site for more information and continues through the process of registration. Web sites also need to be optimised for search engines so that if a potential attendee is searching on-line for an event with keywords, the Web site will show up as close to the top of those results as possible. These tactics are known as search engine optimization (SEO) and search engine marketing (SEM).

Other examples of on-line communication include links on Web sites of partners, meeting and event listing sites, industry publications, and associations' event listings, as well as hybrid sites that act as event-listing sites combined with social networks. On-line advertising can appear in publications, blogs, search engines, social media, and broadcast channels.

Adopting a community mindset is beneficial when participating in social networks. Utilise existing communities or create new ones using groups on various social media platforms. Collect data about how marketing messages are shared between potential participants on social networks so that more informed marketing decisions can be made in the future.

Social media are globally influential and the source for many to learn more about news, brands, products, and services. They change constantly, however, so stay current with the most visited sites and use them to reach your audience.

Setting up a presence on these networks and monitoring for negative comments are not sufficient efforts. Sending messages that are promotional only will not work on these platforms, because the users see them as communication tools, not advertising platforms. They work best when users share the messages for you; however, you need a very passionate audience or a compelling message that is easily shared.

The demographic and psychographic research starts to show some real value when considering social ads. The research that has been done for the event will serve two purposes. First, it will guide the decisions about which on-line social networks are best for that audience and second, it will help maximize the targeting options that social ads provide.

Branding/Messaging/Content

All marketing pieces should have the same look and theme, no matter which medium is used, even if the message is different from one medium to another. Pieces should be dynamic and should integrate the following elements:

- Use active voice, with verbs that encourage the reader to take action.
- Offer specific details.
- Utilise short sentences.
- Highlight benefits instead of features.
- Include testimonials from influential community members.
- Suggest who should attend.
- Describe speakers' credentials.
- Use incentives.
- Caption photos with benefit statements.

- Include contact information for questions.
- Facilitate sharing.
- Construct interactive elements such as video.

Keep written communication simple and straightforward, and do not use slang expressions or jargon. Clichés may work well on home ground, where they are well understood, but they do not travel well.

Even within the social media landscape, the tone of each channel will be different. Samir Balwani (2009) explains this key aspect of social media:

> Social platforms each have an ecosystem of their own. Understanding that each site is different and then customizing your message ensures they do well on each respective site. Not only does customizing messages across sites help the message spread, but it keeps users from receiving multiple identical communications. Be sure to maximize your potential by sending two different messages to a user who follows the business on Twitter and Facebook, instead of the same thing twice. (par. 12)

Today's successful marketers are authentic storytellers who create a personal connection to the organisation or event. Video has become a very popular content format, because consumers are overwhelmed by the amount of data they have to read from their computer screens on a daily basis. A quick and informative video will catch the attention of potential attendees and they may share it across their social networks. Humourous videos can be very effective; however, they should be tailored to the audience and cultural attitudes. This tactic is made possible by careful market segment identification through psychographics and demographics.

Marketing in an International Environment

This section is adapted, with permission, from the *Events Industry Council International Manual, 8th edition*. Organising an event with international attendees requires attention to the following important factors:

1. *Cultures and Customs.* The material used to promote an event may need to be adapted for specific nationalities or groups to reflect their customs, protocols, laws and traditions. As an example, there are different cultural connotations to colours and these, along with other aspects such as direction of reading and depictions of gender roles, should be considered when making advertising and design choices. From a protocol perspective, an invitation from a politician or corporate leader may add great value. Consider economic factors such as access to the Internet and regulations such as constraints on advertising of alcohol or tobacco products. Local advice is recommended.

2. *Countries and Regions.* The political or diplomatic relationship between the host country and the nations of potential attendees should be considered by the event planner. This includes awareness of requirements for letters of invitation to enter a country or obtain a visa. Marketing regulations for data protection vary from country to country.

3. *Languages.* The language used for marketing materials should be tailored to the target country. Translation of marketing materials is recommended, although an exception may be made if the event will be conducted entirely in one language and attendees are expected to be conversant in that language. When translating marketing materials, it is important to consider the specific country, not only the language itself, as clichés, slogans, and expressions may differ from country to country. Hiring a professional translator familiar with the specific country and industry is recommended. The use of on-line translation Web sites for developing marketing materials is not recommended; however, this may be acceptable if a native speaker will then be correcting the translations. Some types of marketing messages—such as

"Register NOW!"—that are common in western advertising may be viewed as patronizing or too direct in some places. In general, communication should be simple and straightforward to facilitate understanding.

4. *Perceptions.* Event planners need to be aware of perceptions and changing attitudes when marketing an event internationally. As an example, one nationality may be viewed with suspicion in one country but regarded with affection in another country nearby. Be aware of different perceptions regarding value, as well as forms of media. These attitudes can change over time and across generations. Seeking local advice is recommended.

5. *Time and Distance.* Plan promotion well in advance for international mailings, as international postal service can have long delivery times. Telephone marketing and social media campaigns should be adapted to the relevant time zones and day of the week, and should avoid religious and public holidays. Press releases should be sent with sufficient lead time to enable translation, if necessary.

Marketing Virtual Events

Promoting a virtual or hybrid event is different than promoting a physical event. Instead of marketing broadcast sessions a week before the event, the virtual portion of the event should be designed and promoted to target the segment of your community that would not have attended the physical event. Messages specific to this audience should be used when promoting the virtual event. This separation in messages should help avoid a situation in which a potential attendee chooses the virtual format instead of attending the physical event.

Sub Skill 24.04 – Implement Marketing Plan

Implementation of the marketing plan involves putting all of the pieces together. The steps before this phase involved a lot of research, and now the plan is put into action. (The steps to managing a marketing plan are in the graphic below.)

In implementing a marketing plan, a timeline should be created that is feasible given the amount of time leading up to the event. In the case of an annual event, marketing should begin prior to the previous year's event, with as much detail about location, dates, etc., as possible and a steadily paced calendar of critical dates, including all marketing activities. In the case of an event with only weeks or months to prepare, a more condensed calendar of critical dates will need to be negotiated with all of the individuals involved in the marketing of the event. Setting up the Web site or on-line registration site should always be the first task, because once a promotional message is sent, the recipient will want somewhere to look for more information. A sample timeline is shown below (adapted with permission from the *Events Industry Council Manual, 8th edition*). This timeline should be adapted for the type of event, the audience, and the amount of time available leading up to the event.

Steps to Managing a Marketing Plan

1 Conduct Situational Analysis   2 Define Target Market Segment   3 Select Marketing Distribution Channels   4 Implement Marketing Plan (putting the previous three steps into action)

Weeks Out	Action
52	For annual events, promotion begins at least a year in advance. Promote the next annual event at the current event. This can include offering a special registration rate, mention of the event during general sessions (if applicable), or a luncheon themed for next year's destination.
40	Send news release #1 to trade publications and influential bloggers.
40	Begin content planning and development for event Web site, including graphical elements that will be used on all promotional materials.
26	Send news release #2 with details about speakers, event theme, exciting destination events, and major benefits of general sessions and seminars to trade publications and influential bloggers.
24	Send mailing #1 – a flyer or postcard about the event – promoting benefits and mentioning the early registration date. Coincide with launch of the event's Web site. Note that this date may need to be adjusted if mailing to international audiences, or if the information is being sent electronically.
24	Place advertisements in trade journals. Include the event's Web site address.
24	Create social media sites and select an event hashtag. Distribute links for these to event partners, sponsors, exhibitors, association chapters or regional offices (if applicable), and speakers so they can promote to their networks.
24	Begin weekly social media promotion.
24	Distribute a video of previous event highlights and attendee endorsements to local chapters of the association, or regional sales offices for the corporation. Place the video on the event Web site.
20	Send news release #3 with more details about speakers, exhibitors, activities, and benefits of attendance to trade publications and blog sites.
16	Send mailing #2 (print or electronic) with full schedule of events, registration, and housing information. Promote registration discounts and downloadable mobile application (if applicable) with programme content.
15	Upload video clips from speakers or entertainers to the event Web site with preview content of the event and distribute links via social media.
12	Place a cover story about the event in your association or corporate magazine (if applicable), promoting benefits of attendance.
10	Send invitations to media list (including influential bloggers if applicable), offering complimentary registration and admission to all functions.
8	Send mailing #3 (print or electronic) with latest information on speakers and other programme attractions, housing, and registration information.
6	News release #4: Send complete details about event, major benefits of attendance, and feature story ideas to trade and consumer press and influential bloggers.
1	Follow up press invitations by telephone.

The challenge with timelines and creating specific marketing messages is the balancing act between organising the logistics of an event and promoting the event. The specific details that participants want cannot be advertised until they are coordinated on the operational end of the event; however, marketing efforts cannot wait until all of the logistics are put into place.

A review of the plan will be necessary from time to time, either to make adjustments due to the timeline for logistics management or if metrics are showing that certain channels are not performing well. Staff and resources that were committed to a particular area may need to be reallocated. Always communicate changes made to the marketing plan to all individuals involved. Measuring the effectiveness of marketing methods can be difficult, because prospective participants may hear about your event from several different sources before registering. Use traffic to the Web site or on-line registration site as a benchmark; Web site analytics can be used to show which channels are most effective. A field on the registration form asking the attendee to indicate how he/she heard about the event is a useful tool for tracking performance. If a different discount code is promoted on each medium and is then entered at the time of registration, a general idea of media performance can be determined. Setting up the plan for how these metrics will be measured before creating a timeline of activities will ensure that efforts will be evaluated appropriately.

Integrate all channels so that your media selections work together and provide a seamless experience for participants. For example, send e-mail and make the information provided and calls to action easily shared on social channels. After someone has registered, the next page that person sees should allow sharing the event with selected social networks such as Twitter and Facebook.

Don't forget that many stakeholders have an obligation to help market the event. If there are sales people in the organisation, make sure they are including the information in their e-mail signatures, talking to people about it, and reaching out to people with a personal invitation to the event. Consider supplying your key partners and sponsors with a toolkit that includes with logos, promotion materials, and Web banners.

References

Balwani, S. (2009, September 30). 5 advanced social media marketing strategies for small businesses. *Mashable*. Retrieved from http://mashable.com/2009/09/30/small-business-strategies/.

Clow, K. E., & Baack, D. E. (2006, March 22). *Integrated advertising, promotion, and marketing communications*. Upper Saddle River, NJ: Prentice Hall.

Events Industry Council. 2011. *Events Industry Council Manual*, 8th ed.. Alexandria, VA: Events Industry Council.

E-mail Campaign Frequency. (2011, March.) *Internet Marketing Blog*. Retrieved from http://www.ecreativeim.com/blog/2011/03/e-mail-campaign-frequency/.

How to create a marketing plan. (n.d.) *Entrepreneur*. Retrieved from http://www.entrepreneur.com/article/43018#.

Master Class Management. (2013). 5 C's and strategic marketing. *Master Class Management*. Retrieved from http://www.masterclassmanagement.com/ManagementCourse-5CsAndStrategicMarketing.htm.

Contributing Author

Elizabeth Glau, CMP
Owner/Consultant
Building Blocks Social Media
Los Angeles, CA, USA
Member of Green Meeting Industry Council (GMIC)

Reviewers

Dr. Rodolfo Musco, CMM, CMP
Motivation & Events S.a.s.
Milano, Italy
Member of Meeting Professionals International (MPI)

Glenn Thayer
Conference Moderator, The Voice of Meetings and Events
Denver, CO, USA
Member of American Society of Association Executives (ASAE) and National Speakers Association (NSA)

Skill 24:
Endpoints

Terminology

Crowd-source
Demographics
Marketing distribution channel
Psychographics
SWOT analysis

Additional Resources

1. Controlling the Assault of Non-Solicited Pornography and Marketing Act of 2003 (CAN-SPAM). FTC's SPAM site: http://www.business.ftc.gov/documents/bus61-can-spam-act-compliance-guide-business.
2. EU Opt-In Directive. EU directive 2002/58/EC. The directive specifies a minimum legislation for the member states. European Law: http://eur-lex.europa.eu.
3. Chen, Elicia. (November 13, 2012). *20 Stats Every Global Social Media Marketer Should Know*. HubSpot. Available at http://blog.hubspot.com/blog/tabid/6307/bid/33819/20-Stats-Every-Global-Social-Media-Marketer-Should-Know.aspx#ixzz2M3nkUBOo.

Skill 24: Review Questions

1. What are the elements of a marketing plan?
2. What are the sources of data used to analyse the position of the event?
3. Why is integrated marketing communication important?
4. Why do attendee goals and expectations need to be considered?

SKILL 25: MANAGE MARKETING MATERIALS

Learning Outcomes

- Review available marketing distribution channels.
- Design materials to be produced.
- Discuss procurement plan and processes.
- Arrange contact distribution lists.
- Schedule promotional activities.

Marketing the organisation, meeting, or event is an ongoing process that is not limited to particular tasks leading up to an event. Building a community around a positive perception of the host organisation and sponsors happens before, during, and after the event. This section will cover the management of marketing materials traditionally found at an event, as well as more engaging tools and tactics for creating the desired experience for participants.

Marketing materials include Web site content, e-mails, printed materials, giveaways and promotional items, signage, educational materials, presentation templates, written pre- and post-event instructions to exhibitors, registration area apparatus, forms, organisers, packaging, surveys, event guides and maps, badges, holders, stickers, ribbons, writing pads, pens, pencils, bags, totes, and lanyards. Essentially, anything that is used to communicate with stakeholders before and after the event, as well as anything brought to the venue, can to affect the experience.

If print materials are selected—such as brochures, postcards, or other mailings to drive attendance—printing projects should be decided upon at one time, as it may be more cost-effective to do multiple orders at the same time. When a vendor is chosen to supply services for the event, the scope of the project should be included in all bids and estimates, and consideration should be given to sustainable materials such as post-consumer recycled paper or Forest Stewardship Council (FSC) certified products. The more information the event professional has about marketing materials needed before the event and on-site, the more accurate the budget will be.

Depending on your target market research and the needs and expectations of various stakeholders, electronic forms of communication may replace the traditional printed pieces. If environmental sustainability is important to the target audience or to the organisation or sponsors, electronic forms of communication should be considered along with recycled paper products and more sustainable printing options. Paper usage is often cited in the production of events; use the ISO 20121 process to identify other potential issues during the communication campaign.

How do the materials that are created for either pre-event marketing or on-site attendee experience support the goals and objectives of the event? The fact that the event has always produced a printed programme is not enough of a reason to continue doing so. At the same time, just because many other conferences are implementing a mobile app in place of a printed programme is not enough of a reason to do that. How do print or electronic materials connect to the stakeholders? As part of a transition to more efficient resource use, a smaller or smarter pocket programme is a good midway option.

More meetings and events are moving toward an environment in which the communication channel is open and transparent before, during, and after the event. Today's consumers expect any organisation they do business with to be responsive in social media. Meetings and events are no exception. Do not treat new media channels as marketing platforms, but do incorporate as much two-way dialogue between the organisation and stakeholders as possible. In this sense, the social media become public relations tools that support marketing efforts.

Social networks serve multiple purposes for the event professional:

1. Monitor feedback, thank participants for their input, and make changes to the programme when possible.

2. Take advantage of the networks to spread important messages (leveraging the ability for your messages to travel outside of the event when shared by participants) and communicate updates and changes.

3. Facilitate the connection among delegates and gain insight into the communities and per-suasive stakeholders inside and outside of your event, either to influence the design of the event or as part of a campaign to attract stakeholder engagement, such as commonly used in events with a strong sustainability focus.

Sub Skill 25.01 – Determine Needed Marketing Materials for Event

Many items support the logistics of a event and are traditionally included in the marketing mate-rials simply because they include the event logo, theme, and message, and are printed by the same vendor who is printing pre-event marketing materials. Logistically important pieces should have the same look and feel as every other experience the attendee has had since his or her first interac-tion with the event.

An audit of these materials against the goals and objectives of the meeting is advisable. Con-siderations include the needs of the attendees, whether or not the item is unique, and whether it supports the event's branding or sustainability commitment. An audit might reveal that the item is no longer feasible as a marketing piece. It is a growing trend for events to innovate with different approaches to types of giveaways, often with a sustainable theme such as a branded, reusable water bottle.

If the goal of the event is to generate positive sentiment among customers, promotional prod-ucts distributed at the event should support that objective. Choosing something participants will use in their daily lives extends the experience and creates an opportunity for brand recognition. If the item is meaningful enough, a logo may not be necessary, because customers will remember where they received it every time they use it. For example, offering a photo booth where par-ticipants can get a professional headshot is a gift that may be greatly appreciated. Focus on the experience participants will have at the event and any extension of that experience you can create for them when the event is over.

Some goals and objectives can be achieved using digital methods instead of hard copy or printed items. As an alternative to printed materials, consider providing the same information in a digital format through a device, such as a smart phone or tablet, that participants will carry with them after the event. This enables them to connect easily with a piece of information or a contact they gained at the event.

Mobile apps or mobile Web sites can be used to distribute the same information typically found in a printed programme, and at the same time, make that information more dynamic by providing links to speakers' Web sites, handouts, and related research. These platforms can also be used to help participants connect with each other. If networking is one of the goals of the event, it makes sense to provide a way for participants to use the devices they are already carrying with them to find the people who can help them achieve their goals and objectives.

Some organisations are using a combination of paper and digital programmex on-site. The in-depth programme and speaker information is included in the digital programme, while a sched-ule-at-a glance is provided in a pocket-size print out for easy access.

Newsletters or newspapers produced by the hosting organisation have traditionally been a great way to recap the day's events, share comments from participants, and highlight the next day's activities. If this is an important form of engagement for the participants and achieves a goal or objective of the event, it should be continued. Digital methods of relaying this type of information are also available in the form of convention television and social networks.

Video is a great way to keep your messaging in front of your prospects or participants. Short videos from your speakers can spark interest in session content. Messages from the organisation's leadership can also be used in the content marketing strategy.

Sub Skill 25.02 – Develop Content and Design Parameters

Content and design for marketing materials, whether they are physical or digital, should follow the theme of the event. If a look and feel have been established at the event design phase, these materials—even though they may seem small and inconsequential—are actually very important in supporting the overall experience. Every single piece should look as if it belongs to the set. If something needs to be produced on-site or at the last minute, ensure that the necessary tools are accessible (i.e., high-quality digital copies of logos, graphics, and fonts).

Double-check the language and phrasing if the event has an audience from more than one country or culture. Remember that some audiences are accustomed to more formal messaging and some audiences respond better to informal messaging. Secure permission to use intellectual property as necessary and obtain permission to use copyright protected and licensed materials, if required.

Visualising the event from the perspective of the attendee will help you determine how much and what information to include in each piece. Signage should not only be appropriately placed but should have the right amount of information on each piece. Smaller programmes can be utilised if a digital platform is provided to participants for more information on each session. Ensure that each piece is appealing to the eye in addition to providing the right content.

When creating the Web site or on-line registration system, consider building features that allow for two-way communication between the organisation and stakeholders, as well as functionality for delegates to start connecting to each other before the event. A sense of community will start to form around the event if participants believe that their opinions are valued and they will benefit from the educational and human resources they connect with through the experience.

Mobile apps or mobile Web sites may be provided by the same company that manages your Web site or on-line registration site, or by a separate vendor. Choose a platform based on research from identified target markets. This will increase adoption if the participants are more likely to own one platform over another. Don't make an assumption about which devices your participants will bring to the event. Before you procure mobile apps and other engagement tools, survey participants and ask which devices they will bring; this will save time and provide a greater return on investment.

Sub Skill 25.03 – Produce Marketing Materials

Branding guidelines for the marketing materials will help keep the branding elements consistent, which helps tie the experience back to the organisation hosting the event. Branding guidelines should include the following:

- Location where official images can be downloaded
- Contact information for the person responsible for maintaining the standards
- Rules for using the logo (e.g., minimum size, ratio, splitting, adding content)
- Colours
- Fonts

Typically, the organisation logo and/or event logo must be included on all pieces, and the guidelines will specify parameters for sizing. Specifications must also be communicated to any stakeholders who will be providing their own marketing materials. This can include sending brand guidelines, a presentation template, or official introduction slide to speakers, so that all session presentations have the same look and feel. Sponsors and exhibitors should also be provided with guidelines for links to the event Web site from their Web site, in addition to any collateral, trade show materials, and giveaways they bring to the event.

When reviewing digital formats for marketing materials, you will find a wide variety of options and prices. Web sites, on-line registration sites, mobile apps, mobile Web sites, and a host of other engagement tools are available. The specifications need to be matched to the goals and objectives of the event, the audience, and the budget, so the final product doesn't end up costing more than necessary. Many engagement features and social networking sites can be built into apps and Web sites. Educate yourself on which features are available and which objectives can be achieved through integration of engagement tools with the mobile app before you start the bid process.

The organisation's policies may require a certain number of bids for any project that is outsourced. The more specific and thorough the request for proposal (RFP) is, the better responses you will get, and the closer the winning bid will be to the final invoice. Requesting that suppliers use a provided template for their proposals will ensure that comparison of proposals does not take extra time.

Create and communicate timelines to vendors as early as the bidding stage of the process. Writing copy, editing, proofing, and, in the case of electronic media, testing the product on various platforms takes time; each stage affects the outcome of the next stage of the process. Several rounds by several people will make the editing and proofing stages more effective. Confirming copy before sending it to graphic designers will help avoid costly changes.

The timeline should also include enough time for shipping. In the case of international shipping, the customs process should be given an ample amount of time for clearance. In the case of electronic media, such as a mobile app or mobile Web site, the finished product should be made available to participants as far in advance of the event as possible to allow for downloading and ready access, especially if the technology is new for that audience.

Sub Skill 25.04 – Distribute Marketing Materials

Delivery of printed and physical items will be coordinated through transportation and venue logistics. Some items may be given to participants at the meeting or during event registration, while other items may be distributed by the venue staff at check-in or delivered to guest rooms. In some cases, registration materials or credentials are sent in advance to the participants so they don't have to queue up when arriving at the meeting. Some items may be offered only to certain participants, so a clear communication plan to all staff is critical.

Establish a delivery schedule for items that should be distributed throughout the event. Keeping the attendee experience in mind, organise and assemble materials in a way that meets their needs and expectations. After a long day of travel, participants will not be in the right frame of mind to be overloaded with information. Consider which materials they need right away and which materials can be given later.

Digital materials often require Internet access, cellular service, and power for the participants' devices. Some apps are fully downloadable to smart phones but not updatable without Internet access. Participants will most likely expect that the one, two, or three mobile devices they are bringing with them to the event will work while they are at the event. Internet cost and bandwidth are issues for many meeting and event organisers; it can be difficult to balance the budget with attendee expectations. Use the Accepted Practices Exchange (APEX) "Bandwidth Estimator for Meetings and Events" as a starting point when speaking to venues and technology providers.

Mobile applications (apps) and mobile Web sites can be set up to require a password if the organisation is concerned about proprietary information. It is easiest to send all participants the same password and ask that they not share it; however, this level of security may not be tight enough. Adding this step to the process should only be necessary for organisations with confidential material in the app, because the more barriers to entry, the lower the adoption rate will be.

The process of promoting the mobile app or mobile Web site should be extensive if the event has not offered this type of technology in the past. Just as printed programmes are typically distributed at registration, a kiosk or dedicated area should be set up to encourage use the mobile technology that is being offered to guide them through the event. On-site assistance with downloading or accessing the mobile app or mobile Web site—or using survey, poll, or other engagement equipment—will be critical for participants new to the technology.

Any materials created should be archived according to the organisation's policies. Records should be kept on the utilisation of physical and printed items to allow for more accurate production of these items for future meetings or events, and recycling facilities should be provided for used or overage printed materials.

All stakeholders should be brought into the process early so they can assist with the promotion of the event and any important features that need extra attention. Speakers, sponsors, and exhibitors all have a role to play in the content of the marketing materials, and it benefits them when the materials are actually used by participants.

Contributing Author

Elizabeth Glau, CMP
Owner/Consultant
Building Blocks Social Media
Los Angeles, CA, USA
Member of Green Meeting Industry Council (GMIC)

Reviewers

Rodolfo Musco, CMM, CMP
Motivation & Events S.a.s.
Milano, Italy
Member of Meeting Professionals International (MPI)

Glenn Thayer
Conference Moderator, The Voice Of Meetings & Events
Denver, CO, USA
Member of American Society of Association Executives (ASAE) and National Speakers Association (NSA)

Skill 25:
Endpoints

Terminology

Branding
Bidding
Bandwidth

Additional Resources

1. ASTM E2746 - 11. Standard Specification for Evaluation and Selection of Communication and Marketing Materials for Environmentally Sustainable Meetings, Events, Trade Shows, and Conferences. http://www.astm.org/Standards/E2746.htm
2. APEX. Event Bandwidth Estimator. http://www.eventscouncil.org/APEX/bwidthestimator.aspx
3. ISO 20121:2012. Event sustainability management systems—Requirements with guidance for use. http://www.iso.org/iso/catalogue_detail?csnumber=54552

Skill 25: Review Questions

1. What purpose do social networks serve for the event?
2. When should an event mobile app be password-protected?
3. What are some examples of marketing materials?
4. Why are branding guidelines created?

SKILL 26: MANAGE EVENT MERCHANDISE

Learning Outcomes

- Collect historical data on past merchandise.
- Define brand guidelines.
- Calculate financial goals.
- Examine legal rights.
- List merchandise specifications.
- Outline launch dates for merchandise.

Events will often incorporate the use of **promotional products** such as giveaways for participants or merchandise sales.

As a planner prepares for an event, promotional products will be developed as part of the marketing strategy. All marketing strategies require a well-thought-out plan with steps necessary to attain success. No strategy is guaranteed to work perfectly. When developing promotional products and merchandise, it's best to follow some basic steps:

1. Know the host organisation. The event's mission statement, goals, objectives, and brand positioning should align with the organisation's mission, goals, and objectives, and the products developed for the event should align with these as well.

2. Research your target audience. Tailoring your product selection to the interest of your customer is essential.

3. Set your budget. This may be related to your costs or, in the case of merchandise sales, the sales budget. Remember to consider international customs regulations that may have an impact on your budget or timeline. Some countries/industries or companies impose a gift policy with specific maximum prices for customer gifts.

4. Select the appropriate vendor. There are a large number of vendors who sell promotional products. Find one who will work within your timeline, responds quickly, and has quality products.

5. Assess the purpose. Determine whether the products are giveaways, sale merchandise, or employee apparel. Be creative at events with a VIP—provide a gift bag and add themed, high-end products to impress these stakeholders.

6. Determine special product needs. Depending on the needs of your company, you may want to order products that are made in a specific country or are sustainable.

7. Determine distribution methods. Creating a plan for distribution to your customers and one to evaluate after the event to gauge success is essential.

Sub Skill 26.01 – Develop Product(s) Design and Specifications

Promotional products and apparel are created to build the brand of a company and increase the value of the company in the eyes of their customers. People keep promotional items if they see them as useful and visually appealing. To begin, let's review the key reasons why you should order promotional products.

- Build your brand.
- Increase customer loyalty (internal and/or external customers).
- Attract new customers.
- Celebrate an event.

- Announce a new product.
- Enhance individual experience/engagement during the meeting.

Many companies develop a brand strategy to define who they are and what they offer to their customer. A brand should also help a company stand out from their competition. The *Entrepreneur* Web site defines branding as "The marketing practice of creating a name, symbol or design that identifies and differentiates a product from other products" (*Entrepreneur*, 2013, para. 1). As you develop promotional product and merchandise ideas, be sure to incorporate elements of your brand to maintain a consistent message. There should also be established brand guidelines for reference. Promotional products that help build your brand can have a tremendous effect on your relationship with your customers; however, they can also damage your brand if chosen incorrectly. Customer loyalty is what every company hopes to achieve when marketing products and services. Promotional products and merchandise can help you connect with your customers and show them that you value their business. When determining the best promotional products to attract customers, you need to think about three concepts:

1. Usefulness
2. Shelf life
3. Applicability to your customer

Start by reviewing previous promotional products and determine which had the best success. Also take into consideration the location of the event where you distributed the products, because some items are targeted to the location. For example, if you have an event at a resort near the water, you might order beach towels. Those items would be extremely successful at that location but possibly not as successful at a ski resort. Depending on the length of time that you will keep and distribute your promotional products, you may want to find items that are useful no matter the destination and that people can easily transport home without customs, excise, or packing challenges.

The shelf life of a product relates to usefulness and applicability. For example, if you choose to order smart phone covers, it is important to know the manufacturing schedules of new iterations of phones. The market share for particular brands changes frequently and it is difficult to estimate the number of attendees that will have a particular type and model of smart phone. Keep the manufacturing schedule in mind so you don't order a product that is obsolete by the time you distribute it.

Last, make sure the product is applicable to your customers. A great way to determine the interests of your customers is to use surveys to gather their feedback. In addition, you can evaluate the competition and gauge their previous successes. Know your audience and order promotional products that meet their everyday needs and that they would enjoy.

Incorporating Social Media and Technology.   Many event organisers incorporate Twitter into their event marketing strategy. It can be used to build traffic at a trade show booth by offering a high-value giveaway and asking customers to tweet a specific phrase to claim it. The phrase should incorporate the event hashtag, your company Twitter handle, and your booth number. This strategy will increase word-of-mouth marketing and identify successful promotional products for future campaigns.

You can use social media to invite your customers to assist with the product-selection process. Most event marketing strategies now incorporate the use of social media. Reach out to your social media followers to gather their opinion on two or three promotional products or sale merchandise to have available at an upcoming event. Tell your followers that the winning selection will be revealed at the event. This encourages increased registration and allows customers to participate in the decision-making process for the event.

Event professionals should be attentive to shifts in the technology landscape to determine the most suitable options for incorporating social media into their event, as these can change rapidly. As an example of technologies used in event marketing, some event professionals are incorporating quick response (QR) codes on promotional products. A QR code consists of black square dots arranged in a square grid on a white background. Scanning the QR code, often with a smart phone or tablet, will load Web-based content. When choosing to incorporate QR codes on promotional products, remember the following tips:

- Let the customer know what to expect when the product code is scanned.
- Test the code and track success.
- Keep it simple: The goal is to scan the code and take quick action.
- Consider whether or not the audience is likely to have a QR code reader and know how to use it.
- Make sure that the Web site code is optimized for viewing on a mobile device.

Sustainability.   Many promotional companies offer environmentally friendly and/or socially responsible products and apparel. These products may be categorized as "post-consumer recycled material," "recyclable," "biodegradable," or made from "organic materials." Considerations related to sustainability and promotional products include:

- Materials used in the product, including being free from toxins.
- Whether the product is organic or local.
- Labour conditions where the product was produced.
- Packaging and transportation.
- Functionality—for example, does the product promote sustainable behaviour, like a reusable water bottle?
- Product quality.

Sub Skill 26.02 – Determine Pricing

Many event organisers will sell merchandise or products at their events. Examples include:

- Souvenir merchandise
- Books or educational materials
- Recordings of sessions

When developing a pricing plan, analyse current pricing on similar products on-line, at local retail stores, and at other industry events. If your company has sold products in the past, review those sales to identify successful products. Study new trends and determine whether those items will be of interest to your customer base. Evaluate your competition to review the merchandise they are selling and the price points. Last, reach out to your network of contacts, especially in other markets, to see if there are any new products that might work for your company.

Recognise that a lot of this process is trial and error. If someone had conducted a survey to see if you would like to buy a high-priced cup of coffee, the results would most certainly not have encouraged the launch of Starbucks. However, the company has been a tremendous success. Some products will be more successful than a survey might suggest. When determining price for merchandise, take into consideration:

- Unit cost
- Estimated shipping and handling
- Market value for a similar product

Some vendors are willing to make adjustments in their pricing in an effort to win new business. Seek out new opportunities or even new products for which a vendor may be flexible on unit cost. Finding unique products can become a huge win for your event, so allow new vendors to get their foot in the door at your organisation.

Sub Skill 26.03 – Control Brand Integrity

Promotional products should help shape your brand, so decisions about promotional products should be made in consultation with the person or department responsible for marketing and should be consistent with brand guidelines.

Promotional products can inspire, motivate, or leave a solid impression on your customer. Promotional products may be used for trade show or event marketing giveaways, as well as for premium gifts. Trade shows are famous for the distribution of promotional items, and customers often expect to receive some type of giveaway if they visit a company's booth at a trade show. Many times trade show participants will discuss with each other which company has the best "swag" available at its booth. If your goal is to increase brand awareness, selecting the best promotional product for your trade show booth is essential. When considering your trade show giveaways, keep in mind:

- Product purpose
- Number of participants
- Trade show budget
- Messaging

Event marketing often utilises promotional products to get the message to customers prior to or upon arrival at an event. Common examples include a product launch, meeting, seminar, or workshop. The promotional products are distributed to all participants, who also may have paid a registration fee to attend; therefore, allow more flexibility in the budget for these items.

Premium gifts are a category of promotional product that is frequently purchased (or in some cases provided free from manufacturers) for VIP participants, committee members, or leadership. They tend to be high-end products and are primarily categorized as executive products. Premium gifts may be used to drive early registration, as well, by offering them to the first 10 or 10 percent of participants.

Sub Skill 26.04 – Acquire Merchandise

Companies in the promotional products industry sell a wide variety of items imprinted with an organisation's logo to increase brand awareness for the organisation's products. Steps to facilitate acquiring merchandise include:

- Establish and follow a budget.
- Follow the organisation's requirements for the number of required proposals and preferred suppliers.
- Know the lead times required for producing art work, printing, and delivery.
- Have a list of suppliers that are able to provide last-minute items if required.

As previously discussed in Sub Skill 25.03 – Produce Marketing Materials, maintaining consistent branding and graphic design elements for your event is very important.

Sub Skill 26.05 – Distribute Merchandise

When ordering merchandise for an event, a planner must take into consideration the time frame for order processing and distribution. Develop a distribution strategy that covers:

- Advance, on-site, and post-event fulfillment
- Shipping costs
- Staffing needs

To manage distribution channels and maintain control over inventory levels, first determine the number of locations where the product will be sold. Some companies choose to sell merchandise in advance of an event, to build up excitement and gauge customer sales volumes for on-site selection. Pre-show sales will require creating and maintaining an e-commerce Web site to sell the product line. It will also require order fulfillment, which you can choose to conduct in-house or outsource to a professional fulfillment firm.

Carefully track the inventory levels for each product sold on-line; those numbers will help with final selection for the on-site store. If you are working with a local vendor or a company with quick turnaround, you may even be able to sell products before you commit to buying a large inventory. However, the customer should be notified on the Web site of shipping delays for specific merchandise. In some jurisdictions there may be requirements for orders to be shipped within a specific time frame once a customer's credit card is charged.

The on-site store needs adequate staffing. Training your team on retail services, including folding and handling clothes, may take some adjustment from their normal office job. In addition, an on-site store will require hired security personnel to address potential theft issues. A risk to your company exists if an employee accuses a customer of theft, even if the employee is correct. The customer could take legal action against the company; therefore, security staff should be hired to manage risk.

Depending on the size and expected sales volume of the on-site store, you may also want to hire temporary cashier staff. Last, be sure to incorporate the local sales tax, based on the city and country where your event is being held and the type of operating license you hold. In some regions, a temporary business license or permit may be required, and taxes may need to be filed in the region where the event is held. If the merchandise incorporates the date and location of the event, you may want to discount the merchandise on the last day of the event to avoid writing off the cost, though doing this regularly will encourage participants to wait until the last possible moment. Another option is to send out an e-mail to participants after the event, highlighting the best sellers and the extended opportunity to buy those products while supplies last.

Event organisers should clearly communicate any point-of-sale restrictions to all appropriate stakeholders, such as selling products on the display floor at a trade show. When you will be selling merchandise at an event, determine beforehand whether there are any restrictions at the venue and that appropriate taxes are collected and remitted.

In some cases, venues may be able to assist with the sale of products. As an example, a college or university bookstore may be able to secure publications and merchandise for your event and set up a satellite location for your participants close to your meetings.

Reference

Entrepreneur Media, Inc. (2013). *Entrepreneur*. Retrieved from http://www.entrepreneur.com/encyclopedia/branding.

Contributing Author

Lakisha Campbell, CAE
Vice President, Publishing and Affinity Programs
National Association of Home Builders
Washington DC, USA
Member of American Society of Association Executive (ASAE)

Reviewers

Dr. Rodolfo Musco, CMM, CMP
Motivation & Events S.a.s.
Milano, Italy
Member of Meeting Professionals International (MPI)

Glenn Thayer
Conference Moderator, The Voice of Meetings and Events
Denver, CO, USA
Member of American Society of Association Executives (ASAE) and National Speakers Association (NSA)

Skill 26:
Endpoints

Terminology

Promotional products
Premium gifts

Additional Resources

1. Thorne, Heidi. SWAG: How to Choose and Use Promotional Products for Marketing Your Business. Booklocker.com. Bangor, Maine, 2011.

Skill 26: Review Questions

1. When determining the best promotional products to attract your customers, what three concepts do you need to consider?
2. When determining price for merchandise, what three concepts do you need to consider?
3. When considering your exhibition giveaways, what four concepts do you need to consider?
4. What three considerations should be included in your merchandise distribution strategy?

SKILL 27: PROMOTE EVENT

Learning Outcomes

- Name official event sponsors, suppliers, and donors.
- Relate impact of event on local community.
- Clarify branding and message of event.
- Interpret permits and legal requirements.
- Identify hospitality protocols.

Promoting the event will involve developing cross-promotional activities, coordinating hospitality, and possibly executing contests. Taking the target market segments and theme of the event into consideration, the budget will likely dictate which tasks are appropriate and necessary to achieve the goals and objectives of the event. Always check the customs and regulations of the stakeholders' countries of origin.

Begin promoting the event as early as possible. Refer to the Web site or registration site and add information as it becomes available. An on-line presence for the event is not optional to attract a public audience. A site optimized for viewing on a mobile device or a mobile application for larger events should be considered strongly.

Different types of stakeholders (exhibitors, speakers, participants, sponsors, and media) should receive messaging that promotes reasons for involvement specific to them. Whether that takes the form of designated pages on the Web site, special mailings, or targeted advertising, each potential attendee should feel as though the event is being produced just for him or her.

More personalized invitations will elicit a better response. When possible, for the participants who are crucial, a phone call from a VIP of the organisation should be considered. Salespeople should invite clients. In this age of digital information overload, individual phone calls and letters get noticed.

This section will highlight a few activities to integrate into the marketing plan to increase participation in the event and ultimately help achieve the goals and objectives of the organisation.

Sub Skill 27.01 – Develop Cross-Promotional Activities

Helping partner organisations promote the event will increase the reach beyond participants your organisation contacts. Obvious partners are those attending the event – sponsors, exhibitors, etc.— who will benefit directly from increasing attendance. Less obvious partners are speakers, other events, and any other organisation that typically cooperates with your organisation.

Start with a list of the potential partners and indicate who in your organisation has a relationship with someone at each partner organisation. These relationships will be the key to a successful cross-promotional strategy. Don't take for granted that a relationship exists and both parties will be willing to help each other. Come up with as many potential partnerships as possible. Not all opportunities will come to fruition.

There are several options for getting partners involved in the promotion of the event. Sometimes an exchange of promotion can be arranged that works for both organisations. Some organisations will see the value in promoting the event because it will directly benefit them. Other organisations will want to see additional value in exchange for promoting the event. Partnerships may exist on which the outside organisation does not benefit from increased attendance at the event, so payment or promotion of its products, services, or event may be appropriate and necessary.

If the event has a positive impact on the community, explore ways to increase the benefits to the local government, businesses, or charities. There may even be ways to partner with environmental organisations that will promote the sustainable aspects of the event. Corporate social responsibility (CSR) programmes will document the effects of the event on the community.

Other meetings or events that attract the same target audience may be prime partners if they are not hosted by competing organisations. This can also be accomplished by engaging in the on-line conversation during another event. In either case, treat this relationship like any other and have a discussion about how the events can help each other.

A multitiered promotion whereby both organisations advertise to their shared target audience with discounts off both is a strategy to consider. One of the sponsors or other partners might offer a coupon or upgrade for its product, along with a discount or membership option for the event. These promotions can run on-line or in traditional advertising channels, depending on the kinds of campaigns that are currently effective for both organisations.

Launch dates of a promotional partnership will vary depending on the goals and objectives of each organisation. Ensure that each campaign makes sense as part of the overall marketing calendar and that there are no overlapping activities to cause a conflict with your partners. The messaging and branding should also align with all other marketing pieces.

Sub Skill 27.02 – Develop Contests (e.g., Encourage Registration, Traffic Builders, Chapter Challenge)

Most people want to feel as though they are getting a good deal. Creating a contest can be a good way to encourage your potential participants to share your event. It can be challenging to strike the balance between a prize that is motivational and giving too much away. A complimentary registration is a common prize for meeting and event planners to give away to the winner of a contest. The question you have to ask is "Will many people participate if they know there will only be one winner?"

The other option is to find something that can be given to multiple winners so that participants think they have a better chance of winning. To get the highest participation, people have to want the prize and feel as though they have a chance of winning. Another option for increasing the attractiveness of participating in a contest is to provide a small discount on the registration fee to everyone who enters. There may be only one free conference registration awarded, but everyone gets the discount.

The sponsors and vendors of the event can be a good source of prizes. Sponsorship of attendee registration fees can take many different forms. For example, Company X sponsors a percentage off the fee for the first 50 people to register. A sponsor could also offer something of value to potential participants when they help you market the event to their customers. (See Sub Skill 27.01 – Develop Cross-Promotional Activities.)

Since a complimentary registration has a cost to the host organisation, this type of prize, or any other prize, will need to be allocated in the budget as a marketing expense, if the goal of the contest is to drive registration. Using codes on on-line registration forms and other ways of tracking the performance of initiatives will help justify the expense of these activities and inform future decisions.

Like any promotional activity, prospective participants should perceive the contest as fitting in with all other marketing materials and branding efforts. If the event needs to be seen as an exclusive event, contests and prizes will not fit well with that message. If a large number of a certain segment of the community (i.e., the buyers) is seen as critical to the success of the event, contests could be geared toward encouraging this segment to register.

When using social media to coordinate contests, make sure you understand the rules and legal issues surrounding contests. In the United States, federal laws governing marketing promotions such as sweepstakes, contests, and lotteries have been in place for decades. To maximize positive results with contests, Hilfer (2013) suggested investigating rules outside the United States: "In Canada, the laws regulating sweepstakes and contests require sponsors to choose winners differently. Rules need to be drafted and publicised with different mechanisms. So, too, each country in Europe, Asia, or South America may have different laws governing these games" (par. 16).

Use a third-party application to administer the contest. Asking people to "like" or "share" your Facebook page is not an effective way to run a contest. A third party application will gather entries (and the personal information that participants share) and allow you to pick a winner from that data instead of the limited data you will have from people who have "liked" your Facebook page.

If you can get people to share the information about your event on social media channels, potential participants who fit your target market might be reached who otherwise would not be. Some people in the community will not be able to attend the event, regardless of what you offer as an incentive: The registration fee is too high, the date conflicts with a previously scheduled event, they can't travel to the location, etc. Consider what might motivate them to promote the event, even if they cannot attend themselves. Are you offering a virtual component? Maybe you can offer a discounted registration for the virtual package if there would otherwise be a cost attached.

Sub Skill 27.03 – Coordinate Hospitality

Other events or attractions at the location of the meeting can help drive attendance to the event. There may be an opportunity for participants to bring family members or other guests along with them. Either a formal programme will be coordinated to entertain these guests or they will be on their own during the hours of the event. Sometimes, a combination programme is set up at which a reception or activity is arranged for all participants, and guests are allowed to attend as well.

Research the attractions of the event location on-line via a Web site hosted by a destination marketing organisation (DMO; also known as a convention and visitors bureau or CVB). The site should list the public events occurring around the same time as your event. This is good information to obtain before a location is chosen so that traffic, parking, and other problems can be avoided when possible. On the other hand, it may be beneficial to the participants of your event to meet in conjunction with another event.

Time may be left open intentionally on the agenda so that suppliers, vendors, sponsors, and so on can host hospitality events during the meeting. Planning for this in advance is advisable so that parameters can be established and additional space or cost reductions can be negotiated with the venue. Work with these event partners so they feel that the option makes the event even more productive and worthwhile for their organisation. Conversations early in the planning process will help determine whether hospitality events will be of interest to the sponsors of your event. Discuss their budget and preferences. A fine line exists between capturing those funds as part of the overall event sponsorship and having those funds go directly toward hosting an "unofficial" hospitality event.

A concierge type of service is often provided by a convention centre or large hotel. If the venue you are using does not offer such a service, consider adding it to your plans. Local recommendations on restaurants and attractions with the ability to make reservations and book tickets are a great resource for participants.

Reference

Hilfer, K. (2013, June 12). *How to Avoid Common Legal Mistakes in Social Media Contests and Sweepstakes*. Maximize Social Business. Retrieved from http://maximizesocialbusiness.com/legal-mistakes-social-media-contests-sweepstakes-9140/.

Contributing Author

Elizabeth Glau, CMP
Owner/Consultant
Building Blocks Social Media
Los Angeles, CA, USA
Member of Green Meeting Industry Council (GMIC)

Reviewers

Dr. Rodolfo Musco, CMM, CMP
Motivation & Events S.a.s.
Milano, Italy
Member of Meeting Professionals International (MPI)

Glenn Thayer
Conference Moderator, The Voice of Meetings and Events
Denver, CO, USA
Member of American Society of Association Executives (ASAE) and National Speakers Association (NSA)

Skill 27:
Endpoints

Terminology

Multitiered promotion
Hospitality event

Skill 27: Review Questions

1. Who are the potential partners for cross-promotional activities?
2. How should messaging be different for each type of stakeholder?
3. What are the disadvantages and advantages of sponsors and vendors donating prizes?
4. What are the considerations for promoting an event in an increasingly mobile society?

SKILL 28: CONTRIBUTE TO PUBLIC RELATIONS ACTIVITIES

Learning Outcomes

- Identify communication, public relations, and publicity strategies.
- Describe emergency response and risk management plan.
- Classify key internal/external issues and social concerns.
- Relate the importance of the organisation's key messages.
- Select media and communication outlets, contacts, and protocols.

The Public Relations Society of America (PRSA) led an industry-wide advocacy campaign to modernize the definition of public relations. The crowd-sourced winning definition is "Public relations is a strategic communication process that builds mutually beneficial relationships between organisations and their publics" (PRSA, 2012). One difference between PR and marketing is gaining exposure to the public, employees, participants, and other stakeholders without paying for the publicity directly. The activities discussed in this section include speaking at conferences, winning industry awards, working with the press, and employee communication.

The changing landscape is blurring the lines between marketing, public relations, and customer service. Most organisations divide these three areas into separate departments; however, some organisations have started to integrate these activities. The PRSA (2011) says, "The reality is that organisations will continue to merge their brand management functions (marketing) with their reputation management functions (PR)."

Public relations strategies should be directly connected to the goals and objectives of the organisation and event. The publicity plan will be based on messaging established in conjunction with the marketing plan. Developing and nurturing media relationships is critical. Sharing news about the event's sustainability plan is a great way to create a positive sentiment about the organisation. Crisis and controversy are more typical than we would like them to be, so always having a plan in place for response to these situations rounds out the topics to include in your public relations activities.

Sub Skill 28.01 – Contribute to Public Relations Strategy

The public relations strategy should be created in collaboration with the marketing and communication plan. Emergency response and risk management plans will provide the foundation for how the organisation responds to crisis and controversy.

A positive perception of the organisation by the public will attract not only customers but potential employees as well. Quality employees will make the organisation's products and services better and, therefore, easier to sell. Every interaction someone has with the organisation leaves an impression of that organisation. You never know who might be a potential customer or employee.

In a corporate environment, customer service is not always considered a public relations strategy but a different department entirely. However, much attention should be given to the subject, regardless of the type of organisation, to ensure that every interaction with the organisation is a positive one. Contact information for questions and issues before, during, and after the event should be easy to find for all stakeholders. Live human response should be available outside of normal business hours if possible, particularly on social media. Participants may be trying to register in the evening or on a weekend, and if they become frustrated with the process, they may decide not to attend. If the audience spans multiple time zones, make sure normal business hours in those time zones are covered at a minimum. PRSA explains the need for personal contact between organisation and customer:

As we move ever closer to a world in which global publishing power lies in every person's pocket, the punishment for failing to listen, engage, anticipate and respond effectively will be severe; and the rewards for an organisation that defines itself through communication will be rich indeed. (2011, par. 7)

Research on target markets should indicate whether participants are likely to contact the organisation by e-mail, phone, or on one of the various social media platforms. Many people these days expect a quick, almost immediate, response to a question or comment via social media. The organisation needs someone to monitor all social networks for mentions, feedback (positive and negative), and questions. Gather social profile information for as many stakeholders as possible and find ways to connect their individual current and future needs and expectations to the event. If potential participants feel as though they are interacting with a human being every time they interact with the organisation, the strategy is successful.

The more training provided to all employees (full-time, part-time, and contractors), along with social media guidelines, the less risk the organisation faces. A social media policy that discourages social sharing only by listing the repercussions and leaving out examples of behaviour that will be rewarded is shortsighted.

The return on investment (ROI) of social media does not come immediately. You have to consider the lifetime value of customer retention. Marketers make the mistake of using the media to push out their messages. Instead, use it to listen to stakeholders and gain valuable insight into their current and future needs and expectations. An event takes so much planning and production that we sometimes forget that the participants' objectives should tie into the organisation's long-term goals.

Sub Skill 28.02 – Contribute to Publicity Plan

Publicity is a rapidly changing field with the focus shifting toward two-way communication with stakeholders. Traditionally, entering competitions for events could mean positive PR. Making presentations at other events is another traditional way to support a partner event and receive positive publicity.

A press release or social media release is a promotional tactic to get the information about an event into the hands of reporters who may want to share the news. Whether the event is B2B or B2C, there are publications for this type of sharing, and those publications should receive your press release. The research done to define the situational analysis might also provide great data for a press release. To generate attention from the media, press releases should include newsworthy elements, not simply event details.

Newer forms of publicity include guest blogging for other organisations in a way that establishes your or your organisation's expertise. Allowing for an exchange of these types of activities with partners in the community is a great promotional tactic. A successful strategy at a cocktail party is to network as though you are only there to help the people you meet. Treat your publicity strategy the same way. Look for ways to help other people, organisations, meetings, and events.

Creating compelling content is the first key to the publicity plan; however, using the tools and technology to figure out how to get that content to the stakeholders when it is relevant to them is the ultimate objective. Most people are experiencing information overload. There's a lot of good content out there, and people are seeing it (mostly on-line) all day, every day. Unless a piece of news crosses their path at a time when they are likely to take action on it (including sharing it with their network), it doesn't matter how good the content is.

Sub Skill 28.03 – Manage Media Relations

Don't forget that having a good working relationship with media contacts helps get stories featured. Sending out press releases and expecting them to get traction on their own doesn't typically work. When an issue arises, media representatives should know to turn to your organisation as the authority and call you for an interview. Positive media relations make this action probable.

In some cases, when a newsworthy announcement coincides with the event, holding a press conference can be beneficial. The spokesperson for the press conference should be knowledgeable, informative, succinct, and adept at answering questions.

Media may be invited to the event in exchange for advertising with their publications. However, many organisations will extend an invitation to the media with no expectation of coverage. Clearly, coverage of the event is the expected outcome of this situation. In fact, some media outlets will be highly offended by a request to attend in exchange for advertising space, as the news segment of that outlet is kept strictly separate from the advertising segment. This is a common position with newspapers but tends to be less the case with trade publications and Web sites.

For the media that attend the event, a press room should be part of the logistics plan from the beginning: "The basic role of the press room is to provide a working area for editors, reporters and columnists pursuing leads. They generally will fall into two categories: editors of special-interest publications that cover your field and representatives of the news media in the host city" (Breden and Chong, 2011, p. 278). A newer strategy is blogger outreach. It can be difficult to ascertain which bloggers might be relevant to your community. Categorising them as media and extending the same benefits provided to traditional media can potentially result in additional exposure for the organisation. Other influential people may warrant this type of invitation, even if they don't have a blog with a large subscriber list, as long as they are influential on-line or off-line.

McMahon (2012) described four categories of influencers who range from having a personal connection to your target market to reaching a broader scope of people. Some will have limited ability to inspire action and others will inspire a high probability of action.

1. Altruistic activators: proactive ambassadors, trusted resource
2. Connected catalysts: massive exposure, immediate action
3. Everyday advocates: sincere endorsement, existing fans
4. Passionate publishers: "buzz" at scale, third-party endorsement

Whether you are dealing with traditional media or on-line influencers, make it a give-and-take relationship. Don't ask for promotion without being willing to help the medium representative. In fact, proactively offering assistance before making a request will go a long way in fostering those relationships. This requires knowing the media well and offering incentives that meet their immediate needs and preferences.

Sub Skill 28.04 – Contribute to Implementation of Sustainability Plan

Sustainability or corporate social responsibility (CSR) initiatives are to the ways in which an organisation mitigates its impact on the environment and increases its positive impact on the event location Including plans and details for these initiatives in your press releases makes the event more newsworthy and might help get media coverage; a though saturation of this type of activity means that innovation is increasingly key. All meetings and events bring economic benefit to the community where they take place, so find a way to measure and highlight that fact and consider a service project to benefit the community beyond the economic realm. Make sure that the efforts are meaningful and verifiable and align with your brand. "Greenwashing"—the practice of claiming or proudly sharing empty sustainability commitments or misleading socially responsible activities without actually doing anything that has real positive impact—can be very damaging to the organisation's reputation.

Sub Skill 28.05 – Manage Response to Crises and Controversies

All events are vulnerable to crises and controversies; however, an effective crisis communication plan can be valuable in helping to mitigate their effects. Information on the types of crises that can affect events are outlined in the risk management domain.

The crisis communication plan has three phases: pre-crisis, crisis, and post-crisis. Considerations in each of the phases are outlined below.

Pre-Crisis

Potential emergencies are handled more effectively when the organisation has a plan in place to respond publicly to the situation. Before a crisis occurs, possible scenarios should be identified and responses to them should be developed. This includes developing a notification system for stakeholders, complete with emergency contact information. Multiple communication methods should be ready to be used, including phones, text messages, social media, e-mail, and fax, in case one form cannot be used. A backup communication plan is essential, depending on the extent of the crisis.

Don't wait to establish a relationship with legal counsel until you need it. Even with the best crisis planning, the type of crisis that occurs may not be one you have planned for and legal may need to be consulted both during the planning stage and as soon as the crisis occurs. The plan should include a point of contact for media inquiries and consistent messaging to be shared with all other stakeholders. All staff should know where to direct media inquiries in a crisis.

A media spokesperson should be designated, whether this person is on-site or back at the office, managing the message with the media, on the organisation's Web site, in voice mail messages, and on social media. Media training for the designated spokesperson as well as a backup spokesperson will benefit the organisation when those people are called to interact with the media in a crisis. If media representatives are on-site at the meeting and the primary media spokesperson is back at the office, crisis communication on-site may need to be delegated to a supplier-partner or professional emergency responder. The person selected should have the authority to speak on behalf of the organisation. There should be someone appointed to monitor and respond to social media, and this person should also receive training in crisis communication. In addition to the event's spokesperson, there may be spokespersons for the venue, the destination, or key partners. These should be identified in advance of the event so that communication can be coordinated or, at a minimum, monitored.

During the Crisis

During a crisis, the first communication priorities are informing emergency response personnel of the crisis and making safety announcements for attendees and on-site staff as required based on the nature of the crisis. Announcements made to internal and external audiences should be timely, accurate, and informative, and should help combat misinformation.

The media spokesperson should make a statement as soon as possible to establish himself or herself as the main point of contact. This is particularly important in an age of social media, when any person at the event can begin sending out notifications that may lead to misinformation. If information is not yet available, the spokesperson should tell the media when the organisation will provide it. All statements by the organisation's representatives should be based on facts not on speculation. The organisation must maintain a reputation for credibility during a crisis.

In many cultures, an immediate expression of regret is expected and should be issued. This is important to help protect the organisation's reputation. Event professionals should consult with their legal counsel during the planning phase and be trained on the legal ramifications of expressions of regret, offers to secure or pay for medical care, and similar crisis responses, as these may vary among jurisdictions.

Post-Crisis

Following the crisis, the plan and its implementation should be analysed and recommendations developed to respond to a future crisis.

References

Breden, C., & Chong, D. (2011). *Events Industry Council Manual*, 8ᵗʰ ed. Alexandria, VA: Events Industry Council.

McMahon, T. (2012, Oct.). *Put up or shut up, beyond social influence.* Session at Social Media Explorer conference. Orange, CA. Retrieved from http://www.slideshare.net/tamadear/put-up-or-shut-up-beyond-social-influence

Public Relations Society of America (2011, Dec. 19). 12 trends that will change public relations. Retrieved from http://prsay.prsa.org/index.php/2011/12/19/12-trends-for-public-relations-in-2012/.

Public Relations Society of America (2012, April 11). Public Relations Defined: A Modern Definition For The New Era Of Public Relations. Retrieved from http://prdefinition.prsa.org/.

Contributing Authors

Elizabeth Glau, CMP
Owner/Consultant
Building Blocks Social Media
Los Angeles, CA, USA
Member of Green Meeting Industry Council (GMIC)

Reviewers

Dr. Rodolfo Musco, CMM, CMP
Motivation & Events S.a.s.
Milano, Italy
Member of Meeting Professionals International (MPI)

Glenn Thayer
Conference Moderator, The Voice of Meetings and Events
Denver, CO, USA
Member of American Society of Association Executives (ASAE) and National Speakers Association (NSA)

Skill 28:
Endpoints

Terminology

Press release
Greenwashing
Press conference

Additional Resources

1. Help a Reporter Out (HARO). http://www.helpareporter.com/.

Skill 28: Review Questions

1. What is the difference between marketing and public relations?
2. How does a positive perception of the organisation affect its success?
3. What are the four categories of influencers?
4. What are the contents of a crisis communications plan?

SKILL 29: MANAGE MEETING-RELATED SALES ACTIVITIES

Learning Outcomes

- Analyse target market segmentation and purchasing behaviour.
- Associate marketing plan with sales activities.
- Discover competitors' sales practices.
- Translate sales objectives, tools, tactics, and targets.
- Share principles of selling, sales communication, and relationship-building.

Certain revenue-generating items require sales tactics in addition to the marketing tactics already discussed in this chapter. While sales and marketing typically fall in the same area or department, they are a bit different in approach and process.

Direct sales of registration fees may be appropriate, depending on the type of event and the target audience. If prospects are already connected to the organisation and their phone numbers, e-mail addresses, or social media profiles are accessible, you can reach out to them directly. Engage in a conversation about why they should attend the event, ask whether they are available and what might keep them from attending, and attempt to register them.

Revenue might be generated from the suppliers, vendors, or other partners in the industry. Sponsorship sales are crucial income for many events. Exhibit sales are another way to generate income from suppliers or vendors, either through a trade show with booths or an appointment-based system with the buyers in attendance. Advertising in the printed programme or mobile application (app) for the event can be sold, if it is not given to sponsors in exchange for their financial support of the programme. Suppliers and vendors might also be interested in purchasing banner ads on the organisation's Web site or on-line registration site, if those are not reserved for sponsors.

As discussed in Sub Skill 26 – Manage Event Merchandise, a number of products may be created by the event that would be of value to participants. On-site memorabilia such as T-shirts, books written by the speakers at your meeting, and educational content such as session recordings can all be sold both on-line and in a retail setting at the event. Session recordings can also be sold to people who did not attend the event. Either archived sessions or a live hybrid event package of some or all sessions can be sold in advance of the event via the Web site or on-line registration site.

Sub Skill 29.01 – Contribute to Sales Plan and Objectives

Sales efforts require a plan, just like the marketing efforts for the event. Look at historical data on what you are selling, whether it is registrations, T-shirts, or anything else. The event budget will account for revenue from sales efforts, so make sure that all previous revenue sources are accounted for or replaced with a new revenue source.

Identify the target market segments for each product. For example, some of the potential participants may not be able to attend the event due to budgetary or travel restrictions. Some attendees might find more value in the networking opportunities the event offers and want access to the education at a later date. Selling them archived session recordings or a live hybrid event package may increase or supplement revenue. Having conversations with potential participants via phone or social media will help you determine whom this option would benefit. This way, the stakeholders will feel confident that the virtual event did not decrease the physical attendance of their target market. Instead, it was a specific niche within the market that was accommodated.

The sales plan should also look at the competitive situation of the event. If it is trade show booths that need to be sold, think about all of the other meetings or events where those suppliers or vendors could be spending time and money. It is possible that the competition is offering them an appointment-based show or other innovative way of connecting with buyers. Their decision on whether or not to buy a booth from you depends on the value proposition of what you are offering and how it will help them increase their sales.

During the sponsorship sales planning process, pricing and packaging will need to be determined before being offered to potential partners. The pricing should consider not only the costs to produce the event but also the value of the event to the sponsor.

After looking at what has been done before and what needs to happen to meet the budgeted revenue, set the goals and objectives for the sales plan. A minimum number or amount should be reached. The sales staff for the organisation will often set a goal of reaching higher than the minimum number for sales or revenue listed in the sales plan. Some organisations will implement a commission or goal-based incentive sales staff, if these numbers can be tracked. If the people in the organisation are motivated to sell more sponsorship, registrations, or advertising, sales will most likely increase.

If any plans exist to sell items, packages, and so on via the Web site or on-line registration site, make sure they are factored into the initial Web site plans, as they could be a costly addition if the Web site administrator has to work them in later.

Have a plan in place to communicate the policy regarding other organisations selling products during the event. If this is a possibility, it should be communicated in advance. Assign staff or volunteers to identify this activity on-site and deal with the situation. The time and resources that sponsors and exhibitors commit to the event should be protected. The opportunities available to them because of their participation should not be available to those who did not contribute to the revenue of the event.

Sub Skill 29.02 – Conduct Sales Activities

The sales plan and marketing plan should be created and implemented together so that efforts are not duplicated and prospects do not fall through the cracks. Using a customer relationship management (CRM) system and tracking every interaction that the organisation has with a prospect will ensure that they feel valued and appreciated. A CRM system will incorporate social media activity and conversations along with telephone calls, e-mails, mailings, and so on.

The sales process may consist of activities such as qualifying leads, conducting sales calls, delivering sales presentations, preparing proposals, and negotiating sales details. This is a typical sales cycle that may or may not work, depending on what you are selling. In the case of the trade show booth or other supplier opportunity, this may be an appropriate use of your salespeoples' skills and abilities. An incentive via commission or bonus would also be appropriate in this case.

For some events, sponsorship packages represent a large sum of money, and top-level executives will be making these purchasing decisions. Once the contract is signed, other activities begin. Benefits tracking, communications during the planning process, sponsor training, on-site management of the sponsor experience, post-event follow-up and reporting will need to be completed.

The salesperson or sales team will be required to attend networking events to grow their base of prospects. When researching potential sponsors, take the event's target market into consideration and find organisations with similar target markets. Then find the events where their C-level executives go for networking.

Packaging products is another tactic that might be used to up-sell or increase revenue. A full conference registration could be offered along with the conference recordings for an additional price but discounted if purchased together. The reverse of that would be to offer something free with the purchase of something else. Give a free T-shirt or book written by one of the speakers with the purchase of an early registration.

Planners should consult the Department of Revenue or other taxation body in the city, county, state or province in which they are planning to make sales to find out how much sales or other tax must be charged, the proper documentation for tax exemptions, and to whom tax collections need to be paid. Even if the organisation doing the selling is (sales) tax-exempt, the person buying may not be.

Contributing Authors

Elizabeth Glau, CMP
Owner/Consultant
Building Blocks Social Media
Los Angeles, CA, USA
Member of Green Meeting Industry Council (GMIC)

Reviewers

Dr. Rodolfo Musco, CMM, CMP
Motivation & Events S.a.s.
Milano, Italy
Member of Meeting Professionals International (MPI)

Glenn Thayer
Conference Moderator, The Voice of Meetings and Events
Denver, CO, USA
Member of American Society of Association Executives (ASAE) and National Speakers Association (NSA)

Skill 29:
Endpoints

Terminology

Customer relationship management
Value proposition

Skill 29: Review Questions

1. Where can advertising be sold to suppliers or vendors?
2. What are the steps in a sales cycle?
3. How do you determine which target markets are unable to physically attend the event but are potential sources of income?
4. What are examples of packaging products together to increase revenue?

Professionalism

SKILL 30: EXHIBIT PROFESSIONAL BEHAVIOUR

Learning Outcomes

- Describe the importance of professional and ethical behaviour.
- Explore best practices for demonstrating ethical behaviour.
- Identify steps for developing and implementing a code of conduct.
- Understand how to arrange security for meetings and events.

Professionalism encompasses both your conduct and how you present yourself. Expectations for these behaviours may vary based on the region(s) in which you live and work. Professionalism, therefore, encompasses meeting the expectations for the region where you are conducting business as well as the expectations for similar behaviours in your normal place of business. (See Sub Skill 19.05 – Manage Protocol Requirements.) Exhibiting professional behaviour sets the tone for how we work and how we are perceived by others. Professionalism in the meetings industry includes the following behaviours:

- having superior knowledge in one or more aspects of the industry,
- treating people and business opportunities fairly,
- maintaining high standards for professional behaviour, and
- being a lifelong learner in, and contributor to, the industry.

Exhibiting professionalism and behaving ethically will help define and protect your reputation in the industry and enhance the overall image of our profession.

In this chapter, the desired behaviours and actions of meeting industry professionals are explored. The chapter is organised into two distinct areas: professionalism and ethical behaviour.

Professional and ethical conduct in our industry are important not only for individuals, but for the industry as a whole. Conversely, unprofessional or unethical behaviour, or the perception of either, is damaging for the individual, the employing organisation, and the industry. Actions resulting in negative publicity put a spotlight on ethical and legal behaviour. Disreputable behaviour, both personal and organisational, can result in lost revenues, dips in stock prices, bankruptcy, and civil or criminal charges. Many Events Industry Council member organisations have principles of professional behaviour or codes of ethics. Professional behaviour is demanded by the professional organisations we join and the organisations that employ us, as well as being the foundation by which our customers and suppliers evaluate us on a daily basis.

Professional Conduct and Standards of Behaviour

There are many resources available to help define expectations for **professional conduct** for the events industry. These resources include Web sites that discuss professional conduct in general and the standards for behaviour that are prepared by the organisation for which you work. As previously mentioned, many Events Industry Council member organisations also provide guidance on this topic. In some cases, referring to the standards of behaviour prepared by the organisations your best customers work for may also be prudent. Standards of behaviour and organisational core values communicate what we expect of ourselves and others in this profession. We are expected to live the values of our organisation and embrace the character of the organisation's behaviour standards. Standards of behaviour can include:

- Integrity – disclosing conflicts of interest and commissions, and fulfilling commitments thoroughly and on time
- Teamwork – respecting diversity and treating everyone with fairness and equality
- Client and supplier relations – demonstrating appreciation and respect for clients and suppliers, even when they are reporting a problem or expressing frustration
- Self-management – maintaining a positive image, and managing time and stress
- Communication – practicing appropriate etiquette in all forms of communication, including verbal, written, and social networking
- Professional presentation – including following locally appropriate expectations for attire, hygiene, smoking, and consumption of alcohol
- Appropriate use of technology – including following organisational guidelines for personal use of equipment
- Ownership/accountability – taking responsibility for commitments and owning the problem when there is one
- Responsible financial management – making sound decisions that ensure the financial viability of the event and a positive reputation
- Respecting local customs – researching expectations for conduct, dress, and protocols prior to an event and communicating these customs to all who need to know

In addition to these general expectations, specific behaviours are also anticipated as a way of demonstrating professionalism in certain settings. For example, during exhibits, exhibitors are expected to be welcoming and focused on the buyers and visitors, as well as respectful of the property (physical and intellectual) of other exhibitors. Buyers and visitors should be respectful of the time they spend with exhibitors, and of their physical and intellectual property.

Sub Skill 30.01 – Demonstrate Ethical Behaviour

Defining Ethics

The late Rushworth M. Kidder was the founder of the Institute for Global Ethics (IGE). According to Kidder, one of the most useful ways for people to think about ethics is as the application of values to decision making. With his work with IGE, he concluded that regardless of differences in religion or social strata, people all over the world talk about the same five values: honesty, responsibility, respect, fairness, and compassion.

Types of Ethical Issues in the Meetings Industry

Ethics are more than just not causing harm (such as spreading rumors about competitors) or avoiding illegal behaviour (such as using intellectual property without permission or citations). It also includes doing good, such as demonstrating care for communities and the environment where our meetings are held. In addition, and perhaps at its most complex, ethics is about making choices between two values, such as choosing between loyalty to a longtime supplier and an open bidding process.

Building on the five values identified by Kidder, the following are a few examples of ethical issues that arise in the meetings industry. This list is not comprehensive, and the types of ethical issues faced by event professionals will vary.

Table 1 Examples of Ethical Issues.

Honesty	▪ Being truthful about potential future business opportunities prior to accepting invitations to participate in familiarization trips or hosted buyer events ▪ Disclosing commissions or incentives such as loyalty programme points to employers or clients ▪ Keeping information confidential ▪ Respecting the ownership of intellectual property, including information in bids or proposals and client lists from past employers
Responsibility	▪ Taking responsibility for the impact of your actions on your stakeholders, the environment, and the community ▪ Fulfilling verbal and written commitments in a timely manner ▪ Accountability
Respect	▪ Valuing diversity ▪ Demonstrating respect for trade show organisers by not suitcasing or outboarding ▪ Avoiding aggressive behaviour
Fairness	▪ Using equitable negotiation practices and fair trade products ▪ Ensuring fair labour practices ▪ Respecting supplier relationships by not requesting special favours ▪ Transparency
Compassion	▪ Speaking out against bullying or mistreatment of others ▪ Supporting the local community through service projects

Special Focus Areas

Professional negotiations. When negotiating business agreements, we have the responsibility to ensure the best possible value for the organisation(s) we represent. We also have the responsibility to ensure that our organisations aren't damaged by our behaviour in the negotiation process. This means that we should treat every negotiation as an honorable business deal, not as a battle to be won; we should treat the person with whom we are negotiating with respect; and we should use language that respects the opinions of others and does not threaten or belittle. Maintaining good relationships also means that there is a high degree of trust—trust that both parties have the authority to make decisions on their organisation's behalf, as well as trust that the details of the negotiations or the results of the negotiations won't be shared with competitors.

Familiarization trips and hosted buyer events.   One of the areas most easily abused in the meetings industry is **familiarization trips** (fam trips). The meetings industry does legitimately utilise these to help event professionals experience a destination, hotel, or other venue and become familiar with the resources available. This experience should make business decisions more effective on behalf of the professional's organisation or client. Ethical behaviour may be questioned if a event professional wants to include others (co-workers, family, friends) who have no bearing on the decision-making process for the organisation. Further, consideration should be given to whether booking business with the inviting party is likely. Specifically, familiarization trips and hosted buyer events should not be used as free vacations or rewards for staff.

For hosted buyer events—where potential buyers are invited to participate in a trade show or some other type of event—the event organisers have a responsibility to qualify prospective hosted buyers properly, and the buyers have a responsibility to truthfully represent themselves and the business opportunities they can reasonably expect to plan. Being present for scheduled appointments in buyer hosted events is an expected behaviour for all professionals.

Gift exchanges.   A gift—offered or accepted—may become ethically questionable based on its financial value, the intent of the giver, the timing, and company standards of conduct. Before offering or accepting a gift, consider the following issues.

- What is the purpose of the gift?
- Is the gift for a group to share or for an individual?
- Does the gift imply an expectation of a return response of some type? Is this response appropriate?
- Is the cost of the gift appropriate to the situation?
- Is the nature of the gift appropriate to the situation?
- Is the gift in keeping with the giver's and receiver's organisational ethics (e.g., a "green" gift)?

A gift becomes a bribe when it is given with expectations of a return favour or decision. When considering whether or not a gift is appropriate, keep in mind the culture in which you are working. In some countries, for example, gift exchange is utilised as a standard and expected element of doing business. If a gift is refused, it can result in loss of face, hurt feelings, and damage to the business relationship. In these cases, corporate gift policies should reflect local practices.

To determine whether a gift is appropriate, use what used to be called the "front page of the newspaper" test: If whatever is in question would appear on the front page of your local newspaper along with your name, would it cause you or your company embarrassment? Today, you might adapt this to the "Twitter test": If your actions appeared in 140 characters and were spread virally, would the consequences be favourable?

Digital technology.   New technology and the digital age have had a dramatic impact on perception of ethical behaviours in the events industry and in society in general. As resourceful as the Internet and social media are, they also present new and unknown challenges, and they can magnify the effects of any ethical misjudgments that might be made. Confidentiality has become more difficult to maintain, and privacy may be difficult to ensure.

Personal information.   Maintaining confidentiality may also refer to the personally identifiable information (PII) of an individual traveling to and/or attending a meeting. Personally identifiable information includes anything that may identify an individual, such as a passport number, national identification number, or credit or debit card number. In the technology world of today, and with the enormous risk of fraud with any one of several pieces of identifying information, it is imperative to keep any PII data secure and confidential. A breach of this data can be devastating not only to the individual but to the organisation that was trusted with the information and allowed the breach. This issue includes both an ethical imperative to protect confidential information and a legal risk. Attitudes and regulations related to personal information can vary across cultures and jurisdictions, and international planners need to do their research in advance. Lawsuits can ruin the organisation that did not keep the data secure. If you intend to share data with others (e.g., sponsors, exhibitors), get permission from the individuals to share their information. This can be done at the time the information is provided, and should specify what information will be shared and with whom.

Intellectual property and bid or supplier information.   Creativity and innovation are increasingly important to provide interesting and new elements in a meeting experience. These elements are critical as we become a design-driven industry. Suppliers compete in this arena and are always trying to stay on the cutting edge of creativity and innovation in their designs. The dilemma arises when suppliers share their creative and innovative ideas with a prospective client who may turn around and disperse these ideas to other suppliers in an effort to obtain a lower bid than the original proposal or to give favour to a competing supplier. This practice is unethical and harms everyone. It might also undermine the relationship and trust that are essential to conducting business. Sharing elements of a proposal can also be unlawful if the proposal states that the ideas contained in it are proprietary and confidential. All parties involved are responsible for maintaining the confidential and proprietary nature of proposals.

Intellectual property and speaker content.   Another new challenge brought about by the digital age is the protection and repository of a speaker's intellectual property, including audio and video content, and images of the speaker or her/his materials. Determine and confirm who may have access to the content and how it can be shared, and draw up an explicit agreement on the extent of and channels for sharing this information. In some cases, meeting organisers are making their expectations related to proprietary content clear to event participants by having them sign non-disclosure agreements. In many cases, at the start of sessions, organisers or the speakers themselves are clearly stating whether their sessions may be recorded in any manner or their remarks quoted in social media. Determine at the outset the conditions under which information may or may not be shared, and insist that audience members comply with the restrictions.

Suitcasing.   According to the International Association of Exhibitions and Events (IAEE), **suitcasing** is the act of soliciting business in the aisles during an exhibition or in other public spaces, including another company's booth, or in a hotel lobby or convention centre space. Trade show managers are responsible for handling situations of suitcasing or allegations of it in a timely, efficient, and discreet manner. A clear policy against suitcasing should be developed and enforced. If this policy is overlooked, it can compromise the support provided by legitimate exhibitors and sponsors. More information on this issue and tools for effectively dealing with it are available at the IAEE Web site (www.iaee.com).

Outboarding.   The practice of conducting an event related to an existing meeting but not approved by the event's host organisation is known as **outboarding**. Prospective participants in the original meeting are invited to the unsanctioned event, resulting in a decrease in event attendance and affecting the host organisation's reputation. Once started, outboarding can become increasingly problematic for event hosts, so a policy regarding outboarding should be developed and disseminated to potential exhibitors, sponsors, and event partners. Meeting with representatives of the organisation that has infringed on the event is an important action that can help curtail future episodes of outboarding. Industry leaders such as IAEE, (formerly the International Association of Exhibition Managers) have publicly identified outboarding as an unethical tactic in the industry (Hatch, 2006).

Transparency.   An element of business that has received more attention in recent years is the idea that transactions should be transparent if they are to be considered legitimate. Every deal we do, every contract we sign, every concession we negotiate, every commission we receive or pay out must be disclosed. The level of disclosure will vary from one organisation to the next, but we cannot afford to have contractual agreements involving business organisations with side deals that we just "keep to ourselves." Even when it appears to be a common practice within a particular market, we must keep our reputation and the reputation of the entire meeting industry in mind, and we must not take any action that can adversely impact the organisations we represent or with which we do business.

It is increasingly common for large-scale public-funded events, such as the Olympics, to be transparent about their costs and their environmental and social impact. The legal mandate for transparency in regulated industries, such as the healthcare field, is growing internationally, and the ethical best practice standard for other organisations is close behind. According to the Global Transparency Reporting Congress, "As practices for spending on healthcare providers have come under increased scrutiny, 'transparency' has become a buzzword with growing weight. Guidelines regulating the disclosure of this spending are rapidly developing across the globe, including association codes that span across borders" (Global Transparency, 2013, para. 1).

Creating an Ethics Code or Policy

To avoid the pitfalls of unethical behaviours, organisations may establish guidelines, processes, policies, and procedures to minimize risk. These tools also provide a framework that is easily understood and to which employees can and should adhere. The greater the specificity (e.g., currency amounts versus the words "nominal" or "limited"), the more readily employees can abide by the code. Recommendations adapted from the Treasury Board of Canada Secretariat in the "Guide for Developing Organisational Codes of Conduct" include:

- **Step 1.** Involve senior management to ensure alignment with the organisation's vision and strategy, communicate the organisation's values and ethics, and facilitate the approval process.
- **Step 2.** Create a diversified and multidisciplinary advisory group to increase the effectiveness and relevance to all employees.
- **Step 3.** Set the objectives for your organisational code of conduct. This will influence the content; these objectives should be tied to the expected outcomes by which the code's effectiveness will be measured.
- **Step 4.** Tailor the code to the needs and values of the organisation. This includes understanding the types of risks posed to the organisation with respect to behaviours that are inconsistent with its values.
- **Step 5.** Validate the draft organisational code of conduct with employees and bargaining agents.

Additional steps to consider in developing the code of conduct include the following:

* Identify written industry standards of conduct and be aware of potential regulations or laws that may govern the industry. Codes of conduct from professional associations can be used as a starting point and should be adapted for the particular needs of the organisation.
* Encourage everyone to be accountable for their own behaviour and for helping co-workers and partners to maintain accountability.
* Create a system for employees to report violations and to be protected when doing so.

Another area to be addressed for event professionals in particular should be the collection and use of reward or earned points from hotels, airlines, or any other vendors offering purchase incentives. This will establish guidelines to ensure that business decisions are not influenced by personal gain. Example: If you are employed by an organisation that asks you to make your own travel arrangements to attend a meeting, and that organisation reimburses your costs after the meeting occurs, do you get to keep the airline points for that travel? The organisation should have a stated policy in the code of conduct or an employee handbook to protect the employee and the organisation from abuse of incentives like these. For meeting industry professionals, being well-versed on these policies in your employing organisation will help make your business transactions transparent and above reproach.

The code of conduct will describe what is expected of employees, members of a board of directors, volunteers, and (in the case of associations) the general membership in the way they conduct business and represent the organisation. The code of conduct should be as specific as possible.

In addition to an internal code of conduct or ethics policy, event professionals should consider the development of specific codes of conduct for suppliers, sponsors, or speakers, as their actions can reflect on the meeting organisers.

For further information about creating a code of conduct, visit www.ethics.org (Ethics Resource Centre); specifically, http://www.ethics.org/search/node/Creating+a+code+of+conduct.

Implementing an ethics policy

In addition to simply having an ethics policy or code of conduct, the organisation must ensure that it becomes a part of its culture. Methods for ensuring this include:

* Make the ethics policy a part of training for all staff and volunteers when they first become active with your organisation.
* Include ethical behaviour as part of the criteria for performance reviews.
* Review the ethics policy or code of conduct in training and staff meetings, discussing particular concerns or examples.
* Assign a review committee to examine the policy on an annual basis and have their report communicated effectively.
* Allow people to submit specific questions or reports anonymously and confidentially.
* Provide easy guidelines with a list of frequently asked questions (FAQs) about ethical challenges.
* Participate in outside training and professional development on ethics to keep up to date with best practices.
* Provide the internal code of conduct to vendors and suppliers or customers with whom your organisation works.
* Specify and carry through on disciplinary procedures.

CMP Standards of Ethical Conduct Statement and Policy

The Code of Ethics for Certified Meeting Professionals establishes basic standards of values and conduct for CMP applicants and current CMPs. As a recipient of the CMP designation by the Events Industry Council, a CMP must pledge to:

- Maintain exemplary standards of professional conduct at all times.

- Actively model and encourage the integration of ethics into all aspects of the performance of my duties.

- Perform my responsibilities in accordance with the laws and regulations of the local, state or national governments under which I reside.

- Maintain the confidentiality of all privileged information, including the identity or personal information of other CMP candidates and the contents of the CMP examination, except when required to do so by law or by court order.

- Never use my position for undue personal gain and promptly disclose to appropriate parties all potential and actual conflicts of interest.

- Communicate all relevant information to my employer in a truthful and accurate manner in order to facilitate the execution of my fiduciary responsibilities.

- Not use the CMP designation or service mark in any way other than that which is authorized by the Events Industry Council, and immediately cease using the designation should I fail to maintain the requirements of the CMP certification or for any other reason have my certification revoked, including non-payment of required fees.

- To abide by all policies and procedures of the CMP Programme as outlined in the CMP Handbook and those that may be set by the CMP Board of Directors in the future.

- To be truthful in all information provided to the Events Industry Council in all applications and recertification applications at all times.

Any action of an applicant or CMP that compromises the reliability of the certification process may be subject to the corrective process described by the *CMP Ethics Policy Disciplinary Procedures*.

Closing

The art and science of meeting management continues to gain recognition in the business world as a disciplined profession requiring knowledgeable individuals. With that recognition comes the responsibility for those individuals to act in an ethical manner and project an image of professionalism at all times.

References

CMP Standards of Ethical Conduct Statement and Policy. (2010). Events Industry Council. http://www.eventscouncil.org/CMP/AboutCMP/Ethics.aspx

Ethical Fitness®—Choosing between right vs. right. (Interview with Rushworth M. Kidder, Ph.D.) (2005, January). Institute for Global Ethics. Retrieved from: http://www.globalethics.org/news/Ethical-Fitness—-Choosing-between-Right-vs-Right/97/

Global Transparency Reporting Congress. (2013). CBI, an Advanstar company. Retrieved from: http://www.cbinet.com/conference/pc13105#.Uehap7afg8h

Hatch, S. (2006, August 1). No outboarding, says IAEM. *MeetingsNet*. Retrieved from: http://meetingsnet.com/corporate-meetings/no-outboarding-says-iaem

MPI Policy Manual and Principles of Professionalism. (2013). Meeting Professionals International. Retrieved from: http://www.mpiweb.org/Portal/Content/20110114/MPI_Policy_Manual

Guide for Developing Organisational Codes of Conduct. (2011). Treasury Board of Canada. Retrieved from: http://www.tbs-sct.gc.ca/ve/code/gdocc-grcco01-eng.asp

Contributing Authors

Pat Schaumann, CMP, CSEP, DMCP
President, Meeting IQ, Present China
St. Louis, MO, USA

Karen Zimmerman, CMP
Training Manager, Maritz Travel
St. Louis, MO, USA

Reviewer

Joan L. Eisenstodt
Eisenstodt Associates, LLC - Meetings & Hospitality Consultant, Facilitator & Trainer
Washington, DC, USA

Member of American Society of Association Executives (ASAE), Destination Marketing Association International (DMAI), Green Meeting Industry Council (GMIC), Hospitality Sales and Marketing Association International (HSMAI), Meeting Professionals International (MPI), Professional Convention Management Association (PCMA) and an inductee into the Events Industry Council Hall of Leaders.

Skill 30:
Endpoints

Terminology

Familiarization trip
Suitcasing
Outboarding

Additional Resources

Global guidance sources for this topic include:

- The Department of Foreign Affairs (may also be known as the State Department)
- Embassies and consulates
- International and national tourism organisations
- Convention and visitors bureaus or destination marketing organisations
- Local destination management companies and professional congress organisers
- Ethics Resource Centre (www.ethics.org)
- Meeting Professionals International's CultureActive™ tool provides valuable information on preparing for international meetings.

Skill 30: Review Questions

1. What are the five values that define ethical behaviour, and how are they reflected in the meetings and events industry?
2. What is suitcasing and outboarding, and how can these behaviours be discouraged?
3. What are best practices for developing and implementing a code of conduct?
4. What are the CMP Code of Ethics and the CMP Ethics Policy Disciplinary Procedures?

Index

Notes